Adopting America

Adopting America: Childhood, Kinship, and National Identity in Literature

Carol J. Singley

OXFORD
UNIVERSITY PRESS

OXFORD
UNIVERSITY PRESS

Oxford University Press, Inc., publishes works that further
Oxford University's objective of excellence
in research, scholarship, and education.

Oxford   New York
Auckland   Cape Town   Dar es Salaam   Hong Kong   Karachi
Kuala Lumpur   Madrid   Melbourne   Mexico City   Nairobi
New Delhi   Shanghai   Taipei   Toronto

With offices in
Argentina   Austria   Brazil   Chile   Czech Republic   France   Greece
Guatemala   Hungary   Italy   Japan   Poland   Portugal   Singapore
South Korea   Switzerland   Thailand   Turkey   Ukraine   Vietnam

Published by Oxford University Press, Inc.
198 Madison Avenue, New York, New York 10016

www.oup.com

Oxford is a registered trademark of Oxford University Press

Library of Congress Cataloging-in-Publication Data
Singley, Carol J., 1951–
Adopting America : childhood, kinship, and national identity in literature / Carol J. Singley.
    p.   cm.
Includes index.
ISBN 978-0-19-977939-0 (cloth : acid-free paper) 1. American literature—History and criticism.
2. Families in literature. 3. Adoption in literature. 4. National characteristics, American, in literature.
5. Children in literature. I. Title.
PS169.F35S56   2011
810.9′355—dc22   2010032159

1 3 5 7 9 8 6 4 2

Printed in the United States of America
on acid-free paper

To my sons,
Cole Kinsey and Ryan Kinsey,
who inspire my journeys into adoption and literature

Contents

Acknowledgments

I am grateful to colleagues and friends who supported this project from its beginnings and who offered valuable feedback at various stages of completion. I particularly acknowledge members of the Alliance for the Study of Adoption and Culture, in particular, Wayne Carp, Jill Deans, Ellen Herman, Emily Hipchen, Margaret Homans, Mark Jerng, Claudia Nelson, and Marianne Novy. I extend thanks to Holly Blackford, Gordon Kinsey, Erika Koss, Caroline Levander, Michael Manson, and Mary Ann Noble, who commented on chapters. Numerous colleagues provided encouragement and suggestions, including Dan Cook, Anna Mae Duane, Chris Fitter, Lucia Hodgson, Elsa Nettels, Susan Elizabeth Sweeney, Lynne Vallone, John Wall, and Fred Wegener.

A Peterson Fellowship at the American Antiquarian Society launched research for the project. I am grateful to the expert staff of librarians, including Joanne Chaisson, Tom Knoles, Marie Lamoureux, Caroline Sloat, and Laura Wasowicz, who helped identify essential primary texts. A Northeast Modern Language Association summer fellowship and an associate fellowship at the Center for the Critical Analysis of Contemporary Culture at Rutgers University-New Brunswick further supported my work. Sabbatical leaves from Rutgers University and a fellowship from the Center for Children and Childhood Studies at Rutgers University-Camden provided valuable time to write.

I especially thank librarians Vibiana Bowman Cvetkovic, Theo Haynes, John Maxymuk, Julie Still, and Donna Wertheimer at Robeson Library, Rutgers University-Camden, and librarians Chris Gebert, Linda Hunt, Alison Masterpasqua, and Mary Ann Wood at McCabe Library, Swarthmore College, for their valuable assistance. Rutgers-Camden graduate students Jamie Gibbs and Jessica Gicking helped to locate sources. David Estrin provided copyediting. Finally, I express sincere appreciation to the editors at Oxford University Press. Shannon McLachlan nurtured my vision for this project, and Brendan O'Neill and Jaimee Biggins guided the book to publication.

Adopting America

Introduction

AMERICAN LITERATURE ABOUNDS with orphaned, homeless, destitute, or neglected children. Many of these characters are either adopted or experience temporary placements that resemble adoption. These stories tell us that adoption matters. To construct a family in the literature of the United States frequently means adoption, and this book sets out to show the difference that adoption makes in the cultural ideology of the family.

Adoption, as a trope or narrative event, is notable in major American literary landmarks. Ishmael observes in *Moby-Dick* that "to any meditative Magian rover, this serene Pacific, once beheld, must ever be the sea of his adoption"; reflects existentially that "our souls are like those orphans whose unwedded mothers die in bearing them"; and concludes with the Rachael's adoptive rescue of "another orphan."[1] Huckleberry Finn's celebrated flight down the Mississippi River is set in motion by his resistance to Widow Douglas's efforts to adopt and "sivilize" him.[2] In *The Scarlet Letter*, Hester Prynne fights off oppressive governmental officials who insist that her daughter, Pearl, would be better raised by adoptive parents than by a single birth mother. The close-knit family of *Little Women* dissolves into an adoptive family unit established in *Little Men*. Disrupted biological families and elective family units are a defining feature of American literature, in a way that is strikingly absent in other national literatures.

Although orphaned and adopted characters appear frequently in Western literature, they have distinctive qualities in American literature, which is persistently shaped around constructions of childhood and images of youthfulness. Historian Ellen Herman notes that since the United States passed the nation's first adoption law in 1851, "observers have attributed curiosity about adoption to its compatibility with cherished national values and traditions," such as migration and mobility.[3] Barbara Melosh, also a historian, identifies a "vibrant optimism" that makes Americans positively inclined toward adoption.[4] Adam Pertman, director of the Evan B. Donaldson Adoption Institute, declares the United States an "adoption nation," naming a process by which adoption is accelerating the transformation of the United States into a more multicultural and multiethnic society.[5] Media coverage of adoption, popular films, and memoirs has recently focused attention on the ways that broken and reformed genealogies define the American child, family, and nation.

Adoption narratives are rooted in the American migratory experience: they reflect politically and culturally the severed ties to Great Britain and the construction of new forms of social and governmental organization. They also derive from a New England tradition of Calvinism and the cultural practices aligned with it, including an emphasis on salvation and good works that appears in representations of adoption from colonial times through the modern period. Analogies between the growth of the nation and adoption appear in myriad sermons, letters, short stories, and novels about disrupted and reformed families. Adoption is a narrative event or trope through which these authors address, often with ambivalence, an evolving American character and nationhood. The rhetoric of adoption is double-edged, and for that reason alone it is a fertile site of inquiry. Adoption draws lines of inclusion and exclusion, entails independence for some characters and dependence for others, and applauds fresh starts while expressing regret over lost origins.

Adopting America: Childhood, Kinship, and National Identity in Literature examines adoptive family formation in selected canonical and noncanonical texts from the seventeenth through the early twentieth centuries. It begins with Puritan writings, when adoption did not exist in the legal sense that it does today and when the word most often appears in the context of spiritual adoption, or redemption, by God. This study interprets adoption broadly to refer to the care of children by nonbiological parents through practices such as placing out, indentured service, foster parenting, and guardianship, and it focuses on the religious and domestic aspects of these placements in order to show how American adoption narratives evolved through the nineteenth century in response to the New England Puritan tradition. An analysis of illegitimacy in the Revolutionary period and the early republic demonstrates the role of class and gender in determining the placements of children born out of wedlock. Portrayals of adoption in fiction of the nineteenth and early twentieth century tell the story of a nation in the grip of social changes including urbanization, immigration, debate over slavery, waning Calvinism, and growing sentimentality. Gender as well as race play a part in the representations of adoption in these narratives, which differ for boys and girls, and for children of color.

Recent work has shown that the child is a potent site of meaning that "absorbs and helps to disseminate the divergent, sometimes contradictory, ideologies that typify particular historical periods."[6] This study adds its voice to the growing body of literary scholarship on the American child as a contributor to social meaning, including Caroline Levander's interrogation of race, childhood, and democracy in *Cradle of Liberty*, and Karen Sánchez-Eppler's treatment, in *Dependent States*, of childhood as an important force in shaping a political and cultural discourse of the nation.[7] These books reinvigorate the critical commonplace, first articulated by John Winthrop in 1637, that "a family is a little commonwealth, and a commonwealth is a great family."[8] *Adopting America* also enters into dialogue with Claudia Nelson's *Little Strangers*, which focuses on the emotional value of nineteenth-century literary orphans; Diana Pazicky's *Cultural Orphans*, about orphancy as a trope for the American experience; and Cindy Weinstein's *Family, Kinship, and Sympathy*, about nineteenth-century adoption and sentimentality.[9] The study is by no means exhaustive; major work remains to be done in order to understand diverse representations of adoptive kinship in American literature, for example, the role of adoption in Indian captivity narratives and boarding school stories, missionary writings of the Southwest, and African American literary traditions.

A cultural as well as literary analysis, *Adopting America* also joins the growing scholarship on children and childhood. It draws on classic studies of the family by Stone, Ariès, Morgan, Demos, and Wishy[10] as well as recent analyses by Zelizer, Coontz, Kincaid, and Berlant[11] that view the child as a complex site of critical inquiry on topics of economic, political, and social value ranging from sexuality to citizenship. It also employs insights and methodologies from the burgeoning interdisciplinary field of adoption studies, a subset of childhood studies, notably the work of literary critic Marianne Novy, anthropologist Judith Modell, and historians Ellen Herman, Barbara Melosh, Julie Berebitsky, and Wayne Carp,[12] to understand how kinship structures reflect and help to shape a sense of personal and national identity.

Adoption takes on various meanings as an element of plot and metaphor in literary texts that span three centuries, yet these meanings are bound together in a developing national and literary culture. Two thematic strains run through American literature about adoption from the seventeenth through the early twentieth century. The first is adoption as a form of salvation that rescues a needy child from poverty, abuse, or homelessness. It begins with seventeenth-century Calvinism and the belief that by adopting others one emulates God and does his will. The second is the notion of fresh starts and the opportunity to realize unlimited potential free of genealogical constraints. It also begins with the Puritan settlers' separation from a birth parent nation, continues through the eighteenth century with the American Revolution, and reaches fruition in the nineteenth-century spirit of democratic individualism. Both of these traditions reflect the lighter side of adoption.

Adoption also has its darker side. In some cases, the child is not saved by adoption or is adopted but remains dependent for reasons such as considerations of race, class, or gender. In this case, the child may be portrayed as unworthy of adoption or unlikely to benefit from its support. Likewise, writers may offset the opportunity for fresh starts and independence by attaching significance to the loss of bloodline. In this case, the child might resist adoption or seek reunion with the birth parents or birth culture in a manner that may be applauded—or be thought regressive and counter to American republican values.

Literary representations of adoption reflect national mythologies. Explorations of family and nation have followed the notion, described by Jay Fliegelman, Jerome Griswold, and others, that the literature of the nation develops as a child does, from a state of dependence, to rebellion, to independence.[13] A critical discourse has likewise developed from Alexis de Tocqueville's observation, first articulated in his book, *Democracy in America*,[14] of an ongoing tension in American literature between notions of inherited and acquired identity. Both these models—of development and tensions between Old World and New, between a self shaped by the past and one open to the future—are embodied in literature about adoption. Writing about modern adoption, Ellen Herman expresses this idea another way: "To the extent that American culture has defined nature as a product of blood-based (now gene-based) identities that are fixed, unchosen, and beyond the scope of social arrangement, adoption illustrates the authenticity crises that plague many forms of voluntary belonging, including democratic citizenship itself."[15]

Adoption gives voice to the simultaneous and sometimes contradictory calls to origins and fresh beginnings, and to feelings of worthiness and unworthiness. Not surprisingly, the primary emotion associated with adoption is ambivalence, which may be experienced as conflicting loyalties to adoptive and birth families, difficulty balancing American customs with English and European ones, or uncertainty over individual versus family or national identity. In the nineteenth century, amidst rapid social change, the versatility of the adoption plot helps to account for its popularity. "American response to change was ambivalent," Anne MacLeod argues;[16] the adoption plot gives form to this ambivalence. Janus-faced, it looks backward as well as forward, revealing problems but also solving them.

Adoption is a complex signifier of difference, but whether the difference is positive or negative is not always clear. The Evan B. Donaldson Adoption Institute finds that "Americans have a favorable opinion of adoption" and agree that it serves a useful purpose in our society,[17] yet many may think of adoption as something that occurs on the margins of society, affecting a few families. This perception follows from the tacit assumption that biological kinship is the social norm. Americans are notably oriented toward blood ties, as David Schneider observes in a 1984 study that draws attention to the manner in which biogenetic representations are privileged in the United States in the determination of what constitutes kinship.[18] Unlike differences such as gender, race, or class, which are obvious markers of difference, adoption may be represented openly as an alternative to biological kinship, or it may be designed as an elaborate fiction that replicates the biologically intact family structure it replaces, as anthropologist Judith Modell observes when she writes about a model of adoption designed in such in a way so that the adopted child would seem "as-if-begotten."[19] Conceptions of nationhood also rely on metaphors of blood kinship. Benedict Anderson, for example, describes a nation as "an imagined political community" and a "style of continuity," discursively created and subject to discontinuities as well as continuities. In tracing the rise of imagined communities that emerged from the demise of religious communities and dynastic realms, he employs the language of birth and development: nations, he writes, are conceived of as limited, sovereign, and involving community or "deep horizontal comradeship" akin to those defined by blood.[20]

Recently, feminists such as Gayle Rubin have criticized the latent biologism of structuralist models of kinship.[21] Marilyn Strathern has argued that kinship is a hybrid formed of nature and culture, a cultural technology that naturalizes relationships as well as turns natural relations into cultural forms.[22] These interrelations of nature and nurture may be observed in literary portrayals of biological and adoptive families and the legitimacy or authenticity ascribed to them. Stefan Helmreich explains the benefit of this kind of critical analysis, writing that "kinship may make reference to biogenetics, but may also implicate political, class, caste, racialized, sexualized, and religious affiliations."[23] Speaking about the power of adoption to signify not only difference but also deficiency, Yanagisako and Delaney show how the process of naturalization is a symbolic activity productive of social inequalities.[24] Adoptive kinship status, which Novy calls "the most invisible minority status,"[25] reveals these social imbalances in the constructions of individual and family identities.

Practiced since ancient times and a matter of historical record, in Western nations adoption was originally designed to provide patriarchs with an heir and ensure peaceful transitions of power. A legal adoption might not occur until the adoptee was grown.

Meeting the needs of younger orphaned or homeless children has motivated adoption in modern times, although specific practices and the cultural values assigned to adoption vary widely across periods and cultures. Temporary forms of adoption, such as foster care, indentured service, and placing out have often been viewed as benefiting the child as well as the surrogate parent, who may enjoy the child's company or extract its labor in exchange for shelter, food, and an investment of time or training. Only recently has the practice of adoption become child-centered, and in this respect American adoption stands out. The United States led Western nations with the passage, in Massachusetts in 1851, of the first adoption law designed to protect the interests of the child. With its strong focus on bloodlines and inheritance, England did not pass a similar law until 1926.[26] Although U.S. family law is influenced by English common law, the Massachusetts statute represents a milestone in the history of American adoption, significant for associating the nation with childhood and rescue, and for validating family and personal identity based on chosen rather than inherited affiliation.

Puritan settlers who left their homeland and migrated to the New World were motivated by the experience of religious and political persecution in England. Hoping to "purify" their faith and rid it of Catholic influence, they ambivalently took leave of their birth country and portrayed themselves as neglected, abandoned children. The first generation of New England colonists mourned the loss of ties to England even as they envisioned and established a permanent settlement in the new land. At the same time that they felt abandoned, Puritans held the religious conviction that they were the chosen children of God. They prayed for salvation, or adoption, by their heavenly Father, worried over their innately sinful state, and sought to emulate God's grace by extending adoption to others. This dual sense—of loss due to abandonment and of gratitude for being chosen—created a dynamic that is visible in literary representations of adoption through the nineteenth century and even today.

As the colonies came of age, won political independence from England, and flourished as a new nation, writers embraced a mythology of fresh starts afforded by the genealogical break with the birth country. By the mid-nineteenth century, they described Americans taking pride in their freedom from the obligations of primogeniture and hereditary rank, even as they emulated English customs and law, and they equated such liberty with an adoptive rather than a biological outlook. In literature portraying white males, adoption is often associated with self-reliance—or self-adoption—and resiliency, often in relationship to nature or the land. In texts depicting white females, it is aligned with obedience, domesticity, home, and family. Adoption fiction of this period, which acknowledges loss and demonstrates inclusion, tells the story of a nation that is cohesive yet elastic, capable of extending its boundaries to absorb new ideas and individuals. The adopted child embodies a belief in individual improvement and national progress deemed not only possible but also divinely ordered. The sentimental and democratic impulses that fueled the production of adoption literature do not serve all children, however. Those born female and out of wedlock or of mixed race enjoy far fewer benefits of adoption than their middle-class, white male counterparts.

The nineteenth-century adoption plot tells the story of an aspiring Anglo-American middle class *and* the underclass it leaves behind, and is associated with social reform. Countless stories portray destitute women and children thrown into poverty by the failure of male heads of households to earn a living, whether because of illness, drinking, dereliction, or business misfortune. These fictions reenact through childhood sufferings the longstanding debate over whose responsibility are the poor, especially the immigrant poor. Destitute and orphaned children face double adversity when, after becoming home-less, they experience strangers' indifference or minimal charity in the form of a casual crust of bread or small coin rather than significantly helpful acts of Christian benevo-lence. This is the case in Samuel Goodrich's *Peter Parley's Short Stories for Long Nights*, about a young Irish boy whose parents have died. In another tale, the narrative simply ends when two girls offer money to a boy who is orphaned by war and then go on their way.[27]Adoption stories, in contrast to these vignettes, are optimistic, with a spirit of adventure about the unknown. Amy Schrager Lang notes that reformist fiction of the antebellum era holds fast to the notion that class can be transcended through individual virtue.[28] Middle-class readers of adoption fiction could entertain sympathy for orphans of various kinds—from genteel homeless girls who have lost their social footing to desti-tute, immigrant "street arabs," as orphaned boys were called. At the same time, they could see these children taken in and held accountable to middle-class standards of morality and behavior.

Despite their egalitarian rhetoric, Americans maintained a patronizing attitude toward the poor, expecting them to express gratitude for personal assistance but seldom ques-tioning the inequities of an economic system that created their poverty. Americans knew, as Emily Graham does in *The Lamplighter*, "how many children were born into the world amid poverty and privation; how many were abused, neglected and forsaken."[29]Although nineteenth-century adoption fiction repudiates snobbishness and favors focused indus-try as the means of success, it also espouses codes of gentility derived from English models and implicitly values good breeding afforded by genealogical continuity. Adop-tion, a side step toward making "all children of one family," is a means by which mid-dle-class families voice anxiety about outsiders and also take action on their behalf. Literary adoption addresses a collective need for improvement, assuages social guilt over inequality, and shows that disparate elements of society can be assimilated without altering the fundamental composition of society itself.

Adoption fiction also represents changes in family structure and gender roles. Histori-cally, a child's status was derived from that of its father, but widespread social changes at mid-nineteenth century saw the deconstruction of traditional notions of family. As Ber-nard Wishy writes, a shift away from patriarchal structures and values accompanied a suspicion that the authoritarian family unit was now useless in a new republic.[30] A child might be termed an orphan if its father died but its mother was still living. For example, after the Civil War, the *Chicago Tribune* used the occasion of a local officer's death to promote society's responsibility to "honor the brave departed soldier" by supporting his widow and orphans.[31] However, shifts in the understanding of the patriarchal family were evident at mid-century in all aspects of society, including the law. Commenting on literary representations of this shift, Jay Fliegelman writes, "the habit of new affection, the habit encouraged by the new world, creates a bond between child and adopted [sic] parent, between immigrant and adopted land as natural as any bond of birth and so permits the creation of a new set of naturalized domestic relations."[32]

Prerepublican Anglo-American law had granted fathers almost unlimited domestic rights, including the right to the custody and governance of their minor legitimate chil-dren. This power was based in a medieval notion of equivalency of property and child, and the assumption that the patriarch was the proper and best guardian of dependent, subordinate entities.[33] As Michael Grossberg writes, "Post-Revolutionary Americans abandoned the hierarchical concept of the family that had dominated English common law and colonial practice. Concurrently, they displayed a new faith in women's innate proclivities for child rearing and in developmental notions of childhood." He notes the "remarkable" impact of these changes on custody law. "Traditional paternalistic custody rules and practices disappeared; an entirely new standard of child placement took their place."[34] In particular, adoption and the attendant issues of illegitimacy assumed a new significance, a point Hawthorne explores in his treatment of Pearl in *The Scarlet Letter*. As Grossberg explains this change:

> Imbued with post-Revolutionary America's increased respect for the individual, [law makers and judges] enlarged the law's concept of a family to include the bastard and its mother, and revamped the common law to aid children who sought legitimacy. A new conviction was being woven into American family law: voluntarily assumed domestic relations provided the most secure foundation for family success.[35]

The increasing attention given to the best interest of the child was reflected in the Massachusetts Adoption Act, which defined the parent-child relationship in nonbiological terms and set the standard for subsequent state legislation on adoption. Adoption fiction reflects the spirit of this legislation, with plots that focus on the child's best interest.

Early American customs, derived from English colonial practices and following Pauline doctrine, unequivocally made the man the head of household. These attitudes especially lingered among evangelicals, who adhered more than moderate or aristocratic parents to patriarchal, Calvinist principles.[36] These methods of child rearing were suited, as Mary Ryan notes, to an agrarian society in which a son inherited his father's occupation and status and thus had every incentive to follow the father's direction.[37] However, a new spirit of liberty challenged traditional authority and redefined the father-son relationship. Daniel Howe notes a rise of interest in independence, self-discipline, and self-improvement at mid-century that cut across class lines.[38] As American society industrialized and sons found new opportunities to build careers different from those of their fathers, it was harder for fathers to exert definitive control. The older generation, once the unquestioned source of income and advice, found itself obsolete as younger men sought their fortunes in ever-expanding markets and topographies.[39] Male adoption stories articulate this cultural shift.

As patriarchal roles diminished, sentimental, maternal ones flourished. A rising emphasis on domesticity and a mother's right—and ability—to nurture children shaped a new approach to child rearing and transformed female roles. With fathers in cities leaving home for longer periods of time, experts fixed their attention on mothers, who were asked to accept "new and portentous responsibilities. . . . The mother was the obvious source of everything that would save or damn the child; the historical and spiritual destiny of America lay in her hands."[40] Christian white women, operating within the domestic realm, played an increasingly large role in advancing not only the family's but also the nation's priorities.[41] Such women play visible roles as birth and adoptive mothers in fiction of the period. Articulating the logic of an ever-expanding sphere of feminine influence, Catherine Beecher wrote, in "An Address to the Christian Women of America," that women's work in the home trained individuals "to obey the laws of God . . . first in the family, then in the school, then in the neighborhood, then in the nation, then in the world."[42] Nurturing, an essential element in the adoption story, gives wide play to women's special talents.

What Ann Douglas labels the "feminization of American culture" at mid-century might well be called a "juvenilization of American culture."[43] Preachers, educators, and writers heralded the importance of the child and focused on child-rearing practices as key to the health of the family as well as of the nation. Since John Winthrop, the nation had conceived itself as the family writ large,[44] but in the nineteenth century, the child, embraced by an all-sacrificing mother and guided by a firm and devout father, moved to center stage as the embodiment of national potential. Anne MacLeod explains this growing cult of childhood:

> Nationalism and optimism, reforming zeal and a concern for the perpetuity of democratic institutions, all contributed to the extraordinary attention Americans turned upon their children. Convinced that young Americans were the inheritors of prospects unique in human history, Americans examined every aspect of childhood and child nurture in an effort to ensure that the rising generation would be equal to the challenges and promises of the future."[45]

A new child-centered philosophy developed around the concept of nurture, which was consistent with idea of adoption. In keeping with the nation's democratic ideals, the importance of genealogy receded: the child was increasingly formed in its own image, not the image of parents. Individually acquired, rather than inherited, traits took priority, with some measure of juvenile autonomy, especially for males, considered beneficial. Adoption motifs in the popular juvenile fiction of Jacob Abbott demonstrate this development. For example, in Abbott's *Rollo on the Atlantic*, the starter book for the *Rollo in Europe* series, Rollo and his younger sister Jane are temporarily orphaned as they set out to join their parents in Europe. The children at first fret over their plight but then revel in the fact that their cross-Atlantic transit is free from adult supervision. They benefit from the kind help of strangers but, more important, they learn to survive by modeling their behavior on that of the adults around them. Unswerving in its belief that good wins out over evil and its advocacy of traditional moral values, Abbott's fiction also celebrates the childhood discovery of right and wrong rather than imposition of rules from authoritarian parents or parent figures.[46] It uses temporary or pseudo-adoptions to help children move from a stage of dependency to that of full-fledged independence.

Adoption narratives also reflect a new religious outlook that saw the dawn of doctrinal perfectionism—a sharp contrast to Calvinist predestination and innate depravity. Nineteenth-century literature about adoption remains essentially conservative in its adherence to the religious doctrines handed down from the Puritans and in its understanding of family as central to the construction of the child and the nation. The call for self-improvement, however, coupled with a sense that progress was not only possible but divinely promised, invigorated attitudes not only about child rearing but also about adoption. Literary adoption combines the religious and the secular. Domestic narratives about adoption frequently open with epigraphs quoting biblical passages about Moses or Jesus or tell the Christian story of a fall from grace depicted as a loss of home or parents, followed by the trial of orphancy, and ending with redemption in the form of adoption. Readers first vicariously experience the plight of a forsaken child and then witness its salvation by adoptive parents who benefit, in turn, from parenting a homeless child.

Although adoption appears in literary texts from Cotton Mather's 1711 sermon, "Orphanotrophium," to Edith Wharton's 1917 novel, *Summer*, it has not been part of mainstream literary discourse about childhood. Yet turning the lens of adoption on American literature results in new angles of vision about the values of genealogical and nongenealogical kinship. Anthropologists have noted how changes in contemporary adoption practices and interest in adoption have reinvigorated kinship studies. Adoption, along with surrogacy and other reproductive technologies, gay and lesbian kinship, and organ donation, can be used to understand culturally specific features of Euro-American practices and even to reconfigure the field of kinship studies itself. Among those changing views are new ways to understand the relation of nature and culture, and the increasing uncertainty about the hegemony of nature as a determiner of kinship. Franklin and McKinnon observe that the "question of how kinship may be conceived of outside its ruling sign of biology has been powerfully explored in recent studies of . . . adoption."[47]

Literary scholars examining adoption can also understand how broken and unbroken genealogies relate to formal aspects of narrative plot. The adoption novel is a subset of the *Bildungsroman*, which developed with the rise of the middle class and its attendant questions of birthright and belonging. Readers of literary adoption also can discover how genealogy and adoption function as signifying tropes in U.S. narratives from the Puritan to the modernist period. Those in American studies and cultural studies can gain, through the analysis of adoptive kinship, critical tools for analyzing concepts related to American identity, experience, and citizenship; those in the emergent field of childhood studies can analyze the social constructions of childhood in the context of kinship and nationhood; and historians and sociologists can see how chronologically organized, close readings of literary texts illuminate past kinship patterns and offer blueprints for charting current ones. Finally, general readers—especially birth parents, adoptive parents, adoptees, and others whose lives are touched by adoption—can find affirmation of their experience and develop tools for a critique not only of their respective roles but also of representations of adoption in an American literary tradition.

Chapter 1, "Abandoned and Adopted in a New World," describes the Puritan settlers' struggles with the first stage in the adoption process: separation from the birth parent. It also establishes a motivational framework for American adoption literature: salvation. Having left their birth country, the founding generation of New England settlers felt both like abandoned orphans and chosen adoptees. The concept of adoption figures prominently in the Calvinist writings that urge immigration to the New World. Sustained by the belief that they were, like the Israelites, chosen and led to a promised land, Puritans emulated salvation—adoption by God the father—by taking in others' children. This notion of adoption as salvation is prominent in the writings of Cotton Mather, whose "Orphanotrophium" helped define the age and power a national literary mythology for centuries to come. Puritans frequently moved children from one household to another as a result of parental death or a plan for the child to receive special education, training, or correction in a practice known as "placing out." However, despite a degree of fluidity in the Puritan household and a public endorsement of the transfer of children, a fear of outsiders, a need for certainty and control, and a patriarchal emphasis on genealogical continuity made early Americans suspicious of adoptive kinship. The result is a conditional embrace of adoption in a religious community as driven to exclude strangers as to admit them.

Chapter 2, "Problems of Patrimony: Benjamin Franklin and Ann Sargent Gage," charts the competing impulses toward adoptive and biological kinship in Revolutionary America and the early republic. Franklin's *Autobiography*, often read as a model for a "go ahead, get ahead" nation, is also a paradigmatic text about the challenges of reconciling birth and adoptive identities. Franklin chose to acknowledge and parent his illegitimate son, William, revealing his attachment to blood. The *Autobiography*'s description of a genealogical search conducted in England also validates the importance of roots. However, when William sided with the loyalists during the Revolutionary War, Franklin lost the genealogical connection he had worked hard to nourish. In contrast, Daniel Sargent, also a prominent businessman, chose not to acknowledge his illegitimate daughter and instead placed her for adoption. Ann Sargent Gage's story, not part of the "official stories [that] constitute Americans," demonstrates the importance of class and gender in helping to shape national narrative.[48] Cut off from her roots, Gage struggled to gain her patrimony but as a woman lacked the social and legal power to define her identity. Her narrative, a study in gender, class, and illegitimacy, bridges Enlightenment literature and the blossoming of nineteenth-century adoption fiction.

Chapter 3, "Adoption Averted in *The Scarlet Letter*," explores nonnormative kinship structures by turning a lens on Hawthorne's landmark novel. Hawthorne's choice to allow an unmarried birth mother retain custody of her child distinguishes his work from that of domestic writers of the 1850s, whom he derided as the "d—d mob of scribbling women."[49] Domestic novelists underline the importance of motherhood by depicting poor or dying birth mothers, whose absences propel a narrative of felicitous adoption by women who better embody the middle-class ideals embraced by a developing nation. In contrast, Hawthorne presents a strong mother who defies convention, resists patriarchal intervention, and retains custody of her child. In championing her cause, Hawthorne is ahead of his time, giving center stage to the plight of birth mothers, an issue virtually ignored in public discourse until the late twentieth century. *The Scarlet Letter*, remarkable for its combination of Puritan and romantic views of family and childhood, also addresses middle-class concerns about changing roles of masculinity and femininity in the construction of the American family. Hawthorne positions Pearl between two fathers: one blood, one adoptive, engaging in issues of birthright and culture without clearly deciding for one or the other. The novel's dual resolution—the reunion of a biological family followed by its disintegration and the daughter's return to the Old World—demonstrates Hawthorne's ambivalence about roots and fresh starts, and his anxiety about the role of bourgeois kinship in mediating tensions between inherited and adoptive identities.

Mid-nineteenth-century social changes created a favorable environment for adoption fiction, as demonstrated in chapter 4, "Plotting Adoption in Nineteenth-Century Fiction." Demographic, religious, and economic changes helped install the adoption narrative as a dominant nineteenth-century form for the articulation of national hopes and misgivings. In portraying families made, not born, writers contributed to an on-going narrative of nation building and set the terms upon which a white middle class would develop. A little known but representative novel, *Laura Huntley*, portrays adoption as an expression both of national anxiety about immigration and urbanization as well as a solution to these challenges. The middle-class adoptive family in this text recapitulates the nation's sense of itself as capable of extending its boundaries and absorbing new ideas and individuals. Adoption fiction also signals a major transition in religious belief and child-rearing practices. The shift from Calvinist to sentimental theology involved movement from imposed external authority to inner guidance and gentle persuasion. Each of Laura Huntley's adoptive parents employs a different strategy, exhibiting in microcosm a debate in society as a whole. Adoption tales such as *Laura Huntley* serve a national purpose: they reflect fears that the family unit—and therefore cultural cohesion—is under threat, and they address these concerns by recreating family structures similar to the ones under siege.

Chapter 5, "Child Saving, Nation Building: *The Wide, Wide World* and *The Lamplighter*," analyzes two bestsellers of the 1850s, not in terms of sentimentality, as they are often discussed, but in terms of family, class, and nationhood. In Susan Warner's *The Wide, Wide World* and Susanna Maria Cummins's *The Lamplighter*, adoption does the "cultural work"[50] of child saving, and more. Ellen Montgomery's and Gerty Flint's adventures reinforce literary adoption as a female experience, affirming the power of nurture, a female domain in the period. This idea is propounded by Horace Bushnell, whose focus on the importance of early nurture influenced the course not only of child rearing but also of nation-building, which was viewed as progressing according to a model of familial support, republican autonomy, and Old World ties.[51] Adoption also provides a blueprint for crossing the boundaries of class and for negotiating Old and New World identities in American society. Ellen rejects British roots to become an American daughter and wife. Her story affirms a vision of American independence guided by a patriarchal and a somewhat progressive Calvinism. Gerty, in contrast, rejoins her birth family in an ending that resembles a European fairy tale. Her American role, and the nation's growing world importance, is signaled by her marriage to Willie Sullivan, a successful world traveler and entrepreneur. The endings of both *The Wide, Wide World* and *The Lamplighter* reflect a sense of American identity as inherited *and* adoptive, and show a nation in dialogue with, but independent of, England.

The role of race as an exempting factor in nineteenth-century American adoption fiction is the concern of chapter 6, "Servitude and Homelessness: Harriet Wilson's *Our Nig*." In Wilson's 1859 novel, adoption is denied Frado Smith after she is abandoned by her impoverished, mulatto mother and enters into service with a white, Northern family. She seeks relief from the cruelty she suffers by turning to religion, but her efforts to be acknowledged by the Bellmonts or by God are continually frustrated. *Our Nig* incorporates elements of the slave narrative and the seduction novel, but its primary model is the narrative of indentured service. This generic similarity is clear when *Our Nig* is juxtaposed with Sarah S. Baker's novel, *Bound Out; or, Abby at the Farm*, which ends with an indentured white girl converting others to faith and being embraced by her adoptive family. Wilson's refusal to write a happy adoption ending for Frado represents a critique of Northern racism as well as an indictment of the exclusion of African American children from dominant literary genres that are aligned with the white, middle-class experience. The fact that adoption is not possible for all children is born out in Harriet Beecher Stowe's *Uncle Tom's Cabin*: Ophelia's disciplined guardianship of Topsy falls far short of the intimate adoptions that Anglo children enjoy, and Stowe implicitly grounds ferocious mother-love in whiteness and genealogy. Regardless of individual merit or effort, Wilson shows, children of color are denied the benefits of adoption and thereby citizenship.

Chapter 7, "The Limits of Nurture: Louisa May Alcott's Adoption Fiction," explores adoption at a transitional moment in nineteenth-century American literature, when the culture of nurture became infused with skepticism and science. *Little Women* earned Alcott a reputation as the premier narrator of nineteenth-century family life. However, viewing her work through the lens of adoption reveals not only the social reform that drove her work but also the novel's genteel, geneaological biases. The boy most resistant to Jo March's reformist agenda is Dan Kean, a street orphan introduced in *Little Men* (1871), who is taken in on a trial basis. Dan appears in *Jo's Boys* (1886) as the most troubled and romantic of Jo's boys, with a sense of adventure and wanderlust that makes it difficult for him to pursue settled career paths that other boys choose. He is fundamentally different, that is, different by nature, and no amount of adoptive care bridges the gap between his original, wild state and the evolved, cultivated young man that Jo expects him to become. Dan's kindred spirit is Huckleberry Finn, who also resists attempts to adopt and "sivilize" him. Both boys are too independent, that is, too severed from geneaological supports, to benefit from adoption. Without the supportive framework of middle-class adoption, both remain adrift. Alcott depicts the limits of adoption and thereby signals a failure of bourgeois ideals to address a complex, late nineteenth-century society influenced as much by Darwin as by nurture and faith.

The final chapter, "Charity Begins and Ends at Home: Edith Wharton's *Summer*," analyzes the death of romantic myths of adoption and nation building. Modernist as well as realistic, Edith Wharton's novel *Summer* (1917) announces a change in portrayals of adoption and citizenship: a transition from the healing power of nurture to reliance on nature and genetics. Rescued from a renegade Mountain community, Charity bears a name that alludes ironically to the acts of child-saving that propel nineteenth-century adoption narratives. Reflecting the context of World War I, during which the novel was written, Charity is first refugee then rebel as she manages adoption by, and then marriage to, her adoptive father. Such marriages, common in nineteenth-century fiction, by the end of the century ran counter to custom and to family law that sought to protect children against incest and child abuse. Charity's inability to curb her adoptive father's alcoholism also signals the end of sentimental reforms such as temperance. Her decision to raise rather than abort her child anticipates twentieth-century issues facing birth mothers, just as her marked ethnicity makes the novel part of a larger dialogue about nationhood and race. Following the views of eugenicists, *Summer* reflects fears that civilized nations were disintegrating as a result of racial mongrelization. Charity survives the trauma of her adoption and, impregnated by a robust young outsider, improves the quality of her lineage and implicitly her nation. However, through adoption and marriage, her bid for autonomy is defeated.

Nineteenth-century adoption fiction is part of a robust literary enterprise aligned with the development of a new nation. By the end of the century, the role of nation-building in literary adoption changes. Gradually, faith in nurture gives way to dependence upon science and psychology to determine the fitness of children to join new families and profit from adoption. In the early twentieth century, with the professionalization of social work, a new emphasis on matching children's traits to those of their adoptive families developed, and many states moved toward sealed records, a process partially underway in the 1940s but not widespread until the 1970s, when adoption practices became invisible and, because of secrecy, stigmatized.[52] Many adoption narratives of this period portray adoption as a matter of individual rather than national identity, as if to deny the tale's ideological import. Yet the cultural tensions between inherited and acquired identity persist in the literature. With the civil rights and feminist movements of the 1960s and 1970s, adoption once again becomes an open topic, partly as a result of adoption rights movements led by both birth mothers and adoptees. Memoirs proliferate as previously silenced family members tell their stories. Increasingly, transnational adoption narratives position the U.S. family in a global arena, requiring negotiation of ethnic, racial, and cultural differences across a wide spectrum of economic and legal divides. In this literature, adoption rises again in importance as a hallmark of a multicultural American society, but ambivalence continues, reflecting both pride in American hybridity and attachment to naturalized, traditionally patriarchal family structures.

1

Abandoned and Adopted in a New World

DRIVEN TO AMERICA by the strength of their belief, Puritan settlers turned to God for spiritual adoption, or salvation. A robust Calvinist theology practiced within a tight social framework created a family-oriented culture conversant with adoptive as well as biological kinship. Puritans placed a high value on children, their neighbor's as well as their own, and followed a model created by their first leader, John Winthrop, who declared in 1637 that "A family is a little commonwealth, and a commonwealth is a great family."[1] High mortality rates among adults and children meant blended families created through remarriage. A system of temporary adoptions, or "placing out," flourished throughout the colonial period. These placements were grounded in religious teachings that cautioned against valuing human ties over heavenly ones, placed checks on the emotional value assigned to blood kinship, and held spiritual adoption as the highest goal. The writings of Puritan preacher Cotton Mather (1663–1728) and jurist Samuel Sewall (1652–1730) demonstrate that raising nonbiological children was normative, supported by a shared vision of church, family, and community.[2]

Despite the open discourse about taking in the children of others, no legal system of adoption existed. Massachusetts Governor William Phips first used the term "adoption" in a will he signed in 1693; colonial legislatures commonly passed individual bills to recognize the adoption of a child.[3] Nevertheless, the attachment to genealogy remained strong, with ambivalent, and sometimes negative, attitudes toward nonbiologically formed families. The seventeenth-century family system was highly regulated and heavily patriarchal, unlike in the 1800s, when adoption narrative was shaped by more feminine principles and a culture of nurture. The early American church fathers privileged bloodline and took rigid stands against unwed motherhood. Mather's and Sewall's writings demonstrate the fluidity of Puritan households in everyday domestic and spiritual life, but their work and that of their contemporaries is also intensely genealogical and suspicious of outsiders. Openness in early American literature toward adoptive practices is moderated by wariness and an inclination to value traditional, patriarchal kinship structures over adoptive ones.

ORPHANS ALL

The Puritans believed that they were a chosen people set on a course of salvation. They viewed themselves as New Israelites, led out of exile on a divinely sanctioned path in fulfillment of scriptural typology. Puritan writers' use of images of birth express the relief of safe arrival: Cotton Mather describes the "ocean crossing as a spiritual rebirth";[4] and Thomas Shepard, according to Sacvan Bercovitch, equates "new life with New World" and "baptism with the Atlantic as a greater Red Sea."[5] However, feelings of fear, abandonment, and guilt over leaving the mother country accompany these joyful expressions. Diana Pazicky observes that the frequent association of the Atlantic crossing with birth is "as deeply rooted in the pain of separation as in the religious signification imposed upon it,"[6] and Patricia Caldwell finds doubt and anxiety in the narratives of those seeking to join the church of New England.[7] For Donald Wharton, the ocean frontier was crossed with an "umbilical" cord to the mother country: "the link was a fragile one, and more than it connected men to their European homeland, it threw them upon their own resources, isolating them from the security and guidance of former practice."[8] Eileen Simpson writes that William Bradford's account of the journey reads "like a fairy tale about the ordeal of children without parents in search of a home."[9] The experience of leaving the Old World was so disruptive, and the challenge of relocation so enormous, that settlers interpreted survival as evidence of God's providence, making migration rather than conversion the keynote in early Puritan life writing.

The first step of separation was a dangerous six-week ocean crossing. Edward Johnson, in "Wonder-Working Providence of Sion's Savior in New England" (ca. 1650), writes that "the ditch between England and their now place of abode was so wide, that they could not leap over with a lope-staff."[10] Homesickness was a common affliction among the first generation of settlers. So profound was the loss of the birth country that Thomas Shepard describes it as a kind of death: "And so I came to this place and coming by sea and having a hard voyage my heart was dead and senseless and I found my heart as stubborn as before."[11] Settlers resisted the terms of orphancy even as they embraced their New World mission. John Winthrop (1588–1649), twelve times the governor of the Massachusetts Bay Colony, refers to the Church of England as a "dear mother" from whom Puritan voyagers cannot depart "without much sadness of heart and many tears in ours eyes."[12] John Cotton (1584–1652), in "God's Promise to His Plantations" (1630), likewise asks fellow Puritans to "forget not the womb that bare you, and the breast that gave you suck. Even *Ducklings* hatched under a *Hen*; though they take the water, yet will still have recourse to the wing that hatched them."[13]

Robert Filmer (ca. 1588–1653) in *Patriarcha* (1680) and Thomas Hobbes (1588–1679) in *Leviathan* (1651), who describe the overlapping duties of father and kings, believed that even though the Puritans were leaving England, they still owed obedience to the paternal authority the Crown represented.[14] Filmer notes that "the desire of liberty was the cause of the fall of Adam" and argues that no men "can be free from subjection to their parents"; the "greatest liberty . . . is for people to live under a monarch."[15] The question of filial attachment to England lasted for generations and became evident in cultural emulation of English customs, laws, and styles.[16] In the eighteenth century, adversaries of the American Revolution used the language of the imperial family and the parent-child metaphor, as Edwin Burrows and Michael Wallace note:

> England enjoyed the rights and duties of parental authority over the colonies while the colonies enjoyed the corresponding rights and duties of children. . . . [S]uch analogies between family and polity . . . lay at the foundations of the English approach to the problems of power and liberty, authority and autonomy.[17]

Kai Erikson writes that the new colonists intended neither to abandon England nor to replace it with a world of their own design, and they hoped that England would not abandon them.[18]

A sense of possession and entitlement in the new land would come in later decades. Perceiving the threat of annihilation everywhere, newly arrived Puritans measured experience by its distance from the mother country and recorded their fear, dependency, and uncertainty. John Cotton describes his reasons for leaving England in *God's Promise to His Plantation* (1630) and repeats them in a letter, leaving Alan Heimert and Andrew Delbanco to wonder "whether his prose is not informed by twinges of regret or remorse."[19] So strong was the connection to the mother country that Cotton calls the migration "voluntary exile."[20] The poet Anne Bradstreet, who arrived aboard the *Arabella* in 1630 at age eighteen and gave birth to eight children in the New World, documents a heart and mind struggling with the loss of home.[21] In a spiritual autobiography addressed to her children, Bradstreet can accept the unfamiliar New World setting only with the most disciplined faith. Her "heart rose" at "a new world and new manners," but "after I was convinced it was the way of God, I submitted to it."[22] In public poetry published early in her career, she celebrates the English culture she left behind and follows stylistic conventions of the Renaissance in a manner that Adrienne Rich interprets as escapist.[23] In private poetry, Bradstreet wrestles with relocation by relying on the language of family. In "A Dialogue between Old England and New; Concerning Their Present Troubles, Anno 1642," the speaker addresses her native England as "dear Mother, fairest queen and best" and promises her allegiance: "You are my mother nurse, and I your flesh." She also calls upon England to join in her sorrow about separation, writing, "Your humble child entreats you, show your grief,/Though arms, nor purse she hath for your relief."[24] Bradstreet alternately denies the distance that separated the Old and New Worlds and asks England to help the colony prosper as an adoptive nation without its mother country.

Hope also meets anxiety in the writings of William Bradford (1590?–1657), who left the Dutch city of Leiden aboard the *Mayflower*. An instrumental founder of the Plymouth colony and its governor from 1621 until his death, Bradford drew comforting parallels between his people's history and that of the children of Israel, as was common at the time. Nevertheless, his strong faith was challenged by the poor climate, disease, and Indian attacks, as described in *Of Plymouth Plantation*. Upon landing at Plymouth Rock, the Pilgrims "fell upon their knees and blessed the God of Heaven, who had brought them over the vast and furious ocean." Once at port, however, the land appeared as threatening and inhospitable as the sea had been. Having withstood "a sea of troubles" before embarking for America, the weary immigrants "had now no friends to welcome them nor inns to entertain or refresh their weatherbeaten bodies; no houses or much less towns to repair to, to seek for succour." Bradford dramatizes the severity of those first years to impress future generations with the founders' stalwart faith and to foster a similar sense of commitment in the younger members of the settlement. Nevertheless, his descriptions convey misgivings that, unlike Moses, who was shown Canaan from a mountaintop, the now homeless immigrants would find no sign from God:

> [W]hat could they see but a hideous and desolate wilderness, full of wild beasts and wild men—and what multitudes there might be of them they knew not. Neither could they, as it were, go up to the top of Pisgah to view from this wilderness a more goodly country to feed their hopes; for which way soever they turned their eyes (save upward to the heavens) they could have little solace or content in respect of any outward objects.[25]

Officially, settlers made little of the challenge of separation. A "conspiracy of silence," Ursula Brumm calls it, was designed to downplay the hazards of relocation and garner support for further emigration.[26] To bolster colonists' confidence, leaders worked out a logic of substitution. Guided by faith in God and their mission, William Bradford asks the newly arrived children of "adversity" to replace their English "fathers" with a divine American one: "Our fathers were Englishmen which came over this great ocean, and were ready to perish in this wilderness; but they cried unto the Lord, and heard their voice. . . . Yea, let them which have been redeemed of the Lord, shew how He hath delivered them from the hand of the oppressor."[27] John Winthrop likewise understates the hardships of migration by matching descriptions of difficulty with claims of fortune, a strategy that laid the groundwork for later American writers to associate the loss of orphancy with the hope of adoption.

As New Englanders settled into their new environment, they found much to be grateful for and took ownership of the land's natural beauty and resources.[28] With this appreciation, the meaning of adoption expanded. Originally conceived as spiritual salvation that connoted child-like dependence or raised the specter of unworthiness, adoption came to represent an opportunity to start anew, prosper, and shape one's destiny. Although his treatise was politically motivated in support of the English crown and church, Thomas Morton, founder of Merrymount, describes the abundance of nature in the New World. "The more I looked, the more I liked it," he writes, taking note of "goodly groves of trees, dainty fine round rising hillocks, delicate fair large plains, sweet crystal fountains, and clear running streams." He notes a country "in a parallel with the Israelites' Canaan, which none will deny to be a land far more excellent than Old England."[29] This new American identity was formed as a result of environmental, not genealogical, good fortune. Robert Douglas Mead reinforces this point, writing that American literature has always resulted from a tension between "the power of ideas and the power of material forces."[30]

Positive attitudes toward relocation were complemented—and complicated—by the settlers' growing perception of the unfitness of the parent country they had left behind. New England colonists increasingly viewed England as incapable of fulfilling its religious and political promises to them. In this respect, the Puritans resembled not orphans but runaways who were leaving their roots and gauging the parent country for its reaction.[31] England, these rebels charged, was theologically untenable. Puritans thus shifted the burden of guilt from children who abandon their parents to parents who deserve their abandonment. Thomas Hooker describes America as a haven for those fleeing a Godless country, writing, "As sure as God is God, God is going from England."[32] John Winthrop likewise writes that when "other churches of Europe are brought to desolation," "who knows but that God hath provided this place to be a refuge for many whom he means to save out the general calamity."[33] Casting England in the role of an abusive or neglectful birth parent, settlers positioned themselves to interpret their adoptive home positively. They did not dwell on the fact that in the biblical story the deliverance of the Israelites constituted a return to the homeland. This biblical pattern was not replicated in the Great Migration that began in 1630 except for a brief period around 1640, the only time when more people returned to England than arrived from there. Instead, the early colonists felt destined to remain in their adopted land, returning to England only in the abstract, through political and cultural emulation.

SPIRIT OF ADOPTION

Of singular importance in Puritan society was the state of one's soul and thus one's candidacy for election, or adoption, by God. The desire to be claimed by God, as Caldwell writes about conversion narratives, was "the speaker's hope to be pure and new and whole in a new and holy place."[34] Puritans persistently describe this prayed-for spiritual salvation in the language of migration, childhood, and family. As Heimert and Delbanco write, "the vaguest and most personal promise of America" was that "it might deliver or revive the *feeling* of belonging to God as a cherished child."[35] Adoption plays a crucial role in this redemptive process.

Belief in salvation was derived from the biblical example of Christ, whose sacrifice transformed the relationship between man and God into one between child and parent, and enabled the believer to enter the kingdom of heaven. Paul writes in his Epistle to the Ephesians about God "having predestinated us unto the adoption of children by Jesus Christ to himself" (Eph. 1:5). In this paradigm, adoption puts an end to spiritual orphancy. "Ye have received the Spirit of adoption," writes Paul; we are "waiting for the adoption, to wit, the redemption of our body" (Rom. 8:15, 23). Romans 9:4 refers to God's chosen people, the "Israelites; to whom pertaineth the adoption, and the glory, and the covenants, and the giving of the law, and the service of God, and the promises." Thomas Hooker explicitly connects adoption, childhood, and salvation when he writes, "We are alive as a child taken out of one family and translated into another, even so we are taken out of the house hold of Sathan, and inserted into the family of God; yea into the mysticall body of *Christ*."[36] Jay Fliegelman observes that according to the Westminster Catechism, the state of grace preceding final sanctification is adoption, which assures the converted of the privileges of spiritual sonship and membership in God's family.[37]

More than a religious symbol, the notion of spiritual adoption informed daily life. The Puritans believed that God's promise continued to be fulfilled through their children, for whom they accepted moral responsibility. As John Winthrop reflects in verse in "A Model of Christian Charity" (1630): "Therefore let us choose life,/that we and our seed may live,/ by obeying His voice and cleaving to Him."[38] Markus Barth likewise observes that Paul emphasizes in Romans "the causative and cognitive power of the Spirit and at the same time juridical-economical implications of adoption: those adopted receive an inheritance."[39] Belief in the power of adoption was so strong that Puritans extended the practice to homeless adults, who were considered orphaned if they were single and who were expected to join themselves to a family.[40]

The role of adoption in spiritual and domestic life is evident in the life and writings of the Puritan preacher Cotton Mather (1663–1728), whose sermons, commonplace books, and letters had great impact in his time and influenced generations of American writers. Kenneth Silverman notes that Mather looms "as the first person to write at length about the New World having never seen the Old," and helped to put America "on the cultural map."[41] Christopher Felker explains that the republication of Mather's 1702 *Magnalia Christi Americana*, a major publishing event when it appeared in 1820, functioned as master text for "considering New England's role in shaping democratic culture." He finds political accents of Mather's texts in nineteenth-century fiction by such writers as Nathaniel Hawthorne, Harriet Beecher Stowe, and Elizabeth Stoddard.[42] The son of Increase Mather and grandson of Richard Mather and John Cotton, Mather was controversial among his contemporaries and subsequently maligned for his fanaticism and complicity in the witchcraft trials.[43] Despite a mixed reception, he conceived of himself as destined for leadership in seventeenth-century Massachusetts and left a full record of his zealous efforts to inspire his parishioners with a no-longer progressive Calvinist theology.

Although best known for theological fervor, Mather also played a significant role defining American kinship. He was no stranger to biological or adoptive parenting and even made a virtue of genealogical disruption. His 1711 signature sermon, "Orphanotrophium," provided a theological and social framework for adoption literature through the nineteenth century and played a part in the United States becoming in the twenty-first century what Adam Pertman calls an "adoption nation."[44]

Mather was a step- and foster-parent as well as a biological parent.[45] High infant and maternal mortality rates in seventeenth-century Massachusetts meant that families frequently confronted the death of loved ones. Married three times, Mather fathered fifteen children, only two of whom survived him. In 1688, his first child died of convulsions at five months of age: that same day, Mather, with characteristic stamina and resignation, set an example for his congregation by preaching on the nature of affliction. "The dying of a Child is like the tearing of a limb from us," he told them.[46] Five of his children by his first wife, Abigail, died. After her death in 1702, he assumed responsibility for his four offspring and parented his second wife's son by her previous marriage. By 1711, he and Elizabeth had four more children, one of whom survived only six months. He lost his second wife, newborn twins, and two-year-old daughter to a measles epidemic in 1713. Later, he took care of a grown, widowed daughter of his third wife, who may have lived for a time with the Mathers.[47]

Mather also served as foster or adoptive parent in his role as minister. In 1688, he agreed to take in a thirteen-year-old girl, Martha Goodwin, who was believed to be possessed by the Devil as a result of her contact with Goody Glover, a local woman convicted of witchcraft and subsequently hanged. After nearly six weeks of devoted effort, Mather declared Martha free of evil spirits and returned her to her family. This event was important, Kenneth Silverman notes, in reinforcing Mather's belief in the supernatural.[48] It is also significant for explaining the make-up of Puritan households, which routinely included nonbiologically related children. Mather met the challenges of biological and nonbiological parenting with equal fervor. A model Puritan in his search for an ever more meaningful one-to-one relationship with his creator, he expected much of himself as well as of the children in his charge and sought to accomplish their betterment through one-on-one interactions. He stressed the importance of reaching each individual child, whether or not the child was related by blood. On Sundays, Mather would single out one of the children or servants, bring him into his study, have him read aloud from the Bible, and engage in discourse to strengthen literacy and faith.[49]

Mather faced myriad problems with children who joined his household temporarily as a result of death, remarriage, or clerical calling, but his greatest trial was with his biological son, Increase, Jr., the first of his male children to survive beyond infancy and the son for whom he held the highest hopes. Chronic disappointment over this child's behavior may have led Mather to think deeply about the bonds that link parents and children and to acknowledge that biological kinship afforded no guarantee of positive outcome. When Cotton himself came of age, he struggled to assume the mantle from his father, Increase Mather, a noted minister. Cotton was therefore doubly disappointed when the son named for this grandfather failed to measure up to his lineage. Creasy (as he was called) caused continual worry despite his father's prayers and efforts: he failed to attend Harvard, as his father and grandfather had done; he kept company with local boys of whom Mather disapproved; he was in legal trouble for public rowdiness; he allegedly impregnated a local prostitute; and he failed to experience a crisis conversion. All manner of disciplinary strategies, including placing his son out with other adults, failed. Mather's vexation over the boy's recalcitrance turned to grief when Creasy was lost at sea in 1723. It then fell to Samuel, the younger son, to carry on the Mather legacy. Although proud of this son's accomplishments, Mather never fully recovered from the sense of failure he felt over his parenting of Creasy. Creasy's failure to measure up to his name may have contributed to Mather's decision to advocate adoption as a way to create positive relationships between parents and children. By 1711, he had contemplated its spiritual as well as practical benefits and was eager to disseminate his ideas to members of his congregation.

"ORPHANOTROPHIUM"

Mather wrote "Orphanotrophium; or, Orphans well-provided for" after the deaths, within three weeks of one another, of congregants John Foster, a magistrate "of Inviolate Integrity," and his wife, Abigail Foster, which left two young children orphaned.[50] The sixty-eight–page sermon reflects Mather's career-long emphasis on not only believing the word of God but also doing his will daily. The importance of personal and public service, the subject of Mather's 1710 "Essays to Do Good,"[51] is reflected in the preface of "Orphanotrophium," which asks congregants to establish "Legacy for Orphans" that will *"befriend their* Temporal *Interests, and their Eternal too."* A focus on doing good is evident in Mather's early writings, stemming perhaps from the social isolation he faced as a result of his unpopular theological stands. In a youthful sermon, written in 1685, he explains, "We all came into the World upon a very important *Errand,* which *Errand* is, To *Do* and to *get Good.*"[52] In 1711, he revised the format of his diaries so that each day he might record a "GOOD DEVISED." In 1713, two years after writing "Orphanotrophium," he declared firmly that the "grand Intention" of his life was *"to Do Good."*[53] The link between adoption and "doing good," so clear in "Orphanotrophium," appears in discourse today, when well-meaning friends or relatives tell adoptive parents that it is good of them to adopt. They may unconsciously reflect the sense that adoption is a secular and sacred blessing, an act of human kindness that reflects divine grace.

During the period in which he wrote "Orphanotrophium," Mather was devoting more of his compositional energies to writing about service and fewer energies to inner spiritual struggle. "Orphanotrophium" shows the influence of German Pietism and exemplifies Mather's aspiration toward generosity as well as faith. He was impressed by the Pietist school's attention to reforming society as well as doctrine. In particular, he was influenced by John Arendt, often called the founder of Pietism, who combined ethical concern and Christian mysticism. He also admired August H. Francke, who organized an impressive educational-philosophical community that Mather publicized in his *Nuncia Bona* (1715). Seeing parallels between Francke and himself, Mather reacted "with wonder [to] the components of Francke's benevolent utopia," which included a school for 1,600 scholars, a free school for poor children, a "Tynaecium" for young women, and a "Cherotrophea" for poor widows.[54] The *Orphano-Tropheum*, or orphan house, that Francke established for 500 students provided the title of Mather's "Orphanotrophium."

"Orphanotrophium" is in the tradition of seventeenth-century conduct literature, a genre to which Mather contributed with his autobiography, *Paterna*, and his advice book, *Ornaments for the Daughters of Zion*, which underlines women's spiritual equality and rational capacity while also prescribing their social subordination to men.[55] "Orphanotrophium" describes a Puritan culture familiar with and hospitable toward adoption within its own ranks. Linking piety and conduct, it expresses the most profound and coveted spiritual relationship—that of God and man—in terms of parent and adopted child. As such, this early American text provides a basis for understanding adoption as a form of salvation among a community of believers with shared goals and perspectives.

The sermon opens with sympathy toward the bereaved children of John and Abigail Foster but immediately places private loss in a larger context of spiritual longing. The orphaned children know full well the desperate pleas made by all the wretched of the earth that God not abandon them, the very fact of their orphancy "challenging that Glorious *Motto; Not Forsaken*" (1–2). Despite feeling forsaken by God, the children should not give in to anger or impatience but rather anticipate deliverance from God, which follows only from acceptance: "if an oppressed man, *Cease from Anger, and Forsake Wrath*, and be a very Patient One; *the Lord is with thee*" (7). Through diligent prayer, orphans will know that *"the Lord will make a better Provision for me, than ever my Parents could"* (9). Mather also encourages adults to reach out to the parentless children. Adults should ask, *"What shall I now do for Poor Orphans? Are there no Poor Orphans of whom you should be able to say . . . I delivered the Fatherless & him that had none to help him? And, the Fatherless has eaten of my Morsel & was brought with me, as with a Father!"* (64).

Mather acknowledges that in the usual course of family life adoption is neither anticipated nor desired. Rather, it occurs when biological parents die or are unable to parent and thus carries the stigma of second choice or second best. However, in a rhetorical tour de force, Mather revises norms to favor adoptive parenting. A high mortality rate in the colonies meant that children frequently forsook their parents; as Mather writes, we see "at least Half the Children of Men dying Short of Twenty" (11). Parental death was also a fact of life. Indeed, to propagate is to acknowledge the ephemeralness of human existence.

Mather advises that "We must then look on our *Parents* as *Mortal*" (15). "That which is most *Natural*, is for the *Parents* to *Forsake* the *Children*, and *Go First* . . . out of the World before them. . . . The *Parents* must make Room for the *Children*" (12–13). Parents who deny their mortality might dread the prospect of a surrogate parent—such as in Anne Bradstreet's poem, about the fear of "stepdame's injury" were the speaker to die in childbirth and leave her children motherless.[56] Mather asks parents to shift their focus from pain at the prospect of death to faith in the knowledge that the true parent is God the father in heaven.[57] He asserts God's providence "at work every where in the World" and "More especially, about *Orphan Children*": "There is a wonderful Providence of God, at work for many Children, when their *Father*, and their *Mother* do *Forsake* them; the *Children* are wonderfully Provided for!" Mather even goes so far as to claim that orphaned children might "Scarce miss their Parents, tho' the Departed Parents had a most unspeakable Fondness for them" (19).

ORPHANCY: A FORTUNATE FALL

For Mather, orphancy is fortunate, not grievous. He refers to "the Orphans Patrimony" and asserts that "no *Singular Affliction* befals them [men of God], without Some excellent *Fruits of Righteousness* brought forth" (4). He enjoins parishioners to see "how easily, how welcome, is the most Grievous Affliction made unto them" and exhorts them to consider "Glorious *Triumphs over Troubles*!" (5). Mather directs his message to the orphaned children and their parents. He reassures both groups that "GOD is their *Guardian*" and "an Alsufficient *Father*" (19). Rather than indulge in self-pity or anger over their loss, congregants should view the plight of orphans as an opportunity for prayer and renewed faith.

Puritans took parental responsibilities seriously. As Edmund Morgan writes, it was assumed that parents would provide their children with food, shelter, and physical and emotional safety and guide them toward an occupation or calling. They borrowed this obligation from nature by observing how their own parents and other creatures cared for their young.[58] Fearful that the convictions that motivated a first generation of Puritans might dissipate in subsequent generations, ministers reminded the older generation of its responsibility to prepare children for the awesome role of God's chosen people. Because parents may not live long enough to see their children grow up, Mather urges them to prepare spiritually for the possibility of their children's orphancy. Preparation involves knowing that comfort comes from faith in God. If God makes children "*Father-less*," he writes in *Paterna*, they will be "*Orphans* well-provided for" since they will be in God's hands.[59] Likewise, in "Orphanotrophium," Mather urges parents to plan for the possibility of their death: "Make a *Testamentary Provision* for them. Let your *Wills* be made, and in a Good order always Lying by you" (40). Focusing on spiritual rather than material inheritance, he asks parents to "lay[] up a stock of prayers," "alms," and "services" for their children (33, 34). In 1721, he elaborates on this point in a sermon: "If your *main concern* be, to get the *Riches* of *this World* for your *Children*, and leave a *Belly full* of this *World* unto them, it looks very suspiciously, as if you were yourselves the People of *this World*, whose *Portion* is only in *this Life*."[60]

In "Orphanotrophium," Mather exhorts birth parents to relinquish feelings of attachment and commit their children in prayerful willingness to God's care. When parents accept other adults as interim caretakers of their children and believe in the honorableness of these adoptive parents, they demonstrate their faith. Just as God attends to motherless ravens and sparrows, so, too, "our Little Birds, when left *Orphans* [are] as much cared for." God sees that they are "*Brought up*" and "their *Education* is provided for" through adoption. God "puts it in the Hearts of those the Law calls *Foster-Fathers*, or Mothers . . . to *Foster* them, & Furnish them, & Cherish them. . . . The *Orphans* have a *Nurture* from such Friends" (21–22). Through adoption, parents emulate God's work, while mindful of their own inadequacies.

Mather likewise encourages orphaned children to find solace in their faith in a heavenly father. He cites Psalms 27.10—"When my Father and Mother forsake me, then the LORD will take me up"—in the epigraph and in the text of the sermon, and urges children to focus on God, not worldly attachments. Orphancy becomes, like any earthly affliction, a test of faith, call to prayer, and occasion for thankfulness. Just as the songs of David were produced by adversity, so, too, orphans might embrace their lot as "*Happy Troubles*," not disastrous ones (5). Alluding to the fall of Adam and Eve and the benefit of experience rather than innocence, Mather offers children divine consolation as compensation for orphancy. When the parents are "laid *Asleep*. . . . Then the Orphans are Savingly Awakened, & brought home unto God their Saviour" (23).

All Puritan children were expected to be pious and obedient toward their parents. Compliance when the parents are alive ensures a blessing in the event of parental death: "*Parents* which have been gratified by Dutiful and Obliging Behaviour of their *Children* do Bless them in the Name of God and Pronounce *Blessings* for them, when they shall be left as *Orphans*" (29–30). Mather holds hope for these orphans, writing, "Such *Orphans* as have been Singularly *Dutiful* unto their *Parents* . . . have singular cause to hope, That *God will take them up*" (29). Exemplary figures, orphans are more afflicted than other children, more mindful of the need to surrender their will, and more aware of God's grace. The injunction to yield to parental wishes pertains especially to orphans, whose pain evokes the sufferings of Christ: "*Orphans*," Mather writes, "You may with a *Filial Familiarity*, make your Approaches unto God; your dear JESUS has led you the way" (49–50). The Christ imagery suggests that the more dire the circumstances, the greater the gain. Living without parents in a "World wherein *Iniquity abounds*" (27), orphans understand in a vivid, concrete way that which is true for all believers: that they are all "the *Foster-children* of Providence" (22). They may then receive grace, of which their adoption is one sign. Mather writes that "when the Children become *Orphans*, Then particularly they reap some of the *Recompense*" (29).

Puritans relied on a variety of child-rearing techniques to ensure children's piety and obedience. For example, in *Paterna*, Mather prays for children and teaches them to pray, tells entertaining stories with pious messages, and imparts brief lessons even at chance meetings. Progressive in his approach, he believed that it was best to appeal to the child's conscience to develop an internal sense of right and wrong. Anticipating the benign methods of child rearing of the nineteenth century, he disapproved physical punishment except as a last resort.[61] *Paterna* advises rewarding a child's good behavior with further opportunities for learning and recommends that parents teach children according to "principles of *Reason* and *Honour*" as well as to the "*Higher Principles*."[62] However, Mather insists that children accept their father's authority: "*My word* must be *their Law*." When necessary he relied upon the separation of child and parent to underline the need for the child to surrender to higher authority. Among his disciplinary strategies, isolating the child from the security of the family was the most drastic measure Mather could take. He writes, "To be *chased for a while out of my presence*" is looked upon "as yᵉ sorest Punishment in the Family."[63] Child-parent separation, a precondition of adoption, thus serves a cautionary function.

Mather's sermon demonstrates that, although not the primary method of forming families, adoption was theologically justified, commonplace, and publicly discussed in colonial society. This open approach continued through the nineteenth century, in contrast to the first half of the twentieth century, when adoption became associated with secrecy and shame.[64] In Mather's scheme, adoption occurs naturally in a Christian context in which family, church, and community have shared goals. Representing orphancy as a fortunate fall—and orphans as beneficiaries of divine grace—Mather articulates a common sentiment in American literature: adoption is a form of child saving. By adopting others, one does God's work. At the same time, however, the adoption of children can only approximate God's power and generosity and falls short of ultimate adoption— redemption. Because they believed that all human endeavors inadequately compare with divine ones, Puritans viewed the parenting of biological and nonbiological children as a spiritual obligation to be practiced as a matter of course, with disinterest rather than with passion. The practice of placing out, a temporary form of adoption, reflects this understanding that all children, including adopted ones, exist not to fulfill human desires but to help answer the call of faith.

FAMILY "RICH AND BROAD"

A natural outgrowth of marriage, children were considered a blessing as well as an economic and demographic necessity.[65] Elaine Tyler May notes that "without children, households would be unable to function as economically productive units, and communities would wither and die."[66] Early American settlers took seriously the biblical injunction to "be fruitful and multiply" and conferred status on fertile men and women. Laura Ulrich writes that "to have 177 descendants" was to be blessed.[67] Nearly all men and women married, and the families they produced were large, often with six or more children.[68] Procreation was so much valued that deliberate attempts to remain childless could be grounds for divorce.[69]

Women assumed primary responsibility for the day-to-day care of children, whereas men took charge of discipline, religious education, and social training.[70] To avoid suspicion, childless women were expected to prove themselves through service to others in ways that their fertile neighbors were not, often by participating in adoptive functions. They helped to rear the community's children, even housing them in their homes. Most children lost at least one parent before they reached adulthood and needed such care.[71] "Never may we write her Barren who is fruitful in good works," wrote Reverend Benjamin Coleman in 1711 in support of adoptive parenting, "the orphans are her children."[72] Although data on the number of childless couples in the New England colonial period are scarce, most adoptive families were childless couples who took in children of relatives. Adoption of orphaned children was generally arranged informally, with blood relatives given preference.[73] There was no legal means of adopting a child, but a fluid, community-based family system made such laws unnecessary.[74] Unlike in England, which followed a system of primogeniture that relied on blood ties and birth order to determine inheritance rights, laws in New England permitted "de facto adoption." Under this system, even children who were not fully orphaned might be placed with a family not related by blood. May cites a story about such an adoption in Plymouth Colony in 1658. On his deathbed, with his wife still living, William Peaks bequeathed their youngest child to John Allin and his wife, Ann. When the Allins asked how long they could keep the boy, Peaks answered, "for ever."[75]

Early American households were far from the tight nuclear structures found in the United States today.[76] As May writes, "colonial families were not private, domestic retreats" but rather intertwined economies that "blended into one another as the needs of each economic unit changed."[77] The size of Puritan households regularly expanded and contracted, with nuclear as well as extended family members, servants, children of friends, and even strangers coming and going at various times. The care of nonbiological children went by many names, as Toby Ditz notes, including fostering, apprenticeship, and guardianship, which referred to jurisdiction over a child's person as well as authority to preserve and account for a minor's inherited property.[78] Among early American families of means, including that of Samuel Sewall, wet-nurses added to the household number.[79] Although the wet-nurse's role was limited, this temporary adoptive mother was on intimate terms with family members. Affluent homes might also include servants and slaves who were treated as family members, with the head of household assuming responsibility for their spiritual training and edification. In this expansive family environment, adoptive care was familiar, not anomalous.

Samuel Sewall (1652–1730), a prominent Massachusetts judge, merchant, and councilor, kept a detailed diary describing a range of bonds under the rubric "family." His experience, both "rich and broad," cautions against monolithic or strictly genealogical constructions of the early American family.[80] Sewall had fourteen children, of whom six survived infancy. He also took interest in children outside his immediate family and expended time, effort, and resources on their behalf. He housed, tutored, and mentored several young men preparing for Harvard College, including two sons of rural ministers and a young Indian boy. He sheltered three orphaned grandchildren and was named guardian of a young man whom he apprenticed to an associate. Nieces and nephews frequently visited Sewall's home, and other young men and women joined his household as servants. A distant cousin's son lived with him and served him in old age, and a niece lived with his family from the time of her youth to adulthood.[81] The affections that each of these children received and bestowed varied according to circumstances, including the children's educational and emotional needs and Sewall's domestic situation at they time they entered his home. Taken as a whole, however, Sewall's busy domicile, peopled by blood and nonblood related kin, attests to the normative nature of nonbiological kinship in early colonial America. Sewall's care of others' children reveals the socioeconomic dimensions of adoption: he was able to take in so many children because, as a prominent Boston jurist and merchant, he had the means to do so. Most of the children who stayed with him came from situations of equal or less affluence and privilege. From early colonial times to today, adoption often involves children moving from less advantaged to more advantaged settings.

Sewall took in his first child in 1676, in the first year of his marriage, before he had biological children, and groomed him for Harvard. Seth Shove, the son of Rev. George

Shove of Taunton, completed his studies in 1687, after which time Sewall and Shove maintained an affectionate association, with Sewall often writing letters to the young man, "who was like a son to him." Graham describes a "bizarre" entry in Sewall's diary about the occasion of Seth's arrival. He is mistaken for a dog and beaten, his experience echoing Harriet Wilson's description in her 1859 novel, *Our Nig*, when Frado Smith, a servant who has a strong bond with the family dog, brings in the wrong size firewood and Mrs. Bellmont "kicked her so forcibly as to throw her upon the floor" (43–44).[82] Sewall writes:

> In the evening, seeing a shagged dogg in the Kitchin, I spake to John Alcock [an apprentice to Sewall's father-in-law], *I am afraid we shall be troubled with that ugly dogg*: whereupon John asked which way he went. I said out at the Street door. He presently went that way, and meeting Seth (who went out a little before) took him for the dogg, and smote him so hard upon the bare head with a pipe staff, or something like it, that it grieved me that he had strook the dogg so hard. There arose a considerable wheal in the childs head, but it seems the weapon smote him plain, for the Rising was almost from the forehead to the Crown, grew well quickly, wearing a Cap that night. 'Twas God's mercy the stick and manner of the blow was not such as to have spilled his Brains on the Ground. The Devil, (I think) seemed to be angry at the childs coming to dwell here.[83]

Sewall takes no personal responsibility for the brutal beating, calling it the work of the "Devil." However, Seth's tale ends happily, unlike Frado's. Despite the inauspicious start, Seth got along well in the Sewall household. A few months later, Sewall accompanied Seth to "gather what herbs we could get, as Yarrow, Garglio, &c.," and in April Seth began formal education under a tutor named Smith. He was admitted to Harvard and received his B.A. in 1687 and M.A. in 1690. During Seth's time at Harvard, he was visited several times by his father, and when the father died in 1687, Sewall's diary records his continuing generosity: "with the news of's father's death yesterday, I let him have my Horse to ride to Taunton." With Sewall's assistance, Seth Shove was appointed schoolmaster in Newbury in 1691, where he taught for several years, clearly rewarding Sewall for his efforts and care.[84]

Sometime before March of 1718 or 1719, Sewall took in another child, the orphaned Grindall Rawson, the tenth child and namesake of a minister-scholar from Mendon, a descendant of John Wilson, founding pastor of the First Church. Grindall joined the Sewall household when he was about eleven and probably remained with Sewall until he entered Harvard in 1724.[85] Sewall's general beneficence, commitment to education, and belief in the religious conversion of Indians were the primary motives for his taking in an Indian boy, Benjamin Larnell, who arrived with only a letter of introduction. Under Sewall's guardianship, Larnell became an excellent student and was admitted to Harvard in 1712. Sewall showed a remarkable commitment to Larnell when he welcomed him back into his home after he was expelled for disorderly behavior. Graham writes that Sewall made "no distinction . . . between the ministers' sons (Shove and Rawson) and the Indian boy."[86] Sewall was instrumental in helping Larnell gain readmission to college, but he died of fever in Sewall's home in 1714, before graduating.[87] Sewall practiced what Graham calls "a spirited humanitarianism in the defense of Negroes and Indians,"[88] a quality that served him well when it came to taking in others' children.

Approachable, fair-minded, and measured in interactions with others, Sewall appeared temperamentally suited for his adoptive roles. Biological parenting proved to be the greater challenge. Sewall was vexed by the behavior of his biological grandson, Sam Hirst. Sam was orphaned when he was twelve years old; he and two of his four sisters joined Sewall's household in 1717, when Sewall was in his sixties. Sam entered the Harvard class of 1723 and succeeded in graduating, but his propensity to create mischief caused concern. Exasperated at Sam's failure to attend to religious duties or obey his authority, Sewall finally ordered his grandson out of his house, taking what Graham calls "a drastic step for the ordinarily forgiving and generous Sewall."[89] Whether the rift would have healed over time cannot be known; Sam unexpectedly died at sea a year later.

There is no record of the feelings of the children Sewall took in—Graham writes that "we can imagine the [distressed] feelings of the young children sent away from their own families and communities to enter a stranger's home in Boston."[90] Evidence suggests Sewall's even-handed treatment of his adoptive children and charges. At least once, Sewall demonstrated a preference for blood kinship. When he required household assistance in old age, he arranged for a niece to be his companion and servant. Graham surmises that "kinship figured directly" in the case of Jane Toppan's coming into the Sewall home and "more remotely" in the case of Benjamin Sweet's staying with the Sewall family. A distant relative, Sweet assisted Sewall in business and received an education in return, exemplifying the economic as well as emotional benefits of the Puritan practice of placing out.[91]

PLACING OUT

The terms "placing out" and "adoption" are not technically synonymous although they can be used interchangeably.[92] Placing out was often temporary; adoption was meant to be permanent. Also, children placed out were often older and closer to the age when they might fend for themselves, whereas children adopted because of parental death or illness might be of any age. However, both occurred in a context in which it was socially acceptable, if not commonplace, for children to move from the household of their birth to another home. Placing out might also resemble adoption in curtailing visits with birth families. Alan Macfarlane, citing English sources, says loss of contact with home was minimal. However, Edmund Morgan notes that although children in New England who apprenticed in close proximity might be able to visit home frequently, especially on Sundays, he found only one apprenticeship contract that specifically provided for home visitations.[93] Both practices developed Puritan families' skills in incorporating strangers into their homes and fostered a fluid sense of family and parenthood. And both adoption and placing out gave adults in all walks of life the opportunity and responsibility to raise children. Arrangements were often flexible and informal, like that in some African American and Native American communities today, and unlike the highly regulated legal procedure in most of the United States. For example, when Cotton Mather's son Sewall (known as "Sammy") was accepted to Harvard in 1719, Mather wrote John Leverett, the college president, to ask him to serve not only as Sammy's president, but also as his tutor and surrogate father. Mather wrote that he unequivocally entrusted his son to Leverett's "wise, and kind, and paternal tuition."[94] Placing out speaks to the permeability of nuclear family boundaries and to ways that biological and nonbiological forms of kinship were put in service to Christian faith.

Colonists inherited the practice of placing out from England, where it has a long history. In Shakespeare's time, upper-class children from about ten years of age onward might be sent to other families to learn manners and cement interfamily loyalties; middle-class children to learn trades and professions; and lower-class children to become servants. Beatrice Gottlieb argues that placement could begin as early as age seven, but ordinary apprenticeship placements—not those precipitated by schooling, illness, poverty, or parental death—occurred at ten.[95] Lawrence Stone describes a "vast system of exchange" peculiar to England in the sixteenth and seventeenth centuries by which parents sent their children away from home and estimates that two of every three boys and three of every four girls were living away from home.[96] Puritan motivations for placing out are the subject of continuing controversy among scholars, but some reasons for the practice echo those for adoption.

As in the case of adoption, children might be moved from one household to another because of critical need, such as death. John Demos writes that children were also placed by birth parents who wished to give the child an education or better material chance than they themselves could provide because of their age or economic fragility. In this case, birth parents might take advantage of kinship networks, especially when another family's social, political, or economic status proved beneficial to a child's education or advancement.[97] Judith Graham suggests that placing out served concrete rather than ideological functions, a view that David Hackett Fischer shares. He also notes practical purposes for placing out, such as situating a child near a school or training for a calling, and instilling good manners.[98] Graham argues that "the parent-child relationship in early New England was marked by warmth, sympathy, and love; that the special nature of childhood was a concept that parents understood very well; and that when children spent time in other households, it was for an entirely practical, clear purpose."[99] Helena Wall views placing out as an economic exchange, with apprenticeship or service in another's home filling a need that biological parents were unable to provide, usually because of poverty, but she also cites bonds of affection that distinguish some placements from those based on financial considerations.[100]

Philosophical views of child rearing also influenced the practice of placing out. In Puritan households in England and in the colonies, education of children started early in order to establish a habit of piety and obedience. Learning began in the home, but questions arose about whether the child would receive better training outside its confines, and a tradition of pseudo-relinquishment developed, based on the notion that birth families were not the best influence for the children. These placements were intended to serve the child's best interest. However, the practice also benefited parents, who saw themselves as contributing to the societal good by alleviating homelessness and need. Thompson speculates that placing out was a mutually agreeable way to mediate intergenerational conflict as children came into their own and questioned parental authority or faced issues of sexuality.[101] Stone suggests that placing out resolved issues of sexuality by removing children from Oedipal tensions and safeguarding them against incest, and protecting them from other intergenerational tensions, a view with which Macfarlane and Illick concur.[102] Macfarlane further suggests that placing out mediated tensions over household authority that developed among the existing and budding adults. These historians connect placing out with issues of puberty, an argument Graham rejects, noting that children were sent out at all ages, not just at puberty.[103]

The widespread Puritan practice of placing out has led to the contested conclusion that Puritans did not love their children as today's parents do, or to the opposite conclusion, that parents consciously took steps to keep themselves from forming too strong emotional attachment to their offspring.[104] Similar theories of motivation surround issues of adoption today, with some praising birth parents for having the courage and selflessness to place a child they feel inadequate to parent, and others judging parents harshly for relinquishing their children. Edmund Morgan posited the now widely circulated theory that Puritan parents harbored a suspicion of the great love they felt for their children, feared spoiling them, and believed themselves the least suitable people to be entrusted with their care.[105] Although he describes dominant parenting practices rather than those associated with adoption, his explanation places the primary focus on children's spiritual salvation, a motivation found in American adoption literature through the nineteenth century.

A corollary of the belief in original sin was the conviction that parental discipline was needed to curb children's natural impulses. Although natural bonds create strong emotional ties between parent and child, they may be insufficient or even counterproductive when it comes to meeting parental obligations. As John Wall writes, believing "that parents' love toward children is, like everything human, deeply 'corrupted,' by original sin," Puritans took pains not to indulge or favor offspring. Adoption and similar acts of surrogacy allowed parents to perform their disciplinary duty, promote their child's well being, and maintain religious and social order.[106] Adoption thus aligns with larger religious and civic goals aimed at strengthening society as well as family.

RESERVATIONS

Despite the Puritan practice of taking in others' children, reservations about adoption were evident in the social dimensions of Puritan culture. These reservations included a suspicion of outsiders, an emphasis on natural bonds between parent and child, and a patriarchal model of authority that enforced a hierarchy of family relations. A child without the security of an intact genealogy could arouse wariness or become the target of disciplinary surveillance or exclusion. This unease toward adoption is found throughout American literature.

A positive view of adoption was supported by two interlocking belief structures about community and faith. First, in Puritan culture, responsibility for raising a family was distributed not just among immediate kin but within the community as a whole. From the beginning, Calvinist leaders sought to knit together the diverse strands of intimate and civic life. In 1637, John Winthrop extended the definition of family to the entire church community in "A Model of Christian Charity":

We must entertain each other in brotherly affection, we must be willing to abridge ourselves of our superfluities, for the supply of others' necessities; we must uphold a familiar commerce together . . . in all meekness, patience and liberality. We must delight in each other, make others' conditions our own, rejoice together, mourn together, labor and suffer together.[107]

Cotton Mather echoed Winthrop in 1699 when he wrote that "[F]amilies are the Nurseries of all Societies. . . . Well-ordered Families naturally produce a Good Order in other Societies."[108] These interlocking definitions of family, church, and society meant that Puritans commonly took interest in domestic matters outside their own households and willingly extended the family unit through adoption.

Second, the Bible, the foundation of Calvinist belief, encouraged a wide and positive interpretation of adoption. Citing lines of scripture such as "Having predestinated us unto the adoption of children by Jesus Christ to himself [for adoption toward him]," according to the good pleasure of his will" (Eph. 1:5), believers focused on divine bonds. They prayed to God as helpless children and sought spiritual shelter under their divine father's care. Edmund Morgan notes that believers thought of God "not as an inscrutable and almighty Being but as a husband or father."[109] A Calvinist emphasis on spiritual filiation blurred distinctions between blood and adoptive kinship. As Constance Post puts the question in regard to phraseology found in Paterna, Cotton Mather's treatise on the subject of the education of children: "when Mather writes 'My son,' as he so frequently does in Paterna, is he invoking Solomon's use of the phrase for his biological son throughout the book of Proverbs, or is he relying upon Paul's use of the phrase to refer to Timothy, as his spiritual son?"[110] Embracing Christ's message that "For unto whomsoever much is given, of him shall much be required" (Luke 12:48), Puritans accepted as part of their mission the responsibility to improve themselves and others in their charge. One way to imitate God is to adopt children who need a home.

Interwoven concepts of family, community, and faith created an environment for non-biologically as well as biologically related children.[111] However, adoptive kinship did not enjoy the same stature as biological kinship. Paradoxically, a theological endorsement of adoption drew attention to biological kinship, for which adoption did not fully substitute. Puritans viewed adoption as a way to serve the needy, expand the family, and emulate God's ways, but adoptive and biological kinship were never synonymous. The result was that adoption by humans was marginalized even as adoption by God was glorified.

Early Puritan society was characterized, as Thomas Bender notes, by uniformity as well as unity. Villages achieved high levels of communal organization and cooperation, which derived from common feelings and experiences. Socially constructed bonds drew people together, and towns were established through the signing of a covenant. Membership was "fundamentally spiritual and experiential," based on long-standing friendship and a decision-making process that acknowledged broad obligations based upon a fusion of reason and emotion.[112] As the number of settlements grew, individual villages tended to be homogenous, somewhat self-contained units. Bender explains the bonds that held these smaller communities together:

> The family and the Christian fellowship provided the basis for local life. . . . One's social roles as father, neighbor, fellow Christian, farmer, town official, all converged. . . . It was a remarkably undifferentiated society, and it was difficult to draw the line between family and community, private and public.[113]

One result of this homogeneity was that anomalies of any kind aroused anxiety or suspicion, a point Nathaniel Hawthorne makes in The Scarlet Letter, in which Salem residents attribute a glow in the night sky to the spirit of their deceased Governor Winthrop, believe the rash on Arthur Dimmesdale's chest is the handiwork of the Devil, and assume that the illegitimate Pearl is Satan incarnate. For Hawthorne, the Puritan tendency to ascribe spiritual significance to natural phenomena suggests a narrow outlook and a desire to control that which seems alien or threatening.

Fear of the unknown applied equally to children and adults, with early settlers relating natural occurrences (e.g., birth deformities) to supernatural phenomena. Samuel Sewall took care to record births that resulted in mothers' deaths as well as anomalous births that drew public attention or sanction. In his diary, a baby born with no tongue and deformed hands and feet is linked to an eclipse of the moon, and a comet in Mexico is noted as coinciding with the birth of a child without arms. Likewise, Cotton Mather thought that his baby son was born with a blocked intestinal tract because his wife had recently been frightened by a specter.[114] Puritans expressed skepticism about nonbiological parent-child relationships. Although a high incidence of mortality among women giving birth rendered many children half-orphans and resulted in the father's remarriage, Puritan writings question whether a stepparent, especially a stepmother, can love her new charges as much as her biological offspring.

Despite social practices that extended the boundaries of family, Puritan perspectives remained provincial. Congregants opened their homes to the orphaned children of members of their own church, as in the case with John and Abigail Foster's children, referenced in Cotton Mather's sermon, "Orphanotrophium." But they were generally distrustful of strangers and wary of adverse influences from outside their ranks. As Alice Morse Earle notes, towns were self-sufficient and made social pacts that included mutual helpfulness based on shared interests and faith; however, "there was one curious and contradictory aspect of this neighborliness, and that was its narrowness, especially in New England." This narrowness was manifested in the way one town treated individuals from another town. Earle continues: "[J]ust as soon as any group of settlers could call themselves a town, these colonists' notions of kindliness and thoughtfulness for others became distinctly and rigidly limited to their own townspeople. The town was their whole world." She notes "a constant suspicion of all newcomers."[115] David Rothman writes that in Rhode Island a "suspicion of strangers [was] so intense as to seem almost paranoid," with strong messages to care for the resident poor but not outsiders. He writes that the "longtime resident, related to a well-established family, known to be a regular attendant at church services, was an important prop of the community. . . . But outsiders posed a more serious problem and warranted scrutiny."[116]

Displaced children easily fell into the category of outsider. London was full of homeless and destitute children who were eagerly sought after in the mid-Atlantic and southern colonies, especially Virginia, often for their labor. However, New England settlers, wary of strangers, admitted relatively few children. John Winthrop, Diana Pazicky notes, "barely mentions orphans in his journal, except to note the arrival of twenty in 1643, one of whom was subsequently abused so badly by his master that he died in 1644."[117] Early Americans felt moral responsibility to adopt others; however, they shaped the English poor laws they inherited to define the "other" in terms that met their own circumstances and priorities. Rothman writes that they enacted provisions that empowered local governments, specified their responsibility "for their own needy," and established mechanisms to exclude others.[118] When Puritans did accept emigrant children into their household, they often came as indentured servants rather than as full members of the family. An entrenched, class-based hierarchy privileged genealogical connections and limited adoption to those already accepted into the fold.[119]

ILLEGITIMATE BIRTH

As a rule, the birth of a child was an event met with pleasure. Linda Pollock, for example, revises Ariès and Stone's argument that the historical child was met with indifference, and argues that Puritan belief about a child's innate sinfulness notwithstanding, children were wanted and welcomed into the world.[120] Graham concurs, noting that "[u]nder ordinary circumstances, the Puritan infant was warmly, if cautiously, received into the family."[121] However, children born under extraordinary circumstances might be less warmly received. Adults responded warily to the birth of "unwanted" children such as those born out of wedlock, especially as a result of rape. The close alignment of family and community made the birth and care of children a public issue, with church and state intervention accepted as a matter of course. By the same token, failures within the family were thought to affect communal health adversely. Ill-ordered families, including those affected by illegitimacy, posed challenges to a commonwealth that, in accordance with Winthrop, viewed the family as a small church and training ground for pious civic life.[122] Meeting the needs of such precariously positioned children could stretch the fiber of the Puritan community.

One measure of the strength of Puritan resistance to adoption is the response to unexpected births. Records of adoption in seventeenth-century New England are incomplete and often anecdotal—few official records of adoptions were kept in the United States until the twentieth century[123]—but the social organization of family life was such that children eligible by contemporary standards for adoption often were not adopted. Three occasions commonly warranted the adoptive placement of a child: parental death, neglect, and illegitimacy. A 1648 Massachusetts Bay Colony law allowed for unruly, incorrigible children to be removed from their home and placed in another one,[124] but adoption was not routinely practiced as a way to alleviate the hardships of parents who were too poor, too young, or unmarried.

On the contrary, Puritan legal and social practice worked to encourage, even force, a mother to rear her child, sometimes with the legislated support of the birth father. The reason was economic as well as moral: Puritan authorities wished to avoid the child becoming a financial burden on the community. Law required that the named father of an illegitimate child pay for its support and education. In some cases, this law, although intended to deter sexual behavior outside of marriage, may have resulted in de facto adoption, as Morgan notes, because a mother who was penniless might claim that a wealthy, innocent man rather than a poorer one was responsible for her child's birth.[125] This system worked to ascertain biological fatherhood. It also made it possible for mothers to raise their children, in contrast to practices at other times in U.S. history, especially the mid- to late twentieth century, when many unmarried, young white women were pressured to relinquish their children for adoption.[126]

Illegitimate births challenged Puritan society, which was built on the strength of marriage and community. As Morgan points out, the penalty for fornication was left largely to the discretion of the court, which could impose marriage, fines, or corporal punishment.[127] Richard Godbeer notes that women were increasingly held more account-able for these crimes than men.[128] Emphasizing the economic dimension, May notes that if a woman's sexual misconduct resulted in offspring who became a burden on the com-munity, she would be severely punished. Servant women who became unwed mothers were subject to fines or whipping, or they might have their term of service extended to compensate for the trouble and lost labor they cost their masters. Servant women might also lose their children at an early age if the court required them to be bound out for ser-vice. These penalties for fornication encouraged women to marry the fathers of their chil-dren, who would then be responsible for their care. Adultery, "the supreme violation of the familial order," was dealt with even more harshly. It was a capital crime and although the death penalty was rarely invoked, colonists were executed for this infraction.[129]

Because adoption was not a ready alternative for unwed mothers wary of raising their children alone, a mother unwilling or unable to parent had few options and could experi-ence extreme distress over the birth of a child. Lyle Koehler describes the desperate situ-ation of unwed mothers who had little chance of finding a husband and faced censure, fining, or whipping for their transgressions. No foundling homes existed; if the child was left at a neighbor's home or public location, authorities would act to track down and punish the mother. Mothers distraught over the birth of a child they could not care for had the choice either of parenting or infanticide. Koehler concludes that in these dire situations, infanticide sometimes seemed the "only tolerable alternative."[130] He further argues that these women, clearly outside approved norms, demonstrated by their refusal to accept the feminine role of motherhood and thereby signaled their discontent with society: "Whether self-consciously or not," he writes, "they were rebels."[131]

Infanticide, a relinquishment of the most severe kind, is a harsh alternative to adop-tion, and clearly required commitment and fortitude. Koehler argues that "mothers who chose infanticide acted out of strong conviction. They had up to nine months to come to their decision and to grapple with the moral consequences of their act. Once their crime was exposed, such mothers rarely expressed much penitence."[132] A woman charged with giving birth to and murdering an illegitimate child had the recourse of confronting the child's father in court, but the burden of responsibility usually fell on her, not the birth father. In one case, Sarah Threeneedles argued to no avail that had the birth father pro-vided support rather than abandonment, he might have prevented her decision to mur-der her child. Her case demonstrates the socioeconomic aspects of unmarried motherhood and adoption, still salient today.

Judith Graham notes the "desperation, hopelessness, and profound emotional dis-tress" of such women and speculates that their lot might have been improved had adop-tion practices been more accepted.[133] Both illegitimate births and infanticide were matters of intense community interest and were investigated and policed, a point Hawthorne ill-ustrates in *The Scarlet Letter*. Graham observes that Samuel Sewall noted all cases that came before his court and those of other magistrates, including executions of women for murdering their illegitimate children. It was common practice to bring a sentenced woman to the meeting house before the execution where her case became the subject of the sermon. There it was hoped the spectacle of her case would edify the community and provide an opportunity for the woman's public expression of repentance.

Despite stigmas attached to illegitimacy, Puritan society was not without its support of mothers. The law evolved in such a way to help unmarried women gain support for raising their children, thus lowering the chance of infanticide. Roger Thompson notes that by 1668, Massachusetts law dictated that an unmarried woman in labor was to be called upon by the midwife to name the father of the child, who then would be charged with the child's maintenance. Although the policy left the door open for women to charge wealthy men who were innocent of wrongdoing, it also gave women the opportunity to retain custody of illegitimate children and progress with their lives with the help of material support. Women who bore children outside of marriage as well as the children themselves garnered little compassion from the community. However, as Sewall's diary shows, the Puritan system took steps to extract confessions and penitence from those guilty of fornication, thereby providing for their reintegration into society.[134] Morgan notes that although Puritans

> ... established a code of laws that demanded perfection ... they nevertheless knew that frail human beings could never live up to the code. . . . [R]ape, adultery, and fornication they regarded as pardonable human weaknesses, all the more likely to appear in a religious community, where the normal course of sin was stopped by wholesome laws.[135]

Illegitimate and poor children routinely remained with their mother, but adoption practices varied with a family's social and economic position. The wages of sin might be lightened or the prospects for adoption increased for families of means. Those who were well connected or had good marriage prospects might be more likely to receive the magistrates' forbearance or to benefit from arrangements that would provide for mother and child in a discreet way. Samuel Sewall's diary indicates that when his ward, Samuel Haugh, was accused of indiscretion with a maid in the household where he was apprenticed, Sewall advised the young man to acknowledge his responsibilities and marry the woman. When a former maid to Sewall's first wife Hannah bore an illegitimate child, Sewall offered the father of the offending son an arrangement by which he would provide for the child and avoid public attention. Another scandal struck close to home when Rebeckah Dudley Sewall, the wife of Sewall's son, Sam, Jr., from whom he was estranged, gave birth to an illegitimate child. Samuel Sewall and the errant wife's father took immediate steps and arranged for the child to be raised elsewhere in an informal adoption. They awarded restitution to the wronged husband, and they helped the couple resume life together. Because of her privileged position, Rebeckah faced neither court nor punishment. As Graham writes, "respectable families often found a way to absorb the problem of illegitimate children."[136] Quietly arranged adoptions, then as now, were alternatives to the inconvenience and shame of rearing an illegitimate child.

INHERITED ELECTION

Pauline doctrine gave a prominent place to adoption yet did not lead to unqualified endorsement. As Constance Post points out, Paul, who was himself childless, configured sonship as a spiritual rather than biological relationship and in so doing established a pattern whereby Christian dogma could reach out to those not already in the fold. The Puritans imagined the Elect as children joined to God as kin, but not everyone was a member of the Elect. To be included in the Covenant, a child had to be born to church members and be baptized, and even then the child was not necessarily saved. The Half-Way Covenant of 1662 helped to relax the requirements for the children of church members, and, Post notes, "paved the way for conflating biological and spiritual sonship."[137] Nevertheless, acceptance of nonbiologically related children was limited.

A commitment to natural as well as communal bonds positioned the adoptee as both insider and outsider. Focused on election, the Puritans created the concept of the chosen child who meets the requirements of spiritual and physical worthiness. A sense of the adoptee as chosen or "special" persists in popular discourse today. However, when Thomas Shepard uses familial language in "The Church Membership of Children, and their Right to Baptism," it is clear that some children are more chosen than others. He alludes to adoption in his description of the "double *Seed*": the external seed comprised of church members and the internal seed comprised of God's chosen ones. Both are adopted children, but the children of the internal seed have the advantage of "saving Grace," which the children of the external seed lack.[138] John Winthrop argues likewise in his 1637 "A Defense of an Order of Court." After asserting that the family is synonymous with the commonwealth, Winthrop draws boundaries around the domestic unit, writing, "a family is not bound to entertain all comers."[139] Adoption, theoretically available to all, in fact extended only to some.

Adopted individuals lacked the quality Puritans most revered: lineage. Puritan preachers who offered spiritual guidance to children routinely emphasized the importance of genealogy. Thomas Cobbett, for example, directs his comments not to all children but to those of proper descent: "Remember, I speak to the Children of the Godly, to the Children of the Church, though not altogether excluding others."[140] To underline the importance of piety, Cobbett elaborates on the child's place in a genealogical system. When he resists evil, the child acts not simply for and by her- or himself, but through, with, and on the behalf of all those who come before and after. Cobbett offers a lock-step method by which children of the Godly might be saved: they must follow in the paths of their ancestors.

> Hereby you become grossly unfaithfull, yea treacherous to your God, to your Ancestours, to your Parents, to posterity, to the whole Church. God made you his Trustees, and so did Ancestours and Parents make you their spirituall Trustees, under God, to hold up Religion, Truth, the Worship, Waies, and Government of Christ.[141]

Preacher William Stoughton likewise evokes genealogy as the true indicator of redemption:

> Consider and remember always, that the *Books* that shall be opened at the last day will contain *Genealogies* in them. There shall then be brought forth a *Register of the Genealogies of New-Englands sons and daughters*. How shall we many of us hold up our faces then, when there shall be a solemn rehearsal of our *descent* as well as of our *degeneracies*? To have it published whose Child thou art will be cutting unto thy soul, as well as to have the Crimes reckoned up that thou art guilty of.[142]

In sermon after sermon, deficient genealogy is synonymous with exclusion from election. The tendency to value the biological parent-child bond was so strong that some religious leaders portrayed the separation of the child from its biological parent as Hell itself. Ministers commonly asked their congregations to imagine the worst possible scenario at Judgment Day: "What a dismal thing it will be," exhorts Increase Mather, "when a Child shall see his Father at the right Hand of Christ in the day of Judgment, but himself at His left Hand."[143] Morgan notes that "[s]uch an argument must have left cold anyone whose parents and ancestors had not been members of the church."[144]

An intensely genealogical belief system led to restrictive rather than expansive understandings of kinship. As Morgan writes: "comparatively few people are saved anyhow, and those who are almost always belong to the same families. Given two generations, the persons who are saved in the second generation will almost invariably be the children of those who were saved in the first."[145] Ironically, even though adoption serves as the dominant metaphor for salvation, a hereditary view of election makes it difficult for children who are not biologically related to be considered eligible for redemption. The Puritans implicitly make salvation conditional upon genealogy. "[I]f a man be not entred into Christs Covenant, how may hee enter into it?" asks John Cotton.

> For the answer of this, consider with your self, whether any of your ancestors have been under this Covenant. . . . If you can say, you have known some of your ancestors in this Covenant, and you have not refused it, but laid claim unto it . . . it is a certain signe this Covenant reacheth to you, for the Covenant of God is, *I will be thy God, and the God of thy seed after thee.*[146]

If the state of one's soul depended upon that of one's ancestor, then a child without family could achieve grace only by joining a family that was saved, whether through service, marriage, or adoption. But Puritan ministers often focused their energies not on promoting an expansive family model, but on describing the dangers that the unregenerate posed for the godly. As Morgan writes, "All the odds, therefore, were against the unregenerate. . . . They were told to get into a godly family, but the doors to such families were closed wherever the ministers could close them."[147] "The church," he argues, "was thus turned into an exclusive society for the saints and their children."[148] Morgan calls this Puritan tendency toward introversion "tribal" and argues that it contributed to the demise of the Puritan project by the end of the seventeenth century.[149] He concludes that the Puritan outlook was so fiercely genealogical, and the belief that natural-born children would honor their parents and be honored themselves was so strong, that "theology became the handmaiden of genealogy."[150]

Belief in the fusion of covenant, church, and genealogy negatively shaped views of adoption. For example, Thomas Aquinas, following an ethics of natural law, maintained that there was a special bond between parents and children on which all other bonds were based. Taking a developmental view of children (that John Wall notes resembles the secular perspectives on child rearing found in Jean Piaget, Sigmund Freud, Erik Erikson, and Lawrence Kohlberg), Aquinas construed the child's growth as a development "from an animal state of irrationality and disorder toward ever greater capacities to order one's own existence using ever more specifically human reason."[151] According to natural law, parents had not only a special affection for but also a special obligation toward their children, with whom they were connected by nature. Aquinas's sense of natural law suggests that parents will "naturally" love biological offspring more than adopted or foster children.

When Cotton Mather recommends adoption to his congregants in "Orphanotrophium," he validates this way of creating family by associating it with divine salvation. Yet in early America and in Mather's own life, genealogy counted heavily. Increase Mather, Cotton's father, based redemption on heredity with a line that became a cliché of Puritan preaching: "God hath seen good to cast the line of Election so, as that it doth . . . for the most part, run through the loins of godly Parents."[152] By adhering to a doctrine of limited election and genealogically proscribed redemption, Puritans implied that children in need of adoption are less redeemable than others.

In imaginative literature that developed out of the Calvinist tradition, orphans and adoptees bear this burden more than children securely positioned in birth families. Simply by needing adoption, the orphaned child becomes associated with sin and unworthiness. Among the paradoxes of Puritan writings in the New World—for example, the search for religious and civic freedom in the context of social restriction and intolerance—that of kinship figures prominently. Believing they were divinely chosen, the Puritans severed ties to a birth nation in order to realize God's promise in a new land. They theorized the rupture and reconstruction of family relations, creating a positive view of adoption. However, despite the emphasis on fresh starts that these ventures entailed, Puritans adhered to a doctrine of descent that tacitly regarded biological rather than adopted children as the rightful heirs of the covenant. In Puritan writings as well as in popular fiction through the nineteenth century, the orphan's plot is driven by a need for adoption, which is represented as a form of salvation. However, patriarchal family structures and a hierarchy of social forms stigmatize adoption and reinforce genealogy, creating ambivalence and ongoing tensions between inherited and constructed forms of identity.

2

Problems of Patrimony: Benjamin Franklin and Ann Sargent Gage

THE LEADING FIGURE of his age, Benjamin Franklin (1706–1790) played a pivotal role in shaping American literature and nationhood. A revolutionary, entrepreneur, inventor, and diplomat, he is credited with creating a national blueprint for innovation and success. However, Franklin might also be understood as an American in lifelong conflict with birth and adoptive identities and a pioneer in the realm of adoptive kinship. Franklin adopted a new city, a business plan, and a model of civic engagement. He led the nation in a radical political break from its birth parent nation. In these ventures, he embraced a doctrine of individualism and fresh starts aligned with adoptive rather than biological kinship. Franklin was also by temperament inclined to value lineage even though his cultivation of blood ties often led to disappointment. Nowhere is his interest in a bloodline and its gendered implications more evident than in his relationship with his illegitimate son, William. Franklin's decision to acknowledge William, raise him in his household, and groom him for public service—choices facilitated and motivated by Franklin's stature as a leading citizen—attests to the importance he attached to having a male heir.

Another American, born four years after Franklin's death, Ann Sargent Gage (1794–1876) also demonstrates the importance of kinship in defining one's place in the family and nation. Less well known than Franklin, Ann was the illegitimate daughter of Daniel Sargent, a prominent Boston businessman. Like Franklin, Sargent faced the risk of damage to his public image because of the illegitimate birth of his daughter. Unlike Franklin, however, Sargent disowned his child, arranged for her adoption by strangers, and discouraged her attempts to claim her patrimony. Denied membership in her family and community because she was female and illegitimate, Ann remained on the geographic and social margins of society. She struggled against this disenfranchisement, eventually finding her voice and gaining a modicum of recognition. She did so despite her father's efforts to erase her identity and deprive her of her birthright.

Gender and class each played a role in the fates of William Franklin and Ann Sargent Gage. Although the male William Franklin was embraced by his father and the female Ann Sargent rejected, both stories document a process of American self-construction and break new ground in the construction of literary representations of adoptive kinship. They demonstrate the importance of genealogy as well as the stigmas attached to illegitimacy in the early republic. They also suggest the range of options, including adoption, available to men of wealth and status faced with managing the social risks of fathering an illegitimate child. Finally, they suggest the unpredictability of even the most carefully considered paternal plans. By acknowledging and raising William, Benjamin Franklin gave his son every advantage and hoped to secure the Franklin lineage. However, he lost the connection with the son he took pains to nurture in a bitter break that left both men disillusioned. In contrast, Sargent's choice to disown his daughter set her on a path of hardship, but one she was able to overcome through will and resourcefulness.

ROOTS

Benjamin Franklin was born in 1706 in Boston, the second to last child in a large, poor family. His father, Josiah, an immigrant from Northamptonshire, England, was a candle and soap maker, one of the lowliest crafts. Franklin's position in the family—the fifteenth of seventeen children and the youngest son—gave him no advantage in an English-based family system that conferred favor and inheritance on the firstborn son. He describes the sting of this genealogical disenfranchisement in *The Autobiography*: "I perceiv'd that I was the youngest Son of the youngest Son for 5 Generations back."[1] Difficult relationships with his father and later his older brother, James, to whom Franklin was apprenticed as a printer at age twelve, added to his frustration. Although apprenticeships were common, the arrangement was, in Willard Sterne Randall's view, "unusual" because it scattered Josiah's children and left him needing to seek apprentices of his own.[2] It was also odd because in a single gesture Josiah not only cast off his son but also reestablished patriarchal authority with James in the role of master. Franklin felt abandoned by his father and disliked his brother, who had mocked him as a child. He chafed at the unwanted placement and the prospect of becoming a printer, even hoping to escape by going to sea, as had his older brother, Josiah, Jr., Randall dubs the apprenticeship "almost a prison sentence."[3]

Rather than languish under James's authority, Franklin used the apprenticeship to gain skills and, eventually, autonomy. In this respect, he exhibited the qualities of male adoptees in nineteenth-century fiction who rise in the world with the help of a mentor or guide and then leave the mentor behind. He bristled under his brother's control and challenged his authority in a series of print shop confrontations that would serve as rehearsals for his larger role in the drama of national independence. He also felt at odds with town authorities and, in response to perceived oppression, began to publish essays and articles anonymously. The writings were politically and personally significant: he added his voice to Boston public discourse, and he signaled his disenchantment with his brother and father by not using the family name. One of the publications landed James in jail because it criticized the Assembly, but Franklin, protected by anonymity, was not jailed. With his brother imprisoned, he was able usurp James's role and become editor of the *Courant*.

Conscious of the importance of lineage in colonial American society, Franklin publicly criticized the privileges associated with bloodline and inheritance. The Mather family, prominent in Boston religious and political affairs, played a role in his thinking. As is evident in *The Autobiography*, Franklin read Cotton Mather's "Essays to Do Good" (58), the name given to Mather's *Bonifacius*; praised it; and used it as a guide for his efforts at self-examination.[4] However, as a deist he took the Mathers less seriously than they would have liked and complained that they could espouse the virtue of doing good for others in part because they were themselves so securely positioned. A Silence Dogood essay lampoons students at Harvard, the Mathers' alma mater, as "little better than Dunces and Blockheads" and objects that the main criterion for admission is wealth, bestowed from father to son, rather than earned through personal effort.[5] In these early writings, Franklin faults an Old World order that links success to accidents of birth in favor of a New World outlook that rewards individual effort and accomplishment.[6] At the end of his life, he was still conflicted about one's emotional and financial responsibilities to heirs, expressing his ambivalence acerbically in a codicil he attached to his will in 1789. Most people, he observed, having received an estate from their ancestors, feel obliged to pass something on to their heirs. "This obligation does not lie on me, who never inherited a shilling from any ancestor or relation."[7]

When conflicts with his brother James continued and conditions in the print shop deteriorated, Franklin escaped the bonds of apprenticeship and made his way to Philadelphia, his adoptive city. The image that he constructs in *The Autobiography* is that of a de facto orphan, poorly clothed, with a loaf of bread under each arm (as if to compensate for the lack of parental nourishment in Boston), making a "ridiculous Appearance" (76). He falls asleep in a dark Quaker meetinghouse and awakes ready to begin a new stage of life. "Born again" in Philadelphia at the age of seventeen,[8] he sets upon the task of remaking himself.

ILLEGITIMACY

Franklin quickly rose in financial and social stature, but his carefully constructed public image was jeopardized by the knowledge that he had fathered an illegitimate son. The facts of William Franklin's birth remain vague. Although Carl Van Doren suggests that Deborah Franklin was William's mother,[9] his illegitimacy is widely accepted. According to Franklin and William, he was born to Benjamin Franklin and his unnamed partner in 1731,[10] one year after Benjamin and Deborah began their common-law marriage. Nineteenth-century biographer James Parton dates William's birth as 1729; more recently,[11] Leo Lemay suggests 1728.[12] Drama, rumors, and mystery, like those found in adoption stories in which a child's origins remain unknown, surround the details of William's birth. Both parents and later William maintained the secret of his origins although speculations about his mother's identity abound.

In eighteenth-century America, as in England and the rest of Europe, illegitimacy was reason for disparagement and prejudice. Lemay argues that contemporaries cared little about Franklin's transgression until William became governor of New Jersey in 1762, whereupon Franklin's detractors and others who were embittered that they had been passed over for posts (or perceiving themselves superior) circulated malicious gossip about William's birth. However, an early reference to William's birth occurs in Provost William Smith's attack in the *Pennsylvania Journal* on May 6, 1756: "The whole Circumstances of his [William Franklin's] Life render him too despicable for Notice."[13] Sheila Skemp notes widespread speculation that William's mother might have been one of the "low women" Franklin frequented when he was a single man in Philadelphia.[14] Franklin's opponents attacked him by circulating rumors that William's mother was a prostitute named Barbara who had been employed as a servant by the Franklins and was exploited by them. Lemay speculates that she was the wife of one of his friends.[15]

The circumstances surrounding William's birth and upbringing speak to an American system of kinship. The fact that Franklin could legitimize his illegitimate son demonstrated the flexibility of the American system as opposed to the British one, in which one could not overcome one's station by birth. Franklin did suffer politically from the stigma attached to bastardy. He lost his seat in the Pennsylvania Assembly in 1764 after attacks on his character, including the charge that he had abandoned the mother of his illegitimate son,[16] but he circumvented these assaults and persisted in making William his legitimate heir. He adroitly managed a domestic arrangement whereby William was parented—in a sense adopted—by himself and his wife Deborah. He prevailed upon Deborah to accept the child despite her embarrassment and apparent reluctance, and, as in the case of many fictional foundlings, he engineered a situation in which William's unknown maternal identity became a source not of shame but of opportunity. The two developed a close relationship, the bond intensifying when Franklin's second son, conceived with Deborah, died at the age of four.[17] William was the only person who accompanied Franklin during the apocryphal kite experiment of June, 1752. He shared his father's dream of an expanded British empire in the American West, riding on horseback to the western regions of Pennsylvania to meet with General Edward Braddock in 1755. And in 1757, he traveled with his father to England and the ancestral homes at Ecton and Banbury, where they collected genealogical information.

Franklin's decision to shelter and rear William underlines the importance Franklin placed on blood ties. Illegitimate children, as Lemay notes, were commonly raised by their mothers.[18] Franklin's taking William into his household was an act of legal, economic, and emotional caretaking commonly found in adoptive kinship, in alignment with early American practices as well as reflecting the ideology of self-improvement of which Franklin himself was a "patron saint."[19] Fluid households were the norm in the colonies, as the writings of Cotton Mather and Samuel Sewall demonstrate. Placing out was common practice. Franklin reached out in fatherly, adoptive ways to others' children, mentoring many girls and women, including a cousin's daughter, Sarah Franklin, whom he temporarily housed in London in 1766.[20] "Everywhere he went," Jan Lewis writes, "he seemed to re-create new families."[21] He also demonstrated willingness to parent others' children: in 1736 he took in James, Jr., his brother's son. At the age of six or seven, James, Jr., joined the Franklin household in Philadelphia at the request of his father, who was in declining health. Franklin housed, educated, and trained his nephew in the printing business, thus making amends for leaving James in Boston.[22] An expanded household of relatives was not unusual at the time. Redeeming others emanated from a concern for character and discipline that began with the self and extended outward in a spirit of individual as well as social improvement.[23]

William's installation in the Franklin home was not without problems, however. According to Deborah Franklin's great-granddaughter, Deborah opposed William's "being a member of the household" but was eventually won over by her husband's desire to raise the child as their legitimate son. The 1755 diary of Daniel Fisher, a young clerk who lived in Franklin's house for a time, confirms Deborah's opposition. Fisher notes that Deborah felt that Franklin favored William over Sarah, their biological child, resented Franklin's attention to him, and behaved like a jealous stepmother, even cursing William in front of strangers.[24] No doubt William felt the smart of Deborah's rejection, although is unclear how it influenced his feelings about his family or his future decision to side with the loyalists rather than his father and the colonists when the Revolutionary War broke out. If Deborah resented the arrangement, did William resent it as well? One oddity suggests that there was a less than harmonious negotiation of birth and adoptive identities. Franklin never baptized William, a decision that Lemay speculates may reflect Franklin's ambivalence about church membership or his concern that questions would arise about the identity of William's mother.[25] Neither father nor son spoke about William's birth, and it is possible that William remained in the dark about his mother's identity.[26] Franklin never mentions the circumstances of William's parentage in *The Autobiography*.

The Autobiography

As the colonies moved closer to war with England, Americans wrestled with divided loyalties. Although Franklin became a leading figure in the Revolution, he, more than many, remained psychologically attached to Europe. His ties to Old World customs are evident in his traditional views of marriage, including his decision to marry for practical rather than romantic reasons; his adoption of courtly ways while serving his nation in France; and his attempts, often unsuccessful, to arrange marriages for his son, daughter, and grandson. As Lewis notes, such "attempts at matchmaking were curious hybrids, grafting a more modern [and American] notion of the family grounded in affection onto the sturdy stock of marriages arranged to serve the family's economic and political interests."[27] These tensions between roots and new beginnings are vividly demonstrated in his signature work, *The Autobiography*.

Franklin wrote *The Autobiography* in the form of a memo and conduct book, a common genre at the time. Models include Horace Walpole's autobiography of Lord Herbert of Cherbury; the work of John Bunyan and Daniel Defoe; William Penn's *Fruits of a Father's Love*, which Franklin read four years after his arrival in Philadelphia; and Plutarch's *Lives*, which he read as a young man. Esmond Wright claims that the work is "uniquely American," with its references to the average workers' wisdom, its "earthy and unbookish" style with biblical resonance, and its references to everyday preoccupations like stoves and smoky chimneys.[28] Written at the prodding of friends (in particular, the Englishman Benjamin Vaughan), *The Autobiography* promotes the self-made American success that Franklin brilliantly illustrated. Vaughan believed the document would invite "settlers of virtuous and manly minds" to migrate to America and adopt the nation as their home. One of its merits is that it "was connected with the detail of . . . a *rising* people" (135, original emphasis).

Although *The Autobiography* is widely viewed as a paradigmatic text of American autonomy and ingenuity, it employs a genealogical logic. It recounts an individual rise to wealth and stature, but its primary rhetorical purpose is to inspire replication. Franklin's life story is an exemplum for others, written in the form of a letter to his son because "my Posterity may like to know [the means to my success], as they may find some of them suitable to their own Situations, and therefore fit to be imitated" (43). *The Autobiography* justifies the American rebellion against the restrictive parental authority of England and proclaims the colonies' right to liberty and self-determination. Paradoxically, however, Franklin draws on lineage—English, paternal, and loyalist—as a basis for his radical departure from models of inheritance. At the same time that he charts the course of national independence, he reveals Old World filial attachments and demonstrates a dual attraction to both ruptured and intact genealogies.

Franklin began to draft the memoir in the summer of 1771, during a visit to the country house of his friend Jonathan Shipley, Bishop of St. Asaph, in Hampshire, England. He composed Part 1 over the course of fourteen days in August; he revised it several times between 1788 and early 1790, while writing Parts 3 and 4. He wrote Part 2 in 1784 during his busy years in France.[29] Each section of the autobiography was influenced by its provenance, and, overall the piece moves from the personal to the public and political. As Wright notes, in the end, accounts of Franklin's "involvement in public affairs, in London, Philadelphia and Paris, . . . could no longer be cast in the fashionable form of a letter to a son";[30] yet even the least personal sections reveal attachment to genealogy, sometimes laced with bitterness that loyalties are neither appreciated nor reciprocated.

The Autobiography opens with Franklin recalling the trip he and William took to the Franklins' ancestral home in Northamptonshire in the summer of 1758. They visited Ecton, the birthplace of Benjamin Franklin's father, having learned from a cousin, Mary Fisher, the story of Josiah Franklin's decision to leave his homeland for the colonies. Benjamin and William explored the grounds of the old Franklin house and examined the church register where the names of generations of Franklins dating back 300 years were listed. The experience was moving and contributed to Franklin's decision to address the autobiography to William. On the opening page of Part 1, Franklin expresses pride in his family tree and details his lineage for his son's benefit. He describes the personal satisfaction of genealogical research, writing that he has "ever had a Pleasure in obtaining any little Anecdotes of my Ancestors" (43). He takes pride in comparing himself to an uncle "who had the same kind of Curiosity in collecting Family Anecdotes" and for the next several pages draws on Thomas Franklin's account of family history as the narrative that shaped his own life. He revels in locating places, names, and occupations of his ancestors. He notes that the family lived in the same village for three centuries or longer, their name originating "perhaps from the Time when the name *Franklin* . . . was the Name of an Order of People" (45). He describes the eldest sons following their father in the "Smith's Business" (46) and enjoins William to remember the inquiries they made about the Franklin family when they visited the ancestral homes at Ecton and Banbury, presenting the fruits of this research as foundational for William's development. Employing "like father, like son" reasoning, he writes that just as it is important for Franklin to learn about his roots, so "it may be equally agreeable" to William to know his family history (43).

Franklin uses genealogy to account for originality as well as continuity. For example, he describes how his place in the family birth order—a fixed aspect of his identity— granted him the freedom to chart his own course. He explains that a parish register from the year 1555 confirmed that "I was the youngest Son of the youngest Son for 5 Generations back" (46), and he makes a virtue of the fact that, unlike the eldest sons, he had the flexibility to choose his profession. The example of his great uncle Thomas supports these dual concepts of blood ties and independence. Thomas "was bred a Smith under his Father, but being ingenious, and encourag'd in Learning" by an esquire who served as mentor, "qualify'd for the Business of Scrivener, [and] became a considerable Man in the County Affairs" (47). Franklin reminds William that Thomas's accomplishments "struck you as something extraordinary from its Similarity to what you know of mine" (47–48). Both broke with the family line and were facile with language.

Franklin also notes the lineage of his mother, whose family dates to the first settlers of New England and is mentioned in the annals of Cotton Mather. Franklin wishes readers to see a connection between himself and these maternal forbears, who were "in favour of Liberty of Conscience" and who advocated on behalf of persecuted "Baptists, Quakers, and other Sectaries" (52). He honors roots as a basis for achieving success independently of roots. He also devotes a passage to his father's "sound Understanding, and solid Judgment in prudential Matters, both in private and public Affairs," traits that undoubtedly were passed on to Franklin and made him a frequent and successful "Arbiter between contending Parties." Franklin implies his inheritance of "an excellent Constitution" from both parents (54), acknowledging the importance of origins as well as autonomy.

Franklin was not unique in attaching importance to personal and cultural genealogy. Visiting Europe was a common activity among colonists of means. England and London, in particular, captured the imagination of people who were born in the colonies but linked psychologically, socially, and politically to the Old World. For example, Abigail Smith Adams waited patiently at home when her husband John Adams was dispatched by Congress in 1778 to rally French and Dutch support for the American revolutionary cause and again in 1779 to help negotiate peace with England. Writing in 1771 to her first cousin, the Rev. Isaac Smith, who was in London and described the sights to her, Abigail Adams admitted that "From my infancy I have always felt a great inclination to visit the Mother Country, as 'tis called; and had nature formed me of the other sex, I should certainly have been a rover."[31]

Franklin's exploration of his English roots shaped his identity and gave him a sense of belonging. However, for him and generations of future Americans, the recovery of roots fueled a process of discovery, resulting in the construction of a self that is independent of origins. This experience is similar to that reported by adoptees who, having searched for and found their birthparents, still find the mystery of identity unsolved. As literary critic and adoptee Marianne Novy writes,

> there are many adoptees who, like me, would testify that they did not find their identity when they found their birth parents. . . . [I]n many cases they were left with more questions to answer. . . . The equation of identity with genetics . . . is not the inevitable way to imagine identity, but an ideology present in various societies in differing degrees.[32]

The Autobiography has been hailed in every age, but for differing reasons. Some see it as a picaresque adventure story with novel-like qualities; others as a fable or secular *Pilgrim's Progress* with a moral attached to each event. To readers in the late nineteenth century it is a rags-to-riches story, circumspect about luxuries even as it details the means to their accumulation. In the twentieth-first century it can be read as an American tale of biological and adoptive kinship, of loyalty to family and nation of origin as well as pride in an independently acquired identity.

REBELLION

Franklin, like some of his compatriots, only slowly embraced the American cause for independence. Gordon Wood, seeking to recover the historic Franklin of the eighteenth century, explains the gradual process by which his Americanization was achieved. Although Franklin became the best known of the founding fathers, "he was certainly not the most American of the Founders during his lifetime. Indeed, one might more easily describe him as the least American and the most European of the nation's early leaders." Emphasizing his ambivalence, Wood writes that "Franklin at several points in his life experienced ... an anxiety of national identity. He was not sure where he rightly belonged. Was he English? Or British? Or did he really belong in France?"[33]

When Franklin shifted his political loyalties to the colonies, he urged William to resign his position as royal governor and join him in the patriot cause. He expected William to follow his lead in an act of filial solidarity. When William refused, intimacy between the two abruptly and permanently ended. Blood, which once had meant everything, now meant nothing. Franklin threw himself into the revolutionary cause with the same fervor he had previously directed toward the preservation of empire, leading Wood to claim that his "emotional separation from England was now final and complete."[34] In fact, however, the anguish of genealogical betrayal continued. Adopting a nation meant losing a biological son.

In taking England's side in the gubernatorial post arranged by his father, William was doing his filial duty to Franklin and the Crown. However, as Philip Dray writes, "In an age when fathers were mentors to their sons, and sons were expected to honor them as such, William's decision was to Franklin a hurtful betrayal, and the source of some embarrassment, given Franklin's celebrated status as a patriot."[35] William's decision was more than a public embarrassment to Franklin; it struck at the heart of his struggle with birth and adoptive identities. William was now an enemy, in Robert Middlekauff's words, "the one causing him the most sorrow."[36] Franklin vehemently turned his allegiance from Britain to America, as if to do less would be to invite more pain. Once the colonies declared independence, he rejected England's appeals for reconciliation, exhibiting toward British commanders a rigid disinclination to reestablish any of the former connections between Old World and New. Gone was the conciliatory Franklin of the early years. For example, meeting with Lord Richard Howe on Staten Island in August, 1776 (Franklin had offered as an alternative meeting place the governor's mansion, from which his son William had been forcibly removed as a prisoner), Franklin noted that irreparable damage already had been done: "Forces had been sent out, and Towns destroyed," he wrote. He defended American independence from England with the staunch assertion that America "could not return again to the Domination of Great Britain."[37] He maintained the same rigidity with respect to William.

Franklin seemed unaware of the irony that he had sown the seeds from which William's British loyalty sprang. Franklin himself had been lured by the promise of Old World patronage when, in November of 1724, Pennsylvania governor William Keith promised to finance him in setting up his own printing firm, a paternalistic gesture common in a colonial society modeled on an Old World patronage system. However, when Franklin journeyed to London to purchase the necessary equipment, he discovered that Keith had reneged on his commitment. Disillusionment over Keith's duplicity laid a foundation for political disaffection toward England; however, for many years, Franklin lived in two worlds. He was inclined to venerate England and affirm his loyalty to the Crown, hoping to remain England's loyal subject even as its colonial rule became a source of increasing irritation.

Having so prospered in his commercial ventures that he was able to retire at the age of forty-two, Franklin was at liberty to accept the colonies' proposal to journey to England on official political business. By the time he made his second visit to England, with William in 1757, he was a wealthy inventor, businessman, and statesman—a far cry from the naïve youth who first visited London on the mere promise of Keith's patronage. The trip was for the elder Franklin a platform from which he could advocate Anglo-American unity, but it was for William a formative experience that laid the groundwork for his later political allegiance to the Crown. It was contact "William, even more than his father, valued" because it came at a developmental time of life.[38] William came of age in England. He completed his studies and practiced law in London, where he took in the full measure of fashionable life. He was a gentleman and an Englishman.

During the interlude of English acceptance, Franklin successfully melded his American and English parts and enjoyed the high regard that followed from success in the colonies. He was respected by members of British society and immersed himself in fashionable London life. The trip had the celebratory feel of a homecoming and became more than the brief stay he had imagined. He remained in England more than five years, very nearly not coming back at all. When he returned to Philadelphia, it was for two years and then back to London for ten years. He began to think of England as "'home,'" and "came close to staying forever."[39] Imperialist and royalist, he strove to solidify connections to the English gentry and, as he wrote, foster "respect for the mother country, and admiration of everything that is British."[40]

Franklin's warm reception in England has elements of traditional fairy tales and contemporary English fiction such as Henry Fielding's *Tom Jones* (1749), in which foundlings discover their true noble origins and are restored to high position in the birth home. He had returned to England not as a poor candle maker's son, but as a wealthy businessman, inventor, and statesman. The reward for innovation and hard work was acceptance into an aristocratic English world. Franklin's immersion in the culture of his birth country was so complete that, in Wood's words, he "was a true-blue Englishman." Long interested in genealogy, sometime before 1751 Franklin adopted a coat of arms. He infused his *Poor Richard's Almanac* with a tone of condescension common to the gentry class.[41] He "stood" rather "ran" for election to the Pennsylvania Assembly ten consecutive times, each time successfully, and, enjoying the patronage system handed down from England, exercised the power available to him by placing his relatives, including William, in public positions.[42] So exclusive was his vision of anglicized America and so seamlessly did he imagine the unity of English and colonial interests that he protested the massive immigration of non-English into Pennsylvania, angrily writing about the influx of Germans, "Why should the *Palatine Boors* be suffered to swarm into our Settlements, and by herding together establish their Language and Manners to the Exclusion of ours?" Admitting partiality to England and wanting to preserve America for those of British descent, he maintained that the country should belong only to the English and Indians.[43]

Franklin had reinforced the importance of genealogy when he returned William to his cultural roots in the 1757 trip to England, but when William sided with England, Franklin denounced him as intensely as he once supported him, his rage fueled perhaps by the sense of a double betrayal: his father and brother had abandoned him, and now his son was doing the same. He refused to help when William was arrested in June of 1776 and responded coolly to his request, after the peace treaty recognizing American sovereignty was signed in 1783, for reconciliation. Franklin could not disentangle the threads of personal and political loyalties, and wrote to his son that, "nothing has ever hurt me so much and affected me with such keen Sensations, as to find my self deserted in my old Age by my only Son; and not only deserted, but to find him taking up Arms against me, in a Cause, wherein my good Fame, Fortune and Life were all at Stake." He could not grant William what he had claimed for himself years ago: the right to self-determination. The bitter tone of a 1784 letter to William reveals how misguided and offensive he considered William's actions to be: "I ought not to blame you for differing in Sentiment with me in Public Affairs. We are Men, all subject to Errors. Our Opinions are not in our own Power." Franklin concludes with a strong emphasis on genealogy: "Your situation was such that few would have censured your remaining Neuter, *tho there are Natural Duties which precede political ones, and cannot be extinguish'd by them.*"[44]

For the rest of his life Franklin treated William impersonally. He left William virtually nothing in his will, acerbically writing, "The part he acted against me in the late war, which is of public notoriety, will account for my leaving him no more of an estate he endeavored to deprive me of."[45] There were recriminations on both sides after the war, but Franklin's acrimony toward the loyalists and his objection to granting them compensation remained far greater than that expressed by other American patriots. Before the Revolution, Franklin had advanced William's prospects in hopes of securing male lineage; after it, he turned his attention to his grandson, William Temple, also born illegitimate. Replicating the pattern, William Temple fathered two illegitimate children, one named Ellen, whom William "preposterously" pretended was his child rather than his grandchild.[46] Filial estrangement continued. Benjamin Franklin had fallen out with his father, Josiah, and had moved to Philadelphia; William Franklin and his father had likewise parted ways during the war. Now Temple and William were at odds. After living in William's London home for eight years after the Revolution, Temple deserted his father and moved to Paris. This breach, like the ones between Josiah and Benjamin, and between Benjamin and William, never healed. William wrote Temple out of his will, just as Benjamin Franklin had left William virtually penniless. Still hoping to ensure a legacy, Benjamin Franklin passed over his son and left a large sum of money to his grandson.

Benjamin Franklin hoped that Temple would be chosen to deliver the Treaty of Paris to Congress and tried to influence the decision in his favor. He asked Congress to appoint his grandson secretary of the new commission created to sign commercial treaties with European nations, envisioning Temple as his successor in France. None of these aspirations were realized, however, as the political leadership in the United States had changed and the government was now being run by men who were more Franklin's enemies than his friends. The Franklin family story ends with Temple immoderate and somewhat profligate, William embittered, and Franklin without a legitimate heir. When Franklin turned again to *The Autobiography* in 1784, he was philosophical and detached about his life experiences. He made an effort to affirm a restored faith in reason and progress, expressing confidence that "even a Man of tolerable Abilities" could make a difference in the world (163), and he struggled to see his life as something in his control. However, as a patriot he had paid a high personal price for political freedom.

Benjamin Franklin exercised his prerogative when he decided to legitimize his son and raise him with every advantage and opportunity, but he could not know how little his efforts would be rewarded. The rift between William and his father reflects not only war-time reality but also a trend in the nation as a whole. Thomas Bender writes that with focus on a common external enemy, the "revolutionary crisis offered Americans an opportunity to rededicate themselves to the ideals of community." Afterward, however, "traditional groups of family, church, and town [became] less prescriptive."[47] Jay Fliegelman notes that a call for "filial autonomy" and "individual identity" echoed in Revolutionary and post-Revolutionary rhetoric.[48] Joyce Appleby observes that fathers lost control of maturing sons as economic opportunities led to cultural change: "Mobility—both geographic and social—cut off young people from the community of their childhood."[49] J. M. Opal describes a sense of ambition as young New Englanders left the family farm.[50] As new occupations appeared and many fathers could not keep their sons at home, families changed.

The political revolution inspired a personal revolution: paternal governance versus self-governance. Advocating American political independence, Franklin applied a theory that had its counterpart in liberal educational practices first espoused by John Locke. His political outlook on the colonies reflects Locke's Enlightenment view of the child as a tabula rasa who, with proper education, will develop into a desirable, mature being. Locke's ideas, articulated in the eighteenth century by John Witherspoon, appear in Franklin's *Autobiography*, where the focus is on self-improvement through self-government. This advocacy of independence required a willed orphancy, which William emulated when he rejected his father's politics and declared loyalty to England.

INCONVENIENT BIRTH

Both William Franklin's and Ann Sargent Gage's experiences demonstrate the stigma of illegitimacy. In Ann's case, however, gender as well as class bias conspired to make her experience of adoption frustrating and her efforts to balance genealogy and adoption difficult. Ann's father, Daniel Sargent (1764–1842) disowned his daughter and rebuffed her pleas to be acknowledged by her birth family. Affluent and socially prominent like Franklin, Sargent chose twice to arrange for his daughter's adoption rather than raise her with her birth family. Franklin, acting with the help of reformed bastardy laws and from a position of stature, was able to manipulate social politics in order to legitimize his son. Daniel Sargent had the same rights and privileges as Franklin, yet he used them to erase his daughter's identity.

Disenfranchised, Ann Gage benefited from neither her family's name nor fortune. As an adult, she wrote poetry to express her feelings and composed letters to her father and to her paternal uncle, her unofficial ambassador, asking to be recognized by the Sargent

family. In this effort she largely failed although she did succeed in obtaining limited financial support for herself and her children. Ann's story demonstrates the significance of gender and class in a rapidly evolving American society and presages the role that these
differences play in popular adoption fiction in the nineteenth century. Her hushed adoption and disappointing relations with her birth family resulted from two separate but mutually reinforcing factors: the legal, social, and psychological restrictions imposed on
women in early American society, and the adherence among genteel members of society to
an English-based set of customs and expectations. Ann's first adoption was motivated by
family illness; her second adoption by her father's fear of scandal, which derived from his
devotion to an English-based legal and social system that valued legitimacy and lineage.

Daniel Sargent's decision to place his daughter for adoption was not only sanctioned by
law but also condoned and abetted by the Boston community. The family of Transcendentalist writer Ralph Waldo Emerson participated in removing Ann from Boston in order to
spare Daniel Sargent public embarrassment. Ann was kindly treated in her adoptive
home, but she was aware that she had been denied her birthright and her freedom. The
Transcendentalist philosophy that Emerson espoused, with its emphasis on individual
aspiration, stands ironically at the center of Ann's adoption story, making her tale one of
tensions between the Old World and the New, and between social orthodoxy and romantic individualism.

Ann Sargent Gage's story begins as the first generation of post-Revolutionary Americans came of age. Her father, Daniel Sargent, was born into a respected Boston family.
The eldest son of a prominent merchant, he became, like his father, a successful businessman and insurance executive. Ann's mother, Hepzibah Atkins, was from a similarly
distinguished Boston family. Her father, Henry Atkins, was a prosperous merchant
who could trace the family lineage to John and Priscilla Alden of Plimouth Plantation.
Hepzibah first married a man named James Brown in 1788; he died shortly afterward. She
and Daniel Sargent conceived Ann before Hepzibah remarried James Durfee in 1796.
Their illegitimate daughter was born on January 16, 1794, when Daniel Sargent was thirty-
four. Because of the stigma attached to illegitimacy, she was renamed Nancy Brown.[51]

When Nancy Brown was two years old, she experienced her first adoption. Daniel Sargent removed her from her mother, who was in poor health, and placed her with the
family of John Hall in Dorchester, Massachusetts. She was not completely cut off from
her roots: she was visited occasionally by her mother and often by her father, who brought
her books and tutored her. When Nancy was six years old, her mother died. W. A. Wheeler,
Ann's great, great grandson, relates the sentimental scene of the death, in which Ann
mourned her mother and fantasized about her father, focusing particularly on his social
standing. Ann "was taken to the funeral and always remembered that a silver plate
bearing her mother's name was placed on the coffin. People told her that her father had
sent it."[52]

Ann continued to enjoy visits from her father until 1802, when she was eight years old
and learned from Mrs. Hall that her father was to be married and she would not be seeing
him much more. His visits became infrequent. Two years later, Daniel Sargent's wife died
after giving birth to the couple's only child, Maria, and Daniel Sargent found himself at a
decision point. According to Lucius Manlius Sargent (1776–1867), Daniel's brother and his
junior by twenty-two years, Nancy Brown's father seriously considered acknowledging
his daughter and taking her home. However, he remained embarrassed by her illegitimacy

and concerned about the scandal that would ensue from the combination of her birth status and great beauty. Ann wrote that "she was attracting considerable notice in some families in Dorchester."[53] Wheeler concurs that Ann's beauty "was the trouble. . . . [P]eople knew who the child was and gossiped about her." Mary Moody Emerson, Ralph Waldo Emerson's aunt, confirmed Ann's head-turning beauty and grace; in later years Count Podbielski, who was a tutor in Metternich's family at the Court of Austria, reportedly said that Ann Sargent was the most "elegant person" he saw in America. Because such attention was unwelcome in the case of an illegitimate child, Daniel Sargent decided "to consult his spiritual advisor, Rev. William Emerson," the father of Ralph Waldo Emerson. After reflection, William Emerson proposed a plan for Nancy's second adoption. Ann would be removed from Boston society and sent to Maine. She would be placed in the home of a "pious, high-minded and gentle" couple, a minister and his wife, who had no biological children of their own.[54]

At this point Ann's story resembles a typical nineteenth-century adoption story in which a homeless child is sheltered by a kind and childless couple, but with gothic overtones. It also takes on the aura of a fairy tale such as *Cinderella*, but without requisite princely rescue. Wheeler speculates that Daniel Sargent "must have agonized long over the decision" to place his daughter far from Boston with relative strangers.[55] However difficult the decision may have been for him, it was heartily endorsed by Sargent family members, who play the parts of the wicked stepmother and stepsisters in the fairy tale about jealousy and abandonment. Daniel Sargent lived with his mother-in-law and two of his wife's sisters, about whom Lucius Sargent writes, "Three more undesirable personages it has never been my fortune to know. They are all now dead, and the neighborhood—is at rest."[56] These women exploited their family's good name and social prominence to deprive Ann of similar advantage. They argued that Ann's return to Boston was impossible given social strictures. Capitulating to them, Daniel Sargent moved forward with the plan recommended by William Emerson. Nancy Brown would be sent to live with William Emerson's sister and Ralph Waldo Emerson's aunt, Phebe Emerson Ripley (1772–?), and brother-in-law, Rev. Lincoln Ripley (1761–1858). The Ripleys' home, in a remote location in Waterford, Maine, was "in those days . . . the other end of the earth from Boston." The decision was the equivalent of banishment: "the little girl sent there would disappear."[57]

Wheeler describes in dramatic language the means by which Ann's adoption—more precisely her removal—was effected:

> Soon after "Nancy's" fourteenth birthday, in 1808, John Turner Sargent (one of Daniel's younger brothers and according to Ann Sargent Gage the "handsomest man that she had ever seen"), riding the "most magnificent horse," came to the Hall's [sic] and told them to have the child ready for a long trip. A few days later he went out with a sleigh and carried "Nancy" to a point where the concoctor of the plan, Wm. Emerson, appeared in another sleigh. He took her to a point where his half-brother Samuel Ripley was waiting in the sleigh that took her to Waterford, arriving there Feb. 4, 1808.[58]

Wheeler also describes Samuel Ripley's anguish and sympathy for the trembling, tearful girl "during the course of that cold and comfortless ride" and his declaration that he "never suffered more for the time on account of any being whatever."[59]

The plan dealt Ann yet one more debilitating blow. It was decided that "Nancy Brown" must change her name yet again, this time to "Ann Brewer." The intent of this name change was clear: Ann would be separated permanently from her birth name and roots. In virtual exile, she was denied access to her father, his family, and Boston. As Ann writes, "I fully understood that the reason for changing my name was that I should be lost to those who had known me."[60] Daniel Sargent ceased communicating with his daughter. Wheeler observes, "thus the gentleman of Boston finally disposed of Nancy Brown."[61]

CONVENTIONS

Ann's adoption occurred during a transitional moment in U.S. history when the republic was moving from authoritative structures to ones that were more democratic and focused on the individual. Her tale is also situated at a crossroads between English and American kinship systems. U.S. legal provisions allowed Ann's father to enfranchise her as a member of his family, just as it allowed Benjamin Franklin to embrace his illegitimate son, William Franklin; but these laws conflicted with social conventions that more closely followed English practices regarding legitimacy and inheritance. As Michael Grossberg explains, English law, which was designed to "repel the challenges that bastardy posed to established family organization and property distribution, and to prevent the public from being saddled with the costs of rearing children born outside wedlock," gradually gave way to a republican-motivated American system that reflected concern over the welfare of children, including illegitimate ones. Gradually, through a growing cult of domesticity, society conferred parental authority on women, who in their maternal roles spiritually guided the family and implicitly the nation.[62]

Ann's circumstances were such that she could not benefit from this social and legal shift. With her mother deceased and her step-relatives hostile to her, there were no close female figures to come to her aid. Her adoption story also illustrates a U.S. legal and social system heavily influenced by British custom and law. Daniel Sargent was comfortably situated in Boston society and benefited from its privileges. By the early nineteenth century Americans had begun to criticize those who affected upper-class snobbishness associated with aristocratic Europe, choosing to accentuate more home-grown forms of courtesy and practicality. "'Genteel!'" says a character in a story that appeared in *Juvenile Miscellany*, "'if there is a word in our language, that means any thing and nothing it is that. I am sure it is a most *un*-genteel word, for it is always in the mouths of the vulgar'"[63] Catharine Maria Sedgwick remarked that the pretentious gentility of a store clerk "served mainly to attract the underbred"[64] and attempted to convince readers "that simple refinement was in the reach of everyone."[65] Even as Americans rejected social hierarchies and embraced new ways, however, European practices were evident in every walk of life. Americans enjoyed material and cultural imports from abroad: for those

> ... born right after Independence ... [n]ew science, new technology, and new literature had come to the colonies with every boat from Europe. The natural rights philosophy embedded in the Declaration of Independence came from English political thought. ... Other novelties that astounded contemporaries were but part and parcel of the industrial process affecting all of western Europe.[66]

For members of society privileged with time and resources, following English social conventions was not only desirable but also expected. For example, aspiring Americans in the early nineteenth century shared the heightened emphasis on marriage found in the larger Anglo-American world and reprinted English novels that prescribed feminine and domestic codes of conduct. These interests included a fascination with rank that resembled the Old World's aristocratic order but was now disguised with more democratically palatable terms. Influenced by French fashion and English styles of speech, a new elite class took the measure of itself according to the elegance of its acquisitions and tastes. Bushman notes that "the notion of gentility was thoroughly entrenched in the middle classes by the mid-century" and was evident in arts, manners, architecture, and other forms of material culture.[67] As Appleby describes this "ideal of refinement": "Most Americans exulted in their abandonment of European snobbery even as they copied European forms of gracious living that enabled them to feel superior to those who had not."[68] In the early decades of the nineteenth century, major cities such as Boston, New York, Philadelphia, and Baltimore saw the rise of various social and cultural organizations such as literary clubs for men and women and fire companies, Masonic lodges, and political and business clubs for men, which offered opportunities for relaxation, refinement, and friendships and created bridges between well-positioned families and the larger society.

The Gage family story thus poses a paradox. As a successful businessman and member of a genteel society, Daniel Sargent felt pressure to keep questions that might arise from his daughter's illegitimacy off center stage. He succumbed to that pressure rather than risk the approbation that might come from defying norms about illegitimacy by twice changing his daughter's name and sending her far from Boston. At the same time, Daniel Sargent was very much the product of a new American republic. Post-Revolutionary economic, social, and geographic mobility had allowed Sargent and his father before him to rise in the world of business and to maintain high position in society. Developments in transportation and communication permitted Ann to be banished to the Maine hinterland and her whereabouts tracked by family members wishing to ensure that she would not threaten their social positions or seek to inherit their wealth. The New World system failed, however, to accept Ann for the child she was.

Ann Sargent Gage reaped ambiguous benefits from her place in the Boston social order. Despite her illegitimate status, she was protected as a member of a genteel class and merchant family. She flourished in her new adoptive home as Ann Brewer. She was well cared for by the Ripleys, who were childless, kind, and deeply religious. Their beneficence, although consistent with their nature, was also supported by regular payments they received from Daniel Sargent. Ann was afforded a moderately good education and fell under the influence of noted mentors. In particular, she was befriended by her adoptive aunt, Mary Moody Emerson (1774–1863), the spinster sister of Phebe Ripley and Rebecca Haskins of South Waterford. Also the aunt of Ralph Waldo Emerson, Mary Moody Emerson was an influential figure in the newly formed philosophical movement, Transcendentalism. As Phyllis Cole explains, she helped lead her nephew Ralph to question traditional Christianity and formulate the tenets of Transcendentalism.[69] Ann was also befriended by Elizabeth Palmer Peabody (1804–1894), a noted educator and Transcendentalist editor and publisher. Ann made a good marriage to a doctor and leading citizen of the town, Leander Gage (1791–1892), on October 7, 1820, in Waterford, Maine. She gave birth to eight children and expressed "gratitude for such a husband" in correspondence to her adoptive mother.[70]

TRANSCENDING ADOPTION

Mary Moody Emerson figures prominently as Ann's mentor, offering valuable spiritual and philosophical support. The two met in 1810 when Ann was sixteen and "struck a mutual chord from their first conversation."[71] Mary Moody Emerson helped Ann to embrace notions of the eminent goodness and perfectibility of human beings. Her uplifting, liberal messages countered what Wheeler describes as the Ripleys' theologically conservative tendency to be "one-sided and very pompous in condemnation." The Ripleys were "as far from the Transcendental intellect as Martin Luther was from the Pope."[72] The devout couple was invested in the Christian notion of adoption as salvation and was motivated to nurture Ann with the mandate to do God's work in mind. However, it is not clear that they experienced spiritual assurance themselves, and thus they may have been hard put to extend it to Ann. Cole writes that Ann's adoptive mother, Phebe, struggled with a long illness and in 1839 "died without religious comfort after a life of rigidly pursued duty."[73] "O may you never know by experience what I endure," Phebe Ripley wrote to Ann.[74] Mary Moody Emerson complemented the Ripleys' austere teachings by imbuing Ann with a spirit of self-sufficiency and a spark of imagination.

The close connection between Ann Gage and Mary Moody Emerson may have formed in part because of their shared experience of abandonment and adoption. Mary had been separated from her birth family at an early age. She was the daughter of Rev. William Emerson, the minister of First Parish Church in Concord, Massachusetts, and of Phebe Bliss Emerson, born to the previous minister of that same First Parish Church. She lost her father when he enlisted as a chaplain in the Revolutionary War and died of a fever in Benedict Arnold's campaign for Ticonderoga and Montréal. Mary, two years old at the time, was sent to live with her grandparents. Her grandmother died in 1779. Her mother married William Emerson's successor at First Parish Church, Ezra Ripley, but Mary remained with her childless aunt, Ruth Emerson Sargent. She seldom saw her half brothers and sisters while she was growing up, but she returned to her birth home when she was nineteen and helped her mother care for the children of her second marriage. An inheritance from her aunt allowed her to purchase her own home in Maine, where she met Ann. She later returned to Boston, at age thirty-seven, to live with the widow of her brother, William, who was minister of First Church in Boston. The effect of early childhood dislocation was profound. Wheeler writes that as a child Mary Emerson "was left about as alone as she would be had she been orphaned."[75] In her last years, she was peripatetic, with no home to call her own.[76] In Mary Moody Emerson's case, a sense of abandonment was the crucible out of which a radical, new outlook on self and society emerged. Espousing Transcendentalism and seeking to turn isolation, often the shared fate of orphans and adoptees, into a positive and edifying experience, Mary Moody Emerson confided to Ann that "to feel alone on earth was one of the highest emotions of my youth."[77]

Ann was an excellent student and easily absorbed the lessons of Mary Moody Emerson as well as those available in her Maine community. She soon outgrew the educational opportunities available in Waterford and was sent to Byfield, Massachusetts, to attend the school of Rev. William Emerson, where she excelled in her studies. She apparently bore no animosity toward the designer of the plan that had resulted in her removal from Boston. She was drawn to abstract ideas, writing to her adoptive mother when she was twenty-one years old, "I had no idea . . . that I could have entered with so much ardour into the study of *philosophy*; for this study attracts me much more powerfully than history."[78] She tutored, instructed members of the Ripley family, and taught at what is now Hebron Academy, although she made barely enough to make ends meet. In 1814, she tutored Waldo's younger brother, Robert Bulkeley Emerson, a difficult child of enormous energy who struggled in the classroom.[79] Ann committed herself to serve the boy and others whom she taught or tutored.

Guided by Mary Moody Emerson and inspired by romantic poet William Wordsworth, who she felt epitomized the expression of the individual seeking truth, Ann began to write poetry. Wheeler speculates that writing provided her with a much-needed emotional release.[80] Her poems reveal an awareness of privilege as well as a sense of sadness. In this respect, Ann's experience is strikingly different from that of less fortunate, friendless orphans who entered asylums and lacked the means or the opportunity to compose their stories. She was well educated and cared for, with a firm foundation from which she could assess genealogical and adoptive losses and gains. Indeed, because there is little literature available from institutionalized or poverty-stricken orphans of the period, her comments on family, self, and adoption are particularly compelling.

Wheeler writes that the act of writing also "must have emboldened Ann," for after producing some youthful poems, she began to use the Sargent name, signing her work "ABS" for Ann Brewer Sargent.[81] However, the power of her pen was limited. Ann struggled to realize the doctrine of self-sufficiency espoused in the romantic writings that increasingly permeated the period in which she lived. She accomplished more than many women of her time: she told her story in two genres—letters and poetry—and she was empowered through the act of writing to lay claim to her birth identity. She made the best of her unwanted adoption. But she only partially succeeded in deciding the terms upon which her family story would be constructed.

Girls born in 1794, the year of Ann's birth, were educated for the role of "republican womanhood." Secondary education expanded and the first colleges for women opened.[82] However, the majority of girls received a "second-class education" that ended, as Harriet Beecher Stowe wrote, where "a boy's education really begins."[83] Essentially religious in nature, education stressed literacy, which was considered necessary, not to aid creativity, but to promote piety and develop womanly codes of conduct that would assist women, as Benjamin Rush wrote, in "instructing their sons in principles of liberty and government."[84] From Puritan times to the end of the nineteenth century, girls' lessons in literacy "helped to support the dominant belief systems of the wider culture."[85] Primers, used to deliver the most basic level of instruction, document this emphasis on moral education. However, they also demonstrate a shift in priorities during the time that Ann came of age. For example, the *New England Primmer* of 1799 emphasizes the religious aspects of education with the letter "J": "Job feels the Rod, Yet blesses God." A year later, a more secular understanding appears. *The Child's First Primer* of 1800 uses the letters "L" and "M" to teach lessons about class, commerce, and gentility rather than religion: "L was a Lady, and had a white hand; M was a merchant to a foreign Land."[86] Reading this primer, Ann would have understood that literacy is put into service both to God and to business. A mercantile-based class-consciousness had inspired her father's decision to expel her from Boston society; it now kept her fed but at the edge of poverty. Deprived of the Sargent family's connections and wealth, Ann had to earn her own way after completing her schooling. She also lacked family to help her find a husband. She writes that "I had no outfit at the time of my wedding, with the exception of $20 at the time with which I bought some silver."[87]

It is impossible to know whether Ann's illegitimacy and adoption negatively influenced others' opinions of her. It is possible that it did. Mary Moody Emerson mentored Ann and openly acknowledged her poetic gifts; however, she extended less support to Ann than to her contemporary, Sarah Bradford. Of the two women Mary Moody Emerson tutored, only Sarah was encouraged to develop her full intellectual talents. Cole writes that Mary "took Sarah's intellectual life as a given, even a personal resource, while trying to bring the younger woman to share her faith, whereas she took Ann's faith as a given and tried to perfect it, while warning her off from intellectual life." Eventually Mary would refer glowingly to Ann as a "poet bro't up in the pure mountain air,"[88] but when Ann was eighteen, Mary discouraged any pursuit except that of moral perfection.

Like fictional adoptees who populate the domestic fiction of the mid-nineteenth century, Ann was expected to earn her place, practice humility, and exhibit feminine decorum. Her illegitimacy and controversial birth history may have worked to her disadvantage. When Ann expressed a yearning for knowledge, Mary responded that its "sybil leaves" were "never destined to be unrolled to you or me."[89] One must wonder whether Mary Moody Emerson's lower aspirations for Ann were related to her illegitimacy and adoption. In her mentorship of Ann, we see a common pattern: female adoptees, more than counterparts raised with biological parents, were expected to conform to accepted feminine norms and, in particular, to subordinate their own ambitions and serve others with obedience and piety. It is difficult to know whether Mary Moody Emerson was responding to traits she genuinely perceived in Ann when she directed her to a life of faith and service rather than of intellect and questioning, or whether she sought to lower Ann's horizons because she deemed them appropriate to her illegitimate status. Whatever the reason, it fell upon Ann to marshal the resources necessary to shape her future.

RECOGNITION

Ann began to work to recover her birth name and secure a legacy for herself and her children. Her mission had actually begun with her arrival at the Ripleys' farm in Maine. As W. A. Wheeler writes, "[f]rom the moment that Ann Brewer arrived in Waterford, she started a campaign for recognition by her natural father."[90] In so doing, she created a voice for herself, a rarity for adoptees in the nineteenth century. She regularly wrote to her father, asking him to acknowledge her as his daughter. When he did not reply, she saved the envelopes that contained the money he sent to the Ripleys for her care. On one occasion he sent a few unsigned lines from the Bible scripted in his own hand, which she kept. Ann adroitly exploited what few advantages came to her. Upon her betrothal to Leander Gage in 1819, she wrote to her father, stating her desire to marry with the Sargent name. She told her father that if she did not hear an objection from him within two weeks, she would assume his agreement with her decision to marry. The tactic was clever: If Daniel Sargent responded affirmatively, then Ann had earned the right to the family name. If he protested, then she had won his admission of paternity. Before the wedding in 1820, Leander made a trip to Boston presumably to ask Daniel Sargent for Ann's hand in marriage. Leander reported that he was gracefully received by Daniel Sargent although the outcome of the meeting is unclear.

Ann continued to seek acknowledgement until her father died in 1842. She then pursued her case with Daniel Sargent's son-in-law, Thomas Curtis, and with his grandson, Daniel Sargent Curtis, writing to him, "It was clearly not my fault, however much it may have been my misfortune, to be born out of wedlock. . . . I am now in my sixty-first year & a widow . . . some addition to my limited means would not be unacceptable."[91] She also enlisted the help of Daniel Sargent's younger brother, Lucius Manlius Sargent (1776–1867), who became her supporter. She wrote, in the guise of her husband, to her half-sister Mary Durfee (Walker), asking for information about her mother Hepzibah. Later writing under her own name, she asked Mary to "answer every question as fully as you can, and many more, which you will know I long to ask."[92] She inquired of "Mr. Hall's family where I used to reside in Dorchester."[93] Although her attempts at recognition subsided while she raised her children, Ann never abandoned the "melancholy pleasure in gathering up fragments of my childhood's history."[94] As she explained to Lucius Manlius Sargent:

> I wrote to him [Daniel Sargent] many times ranging all the way from the impulses and yearnings of orphaned childhood, to such maturity of mind as came with years, & such chastened feeling as was produced I trust by the Holy Operator. I had said many times that one line or word of recognition would be infinitely more precious than a bank note.[95]

By most measures, Ann's adult life was full and productive. Her marriage to Leander lasted twenty-two years and produced eight children who reached maturity. Leander was a physician and an active Waterford town leader, at one point president of the Waterford Lyceum.[96] Ann was a devoted mother and committed housewife, embracing what Barbara Welty and others have dubbed the "cult of true womanhood," as was expected at the time.[97] Wheeler notes that her husband's uncle described her as "a person of strict morality, sincere piety, of an amiable disposition and friendly feelings." Her household was stimulating and engaged with current issues. A part of the lively literary and cultural circle in New England, she and her husband hosted notable figures, including Ralph Waldo Emerson and Abigail Alcott, wife of Transcendentalist Bronson Alcott, and her daughter, the author Louisa May Alcott.[98]

A lively interest in people and issues of the day did not make the family immune to external pressures, however. A wide-scale economic depression in the 1830s and early 1840s took its toll on the Gage household. Leander failed to receive payment from many patients and fell into debt. When he died in 1842, he left his widow and eight children with no means of income. Leander's brother was appointed trustee of the estate and vowed to help Ann collect debts. Largely successful, he obtained roughly half of the doctor's yearly income. Again, Ann's writing proved cathartic. In grief over her husband's death, she turned to poetry, penning "Seasons," which was later renamed "Meditations of a Widow" at the suggestion of Elizabeth Peabody. The poem appeared in the literary journal *Aesthetic Papers* in 1849 and attracted the attention of Ralph Waldo Emerson. Impressed by its sentiments, Emerson quoted excerpts of it in a letter to Thomas Carlyle, as part of his condolences on the death of Carlyle's wife.[99]

Ann also began a friendship with Elizabeth Peabody, the sister of Sophia Peabody, wife of Nathaniel Hawthorne, and of Mary Peabody Mann, wife of educational reformer Horace Mann. Elizabeth Peabody gained a reputation for being a meddler and busy-body;[100] however, her unlikely friendship served Ann well. It helped to bring her into greater contact with intellectually enlightened ideas associated with Transcendentalism and further guided her on her chosen route: a "Yankeeism" made up of aggressive and personal responsibility coupled with a deep respect for individual beliefs.[101]

Transcendentalist ideas freely circulated in Ann's Waterford, Maine, community. Ann formed a personal philosophy derived from her upbringing with the devout Ripleys and from the more experimental mentoring of Mary Moody Emerson. Aided by frequent visits from notables, networks of relatives and friends, and on-going exchanges of read-ings, she developed a unique form of Transcendentalism. In prose and poetry, Ann expresses curiosity about the interplay of traditional and liberal religious beliefs. Her writings not only follow the tenets of Transcendentalism but also speak to her feelings as an abandoned daughter and adoptee. In 1839, Mary Moody Emerson noted that she sent a poem of Ann's entitled "Transcendental Sentiment" to Samuel Ripley, who had escorted Ann out of Boston. Soon afterward, Cole writes, "Ann recorded her view of the struggle between Tradition and Spirit, her 'diviner name' for Emerson's Soul."[102] The Trinitarian Calvinists had neglected their own essential truths:

A system which used to create and sustain the most fervid enthusiasm, as is its nature, for it makes God all in all, leads in crusade against all even the purest enthu-siasm. It fights for the letter of orthodoxy, for usage, for custom, for tradition, against the spirit as it breathes like healing air. . . . The Transcendentalists do not err in excess, but in defect, if I understand the case. They do not hold wild dreams for realities; the vision is deeper, broader, more spiritual than they have seen.[103]

Ann's personal battle with adoption is evident in the passage. She had been a victim of a social "orthodoxy" and "custom" that attempted to consign her to genealogical oblivion. Understandably, she sought a philosophy with more expansive alternatives. In a warm letter to Samuel Ripley she combines prose and poetry to express faith inspired by Tran-scendentalism: "I feel encouraged to put forth to you the gratitude that is in my heart, and you will let me assure you, that in my orphan course, it cheers me that . . ."

> The spirit hast a Father
> "Father of Lights" He is, and no dark ban
> Shall interdict the soul. He ranges free,
> With the great family of spirit, one . . .[104]

Ann also aligned herself with the needs of the oppressed, becoming interested in the ab-olition of slavery and other reform movements of her time. She and her husband were targeted for "conversion" to abolitionism and were successfully won over to its cause.[105] Mary Moody Emerson sent Ann her manuscript on slavery and urged her to study slavery with religious devotion. When Ann's daughter, Phebe, accepted a teaching position in Louisville, Tennessee, in 1840, Mary Moody Emerson advocated social action, writing, "If you do go—God will guard, guide & bless. And in that very land of slaves & slavery you may plant, thro' His agency, some of those seeds w'h are destined to cover our wretched land with the glory of their freedom."[106]

Ann's interest in social reform not only helped others but also facilitated her own genealogical search. While reading *Temperance Tales* by Lucius Manlius Sargent, she discovered that the author was her father's younger brother by twenty-two years. Writing under the guise of congratulating him, she commenced communication with her relative, offering information about herself and posing questions about her father. At first stiff and reluctant, Lucius Sargent was moved by her situation and became one of her closest allies. He was, Wheeler writes, "the next thing to her real father."[107] The correspondence between Ann and Lucius continued for thirty years, ending just six months before Lucius died in 1865. Lucius helped Ann by confronting Daniel Sargent about his responsibility to his daughter. He also advanced her cause to Daniel Sargent's son-in-law and grandson, and he gave sympathetic, measured advice when more concrete forms of support were not forthcoming. When Daniel Sargent's son-in-law Thomas Curtis refused to grant Ann's request for recognition, Lucius sent her an anecdote aimed at lifting her morale as well as her poetic aspiration. "For seven years of my early married life, I lived in the neighborhood of John Adams, the first President Adams; & I remember a few words of his to me— "'You want only one thing to make a good poet."—"What is that, sir?"—"misery!'"[108]

Ann was well acquainted with misery. The failure to gain her patrimony had significant financial as well as emotional consequences. As noted above, as a widow, she struggled to feed her family. During the cold winter of 1852, she reported that the "long severe season is very expensive in many respects. We have not an ear of corn and, I think, very little hay."[109] She took in boarders, including at one point Elizabeth Peabody. By 1854, she had sold her home in Waterford, Maine, and taken her "thirds" (i.e., a widow's entitlement). She was without additional means of income to support her daughter, Phebe, who was mentally ill.[110]

In contrast, the Sargent family was thriving in Boston. Daniel Sargent's estate had grown to be one of the largest in the city and was managed by his son-in-law, Thomas Curtis. As mentioned above, Lucius presented Ann's case with no initial success although Curtis eventually acknowledged that "This lady is clearly, on every score, entitled to respect and sympathy." One month later, as Daniel Sargent's legatee, Curtis sent Lucius Sargent a check for $100, with the instruction to deposit it in his own account and write a personal check for that amount to Ann. Ann had received recognition although the money's circuitous route demonstrated Curtis's reluctance to connect his name with hers. In 1856, Ann again wrote requesting monetary assistance because she lacked the means to place Phebe, whose condition had worsened, in a mental asylum. Once more Curtis sent a check, this time for $50, stipulating again that his identity not be "known in the operation."[111]

ADOPTIVE IDENTITIES

It is impossible to know how much of Ann's determination and resiliency derived from her experience as an adoptee and how much from her basic temperament. It is clear, however, that her early experiences of abandonment and relocation set her on a path of personal discovery. Denied an inheritance and the comforts of living with a birth family, she became preoccupied with issues of identity. Wheeler describes Ann as possessing uncommon "stubbornness," concluding that the "greatest and longest act of intractability was her continuous search for herself, her position in her family and the self esteem that she felt she would gain from recognition by the Sargent family."[112] Today experts in the field of adoption have language to explain the experience of adoption. For Betty Jean Lifton, an adoptee and an author, being adopted is like being "twice born."[113] Ann experienced this dual, even triple, sense of identity. Born a Sargent, she was adopted and renamed twice, first as Nancy Brown and then as Ann Brewer. In disposition and outlook, she was a child of Daniel and Hepzibah, with a sense of refinement and urban gentility. But she was also a product of Maine simplicity derived from her life with the Ripleys. She negotiated the extremes of Calvinism and Transcendentalism, and she wrote in two genres, prose and poetry. She moved fluidly, Wheeler writes, between one form and the other: "not just satisfied with the stand alone poem, she would often work an emotion or thought to the point in a letter where she interrupted the prose to insert a poem."[114] Adoption, by definition a story of dual parentage, provided her with the ability—and perhaps the imperative—to hold opposing views and forms in tension.

Ann also demonstrated what psychologist David Brodzinsky describes as an ongoing search for self.[115] Her search took concrete form as she sought acknowledgement from her birth father, but like many adoptees, she also sought answers to larger questions of identity and purpose. Throughout her writing one theme stands out: an abiding emphasis on truth, an ideal consistent with the Transcendentalist movement and of special significance to an individual forced for much of her life to assume false names and identities. A particular poem, one of Mary Moody Emerson's favorites, demonstrates this preoccupation. In a blank verse sonnet written about "the Basins," a river and forest scene near Waterford, Maine, Ann repeats the words "true" or "truth" three times in three lines. She describes naturally beautiful settings as "God's true temples" that inspire and ennoble, and she recounts the heart's longing for transformation, harmony with truth,/With all true forms." The poem is both a paean to the healing qualities of nature and a cry from one who suffers from separation and longs to join her "song in unison" with that of divine form and purpose.[116]

Ann's quest for validation from her birth family also demonstrates tensions between Old World blood ties and New World individualism. As an adult with a husband and children in a new republic, Ann single handedly launched a campaign to reestablish her identity. In this respect she epitomizes the self-reliant, self-made American that her age revered. However, her mission—to restore her place in her family's lineage—aligns her with European traditions. She wished to reinstall herself in the Sargent family line and benefit from its English-based genealogical system. As a woman in early nineteenth-century America, Ann was also pulled in two directions, between an incipient movement for women's rights that affirmed women as different from but fully equal to men—an assumption that drove her objections to the stigmas of illegitimacy, which were based in patriarchy—and a more traditional view of womanhood, marriage, and motherhood that required women to defer to masculine power.

Ann's adoption occurred at a time of major change and intense generational tension in American society. For the first time, the older generation was only minimally helpful to a populous newer generation, for whom the concept of independence meant a greater reliance on peer groups than on elders and a sense that the Revolution had truly given birth to "a race of Americans," as Gouverneur Morris put it.[117] As the new nation developed industry, expanded markets, and welcomed technological innovations as well as geographic and social mobility, England became more a competitor and less a supplier of manufactured goods. New England, in particular, once dependent upon England for ideas as well as goods, forged a new economic independence and a corresponding confidence about the future of the United States. Ann's relocation from Boston to Maine was emblematic of this national mobility. But her story also demonstrates the limits for those born female and illegitimate. Ann could validate her identity only through a father or a husband; she had little recourse when her father denied her existence. Despite advances in virtually every aspect of society, women still had little legal control over their own lives.[118] Genteel society in post-Revolutionary Boston conferred status through legitimacy, which in turn derived from patriarchal structures found in the English or European aristocracy. In the early to mid-nineteenth century, these international influences were strong despite the fact that Americans had since the Revolution confidently embraced notions of freedom and individual opportunity.

Ann was no radical. She was raised in a manner that led her to accept gender roles of her class and time. Evidence suggests that she did not question the socially inscribed biases that led families, including her own, to value sons over daughters. She voiced concern that, after giving birth to three daughters, she still had no sons. When her husband Leander began to despair and expressed impatience, she wrote, "Husband says *no hope!*" After the birth of her first male son, Thomas Hovey Gage, she enthusiastically penned a note to her adoptive mother, Phebe Ripley, saying, "You can judge faintly of my joy. . . . It was much to me who have passed [?] on my journey without parents, or brother or sister."[119] However, she was introduced through Mary Moody Emerson to romantic theories of individualism as well as abolition, both of which coincided with the rise of the women's movement. Participation in these movements required courage and forward thinking and helped her construct a sense of self that could challenge the status quo. Support of these reforms, like the need to adjust to her adoption, demanded resourcefulness, tested resilience, and set her on a course of her own making.

Ann's spirit of independence, necessitated by her adoption, led paradoxically to a search for roots. She thus worked in a manner counter to that outlined by Michael Ragussis in *Acts of Naming* but consistent with her own experience and feminist goals. Ragussis writes that "[e]arning one's name, instead of inheriting it, is the core of the democratic American plot" and is the feature that sets the American plot apart from the British one. In American fiction, he continues, "when you earn your name yourself, you bear a 'natural' name, while in the British system your name is merely nominal and depends entirely on your family." In American mythology, "we see the protagonist successfully live beyond names." Ragussis adds that these "American 'solutions' to the naming plot are male plots."[120] Ann's adoption story is distinctive in its display of American and British, and male and female, plot conventions. Ann demonstrates what Ragussis describes as the masculine drive and courage necessary to establish identity and challenge conventions that disenfranchise her, but she does so in a feminine way, not in order to distance herself from her family of origin but to realign herself with it.

Ann's quest for recognition from her birth family was in the spirit of liberty and reform that swept the young United States. Her generation, fueled by the conviction that a combination of democratic principles and Christian faith could shape a world already transformed by the Revolution, gave birth to a wave of reforms ranging from the temperance movement to foreign missions, antislavery campaigns, urban charities, and female suffrage. Ann embraced these movements. However, despite the energy she poured into various causes and missions, her experiences make it clear that liberty was not available to all. Individual women were capable of making impressive gains: Mary Moody Emerson, Ann's adoptive aunt, became a noted intellectual, and Elizabeth Peabody, a noted educator. Ann herself was an exemplary wife and mother as well as a modestly successful poet, combining marriage, motherhood, and authorship in a manner few women of the time managed. She even became a noted civic leader instrumental in creating the Waterford Temperance Group. However, her failure to gain her patrimony underlines the social stigma attached to illegitimacy generally and to female illegitimacy especially. She stands in striking contrast to William Franklin, who as a child enjoyed the lavish attentions of his father.

An American mythology of success based on merit, not on inheritance, was emerging in nineteenth-century American society, nurtured by a revolutionary zeal for freedom and movement. Such a spirit invigorated adoptive practices and shaped an outpouring of literature about "little strangers," as Claudia Nelson calls orphans taken into households in American fiction of the period.[121] Not only orphans, but also slaves, settlers, migrants, adventurers, and travelers left the emotional matrix of traditionally organized families for new homes of all types. Ann resembles them by embarking on an adventure away from home, albeit involuntarily. Her conflicted story is a testament both to the strength of Old World ties and to the dynamic energies of the new republic.

Ann Sargent Gage was bold enough to claim her birthright, yet her attempt failed. An obscure figure in American history and literature, she valiantly resisted a gendered political and social system in order to restore her reputation in the public eye and secure a legacy for her children. In this respect she keeps company with Hester Prynne of *The Scarlet Letter* (1850), whose romantic individualism also challenges the patriarchal status quo. Although Hester's story is set in colonial times, the predicaments of the real Gage and the fictional Prynne reflect shifting terrain in familial relations and custodial law of the mid-nineteenth century. Michael Grossberg notes the strength of traditional legal patterns. In post-Revolutionary America, "[j]udges were extremely cautious in allowing bastardy reform to upset an existing scheme of family inheritance." When evidence supported a man's desire to legitimate an illegitimate child, the court generally complied with his wishes. But if a father renounced the child, as Daniel Sargent renounced Ann, then the child "dwelt in a kind of legal purgatory," alive but without acknowledged relatives.[122] Nineteenth-century juridical codes increasingly recognized maternal custody rights and gave women the opportunity to legitimate illegitimate children and make them their heirs, assuming no legitimate children laid claim to the estate. By the mid-nineteenth century, illegitimate children were beginning to seem "less of a threat to social order, sexual morality, and domestic life, and more compelling objects of compassion" than they had in the past.[123] In popular fiction of this period, orphans, including illegitimate ones, elicit sympathy from readers even though they continue to be stigmatized.

Such transformations in domestic life may have been on Nathaniel Hawthorne's mind when he created in *The Scarlet Letter* another illegitimate American daughter, Pearl Prynne, who is also denied her patrimony. Both Ann and Pearl resist the shame associated with their illegitimacy, seek the truth about paternal identity, and ask their fathers to acknowledge their existence. Ann made these appeals on her own. One wonders what her success might have been had her mother lived and been able to support and defend her. These are the questions—of illegitimacy, mother right, and paternal detachment—that Hawthorne takes up in *The Scarlet Letter*.

3

Adoption Averted in *The Scarlet Letter*

IN CHAPTER 7 of *The Scarlet Letter* (1850), Hester Prynne hurries to the governor's mansion after hearing rumors that the Puritan magistrates plan to transfer Pearl from her care to "wiser and better guardianship."[1] Hester protests the decision and success-fully pleads her case, demonstrating here as elsewhere her ability to challenge male authority. Hawthorne does more than comment on the politics of gender in this drama between the mother of an illegitimate child and Salem officials. He explores the nature of childhood, child-rearing strategies, and the child's place in American society. New atti-tudes toward children and the family emerged at mid-century in response to widespread social changes.[2] Hawthorne observed these changes both as a writer of romance and as a parent of an unexpectedly strong-willed daughter, Una.[3] In the novel, he explores the strength of bonds of blood and care necessary to form a stable foundation for the family and the republic. The trope of adoption—in this case threatened and averted—permits this examination of kinship. It also provides a previously unrecognized link between Hawthorne and popular writers of his day.

Hawthorne rejects the adoption plot as practiced by nineteenth-century domestic writers. In fiction by the "d—d mob of scribbling women"[4] that Hawthorne famously de-rided, birth mothers relinquish their children because of sexual transgression, illness, or misfortune to others presumably more able to support the child's growth. First orphancy, then adoption, launch the protagonists on a wide narrative arc that, even as it involves hardship, models a sense of progress and optimism appropriate to the aspirations of an expanding, democratic nation. Hawthorne's portrait of an adulteress in control of her motherhood is striking in a body of fiction known for strictly enforced codes of feminine purity and sundered mother-child bonds. Hester is unlike the ill and retreating Mrs. Montgomery, who is persuaded by an autocratic husband to relinquish her daughter, Ellen, in Susan Warner's popular *The Wide, Wide World*, which appeared in the same year as *The Scarlet Letter*. Hester is a present, potent force, unlike Gerty Flint's absent birth mother in Susanna Maria Cummins's hailed novel, *The Lamplighter*, published four years later. Hawthorne takes exception to these novels, which "express an ethos of conformity."[5] He is progressive—even radical—in depicting a mother outside the social norm who defies authority in order to keep her child. In championing her cause, he gives center stage to an issue virtually ignored in literary discourse until the late twentieth century.[6]

The adoptive aspects of *The Scarlet Letter* have been overlooked even by critics who focus on family relations. Emily Miller Budick, for example, writes that the novel "dramatizes a relationship between issues of birth (Whose child is Pearl?) and questions of interpretation (What does the letter mean?)."[7] She focuses on the adultery that the letter represents rather than on the child-rearing issues that result from Pearl's illegitimate birth. However, the novel also dramatizes the tension between issues of illegitimacy (Whose child is Pearl?) and those of care (Who is responsible for her?). When custody and child rearing are viewed as foremost, the question that emerges is not "Who or what has produced Pearl?" but "Who will raise Pearl, and what will she become?" The novel becomes a study not simply in gender, but also in genealogy. Adoption—averted in chapters 7 and 8 but indirectly acknowledged in chapter 24 when Pearl receives Chillingworth's inheritance—becomes emblematic of Hawthorne's anxieties about his own family dynamics as well as those confronting the mid-nineteenth-century bourgeois U.S. society of which he was a part. His portrayals of severed and repressed biological ties have their basis not only in widespread cultural changes but also in his personal experience of rootlessness. These feelings were generated by childhood dislocation; a troubled relationship to Puritan forbears; and an ambivalent attachment, as an American, to the cultural and literary traditions of Europe.

The novel's historical setting allows Hawthorne to deliver a critique of Puritan repression and control commensurate with nineteenth-century literary nationalism and romanticism.[8] The time period also permits him to deflect onto a bygone era his more subtle worries over shifting conceptions of childhood and parenthood that affected middle-class family life as result of a rapid economic and social expansion. Hawthorne presents a fictional family in alignment with both seventeenth-and nineteenth-century domestic customs and law. From dual historical perspectives, he explores the challenges of raising children to become virtuous, responsible citizens. These challenges are visible in his portrayal of the four main characters. Pearl, a "spirit-messenger" as well as an "earthly child" (123), represents not only her parents' sexual transgression but also the liberties extended to American children and the instability that was a consequence of newly configured bourgeois values. Hester's maternal conviction affirms the primacy of the mother-child bond but resists accepted sentimental representation because her unwed motherhood associates female sexuality with sin. Dimmesdale and Chillingworth embody the shifting grounds of masculinity in the mid-nineteenth century. Their divided paternity—one biological and one adoptive—suggests Hawthorne's misgivings about traditional patriarchal authority, on the one hand, and the uncharted territory of republican fatherhood, on the other.

Hawthorne affirms biological kinship in a plot that climaxes with a birth father's acknowledgement of his daughter. Despite this affirmation of genealogy, however, the center of this family unit does not hold. Arthur Dimmesdale is an intimate who remains an outsider, incapacitated by guilt and the conflicting demands of public and personal roles. Throughout the novel he denies family ties, and he dies the moment his identity is known, abandoning his family. Roger Chillingworth, his companion and nemesis, is Hester's legal husband, whose money helps to transform Pearl from Puritan pariah to lady of stature. However, Chillingworth creates domestic havoc, his malevolence as self-diminishing as it is vengeful. Pearl, caught in a parental triangle, is also conflicted. The Puritans' own American child, she is both representative of its most feared sin—illicit sexuality—and symbolic of its most ebullient, youthful hopes. But Pearl does not remain in America. She moves not forward but backward, to Europe. Only Hester abides, but on the social margins, worthy but muted, waiting for an unspecified time that can accommodate the full force of her feminine power. These mixed outcomes combine to make *The Scarlet Letter* more skeptical than optimistic about intimate relationships and the future of the American child, family, and developing republic. Exploring the strength of blood kinship and adoptive bonds, Hawthorne is ultimately ambivalent about both.

CHILDHOOD ROOTS

Although Hawthorne was deeply connected to his family of origin, he suffered anxieties associated with orphancy and adoption. As Gloria Erlich notes, he experienced "a series of losses and dissociations," including the death of his father and separation from his mother.[9] In a fictional account, he describes the process of growing up as painful and alienating: "[Y]ou know how I sprang out of mystery, akin to none . . . how, all through my boyhood, I was alone; how I grew up without a root, yet continually longing for one."[10] Hawthorne's relationship to his ancestral family history also created tensions, such as found in adoption narratives, between inherited and acquired identity. He was proud but also wary of his ancestral legacy, which afforded a sense of belonging as well as isolation. Hawthorne's choice to become an author further distanced him from well-meaning relatives who expected him to pursue a vocation in law or theology.

Descended from the first New England settlers, Hawthorne was part of a lineage that venerated genealogy even while finding it of little practical use. His ancestors included the eminent John Hathorne, judge at the Salem witchcraft trials of 1692, but by the early nineteenth-century the family had lost its prominence. Hawthorne's great-grandfather, Daniel Hathorne, was a Massachusetts farmer "of modest means whose sons commanded ships they did not own."[11] His father also went to sea. His father's death in Surinam when the future novelist was four years old meant the loss not only of a parent but also of the family home. He became dependent on the kinship care of his mother's family, the Mannings, whose fortune had been made through their ownership of the Boston and Salem Stage Company. He relied specifically on the adoptive good will of his aunts and uncles. His pragmatic uncle, Robert Manning, supervised his schooling but discouraged his art.

When he lived in Salem, Massachusetts, separated from his mother except for visits at the family home in Raymond, Maine, the young Hawthorne faced orphancy again. In 1821, he wrote longingly of his desire to spend uninterrupted time with his mother. If she could remain in Maine rather than return to Salem, he wrote that it should be as "a second Garden of Eden" for them.[12] He was not successful in persuading her to stay with him, and the trauma of this abandonment stayed with him, marring his adult life. Writing about the impact of dislocation, Elizabeth Goodenough suggests that Hawthorne's "parental loss and early sense of displacement may explain his nostalgia, as well as his need to remain at home" for twelve years once he graduated from Bowdoin College.[13] The early disruption of his family life also produced a peripatetic adulthood. His son Julian wrote that necessity, convenience, or "his own will, drove him from place to place." He was "always wishing to settle down finally, but never lighting upon the fitting spot."[14] His children, subjected to this vagabondage, knew their childhood home as "The Wayside," a name that conveys its impermanence. Deprived of maternal contact, Hawthorne imaginatively fulfills this childhood void in his depiction of isolated intimacy between Hester and Pearl.

Hawthorne's wife Sophia was also descended from a downwardly mobile gentry-class family. Her mother, Elizabeth Palmer Peabody, had married Nathaniel Peabody, a doctor turned dentist who enjoyed only "fitful success."[15] Changes in American class structures were very much on the couple's mind as they began married life together. Nathaniel and Sophia Hawthorne, described by T. Walker Herbert as "descendents of the pre-Revolutionary elite," found themselves supplanted in the antebellum period by the "rising culture of the urban Northeast."[16] These quickly changing social circumstances bred a sense of disappointment and longing for the past, but they also created the conditions for an American self-sufficiency. In a new republic, the genealogical past no longer determined their future. For example, the family's experience of decline led Sophia to make a Tocqueville-like observation that in America "greatness can never be predicated of a man on account of position—but only of character, because from the nature of our institutions, place changes like the figures of a kaleidoscope."[17] Without a patrimony, Hawthorne had no choice but to become self-made, aided in his pursuit of worldly success by his wife. Together he and Sophia fashioned a new, middle-class family life. As Herbert writes, "The Hawthornes became shamans of domesticity."[18] Yet the inner stresses and contradictions of this life were palpable and became material for the psychological romance in *The Scarlet Letter*. As Herbert writes about problems afflicting the Hawthorne clan,

> The Hawthorne family vividly exemplified the domestic ideal of family relations that became dominant in the early nineteenth century.... Yet this union of perfect beings was simultaneously a battlefield of souls, marked at times with scenes of cruelty and agony; this ideal model of middle-class normality embraced fierce collisions of opposing psychic, social, and religious forces, and it produced a madwoman, a criminal, and a saint.[19]

Hawthorne's childhood traumas and aspirations found expression in his early fiction. He began his career by writing for young people, contributing pieces for the popular Peter Parley stories of Samuel Goodwin Goodrich and producing, as Karen Sánchez-Eppler explains, "more pieces directly aimed at a juvenile audience than any other canonical male author of the antebellum period."[20] At Goodrich's invitation, for a brief time beginning in 1836, Hawthorne served as editor of the juvenile periodical, *American Magazine of Useful and Entertaining Knowledge*. In 1838 he planned a collaborative children's literature project with Longfellow, which did not materialize but that Hawthorne enthusiastically claimed could "entirely revolutionize the whole system of juvenile literature."[21] His adaptations of New England history for children appeared in *Grandfather's Chair, Liberty Tree*, and *Famous Old People* (1841), which was later collected in *The Whole History of Grandfather's Chair*. His sketches, *Biographical Stories for Children*, appeared in 1842. He made lasting contributions to children's literature with two collection of classic myths, *A Wonder-Book for Girls and Boys* (1851) and *Tanglewood Tales* (1853). Although he initially considered writing for children a form of "drudgery" necessary to make a living, he later embraced the task as a vocation, approaching it with confidence in his writing ability and in the capacity of children.[22] The Wonder Books, he wrote, were efforts were to "raise the intellect and fancy to the level of childhood."[23]

The juvenile collections pleased him: "I never did anything else so well as these old baby stories," Hawthorne wrote to Richard Henry Stoddard just before the publication of *Tanglewood Tales*.[24] He took pride in his accomplishments in the genre of children's literature, seeing the form, as Sánchez-Eppler notes, as compatible with "a new kind of literature for children" that "resists hierarchies and control, and that celebrates storytelling as the most effective ways of knowing." Children, she concludes, enabled "not only publicity but authorship itself."[25] Other critics note the importance of the child in Hawthorne's writing. Goodenough observes that his "temperamental affinity . . . centers on the child" and is related to "concern with origins and the past."[26] Gillian Brown and Laura Laffrado point to Hawthorne's interest in adult influences on children. What is unique in Hawthorne's work, Laffrado writes, is his focus not on the saintly death of children, but on their "pollution" by adults.[27] Adult responsibility toward children, or the lack thereof, drives the plots of diverse tales such as "Rappaccini's Daughter," a story of literally toxic birth parenting, and "The Gentle Boy," an account of religious strife, child abandonment, and adoption.

Hawthorne's juvenilia are set against a lively cultural discourse about American childhood. The Hawthornes were immersed in current New England thinking about child rearing and education. Hawthorne's sister-in-law, Elizabeth Palmer Peabody, was a pioneer in early childhood education with Bronson Alcott, the founder of the Temple School in Boston, and the author of a children's version of Spenser's *Faerie Queen* (1836). A noted teacher and educational reformer, who followed the theories of Transcendentalism, Elizabeth Peabody founded the first kindergarten in the United States. His other sister-in-law, Mary, married educational reformer, Horace Mann, and published a treatise on early childhood education, *The Moral Culture of Infancy* (1863). The Hawthornes were fiercely committed to home schooling, in contrast to Horace Mann, who led the way in the creation of public schools.[28] Yet they shared with the Manns the Transcendental belief in the intuitive nature of knowledge and the importance of educating the whole person by drawing out rather than imposing ideas, and of disciplining children through nurturing love rather than corporal punishment. Reflecting a romantic emphasis on the natural goodness of children, they followed contemporary views of the child as not only in need of adult guidance but also able to lead adults to higher moral ground. At the same time, they were concerned over troubling aspects of childhood, which they tended to view as their Calvinist forbears might, as inherited "sins of the fathers."[29] These issues of child rearing, including the proper balance of paternal and maternal influence, become the thematic center of the custody scene in chapters 7 and 8 of *The Scarlet Letter*.

CUSTODY RIGHTS

After three years of living in relative isolation and calm on the outskirts of Salem, Hester learns that, as in the opening scaffold scene, she is the object of official scrutiny. There is "a design on the part of some of the leading inhabitants, cherishing the more rigid order of principles in religion and government, to deprive her of her child" (69). Panicked,

Hester hastens to the governor's mansion, her appearance before Bellingham and other officials paralleling the scene in chapter 2, when she leaves the prison with Pearl and ascends the scaffold in a Foucaultian display of public surveillance and discipline. Both scenes call Hester's maternity into question and constitute what Jamie Barlowe terms "noisy" moments, when her force of character stands out in relation to that of the established authorities.[30] In both scenes, the mother-child bond is prominent, with Pearl both protected by Hester and protective of her. In chapter 2, Hester clutches Pearl to her breast in the prison doorway to defend herself and her child from the gaze of a vindictive mob. In chapter 7, Pearl asks to be "taken up in arms" (70) as the Puritan children stare and taunt. She defends Hester by responding aggressively to their attacks, a "half-fledged angel of judgment,—whose mission is to punish the sins of the rising generation" (71). In both encounters, Pearl is an extension of Hester, both bane and blessing, cause of maternal suffering and source of its relief.

The scene reinforces the contrast between the lone Hester and the Puritan establishment. Mother and daughter make their way from a modest "solitary cottage" to the governor's large wooden house, a structure whose "brilliancy might have befitted Aladdin's palace." The path divides, with "the public, on the one side, and a lonely woman" on the other. The dark mud that "sombre little urchins" fling at both mother and daughter contrasts with the gold and crimson splendor of their dresses (70–71). Governor Bellingham is relaxed and at home "in a loose gown and easy cap" (74), whereas Hester is beside herself with worry. Inside the hall, the magistrates interrogate her with a proprietary air, conscious of their right to decide her fate in all civic and religious matters. The men have the advantage of previous conversation among themselves—"'This is the self-same child of whom we have held speech together,'" whispers the Reverend Wilson to Governor Bellingham (76)—but Hester faces the august group alone and without counsel.

The magistrates explain their concern over the state of Hester's soul and the quality of Pearl's moral education under her tutelage. Leading citizens in Salem already have judged Hester to be unfit. They believe that Pearl is of "demon origin," sent "to promote some foul and wicked purpose," and they follow a logic born of this belief. If, on the one hand, Pearl is demonic, they reason that "a Christian interest in the mother's soul required them to remove such a stumbling-block from her path." If, on the other hand, Pearl is capable of salvation, they conclude "that a wiser and better guardianship than Hester Prynne's" would provide Pearl with the necessary moral education (69). Governor Bellingham uses the language of law—"We will judge warily . . . examine this Pearl"—and he questions how "one who hath stumbled and fallen, amid the pitfalls of this world" can presume to raise a child to follow a Christian path (76–77). Bellingham has civil and religious doctrine on his side. Hester, in contrast, is "backed by the sympathies of nature" (70), as she is throughout the novel and most famously in the forest scene in chapter 18. She speaks from her heart and experience: "I can teach my little Pearl what I have learned from this," she replies, pointing to the letter A. "This badge had taught me,—it daily teaches me,—it is teaching me at this moment" (76).

Hawthorne presents a lively debate about maternal fitness in what is arguably the most famous custody case in American literature. Hester's suit seems lost when Pearl refuses to recite her catechism rather than exhibit the salutary effects of her mother's instruction. The governor asks, "who made thee?" whereupon Pearl disavows her Christian origins in favor of natural ones, proclaiming that she "had been plucked by her mother off the bush of wild roses" (83). In desperation, Hester evokes her natural, maternal prerogative, which she instinctively and romantically associates with divinity. "She felt that she possessed indefeasible rights against the world, and was ready to defend them to the death." "God gave me the child!" she shrieks twice, "I will not give her up!" "Ye shall not take her! I will die first!" (78). Pearl likewise affirms, "I am mother's child" (76).

Social practice in the novel's two time periods—the seventeenth and nineteenth centuries—would support Hester's guardianship but raise questions about Pearl's best interest and the nature of American childhood generally. From colonial times onward, women's virtue was understood in terms of marriage, and marriage in terms of domesticity and motherhood. Within this context, children were expected and welcomed, with responsibility for their physical and spiritual care falling mutually but differently on both parents. However, children born out of wedlock presented a special challenge. In early America, mothers of illegitimate children often retained custody of their offspring rather than relinquish them for adoption but faced rigid, punitive controls by male magistrates.[31] Custody was granted for economic as well as moral reasons. The official sanctions against Hester are consistent with the understanding of law that early American colonists imported from England. An illegitimate child, Pearl is both the instrument of Hester's shame and punishment for adultery *and* a potential public financial burden. Michael Grossberg explains that the Elizabethan Poor Law and its related common-law definition of the bastard applied in North American provinces as well as in Britain:

> Colonial officials transferred to the New World the English policy of using illegitimate children to enforce proper sexual conduct, protect public solvency, and aid the patriarchal distribution of property. The Atlantic migration of the law ensured that the bastard and its mother bore the brunt of punishment and social ostracism, without compensating rights or benefits.

Paternalistic English law granted fathers custody of legitimate children, but it assumed that illegitimate children outside the patriarchal household were not subject to statutes or entitled to their protections. Women were encouraged to raise their children as single mothers so long as they remained under control of the state. Officials frequently took steps to locate the birth father and make him financially responsible for the child's upkeep in the interest of "keeping baseborn offspring off the public rolls."[32]

Hester's successful battle for custody also reflects the transforming landscape in child-rearing practices and child-custody legislation as it developed from the colonial period to the mid-nineteenth century. The debate over Pearl's placement represents the American legal system's growing interest in the welfare of the child and an increasing reluctance, in contrast to England's system, to punish children for the sins of the fathers. Such a transition was already underway in the mid 1700s, when Benjamin Franklin challenged public opinion and secured a bright future for his illegitimate son, William. The expanded roles for women as custodial parents are also apparent in Franklin's political satire about the fictional Polly Baker, an unmarried mother who has just given birth to her fifth illegitimate child. Prosecuted for licentiousness, she protests to a Connecticut court that her actions are not only natural but also patriotic. Polly Baker challenges the sexual double standards prevalent at the time. She rationalizes that officials should decline to sanction her out-of-wedlock maternity and instead acknowledge the duty she does to the

"Command of Nature, and of Nature's God, *Encrease and Multiply*" the population of the new nation by arranging "to have a Statue erected to my Memory." Maintaining her children not on charity but by her own "Industry," Polly Baker argues that she is a contributor to society, not a burden on it. Her arguments are so convincing that they elicit a marriage proposal from one of the judges who hears her case.[33]

The English legal system, despite its paternalistic leanings, favored maternal custody of children under the age of seven. American juridical decisions extended these custodial rights unless the mother was proved unfit. Traditionally, however, the illegitimate child was a relative of no one and resided "in a kind of legal purgatory,"[34] "as if he were dead and his relatives had never existed."[35] As Grossberg notes, a bastard's only rights were extracted from poor-law authorities, and from the customary practice of being left in the care of its mother for its first years of life. U.S. republican law altered this situation, creating new binding relationships that secured and extended the illegitimate child's inheritance rights and fortified the mother-child bond. These changes began with courts supporting the rights of mothers to gain custody of their children born out of wedlock. As early as 1807, the courts ruled that in the case of illegitimacy, especially of females, "the mother appears to us to be the best entitled to the custody of them; but this right is not of such a nature as to prevent the court from interfering to take the infant from the custody of the mother, under special circumstances of ill-treatment."[36] Hawthorne reflects this shift with the magistrates' ruling in Hester's favor. Although illegitimate children never fully gained the rights of legitimate children, "barriers keeping them outside a legally recognized family began to crumble" and continued to do so throughout the century.[37] By mid-century several states had established direct lines of inheritance between the mother and her illegitimate child, including Massachusetts, although provisions varied widely.

This new view of childhood challenged traditional family structures by putting the child's needs, rather than the father's inheritance, in the center of the family picture. As Grossberg writes,

> Post-Revolutionary Americans abandoned the hierarchical concept of the family that had dominated English common law and colonial practice. Concurrently they displayed a new faith in women's innate proclivities for child rearing and in developmental notions of childhood.... Traditional paternalistic custody rules and practices disappeared; an entirely new standard of child placement took their place.[38]

The implications of this shift for adoption and the related issue of illegitimacy were enormous. As post-Revolutionary American society . . .

> increased respect for the individual, [legislatures] enlarged the law's concept of a family to include the bastard and its mother, and revamped the common law to aid children who sought legitimacy. A new conviction was being woven into American family law: voluntarily assumed domestic relations provided the most secure foundation for family success.[39]

In a break with English tradition and in keeping with republican attitudes toward the family, U.S. law provided for the legitimization of children through a variety of means, including adoption.

Money as well as morality remained motivating factors in resolving nineteenth-century child-custody issues. Solvent mothers benefited more from the new statutes because a primary concern of the courts was to ease the financial strain of public support of illegitimate children, as was the case in colonial times. Hawthorne reflects these issues by depicting Hester as a self-supporting seamstress capable of providing for Pearl. Her needlework meets the demands of such dignitaries as Governor Bellingham, a clergyman with "a long established and legitimate taste for all good and comfortable things" (75). The original purpose of Hester's visit to the governor's house is not to plea for custody of Pearl but to deliver embroidered apparel that Bellingham has commissioned. The scarlet "A" has not made Hester financially dependent on the town; on the contrary, she survives economically through her skilled labor. Earning her own way, she frustrates the efforts of officials who would deprive her of her child for pecuniary reasons.

MATERNAL FITNESS

The Scarlet Letter reflects mid-nineteenth-century societal trends, outlined by Bernard Wishy and others, in which the grounds of family governance shifted away from masculine, legal-based frameworks toward more feminine ones based in emotion and spirituality.[40] These domestic sentiments helped to secure women's legal rights to their children and reflected a movement from culpability to accountability. In a cultural environment in which womanhood was increasingly considered equal to motherhood, maternal rights were expanded to enhance the welfare of children. Accordingly, Hawthorne shows Hester not only enduring but also rising above circumstances and transforming the meaning of the scarlet "A." In chapter 2, Hester is compared to Anne Hutchinson, a first-generation Puritan settler and religious renegade who followed the dictates of her own mind rather than comply with religious orthodoxy. She also evokes the Madonna, the Christian model of divine maternity. In chapter 7, Hester is "self-ordained a Sister of Mercy," her nature "warm and rich; a well-spring of human tenderness." The scarlet letter itself undergoes transformation. Initially denoting "adulteress," it now means "Able; so strong was Hester Prynne, with a woman's strength" (110–11). In chapter 7, the scarlet letter acquires another meaning: that of "advocate." Committed to raising her child, Hester transforms her badge of shame into one of power historically denied mothers.

Hawthorne's allusion to the Madonna would seem to inscribe Hester within a cultural ideology of motherhood that is synonymous with nineteenth-century domesticity and with American republican values. Shirley Samuels demonstrates that the post-Revolutionary family, "made public and publicized," appears in the early sentimental novel as a model for the nation.[41] In the preface of *The Scarlet Letter*, the symbol of the eagle perched over the Custom House door helps to write this iconography of mother-as-nation (6). There are frequent references throughout American literature to Mother Britain, to Columbia as a maternal figure, and to the "motherhood" of the Statue of Liberty.[42] Stephanie Smith observes, however, that "critical articulations of maternal iconography remain scarce."[43] Threatening as well as comforting, demonstrating hopes for union as well as "fears of disunion," figurations of the national maternal are unstable.[44] Smith notes, in particular, the "troubling antinomies" that the image of the Statue of Liberty inspires: "stony, frowning brow and her alarmingly spiked crown. Such a medusan image unsettles."[45] Lauren Berlant likewise argues that the Statue of Liberty inhabits a national fantasy of the timeless, indivisible iconic maternal body, but her importance or "positive 'agency' lies solely in her availability to be narrativized—controlled."[46] These varying conceptions of maternity and nationhood are formed from an idea rooted in biology and reproduction: to conceive an idea of liberty is also to give birth to it. However, surrogate and adoptive motherhood also play a part in creating this American cultural narrative. For example, in a recent, well-publicized adoption case, the Baby M case, Mary Beth Whitehead-Gould, a surrogate mother, unsuccessfully defended her right to break her contract with the biological father and adoptive mother of her child by saying, "Mother and child—that is what America is built on."[47]

Hawthorne calls forth a variety of meanings by associating adulterous, unwed motherhood with domestic and national ideals. Thus, Hester's outlaw status invites not only the question, "What is the iconic value of a mother who breaks moral, legal, and social boundaries?" but also, "What kind of parent is this mother?" Hester's victory in her battle for custody of Pearl positions the novel in a social movement that supports maternal rights regardless of whether the mother is chaste, reverent, or submissive. Hester herself expresses a romantic belief in individual autonomy that questions society's right to define interpersonal relationships. However, Hawthorne is ambiguous about the effects of Hester's parenting. Although he demonstrates a traditional adherence to the sanctity of bloodline, he is less clear whether the magistrates' ruling ensures Pearl's well-being.

Hester wins custody, but she does not earn Hawthorne's unqualified endorsement. Like the domestic writers he criticized, Hawthorne affirms motherhood as an essential feminine practice. As Ann Douglas, Mary Kelley, and others have documented, experts increasingly assigned to women the role of domestic and spiritual caregiver, expecting them to find fulfillment in self-sacrificing service to others, and promising that this behavior, in contrast to participation in the more masculine public arena, would ensure their families' success and counter the competitive, aggressive forces of the marketplace.[48] Hawthorne frowns on adultery, subscribing to the view held throughout the history of Western literature that vilifies and punishes unmarried women with children for transgressions against established rules that require conformity and limit women's access to and expression of their sexuality. Despite the new elevation of womanhood, these issues were as pressing in nineteenth-century society as they were in previous periods. As T. Walter Herbert writes about the cult of femininity at this time, "[t]he domestic ideal gave adultery an enlarged significance."[49] A problematic mother on many grounds, Hester never overcomes the stigma associated with the scarlet letter.[50] Specifically, Hawthorne's representation of her reveals his anxieties over how changes in nineteenth-century domestic life were affecting family life. As Gillian Brown explains, "What most concerns Hawthorne is adultery's effect on children."[51] Brown analyzes issues of rightful inheritance and transference of property, but Hawthorne targets child-rearing practices themselves. Hawthorne is vague about whether the fault lies exclusively with the parent or with both mother and child, but despite Hester's unquestionable love for her daughter, there is something amiss in Hester's parenting of Pearl.

The cult of domesticity invested the parent, and especially the female, with responsibility for the moral state of the child. Hester's principles of pure individualism conflict with the Christian precepts espoused by leading child development experts such as Horace Bushnell, author of the influential treatise, *Christian Nurture* (1847). There is no doubt of Hester's love for Pearl, but her indulgent, passionate, and erratic discipline puts her daughter at risk. Hester's "haughty spirit," inherent waywardness, and recalcitrance lead to penance without penitence; in the end, "the scarlet letter had not done its office" (114). An abundance of natural affection, Bushnell warns, jeopardizes the child's moral well-being: "I know not any thing more sad to think of, than the cruelties put upon children in this manner" "of over-fond motherhood."[52] Hawthorne questions Hester's maternal fitness at the time when feminine influence on childhood was in its ascendancy in the world outside the novel. Likewise, from a seventeenth-century perspective, the magistrates' inquiry into Pearl's guardianship reflects a fear that inadequate parenting would fail to secure a generation of pious, law-abiding citizens needed to further the mission of the commonwealth. In both contexts, inconsistent or deficient mothering threatens the national order.

CHILD REARING

One measure of Hester's maternal fitness is Pearl herself, but as critics have noted, Pearl defies explanation and remains a challenging figure of study. Barbara Garlitz's early proclamation that Pearl is "the most enigmatic child in literature" still holds true.[53] Reinhard Kuhn likewise calls her an "enigmatic figure," with the power, sometimes beneficent, sometimes malicious, to transform those who cross the child's path.[54] Early perspectives on Pearl are mixed, with some critics exploring Pearl's evil nature as consistent with Calvinist theology and others viewing her angelic qualities as compatible with Romanticism. For Kuhn, for example, she combines the conflicting traditions of Rousseau-like childhood innocence and goodness with more Calvinist associations of the unredeemed child given over to the forces of Satan and redeemable only through austere training that will eliminate its spontaneity and whimsicality.[55] More recent focus on Pearl's multivalence as a linguistic or cultural sign aligns her with the novel's indeterminacy. Goodenough writes that Hawthorne's "shifting representations of the child mirror multiple qualities of the author: his artistic calling, bizarre feelings of unreality, and obsession with 'the foul cavern of the heart.'" She finds that Pearl "prefigures the use of indeterminacy by modernist writers like Woolf."[56] For Cindy Lou Daniels, Pearl is a feminist prototype who "demonstrates a new type of woman—one capable of answering whatever needs society may have."[57]

The "major symbol"[58] approach to Pearl has its uses, even if, as Darrell Abel claims, it "tends to make her unmanageable and seriously defective as an active character."[59] The fact that Pearl is frequently associated with light—especially in the forest scene, where she "did actually catch the sunshine, and stood laughing in the midst of it"—suggests her natural goodness and ability to heal (125). Pearl so brightens her mother's outlook that Hester thinks of her as a redemptive force: "might it not be her errand to soothe away the sorrow that lay cold in her mother's heart, and converted it into a tomb?" (123). Yet Pearl also exhibits punitive and tormenting qualities, which are related to the notion of original sin as socially manifested in her illegitimacy. As Hawthorne writes, "The child's own nature had something wrong in it, which continually betokened that she had been born amiss,—the effluence of her mother's lawless passion,—and often impelled Hester to ask, in bitterness of heart, whether it were for good or ill that the poor little creature had been born at all" (113). The Puritans think of Pearl as "an imp of evil" (65), a "demon offspring" (69), and an "infant pestilence" (71), whose odd visage puts her very humanity into question: "It was a look so intelligent, yet inexplicable, so perverse, sometimes so malicious, but generally accompanied by a wild flow of spirits, that Hester could not help questioning, at such moments, whether Pearl was a human child" (64). By labeling Pearl demonic, Hawthorne may wish to convey the small-mindedness and senseless superstition of the early American Puritans. His portrayal of Pearl also has roots in his personal experience of his daughter as a wild, unfathomable creature who was six years old when the novel was published. As Herbert explains, Pearl reflects Hawthorne's wonder over the enigma of childhood generally and befuddlement over his daughter Una's failure to conform to adult expectations specifically. A frustrated, sometimes incredulous Hawthorne wrote: "I now and then catch an aspect of her, in which I cannot believe her to be my own human child, but a spirit strangely mingled with good and evil, haunting the house where I dwell."[60]

The notion of Pearl as a "demon child" also reflects nineteenth-century worry over the new emphasis on the importance of child rearing. Such concerns were part of a debate promulgated by clergymen such as Bushnell, who asks: is the infant child "to become a *demon* let loose in God's eternity, or an angel and free prince of the realm?"[61] Like the Puritans, Bushnell links the child's condition to that of the parents, but in his view, Pearl's character depends not on Hester and Dimmesdale's sinfulness at the time of conception but on their care of her once she is born. Bushnell emphasizes that proper nurture is necessary to quell the child's naturally independent and headstrong qualities. Wildness in all children was to be tamed by firm but gentle persuasion.[62] However, in popular fiction of the era, illegitimate children and orphans become special, even ideal, candidates for moral and social renovation.

Unfortunately, Pearl is not as malleable as child-rearing experts would like. Strongly connected to nature, she is impermeable to cultural influences and does not develop according to the norm. Conceived in an act of impulse and passion, she is impulsive and resistant to disciplinary strategies. Declaring herself immune to Puritan law, she frustrates Hester's attempts to guide or control her:

> After testing both smiles and frowns, and proving that neither mode of treatment possessed any calculable influence, Hester was ultimately compelled to stand aside, and permit the child to be swayed by her own impulses. Physical compulsion or restraint was effectual, while it lasted, of course. As to any other kind of discipline, whether addressed to her mind or heart, little Pearl might or might not be within its reach, in accordance with the caprice that ruled the moment. (64)

Pearl is strong-willed, changeable, and given to extreme emotional states and behavior. When taunted by other children, she would "clench her little fist" and return their scorn with "the bitterest hatred." Alternatively, "she would laugh anew, and louder than before, like a thing incapable and unintelligent of human sorrow," or "more rarely," "she would be convulsed with a rage of grief, and sob out her love to her mother, in broken words, and seem intent on proving that she had a heart, by breaking it" (64–65). Loving discipline neither comforts nor corrects her.

For seventeenth-century Calvinists, Pearl's behavior is evidence of evil that stems from innate depravity. From a nineteenth-century romantic perspective, it reflects the unintended side effects of unchecked individualism. However, contemporary analysts interpret Pearl's antisocial gestures as a response to parental abandonment or neglect. As Herbert writes, "Pearl is demonically rebellious because her father does not acknowledge her."[63] The ever-present Hester only partially meets Pearl's needs. Semi-orphaned, she seeks the father who abandoned her; and whether she is viewed as "sprite," "demon," "angel," or "hieroglyph," she is first and foremost a child in search of her roots. Like many orphans who join their adoptive families with legally closed birth records and no information about their origins, Pearl seeks a name and an identity. "Withholding a name," Ragussis writes, is itself "a kind of orphaning." In *The Scarlet Letter*, he continues, such acts "become criminal when we realize how meaning becomes human."[64] Despite Pearl's insistent questioning, Hester and Dimmesdale conspire to withhold information about her paternity, and this lack of knowledge puts her at odds with the world, reducing her, as Ragussis writes, to a "disembodied string of questions."[65]

Acknowledging Dimmesdale's importance in the novel, some critics have claimed that paternal absence is a hallmark of the American romance. In a typical Hawthornian text, Erlich writes, "maternal presence and paternal absence are the positive and negative poles that generate this historical romance. . . . The absence of a father becomes the dominant question for . . . the child."[66] David Leverenz likewise argues that in the intensified version of domesticity found in *The Scarlet Letter*, the mother is "overpresent" and the father "absent."[67] However, *The Scarlet Letter* does not pose a simple case of paternal absence. Dimmesdale is physically present but intent on remaining anonymous and evading responsibility for Pearl. In fact, Pearl's identity—and legitimacy—rests not on one father but on two. Dimmesdale is the rising civic and spiritual leader of the Salem community, yet he fails in the role of pater familias when he refuses to recognize Pearl as his daughter. Chillingworth is Hester's legal husband and the source of a legacy that allows Pearl to construct a life in Europe, yet he aligns himself with savagery, occult science, and cold materialism. Neither the biological nor adoptive model of fatherhood suffices. Splitting fatherhood between two characters, Hawthorne complicates notions of masculinity and questions simplistic equations of paternity and nationhood. These portraits reflect Hawthorne's anxiety about changing social mores that saw a decline in patriarchal authority while remaining vague about its replacement.[68]

DIVIDED PATERNITY

In chapter 8, Hester's appeal for custody appears to be failing until with "sudden impulse" she turns to Arthur Dimmesdale, who has been mute during the magistrates' interrogation. Startled out of passivity by her frenzied command, "Speak thou for me! . . . Look thou to it! I will not lose the child! Look to it!," the minister comes forward. "Pale, and holding his hand over his heart" as he does in circumstances of nervous "agitation," he speaks eloquently about the "awful sacredness" of divine, maternal, and natural rights: "God gave her the child, and gave her, too, an instinctive knowledge of its nature and requirements . . . which no other mortal being can possess." Pearl should remain with Hester, he argues, because she is both "blessing" and "torture," meant to "keep the mother's soul alive, and protect her from blacker depths of sin" (78–79). Persuaded by his argument, Governor Bellingham leaves Pearl in Hester's custody on the condition that

Dimmesdale oversee her catechism. Authority is thus transferred from town father to birth father, with Dimmesdale in the position, as he is in chapter 2, of publicly denouncing Hester's behavior while secretly sharing her blame.

Dimmesdale's successful intervention on Hester's behalf makes the power of the father clear, even though his true identity remains concealed. In the Western literary tradition, fathers have this power and means to decide where their children will be raised and by whom. In Susan Warner's *The Wide, Wide World*, for example, Ellen Montgomery's father overrules his wife's and child's objections and sends Ellen to live with a paternal aunt who proves indifferent to her needs. In a long biblical tradition, particularly in the Old Testament story of Abraham and Isaac, fathers relinquish children with impunity. When Abraham is forced to choose between love of God and love of his son, he decides to kill his son to prove his love of God. This story, about the impossible choice of serving one's own will or God's, speaks to a parent's anguish over losing a child and has implications for adoptive as well as genealogical kinship. By suggesting that the act of killing a child is the means of saving it, the Bible offers a context in which relinquishment—the first step in the adoption process—becomes a form of sacrifice put in service to a higher goal. The magistrates seek to address this higher need when they tell Hester that under their adoptive plan, "the child shall be well be cared for!—far better than thou canst do it" (78).

As Carol Delaney points out, the right to sacrifice a child is historically a male right.[69] The unwritten law of paternal ownership entitles Abraham to make decisions about his son that a birth mother rarely can make. If a woman assumes the right to abandon, place, or kill her child, she is thought to be unnatural and is pitied or demonized. Historically in Western culture, the birth father—and by extension all men—have the authority to transact business on behalf of the child. The biblical patriarch can best show his love for his children, not by paternal kindliness, but by his willingness to sacrifice them. This Old Testament narrative offers immunity to patriarchs such as Dimmesdale, who place their children in jeopardy by abandoning them in order to answer the call of the ministry. His part in this mythic narrative is complicated, however. The Salem community invests him with clerical powers that conflate the roles of biological and spiritual father, as the unsuspecting Mr. Wilson indicates when Dimmesdale affectionately lays a hand on Pearl and kisses her brow. Mr. Wilson says that "every good Christian man hath a title to show a father's kindness towards the poor, deserted babe" (80). Dimmesdale exercises both his priestly and fatherly prerogatives when he offers Pearl this blessing. However, unlike the patriarch in the story of Abraham and Isaac, Dimmesdale must conceal his identity. After defending Hester's claim, he retreats and stands apart from the group, shielded by a curtain, half in shade—a divided self. Terrified of being found out, he keeps his distance from both Hester and Pearl, and, in a reversal of normal parent-child roles, he receives comfort from his daughter. She "stole softly toward him, and taking his hand . . . laid her cheek against it" in silent, affectionate recognition (80).

Dimmesdale denies his paternity despite Pearl's driving need to know her origins. Not only "the pearl of great price" (77) but also the irritant around which a pearl forms, she presses to learn her identity with her unpredictable chatter and behavior. She is a sharp-witted sleuth and a precocious learner, who at the age of three "could have borne a fair examination of the New England Primer, or the first column of the Westminster Catechism" (77). Her object of study is the letter "A," the first thing she sees when she comes into the world and the only clue to her identity. Intent on deciphering the letter's meaning and the truth about her parents, she persistently asks Hester, "What does the letter mean?—and why dost thou wear it?—and why does the minister keep his hand over his heart?" (123). When her search is thwarted, Pearl's anger is palpable, expressed in her passionately erratic behavior toward Hester and her defiant assertion, "I have no Heavenly Father" (68). To compensate for Dimmesdale's abandonment, Pearl claims nature as her metaphoric parent. She uses nature to express her emotions, throwing wild flowers on Hester's embroidered bosom (67) and uprooting weeds in violent protest against the Puritan children who torment her. When she communes with the natural world, it reciprocates: "The great black forest . . . became the playmate of the lonely infant, as well as it knew how. Sombre as it was, it put on the kindest of its moods to welcome her" (139).

Nature also affords Dimmesdale the opportunity for truthful self-expression. The "sympathy of Nature" (138) appears in the flood of sunshine that surrounds Hester and Dimmesdale during their forest meeting. At ease in this natural setting, Dimmesdale confesses his fear of what would happen were he to disclose his paternity. He and Hester gaze proudly at Pearl as she approaches them adorned with flowers. "Dost thou not think her beautiful?" Hester asks. She tells him, "I know whose brow she has," but he deflects the compliment, saying, "But she is mostly thine!" and admits that for seven years he has dreaded seeing his likeness in Pearl's face because it might reveal his identity. Her looks, he says, have "caused me many an alarm" (140). Dimmesdale betrays Pearl with these words and they have an immediate, negative effect. When she wanders back to her parents, she loses her bearings: she "could not find her wonted place, and hardly knew where she was" (141). The novel's refrain, "Be true! Be true! Be true!" (175), is made manifest only when Dimmesdale admits his paternity in the final scaffold scene, and the family circle is complete. Dimmesdale calls her "My little Pearl," and when she kisses him, "a spell was broken." Tears fall that "were the pledge that she would grow up amid human joy and sorrow, nor forever do battle with the world, but be a woman in it" (173).

However, at the moment of reunion, when natural ties are affirmed, they also disintegrate. Hawthorne's family portrait thus differs from those found in the popular novels of the 1850s. Hester entreats Dimmesdale to escape with her to a land where they might live together as mother, father, and child. This proposition can be dismissed as an expression of romantic idealism or feminine emotion over masculine reason. From the perspective of the child, however, it is a sound plan because it is the only means by which Pearl can receive support of both parents. Hawthorne is ambivalent about such an ending. Throughout the novel, he emphasizes the importance of traditional family structures, but he denies the biologically intact family a future in Salem or elsewhere. Dimmesdale only half-heartedly agrees to Hester's plan to escape and in the end cannot follow through with it. With his death, hope of escape evaporates and Pearl is abandoned once again.

Dimmesdale's death creates a gap filled by Chillingworth, who watches the scaffold scene from a distance. He provides Pearl with a financial legacy that ensures her future and supports her progeny in ways that Dimmesdale, her biological father, does not. Chillingworth's gesture does not constitute adoption, but it demonstrates Hawthorne's awareness of alternative forms of family formation that were becoming acceptable in mid-nineteenth-century middle-class society. In 1851, just one year after the publication of *The Scarlet Letter*, Hawthorne's home state of Massachusetts passed the nation's first adoption law, which focused attention on the best interest of the child rather than the parents. The novel reflects the spirit of this statute although Hawthorne remains ambivalent about whether adoptive parenting is as beneficial to the child as biological parenting. Chillingworth provides money but no emotional support. His limitations are foreshadowed in chapter 4, when he visits Hester in prison and offers a draught to calm Pearl's cries. He is the first person aside from Hester to touch Pearl, yet he does so with cold indifference. Hester fears that his potion may be poison, but Chillingworth shrugs off her alarm, as if to say that Pearl is of such little importance that he would not bother to harm her.

Hawthorne's resolution is also problematic in its failure to symbolize fresh starts, as adoption does in the popular American domestic fiction that Hawthorne reviled. Pearl uses her inheritance to succeed not in the New World but in the Old. Her return to Europe reverses the usual American migratory pattern. She and Hester depart Salem, and little is heard of them until Hester quietly resumes residence in her little cottage. She receives letters and gifts, presumably from Pearl, who has married well in Europe and is now the mother of an infant for whom Hester embroiders beautiful clothes. "The elf-child" is transformed into "the richest heiress in her day," her fortune producing, in turn, a "material change in the public estimation" of her (176). Pearl thrives not as an American but as a European. Her literary descendant is Isabel Archer, the protagonist in Henry James's *The Portrait of a Lady* (1881), who despite not wanting to be "a candidate for adoption," inherits Paul Touchett's fortune.[70] Both Pearl and Isabel inherit wealth, become aligned with an aristocratic tradition, and lose their connection to America. Pearl is transformed from a Puritan to an exotic, who sends Hester letters with "armorial seals . . . of bearings unknown to English heraldry" (176).

The ending of *The Scarlet Letter* is fairy tale-like in its affirmation of Pearl's success. However, in returning her to the Old World, Hawthorne suggests that she cannot live in the new one. Her displacement reveals his discomfort with the kind of woman she has become. This ending prefigures that of Edith Wharton's *The Age of Innocence* (1920), in which a beautiful orphan, Ellen Olenska, also finds herself at odds with a repressive American society. Ellen's blood, like Pearl's, is "too rich" for staid, old New York society,[71] and she ultimately settles in Europe. Had Pearl remained in the New World, Hawthorne writes, she "might have mingled her wild blood with the lineage of the devoutest Puritan among them all" (176), but this commingling is not to be. Individualistic, potent, and captivating, Pearl exceeds the limits of social conformity and is precluded from serving as harbinger of the American future. Described in terms of wealth and beauty, sending "articles of comfort and luxury, such as Hester never cared to use," she comes to represent opulence without moral meaning. She undergoes, like an element in Chillingworth's alchemical experiments, material rather than spiritual transformation.[72]

AMBIGUOUS FUTURE

Throughout nineteenth-century American literature, the child is symbolic of the future of family and nation. Cindy Lou Daniels argues that the eagle depicted in the novel's preface, "The Custom-House," represents Pearl well as Hester and points to the influence that both will have "for Pearl's generation and beyond."[73] Yet Pearl's energies exceed what Hawthorne is willing to consign to the next generation. She is opposite Horace Bushnell's image of the ideal child, who is "passive and plastic, living in the will of the parents."[74]

Hawthorne minimizes her influence on American society through her absence. His discomfort with the increasing independence of children reflects a skeptical rather than forward-looking view of change in middle-class American society.

Although Hawthorne questions the harsh, Puritan conception of original sin, Pearl remains a living symbol of her parents' transgression against God and society. Herbert associates Hawthorne's reservations about inherited characteristics "transmitted" from "the mother's impassioned state" to the child (63) with issues of gender.[75] Goodenough likewise claims that Pearl expresses "antipatriarchal rage,"[76] and Fanny Nudelman argues for greater critical acknowledgement of Hawthorne's "alarm over the problem of indeterminacy . . . as it applies to the representation of unruly women" and mother-child bonds.[77] However, unruly childhood is as much a concern as disorderly motherhood, a point Monika Elbert makes in her study of bourgeois sexuality and the Gothic plot. Both Hawthorne and Wharton, she argues, engage a female body to explore their concerns with "replicating and reproducing, on a figurative level, good ancestral blood and, on a biological level, good hereditary genes," as well as the class anxieties that emerged in the nineteenth-century clash over republican and aristocratic values. In order to avoid becoming "a deteriorating New England maiden," she argues that Pearl "needs to mate with someone from the Old World, to invigorate the family line."[78] Elbert does not observe, however, that with Pearl's exodus, the American future is deferred, not redeemed. By banishing Pearl, Hawthorne evades rather than resolves questions about bloodline and care in nineteenth-century middle-class society. He no sooner affirms Pearl's flesh-and-blood status than he exiles her from her native land. Hawthorne's concerns in *The Scarlet Letter* reach beyond gender to genealogy, as they do in his next novel, *The House of the Seven Gables*, to parent-child relationships and the effects of greed across generations. Issues of parentage are also evident in his story, "The Gentle Boy," first published anonymously in 1832 in Samuel Goodrich's annual, *The Token*. Critical of the Puritans, this story is notable, Erlich writes, for its representation "of the dissociation between home and parents"[79] and describes the failure of adoption to substitute for the mother-child bond.

Hawthorne's anxieties about contemporary child rearing are also evident in his personal parenting dilemmas. Herbert argues that if "Pearl is made to enact the qualities that most troubled Hawthorne in his daughter," she is also the target of his "therapeutic program, which includes a diagnosis of her difficulty and a prescription for cure."[80] This cure, grounded in theories of childhood, family, and nation in circulation at mid-century, includes tracing the identity of a missing birth father and installing origins as central to the American experience. Hester's insistence on custody and Dimmesdale's eventual admission of paternity reflect the prevailing ideology that a home and parents are necessary not only to help the child grow but also to make it human. However, Hawthorne's biological family is still askew. In his anxiety-ridden domestic sphere, the mother violates feminine moral conventions, the father splinters into parts, and the New World child abandons her American family and society altogether.

Hawthorne's complicated treatment of kinship sets his novel apart from those of rival domestic novelists, who employ adoption as a means of celebrating the resiliency of the American child and family and the expansionist ambitions of the nation. Hawthorne rejects these popular conventions and with them the optimism that characterizes the typical adoption narrative. He gives center stage to an adulterous mother who retains custody of her child; but his tale, which begins by focusing on motherhood, ends by making patriarchy its foremost concern. Although he preserves the mother-child bond, Hawthorne undermines the traditional rights and responsibilities of fatherhood, showing the insufficiency of either a biological or adoptive model to hold the family together. These depictions of split paternity express concern over a breakdown of family structures and republican virtues as well as ambivalence about the effects of new views of childhood and femininity on the American family. Pearl, an enigmatic, unruly child so opposite the ones popularized in fiction of the period, defies interpretation at every stage of life. Viewed as the embodiment not of Hester and Dimmesdale's sin but of Hawthorne's bourgeois anxiety, she ambiguously benefits from both biological and adoptive parenting. This difference in the treatment of kinship, as much as his abstract romanticism, accounts for the distinction that *The Scarlet Letter* enjoys as the first American novel.

4

Plotting Adoption in Nineteenth-Century Fiction

BY THE 1820S, novels and short stories had displaced sermons, essays, and autobiographies as the predominant forms of American literature. By the 1850s, the historical romance had had its day, and the domestic novel Nathaniel Hawthorne famously excoriated was enjoying widespread popularity. Orphancies and adoptions figure prominently in these stories of white, middle-class American childhoods. Why did so many stories of displaced and relocated children develop out of the Jacksonian era? The answer involves more than formal considerations of plot: children without parents, who have more adventures than those securely nestled in a family circle, gave range to a writer's imagination. The outpouring of mid-century fiction about finding a home was a response to widespread changes in American society. Writers enlisted the trope of adoption to represent anxieties and hopes associated with these changes.

The adoption plot emerged as a literary form commensurate with and demonstrative of a new republican conception of the family as a nonhierarchical group of individuals whose will to be together is at least as important as blood ties. Massachusetts passed the nation's first adoption law in 1851, but such statutes were nonexistent in many states and there were few formal adoptions in today's sense. In the absence of legally sanctioned procedures, the relationship between adopted children and adoptive parents remained undefined, as Cindy Weinstein observes in her analysis of *The Lamplighter*.[1] Yet writers devised myriad plots in which children separate from parents and experience the challenges and benefits of placements with a range of adults not related to them by blood. The proliferation of adoption fiction occurred at a time when Americans were celebrating democratic individualism, freedom from English influence, and a sense of unlimited potential.

Fictional adoptions often reflect these sentiments by demonstrating how a child severed from biology acquires a new identity through a combination of effort, resourcefulness, and opportunity—all qualities aligned with the nation's sense of itself as a young, growing republic. At the same time, adoption fiction addresses widespread societal fears and concerns. By definition conservative and recuperative, adoption replicates the child's original family structure and thereby has the potential to calm middle-class fears over instabilities caused by demographic changes and unprecedented national growth. Apprehensions over urbanization and immigration are assuaged by narrative plots that open with disharmony or rupture but end with domestic security. If orphans symbolize unchecked liberty and the threat of social disorder, then well-placed adopted children illustrate the positive effects of freedom suitably restrained. Literary adoptees such Ellen Montgomery in Susan Warner's *The Wide, Wide World* (1851) and Gerty Flint in Susanna Maria Cummins's *The Lamplighter* (1854) experience this kind of adoption, which is especially available to white girls and entails dependence as well as independence. Topsy in Harriet Beecher Stowe's *Uncle Tom's Cabin* (1852) and Frado in *Our Nig* (1859) are sheltered but deprived of the full benefits of adoption because of their race, and later figures such as the boys in the Horatio Alger's *Ragged Dick* series (1868–), Huck Finn in *Adventures of Huckleberry Finn* (1884), and Dan Kean in Louisa May Alcott's *Jo's Boys* (1886) resist the ameliorative effects of adoption or make their way with minimal assistance. All these tales demonstrate in different ways what might be done on behalf of poor, abandoned, or neglected children. At the same time, the adoption narrative's "back story"— the tale of origins and birth families—keeps genealogy firmly in view.

Adoption literature also developed in the context of shifting religious attitudes and changes in the understanding of the family as a traditionally organized unit with strong patriarchal authority. Increased geographic, social, and economic mobility challenged the authority of male heads of household, and power devolved to women and to children themselves. New views of children and childrearing emerged, which adoption fiction often reflects by juxtaposing disciplinary strategies informed by different religious views. For example, if the wayward, destitute, or orphaned child suggests the innately flawed being familiar to Calvinism, then the child saved by adoption evokes a sentimental discourse aligned with a gentler form of Christianity. Transitions in faith and family correspond in turn with gender roles that make the domestic life of girls and boys, especially adopted ones, discrete experiences. These diverse social changes created a favorable environment for adoption fiction and helped to install the adoption narrative as a key form for the expression of national hopes and misgivings. By portraying families that are made, not born, writers explored the tensions between inherited and acquired identity and contributed to an on-going story of nation building among an increasingly visible white, middle class.

NEED

The large number of literary adoptions in the mid-nineteenth century owed something to the social reality that death was still a common fact of life for adults as well as children. Well into the nineteenth century, high maternal mortality rates left many children without parents and in need of adoption. Accounts of informal adoptive arrangements soften the pain of abandonment in nonfiction as well as fiction and evoke similar sentimental responses.[2] For example, Edward Hicks (1780–1849), the Quaker painter of the "Peaceable Kingdom" series, might well be penning a popular novel when he describes how his mother, just before her death, "leaving her poor little feeble infant under the care of her colored woman, Jane, who had been a slave in the family, and being left to shift for herself, took me with her like her own child," because "my father was now broken up, having no home of his own, or any business by which he could support and keep his children together."[3] A statistically high incidence of parental death contributed to the proliferation of adoption stories in the mid-nineteenth century. However, it does not entirely account for these stories' popularity.

The adoption plot grew in importance in American literature at a time when asylums, including refuges for delinquent, poor, and neglected children as well as orphanages, were also on the rise.[4] In American society as a whole, children were increasingly directed to externally organized institutions, yet authors chose to write about homeless children taken in by families. Popular literature of the period seldom portrays institutional care except as a setting from which the orphan soon departs. The number of stories that privilege family adoption suggests a strong link between this form of family construction and the expression of cultural values and expectations. To use Jane Tompkins's term, adoption literature does important "cultural work."[5]

In the United States, poverty caused by immigration, urban crowding, illness, and lack of employment opportunities created a population of poor children who, if not orphaned, were in need of basic support. A similar situation existed in England, where destitute children fell under the government-sponsored Board of Guardians, which both provided shelters and placed children in homes.[6] American ministers, doctors, and philanthropists responded to the needs of orphaned and destitute children by developing asylums for needy children. Often modeled roughly along the lines of families, these facilities, such as the newsboys' homes in New York City that inspired Alger's *Ragged Dick* tales, took children off the streets and offered them a modicum of comfort and nurture.[7] These societal efforts to alleviate the needs of a growing number of destitute or orphaned children represented a significant change in the treatment of homelessness. As David Rothman notes in his history of the asylum, beginning in the eighteenth century, confinement in the form of prisons, mental hospitals, reformatories, and almshouses became the preferred response to deviancy and dependence. Although often deficient in practice, the nineteenth-century asylum reflected a utopian vision born of humanitarian intent and one far superior to previous centuries of public torture and execution that deviants often faced.

Asylums in the United States, Rothman argues, emerged as a response to "a crisis in confidence in the social organization of the new republic" and to anxieties that the community, church, and family bonds were loosening.[8] Children were the specific focus of these misgivings, with experts investigating the early years of delinquents and dependents and often locating the cause of trouble in parental neglect. It was a pursuit, Rothman argues, that "turned everyone into a child."[9] With its characteristic structure, order, uniformity, punctuality, and habits of discipline, the asylum was meant to rehabilitate offenders; reduce crime, insanity, and poverty; and set an example for the larger society. Despite the best intentions, however, and even though they met tangible needs, after mid-century, by Rothman's account, orphan asylums had degenerated into "warehouses that were understaffed, overcrowded, harsh, and corrupt."[10] Anne MacLeod likewise notes that in many communities institutionalized care or town- and church-supported charities were either nonexistent or so haphazardly and carelessly organized that potential beneficiaries consciously avoided them.[11]

From a literary perspective, asylums are poor choices to represent a nation proud of its independence and its opportunities for fresh starts. Despite the widespread public acceptance of asylums, writers' imaginations were stimulated not by tales of impersonal, institutional care but by stories of individual rescue from such fates. Adoption, in contrast to the asylum, provided a reassuring fictive solution to the threat of social disorder. Just as abolitionist author Harriet Beecher Stowe urged readers of *Uncle Tom's Cabin* to *"feel right"* and abolish slavery one reformed conscience at a time,[12] so, too, authors showed how adopting a child reforms the nation one family at a time.

MOBILITY

Adoption plots make a virtue of dislocation by celebrating the creation of roots separate from original ones. The adoptee journeys to a new home, reflecting a fact of life for many Americans as they left familiar domestic scenes for promising, unfamiliar ones. As the nation moved away from an agrarian economy and toward an industrial one, people encountered new opportunities to alter their geographic situation. Increased mobility occurred with migrants arriving from Europe; Easterners moving westward; adventurers and travelers sampling new climes and locales; and slaves cut off from roots and families. Daniel Howe writes that with these relocations came new attitudes toward "self-construction," especially among groups of people traditionally excluded from these opportunities; this rise of individualism was "accompanied by a growing nationalism."[13] The drive for "self-making," Joyce Appleby writes, was "wondrously broad," taking in such diverse interests as the African American campaign for freedom from slavery; a reform movement motivated by a sense of religious revival in which people spiritually discovered themselves anew; and a rags-to-riches narrative,[14] which became the hallmark of orphan and adoption fiction.

Whereas the orphan's tale demonstrates what a child can do without traditional supports, the adoption story confirms safe arrival, often after a series of temporary placements, expressing a positive outcome to the realities of increasingly mobile groups of Americans who were leaving farms for cities, traveling westward, and striving to improve their economic and social status by leaving home. By definition interfamilial and often multicultural, adoption fiction also reflects, on a small scale, larger demographic changes as increasing numbers of immigrants arrived from Europe. The homeless child's successful adoption into a financially secure, Protestant family represents a positive outcome to the nation's struggle to accommodate immigrants in urban areas ill-prepared to employ or house them. Portraying migration within a narrowly defined range, adoption literature offers a fantasy of assimilation.[15] It validates the aspirations of the middle class and communicates the sense that there is a home for everyone in an expanding nation.

Adoption fiction reflects social as well as geographic mobility. It resonates with the national refrain, which, despite institutionalized practices such as slavery, Indian removal, and the restriction of women's rights, was opportunity for all. "Unlike other countries, our law and institutions do not favor the rich and great," writes Catharine Maria Sedgwick; Americans are "all children of one family."[16] In the Jacksonian era, traditional parental ties and authority weakened or even threatened to become obsolete. As Mary

Ryan writes, by the 1830s "parentage did not determine 'place.'"[17] Increasingly, the child relied on his or her own initiative and resourcefulness to make a place in the world. Edouard de Montulé wrote in response to this growing sense of individualism that in the United States, money, reputation, and pretensions often went unappreciated. Success was measured not by identity bestowed through birthright but by accomplishment. Doing something with one's life made one a contributor to the resources of the nation, he observed.[18] Noting the importance of career early on, Montulé inadvertently made the case for the adoption plot, in which the orphaned child's vocation is to find a home.

In most adoption fiction, adoption represents an opportunity for the child to improve its economic status. Adoption fiction thereby addresses the material and social concerns of a growing, nineteenth-century middle class, a recognizable if somewhat uncongealed entity, as Stuart Blumin notes.[19] Political, industrial, and commercial revolutions had produced a flourishing group of merchants that composed this new class, situated between workers and aristocrats. Identifiable but still unstable, the middle class faced a series of challenges, including the financial Panic of 1837, an increase in immigration, urban riots in the 1840s, and increasing tension over the practice of slavery, all of which contributed to class unease. The middle class met these challenges by solidifying itself politically, as evidenced by the Whig Party's Franklin-like philosophies of pragmatism and the concept of the self-made man.[20] Fictional accounts of circumstances that created a need for adoption, such as death, illness, and poverty, give expression to middle-class concerns over the unsettling effects of social change. Conversely, the fact that adoption usually represents a material change for the better sends a reassuring message about economic and social advancement coincident with the desire for self-improvement.

Both informal kinship adoptions and formal stranger adoptions appeared in American fiction at a time when class structures were both more visible and more permeable. As the nineteenth century progressed, distinctions among the classes became more ambiguous, as evidenced by the imprecise use of such terms as "aristocracy," "upper," "working," "producing," and "lower" classes. However, as Diana Pazicky notes, "there was a distinct limit on its upward mobility, a glass ceiling of hereditary privilege that constrained the ability of the middle class to penetrate the upper." Between the 1820s and the 1850s, the "frightening reality for the middle class was that downward mobility exceeded upward, at least in cities."[21] Historian Edward Pessen bluntly asserts that during the second quarter of the nineteenth century, in northeastern cities as well as small towns, "the rich appear to have been a true 'governing class.' . . . Far from being an age of equality, the antebellum decades featured an inequality that appears to surpass anything experienced by the United States in the twentieth century."[22] If the middle class imagined itself on a social escalator leading to greater wealth and prestige, it was all too common, Karen Halttunen writes, that "the middle class escalator was at least as likely to go down as up."[23] In a climate in which the bourgeoisie envisioned success but saw the gap between haves and have-nots appear to widen, adoption stories appealed to readers because they offered a socially sanctioned, controlled transgression of class boundaries.

The negative as well as positive associations of adoption made it a powerful tool in antebellum national mythmaking. On the one hand, successful placement validated the notion that the child's identity is constructed and can be reformed regardless of blood or circumstances of birth. On the other hand, if maladjustment or misbehavior persisted, the child could be blamed for inheriting problems from the birth parents. An argument thus could be made either way about the power of both nurture and genealogy. Imitating the traditional biogenetic structure, adoption was conservative and did not signal a radical reconfiguration of family or nation, as did the child-rearing practices of the communitarian and utopia societies that appeared during this period. The Shaker and Oneida communities, for example, assigned child rearing to specific caretakers who worked in separate children's quarters. The arrangement was believed to best serve the needs of children and also provide for the intellectual and educational development of women. This practice met with general condemnation in society as a whole, as it was thought to work against maternal affections. Even John Humphrey Noyes, founder of the Oneida community in 1842, wrote of "melodramatic scenes" that ensued when mothers and children were forced to separate, although he argued that mothers soon found satisfaction in being able to pursue their own education and children prospered once they were denied "the luxury of a sickly maternal tenderness."[24] Such radical forms of adoption did not make their way into the mainstream literature.

CULTURE AND NARRATIVE FORM

Narratives about adoption constitute a particular subset of the *Bildungsroman* (novel of development). The adoption story and the *Bildungsroman* are not identical forms, however. Adoption narratives oppose the idea, derived from the *Bildungsroman*'s eighteenth-century German origins, that the genre is concerned, in Martin Swales's words, with "the whole man unfolding *organically*."[25] The romantic innocence of the kind Gillian Brown describes—a growth that implies cumulative, gradual development—must be modified to account for the disruption of the adoptive experience. The fictional adoptee does not reflect "the belief in childhood as a special realm, a place to which adults can never return but which they can always remember."[26] Rather, adoption brings with it a specific set of circumstances that leads to the need for adoption. Even though most nineteenth-century adoption fictions end happily, they challenge the romantic theory of the innocent child transcending time, in the sense envisioned by William Wordsworth and other nineteenth-century writers.[27]

Rather than avoid or transcend history, adoption plots demonstrate that families are socially constructed and maintained. Because they involve a disruption of genealogy and a grafting of new lineage onto the child's present one, they look backward and forward, simultaneously engaging issues of origins and new beginnings. Whereas the idealized romantic child trails "clouds of glory," the adopted child has already experienced a fall from innocence; orphancy is at best a waiting period, at worst an ordeal. Even if not narrated, the losses that the child experiences before joining a new home become part of the adoption story. Orphans and adoptees therefore call attention to themselves as historically situated beings. Their status invites questions: What happened to their parents? Why were they abandoned? How does biology affect their personality? What kind of adults will they become?

One purpose of the *Bildungsroman*, according to Carolyn Steedman, writing about the work of Franco Moretti, "is to make time circular, to bring a linear series of events—a chronology—into a system of relationships . . . in which the protagonists find a home to replace the original one."[28] The sentimental novel about adoption falls into the category of *Bildungsroman* that is "designed to make people cry" and owes its popularity to this larger literary development.[29] Moretti explains that the power of the child to produce tears is salient at the moment of the protagonist's death, a "state of affairs" he calls "the 'too late'": "This is what the protagonist's death is for: to show that time is *irreversible*."[30] However, in adoption novels, it is not too late. A small death occurs in the form of the loss of the child's parents, a loss that may be impossible to reverse; but change *is* possible. There is life after death, so to speak, in the form of the child's adoption. These novels are examples of "'moving literature'" that elicit tears but also end happily, as romances do, with a completed search for home.[31] In an ideal sense, they allow readers to mourn the loss of roots (i.e., preadoption), and they cultivate pleasurable feelings of harmony, inclusion, and unity deemed essential to a properly ordered subjectivity and developing family and nationhood (i.e., postadoption).[32]

Plots involving adoptees offer many narrative possibilities, with the children free for adventures that would be impossible if they were living with their parents. Subplots emerge as children search for a new home, adjust to a family's behaviors and values, and experience temporary placements before finding a permanent home. The adoption story brings about narrative closure: A child is taken in by a family with the acknowledgment— legal and emotional—of the benefits and finality of this domestic arrangement. Although some adoptees resist placement, for example, Mark Twain's Huckleberry Finn, who rejects the Widow Douglas's attempts to "sivilize" him,[33] in fiction after fiction children look forward to joining their new families, often as a relief from a burdensome past. For example, in a story about two homeless children, adoption is "good news" that "gladden[s] the hearts of the little orphans." In another narrative, a boy who was once passed over for adoption gratefully acknowledges his new home, saying "'the old life was . . . a hard bitter reality from which you saved me'"; and the heroine of another tale, when asked if she wants to be adopted, responds, "'Glad? . . . It's just next to having God for my father.'"[34]

A different form of narrative emerges when the orphan discovers his or her birth parents and is reunited with the family of origin. In this case, the narrative follows the lines of a mystery story, with the orphan seeking to answer the question, "Who did it?"—that is, "Who brought me into the world?" This kind of narrative has ideological as well as formal functions. As John Cawelti writes about popular literature, formulaic fictions such as the mystery story serve to affirm current attitudes and interests, resolve cultural tensions and ambiguities, explore forbidden worlds, and assist in assimilating change.[35] The return-to-origins plot resembles those found in European fairy tales, in which the child discovers that he or she is actually of noble birth and is restored to a position of wealth and high status. In American literature, the *Bildungsroman*, with its implied forward progression for the protagonist, is more common than the European fairy-tale ending; however, many American authors exhibit ingenuity in allowing their characters to try out new homes *and* reconnect with their origins. For example, in two nineteenth-century juvenile fictions, Sarah S. Baker's *Coming to the Light* (1862) and Asa Bullard's *The Lighthouse* (1863), orphaned girls are adopted by families who learn that the children have wealthy relatives living abroad. In both stories, the girls return to England, but in a qualified way. In *Coming to the Light*, the return is temporary. Once her wealthy English grandfather dies, the protagonist resumes her life with her American adoptive family. In *The Lighthouse*, the adoptive parents, who are elderly and more like grandparents than parents, return to England with the birth father and daughter.[36] Both novels incorporate Old and

New World elements in their endings. They offer an American fantasy in which ties to England are simultaneously renounced and renewed.

Nineteenth-century adoption stories also promote the virtues of middle-class domesticity. As Rachel Blau DuPlessis observes, "narrative may function on a small scale the way that ideology functions on a large scale."[37] The contrast between impoverished, vulnerable, or solitary adoptees and their loving adoptive families serves to glorify middle-class life, making adoption, in contrast to orphancy, seem "utopian"[38] or heavenly. These narratives reinforce religious belief by positioning children and their adoptive parents in tight narratives of salvation in which the adoptive parents rescue the child, and the child becomes a catalyst for the parents' spiritual growth. The adopted child plays a distinctive role in this sentimental literature, a discourse that tends to flourish, as Gillian Beer notes, during periods of rapid social change.[39]

With its focus on recovering home, adoption literature aligns with domestic fiction and its corollary: the sentimental commemoration of childhood innocence, suffering, and death. Accounts of holy child death are found as early as the 1670s, with James Janeway's *A Token for Children*, and became standard fictional fare by mid-nineteenth century.[40] They appear famously in Stowe's description of Eva St. Clare in *Uncle Tom's Cabin* and Alcott's portrayal of Beth March in *Little Women*. Plots in which parents die also become associated with sentimentality, which is located, as Shirley Samuels argues, "literally at the heart of nineteenth-century culture," and "intimately linked individual bodies to the national body."[41] Adoption not only supports the ideological framework of sentimentality through the requisite excess of feeling produced when a child loses both home and parents, it is also essential to this body of work. If, as Glenn Hendler argues, the legibility of the body is a central tenet of sentimentality,[42] then the corporal sufferings of orphaned, poor, or neglected children place adoption literature squarely in the sentimental discourse of the time.

Adoption stories do more than elicit the reader's sympathy. They are forms of social practice that, as Jane Tompkins writes about domestic fiction, can be "preoccupied, even obsessed, with the nature of power."[43] These power dynamics appear in the descriptions of the social or economic causes of orphancy and in the behavioral expectations that adoptive families set for all children and for adopted children in particular. Based in religious faith, these include the requirements to obey the parents, express gratitude for adoption, and be of useful service. Inscribing these expectations, adoption narratives provide socially acceptable views of the family, the child, and the republic.

GENDERED ADOPTION

Conformity is a hallmark of the nineteenth-century adoption plot. It is not surprising, therefore, that adoption stories reflect the gender expectations found in society as a whole. Not only are adoption plots ending with in-home placements highly gendered, they are also overwhelmingly feminine. Female protagonists vastly outnumber male protagonists,[44] and, as Anne MacLeod notes, the majority of didactic fictions were penned either by women or clergymen.[45] At a time when Americans were most proud of their political and economic independence, writers use the trope of adoption not only to signify unfettered potential but also to set the limits of gender. In many narratives, adoption is associated with feminine rather than masculine values and connotes dependence rather than independence. Reflecting cultural views, authors often portray females seeking affiliation through adoption, needing the security of home, and settling into their new families' routines with model behavior. Indeed, in some texts adoption serves as a disciplinary strategy aimed at ensuring a girl's piety, passivity, and obedience.

In contrast, writers portray males as benefiting from the help of a parent, teacher, mentor, or friend, but resisting permanent integration into adoptive households. Female characters experience placements as training grounds for their roles as wives and mothers, whereas male characters measure their worth by self-sufficiency and autonomy.[46] As Lois Keith writes, "the fictional orphaned boy set off on his adventurous journey without any sense of callousness or irresponsibility to a family left at home. He proved himself by his self-reliance and his success in conquering the world."[47] These gender expectations were consistent with nineteenth-century "separate spheres" ideology, in which men's and women's lives were viewed as essentially different and complementary.

Gender also plays a major role in the amount of parental control that is warranted in an adopted child's upbringing. In most fictions, subduing the child's will is still a priority, although a changing U.S. economy made this approach to child rearing seem old-fashioned and perhaps disadvantageous to a child for whom ingenuity and ambition are traits that lead to success. Adoption provides a prime opportunity for breaking a child's will. Adopted children might be seen as having inherited their birth parents' flaws or having picked up evil habits during years of neglect. If left to their own devices, they are at risk for waywardness. Girls and boys are not equally amenable to correction, however. It is possible to conquer the will of girls, as in case of Ellen Montgomery in Susan Warner's *The Wide, Wide World*, who ends her narrative at home. However, this idea makes little practical sense for fictional boys who no longer stand to inherit their father's lands or status but achieve these things for themselves. For boys, the very notion of adoption might seem redundant when the entire world beckons.

Nina Baym's description of the female "overplot" commonly found in American fiction from 1820–70 offers a model for female adoption fiction. A young girl is deprived of family supports and forced to make her own way in the world, often with a series of pseudo-mothers or adoptions. Intelligent and resourceful, she overcomes obstacles and, through loyalty or service to others, proves her worthiness and is rewarded with a socially acceptable marriage.[48] Sarah S. Baker's *Bound Out; or, Abby at the Farm* (1868), discussed in chapter 6, follows Baym's model and typifies the nineteenth-century female adoption story. An orphan named Abby lives in an asylum and hopes to be adopted. A farming family needing help takes her in but values only her labor and offers little affection. However, Abby's faithful service and Christian piety eventually win over not only her adoptive parents but also their hired hands, and the tale ends with Abby embraced by her new family. In *The Wide, Wide World* and *The Lamplighter*, discussed in chapter 5, the protagonists likewise experience a series of domestic adoptions that lead to their rightful places in homes as wives as well as daughters.

Although stories about boys and girls may begin with sentimental portrayals of departures from birth parents followed by trial adoptions, virtually all stories about girls end with the protagonist safely inscribed within the boundaries of family and home. Such is not the case in stories involving boys. As Robert L. Griswold notes, an industrializing economy drew aspiring middle-class fathers to jobs away from home, with the result that father-son ties weakened. Farming fathers also found it difficult to exert influence over sons who were no longer dependent upon paternal legacies and could make their fortunes in expanding markets and territories.[49] Economic changes and a spirit of liberty challenged the traditional authority of the father and redefined the father-son relationship. As sons surpassed their fathers, the patriarchal role diminished.[50] In male adoption stories, the protagonist proves himself and succeeds in the world not through obedience to his father but through his own ingenuity and effort.[51] Horatio Alger's Ragged Dick stories belong to this narrative model, as does the tale of a young boy, Little Bob True (1858). The novel opens in typical sentimental fashion, with a tearful, thirty-page description of Bob's mother's death. However, from early on, Bob focuses on making his own way. Even on the sorrowful trip to a neighbor's house, where he finds refuge after his mother's death, Bob exhibits interest in people and events around him. He experiences a succession of temporary placements with families and single men who help him gain confidence and skills that he later uses to make his fortune. By the end of the novel, having worked as a miner and canal boat driver, Bob is heading West on horseback, assisted—but not actually adopted—by a former male schoolteacher. Significantly, his direction is westward toward the frontier, a typically masculine American domain of adventure and opportunity.[52]

In another story, My Teacher's Gem (1863?), a boy named Joe develops a mutually beneficial relationship with a man, but the alliance falls short of adoption. After Joe's father dies of alcoholism and his mother of complications from Joe's birth, he manages on his own until one evening he meets a drunken gentleman on the street. Joe inspires the man to renounce his profligate ways; in return, the man provides Joe with a good home, schooling, and an apprenticeship. This "patron"—he is never referred to as "father"— tells Joe that "'you and I are alike.'" Even though the man is the boy's senior, the relationship is more a partnership than an adoption, with reciprocal, practical benefits. The narrator states that "the principal thing was this: Joe was useful to the gentleman, and the gentleman was useful to Joe."[53] In another tale, the title story in the collection Orphan Willie, the author dispenses with the male guardian figure altogether, allowing the boy to pursue his own interests. After Willie's mother dies and his guardian uncle becomes destitute, Willie, who has a strong desire for "roving," sets out by himself with "no fear for the future." Equipped with only a song and a guitar, he plans to travel the country and become "a pioneer among the minstrels of America."[54] Huckleberry Finn also decides to "light out for the Territory," his exact destination and motivation unspecified.[55]

FAITH AND WORKS

Changing attitudes toward child rearing were part of a major theological shift in American society, as Ann Douglas notes.[56] A new sentimental approach—what Richard Brodhead calls "disciplinary intimacy" and Bernard Wishy "gentle" Christianity[57]—emerged as Calvinist holds weakened. Increasingly, what ruled the family was not a Calvinist, patriarchal, authoritarian model, but a new, more benevolent form of governance inspired by a firm but loving Christianity. In English literature these influences were evident in the liberal juvenile fiction of writer Maria Edgeworth, whose blend of entertainment and instruction in such books as The Parent's Assistant (1796) and Moral Tales for Young People (1801) helped to make the transition from strictly Puritan writing to more generalized moral writing. Edgeworth's stories, reprinted in numerous editions through the 1840s and 1850s, emphasized self-reflection and self-improvement and paved the way for more adventuresome literature that appeared by mid-century. After 1820, American authors, dissatisfied with the imported books that had set the standard for literature, made a concerted effort to write what they considered American rather than English fiction.[58] In contrast to English models, American authors attempted to minimize class difference and emphasized egalitarianism and opportunities open to all.

By the 1830s and 1840s, the practice of breaking the will of children through physical force (if necessary), inherited from the Puritans, gave way to more benign methods of discipline designed to set the naturally erring child on a pious path through the internalization of desired qualities. Parents still expected a high measure of obedience, but now preferably accomplished by the child's willing subjection to authority. Replacing punishment with love, affection, and manners, parents responded to a growing romantic sense of the child's innocence and openness to the world while at the same time enlisting the child's participation in developing a moral code. In keeping with changing religious sentiments and a sense of democratic individualism, the key to the child's success was self-governance, which was first espoused by John Locke, and later articulated in eighteenth-century America by John Witherspoon, and touted by Benjamin Franklin in his *Autobiography*. As Mary Ryan notes, noted educators, philosophers, and writers all espoused self-governance. Catharine Maria Sedgwick, its vigorous proponent, wrote: "Again and again I repeat there are none educated but the self-educated."[59] Heman Humphrey noted the importance of affection in developing conscience, and Catherine Beecher declared the supremacy of this kindly emotion: "affection can govern the human mind with a sway more powerful than the authority of reason or the voices of conscience."[60]

Adoption stories of the mid-nineteenth century document this transition from austere approaches to a softer focus on the child's ability to progress morally. Early New England writers had emphasized the role of adoption in Christian salvation and held to the notion of covenant between God and all family members; nineteenth-century adoption fiction shows the transition from a concept of sin as fixed or inherited to a belief in the infinite possibilities of moral and social reform. In many adoption stories these competing religious influences vie for prominence. A child may experience placements with multiple families, each at a different point on the continuum between strict and liberal theology. The various situations allow readers to weigh the benefits of different religious beliefs and childrearing techniques. Sometimes, as in the case of Maria Browne's novel, *Laura Huntley* (1850), discussed below, the adoptive parents themselves embody dueling religious and childrearing perspectives. In this juvenile novel, a couple disagree about how to discipline their adopted child, documenting in miniature the debate between Calvinist and gentler forms of Christianity. Laura's adoptive mother responds to bad behavior with characteristically sentimental, feminine patience, whereas her father favors a harsher solution. The reader is left to evaluate the effectiveness of each approach by observing the adoptee's success under each parent's tutelage.

Laura Huntley

Changing demographics, family structures, and religious values all find imaginative expression in a little known but representative novel, *Laura Huntley*, published in 1850 by Massachusetts author Maria Browne. In this short fiction, a childless couple finds an abandoned infant on the street.[61] The child's orphancy is represented as a mythic fall from innocence; her adoption as a form of salvation that shapes the child's morals and makes her worthy of the family she joins. Laura Huntley secures her place in the family, and thereby the nation, through self-discipline, Christian piety, and obedience. The plot hinges first on Laura's rescue from orphancy and then on her struggle to mend her errant ways and follow the example of her Christian adoptive family. The challenges inherent in her adoption are historically situated. They reflect class-consciousness, a "separate spheres" ideology of gender, and on-going religious debate. For a growing white, middle-class readership, Laura's adoption bridges social and economic divides. As a tale of opportunity, it also tells a story about the disadvantages of low birth and broken genealogy.

The Huntleys, a couple whose child has died, go for a walk in the city and discover an infant, presumably abandoned by immigrant birth parents. With no consideration of legalities, a point that reflects the amorphous nature of adoption law in the mid-nineteenth century, the couple takes the child home to raise "as if she had been their own."[62] The Huntleys offer their new daughter religious nurture as well as domestic stability. However, despite their loving attention, by the time Laura reaches thirteen, she shows signs of deviating from the Christian path that the Huntleys have set out for her. Vexed by Laura's numerous displays of disobedience and deceit, her adoptive parents pursue various disciplinary strategies that eventually produce the results they desire. Laura finally acknowledges her wrongs, resolves to offend no more, and shows signs that she will "become a virtuous and respectable woman" (143). The story ends happily with Laura embraced by her adoptive family and renewed in her commitment to be a model daughter.

Laura Huntley represents adoption as salvation. At the same time, the novel reflects the tensions between an older Calvinist-derived sensibility and a newer form of Christianity. It also reflects an increasingly child-centered notion of family and an awareness of gender differences, with harsh masculine will juxtaposed with gentle feminine suasion. That the novel is in dialogue with the religion and culture of the Puritan past is established early on, in a preface that includes a quotation from Psalms 27:10 that links earthly and heavenly adoption. The same verse opens Cotton Mather's "Orphanotrophium" of 1711: "When my father and mother forsake me, then the Lord will take me up."[63] The quotation, as well as the Huntleys' rescue of a crying infant, alerts the reader that nineteenth-century adoption fiction is, like early American literature from which it derives, an act of redemption, transposed from a religious to a secular setting.

Echoes of Calvinism resonate in the novel, beginning with the Huntleys' discovery of their adoptive child. The narrator comments that Laura's rescue is a function not of human intervention but divine will. The Huntleys "happened to be walking by" and hear an infant's cry. The narrator attributes their discovery of Laura not to the Huntleys but to God, writing, "ought I not rather to say God directed them" to the child. Using language similar to that found in Mather's "Orphanotrophium" and the biblical text of David, on which his sermon was based, the narrator writes that it is God "who feathers the soft breast . . . of the little helpless bird in the wild depths of its native forest. . . . He saw the deserted child, when she was forsaken of father and mother, and he provided for her" (19–20). Browne treats the subject of orphancy and adoption with candor. The Huntleys make no secret of the fact that Laura is adopted, nor do they pretend that their love for her is the same as for their biological child. As in Puritan texts, the novel uses terms such as "adopted daughter" and "foster parents." The narrator explains without apology or embarrassment that the Huntleys "loved [Laura] *almost* as well as they could have done if she had been truly their own" (29, emphasis added).

The context for Laura's adoption is consistent with Calvinist understanding of original sin. Nothing is known about Laura's birth parents, but the narrator associates their abandonment of their child with sin and an inability to accomplish good, no matter how well intentioned. To describe Laura's abandonment, the narrator evokes the fall of Adam and Eve in the Garden of Eden, asking the reader to imagine him- or herself in Laura's fallen position and equating the adoptive home with heaven:

> Think a moment, of being cast off in your early childhood from your mother's bosom, and your father's care, and of being dependent for your daily food . . . on the cold and stinted charity of the world—of resigning your soft white pillow for a restless bed on a board or the cold pavement—your clean nice clothing for a scanty covering of rags—your lovely home with all its refinements, and all its comforts—the home that seems to you as happy as a Paradise; to be a houseless and homeless wanderer. . . . (13)

If orphancy is a fall from grace, then the birth parents' relinquishment of their child is also sinful. The narrator suggests their low moral character by describing them in animal rather than human terms and by imagining their origins in "heathen lands, rather than in a Christian city" (19). These derogatory comments reflect religious sentiments as well as social anxieties about immigration and its effect on a rising middle class. A burgeoning middle class was eager to manage its success by projecting its fears onto poor or immigrant groups, whose individual members it then rescued through adoption.

In *Laura Huntley*, the mention of the birth parents' foreign provenance reveals nineteenth-century bias against non-Protestant immigrants generally and immigrant mothers in particular. Although both of Laura's birth parents are portrayed as deficient, the narrator targets Laura's birth mother, reflecting sentiments that align nurture with feminine principles.

> Laura Huntley's parents were probably very degraded, vicious people, without the fear of God before their eyes, who did not want the care and trouble of a poor little helpless infant; so she was wrapped in a miserable old filthy blanket, and laid behind a pile of rubbish near a wharf, where some decayed buildings had lately been torn away. There she lay in her helplessness, unconscious of the inhuman treatment she had received from her natural protectors—more inhuman than the most savage beast was every [sic] guilty of . . . exposed in all human probability by her own mother! (17–18).

The passage ends with a specific attack on Laura's birth mother, whose abandonment of her child is no better than that of "the most savage beast." The mother's "inhuman" treatment contrasts with Laura's poor "helplessness" (18).

Given the deplorable circumstances that led to Laura's orphancy, the outlook for her future is uncertain. On the one hand, Browne subscribes to beliefs that associate Laura with her birth parents' flaws. On the other hand, she suggests that through her adoptive parents' guidance and the inculcation of middle-class, Anglo-European, Christian values, Laura can rise from her sordid beginnings. The Huntleys become agents of God's will, charged with a mission to nurture and discipline Laura so that she will follow a Christian path. In exchange, they expect Laura's obedience and gratitude. Mid-nineteenth-century adoption narratives commonly show the movement from structural impositions of external authority to individual development of conscience; from adherence to the Bible as a text outside the self to attunement to one's inner voice; and from a prescribed code of behavior to a personal standard of ethics. However, despite the fact that the Huntleys groom Laura "to act the part of a dutiful and faithful daughter, and to return the love and kindness which had rescued her from such a deplorable destiny, and procured for her a heritage of so much blessedness" (30), Laura fails to achieve the standards of self-governance required by both her family and nation.

Steadily falling short of her parents' expectations, Laura has by age thirteen become "selfish, wayward, and full of concealment." When she breaks a glass, she lies, claiming that the servants broke it. The narrator laments about her indiscretion, "first deceit, and then falsehood!" (33). The narrator does not explicitly attribute Laura's misbehavior to her adoptive status—all children, not just Laura, require guidance and discipline. But unlike biological children, Laura has a tenuous place in the household and must behave in order to keep it. She becomes an example to young readers, who learn from her trials the need for obedience and self-restraint. In literature of this period, the adoptive child often must earn a place in the home, even starting out as an indentured servant or temporary laborer. As one character muses about her prospective adoptive daughter, "'I should so love to dress her and teach her and have her always near me. . . . I could learn her to dust the things, and feed the canaries—and soon she could run of errands. I do n't believe she'd be so much care after all.'"[64] The care and expense of adoption are repaid when the children help with chores, obey their parents, and mature into virtuous, responsible adults.

Narratives such as *Laura Huntley* are clear about the adopted child's shortcomings and the adoptive parents' need to provide guidance. When Laura misbehaves, each parent responds according to nineteenth-century gender roles. Laura's mother, taking a sentimental approach, attempts to reform Laura through gentle persuasion and positive example. Her father, in contrast, reacts with masculine firmness derived from seventeenth-century Calvinism. The task of harsh discipline traditionally belonged to the father, who according to Pauline doctrine was the indisputable head of the family. It fell upon him, even more than the clergy, to carry out the responsibilities of creating and maintaining family piety. The emphasis on patriarchal control persisted into the nineteenth century, which we tend to think of as a sentimental age, but women still lacked political rights and were understood to participate in a social order in which it was decreed by God that they be subordinate to their husbands.[65]

Mr. Huntley's sternness eventually accomplishes the parents' goal, leaving readers to appreciate not a romantic belief in the self-governing child but a more austere approach to punishment. When Laura's school behavior becomes so disruptive that her mother despairs of correcting it, Laura's father steps in with a plan reminiscent of the forced isolation that Cotton Mather employed with his children. Mr. Huntley threatens to punish Laura by putting her out to service. His threat "to send her to the work-house—to service any where" is potentially as terrifying to an adopted child who has already experienced abandonment as hell might be to a Calvinist believer. In contrast, Mrs. Huntley "mildly and tenderly" intercedes on Laura's behalf, stressing the importance of parental kindness and a loving, nurturing environment. She argues that "if they sent Laura away from them, at least, until every effort in her behalf proved unavailing, she might become worse and worse, and grow up into an abandoned and ruined woman. Wrong as her conduct had been, it was still their duty to be forbearing" (138). However, Mr. Huntley's sterner approach prevails. He requires Laura to confess her wrongs publicly and resolve to offend no more. She is expelled from school until she changes her behavior. The narrator reports that Laura "*did improve* under her severe discipline" and her outlook brightens, although the narrator cautions that such "reformations are always of an uncertain character, until the heart is regenerated by the Holy Spirit" (143, original emphasis).

Laura Huntley demonstrates that Puritan notions of sin, salvation, and community persist in nineteenth-century adoption narratives. Puritan doctrines of salvation continue to make adoption normative—the Huntleys casually and confidently rescue the infant they find on the street and extend their sense of family beyond the biological one. However, just as Puritan believers narrowly defined community and used it to justify exclusion on grounds of unworthiness, the Huntleys exhibit ethnic and racial biases against Laura's birth parents. *Laura Huntley* thus subscribes to a Calvinist-based theology that restricts the notion of adoption, or election, to a select few even while promoting a sense of civic and religious responsibility in which adoption can be practiced. Nineteenth-century American literary adoption continues to rely on these contrasting notions of exclusion and inclusion, sin and redemption, although in more secularized forms.

Adoption performs a disciplinary as well as a redemptive function in *Laura Huntley*. It is enacted by pious individuals who believe in innate depravity yet expect Laura to progress through nurture. Laura's plight—she is presumably orphaned or abandoned because of parental illness, drinking, dereliction, or business misfortune—reflects economic and demographic unease as cities swelled with newly arrived immigrants. But *Laura Huntley* also shows how a child may rise with care, faith, and discipline to become an upstanding citizen. Browne imagines a world of familial and social cohesion achieved through adoption that the law had not yet specified, and even while she constrains the female character to pious domesticity, she registers a confidence resonant with that of a youthful, expanding nation.

Fictions such as *Laura Huntley* represent a watershed moment in literary portrayals of kinship. They teach by example Christian doctrines of charity and redemption. Depicting adoptive parents as those who emulate God's benevolence and generosity, domestic novels such as Browne's work to bring nonbelievers to faith within the context of rapid social and economic change. These novels reinforce the notion of family as a microcosm of the community and help guide parents and children in proper fulfillment of responsibilities, which, based on Pauline doctrine, includes feminine piety, patriarchal authority, and juvenile compliance. The key question about this sentimental discourse may not be whether it supports or subverts mainstream gender roles, a topic of much recent criticism,[66] but how it mediates opposing views of childhood, family, and society.

Adoption fiction is ultimately ambivalent about the function it describes. Adoptive placements are not only loving but also disciplinary and sometimes coercive, informed as much by belief in childhood insufficiency and deficiency as by belief in its goodness and potential. Featuring at least two families and four parents, birth and adoptive, adoption stories provide multiple viewpoints from which to analyze and judge human motivation and behavior. Exemplary tales such as *Laura Huntley* demonstrate how powerfully literature of the period reinvigorates the Calvinist salvation narrative and how seamlessly austere as well as sentimental concepts of kinship and childhood are woven into the fabric of nineteenth-century fiction. At the same time that they signal dependency, especially for females, mid-nineteenth-century adoption narratives reflect an increasingly romantic, child-centered sensibility that grants juveniles the opportunity for unprecedented adventure. Demonstrating both the importance of roots and the benefits of fresh starts, domestic adoption fiction tells an American story.

5

Child Saving, Nation Building: *The Wide, Wide World* and *The Lamplighter*

AS THE NATION grew, so did the number of published fictions about adoption. These popular narratives do more than celebrate the child as emblematic of youthful American nationhood. Mediating tensions between inherited and constructed forms of identity, adoption fiction expresses white, middle-class hopes and misgivings about changing definitions of family, faith, and nationhood. Girls rather than boys figure prominently in these stories, reflecting the fact that adoption's goal—a home—was a domain increasingly shaped and occupied by women.

Two bestselling adoption novels of the 1850s, *The Wide, Wide World* by Susan Warner and *The Lamplighter* by Susanna Maria Cummins, reward their heroines with new families, affluence, and social standing. In these novels, a series of adoptive homes serve as way stations on the protagonist's path to fulfillment and abundance, allowing the authors to equate successful adoption with a Franklin-like rise in the world, albeit one inflected by gender norms.[1] The question for protagonists Ellen Montgomery and Gerty Flint is not how to function independently, as it is for boys, but how to gain the insights and skills necessary to meet society's domestic ideals. Not only adoption but also marriage is the reward at the end of each girl's journey. Nurture, in the context of Christian faith, is the means by which both learn the combination of selfless service and proud individualism necessary to take their place as female citizens in the developing republic.

No educator or preacher did more to stress the importance of interlocking concepts of nurture and faith in children's lives than Horace Bushnell. His aptly titled *Christian Nurture* (1847), which appeared three years before Warner's bestseller, provides a framework for the training that the protagonists in *The Wide, Wide World* and *The Lamplighter* receive to become pious, compliant, and civic-minded female adults. In both novels, adoption is associated with salvation. Both novels reflect shifts from austere Calvinism to a gentler Christianity with descriptions of old and new methods of child rearing and portrayals of masculine authority versus feminine sympathy. Whereas some adoptive settings emphasize the child's submission of will in ways evocative of seventeenth-century child-rearing practices,[2] other settings offer more progressive advice to nineteenth-century parents: to treat children with loving firmness so that they come by their own volition to embrace virtues that the family and the republic hold dear. Central to this process is Bushnell's emphasis on the power of Christian nurture and its corollary: the strength of American values and institutions in relation to European ones. Both Ellen Montgomery and Gerty Flint learn to check their anger over loss and injustice and practice pious submission: "Though we *must* sorrow, we must not rebel," Ellen's mother advises, for our truer "home" is in heaven.[3] Gerty likewise learns from trials that "it is through suffering only we are made perfect."[4] In both cases, nurture through adoption leads to a new kind of American family, one that celebrates republican autonomy while honoring Old World tradition and authority.

Despite their similarities, *The Wide, Wide World* and *The Lamplighter* rely on patriarchal models and configure the adoptive child's relation to the republic differently.[5] Warner's novel reflects a Calvinist adherence to Pauline doctrine, with men as heads of household and women and children spiritually equal but socially unequal, a model based on Old World concepts of family. Nevertheless, at the conclusion of *The Wide, Wide World*, Ellen affirms New World possibilities rather than Old World certainties. She rejects European claims and instead uses adoptive kinship to forge an American identity that is sororal or fraternal rather than strictly hierarchical. Although still subject to masculine authority, Ellen evolves from a position of abject submission to one of willing acquiescence within a consensual model of gender relations.

The Lamplighter develops a relationship to American identity in a complementary way. At the beginning of the novel, Gerty exercises more autonomy than Ellen, but when she arrives at a point of selfless service to others, she is rewarded not with an opportunity for fresh starts but with a genealogical connection. Although the novel expresses distaste for European-based fashion and pretension, it relies on Old World order by reuniting Gerty with her birth father. *The Lamplighter* follows a plot pattern found in European fairy tales, in which multiple adoptive placements precede the child's discovery that her true place is with her family of origin. In different ways, both novels affirm American qualities by simultaneously fulfilling desires for connection and independence.

FAMILY: "THE CHURCH OF CHILDHOOD"

Horace Bushnell (1802–1876), a recognized leader in the Christian education movement in the United States, had a profound impact on the moral qualities of nineteenth-century domestic literature. Influenced while attending Yale College by his reading of Samuel Coleridge's 1825 "Aids to Reflection," he came to believe in Christian faith not as a knowable intellectual problem, as had the eighteenth-century thinkers before him, but as a matter of intuitive understanding and ethical feeling.[6] His ruminations, laid out in *Christian Nurture* in 1847 and revised in 1861, served as a theological framework for an age in transition from Calvinist austerity to Christian sentimentality: a religion of the heart, a notion of God as a loving rather than angry patriarch, and a sense of family "as an avenue of God's grace."[7]

Bushnell's notion of Christian nurture was well suited to Warner's and Cummins's middle-class readers. His theory addresses two challenges simultaneously: it confronts

Calvinist austerity, and it emphasizes the spiritual in the face of increasingly secular and material culture. In the years following the 1847 publication of Bushnell's *Christian Nurture*, the debate over infant depravity became pronounced. The New England Calvinists held to the notion of original sin. Jonathan Edwards likewise describes the "child of wrath."[8] But the Swedenborgians argued for innate goodness: "at birth the child is . . . but an incipient receptacle of that thought and affection, the proper protection, nourishment, and exercise of which are capable of forming it into an angel."[9] Like the Swedenborgians, Bushnell adhered to the power of example, writing, "And your life is more powerful than your instructions can be."[10] He also shifted the conception of a child as essentially alienated from God's grace until the moment of conversion to the idea of a child of God whose membership in a Christian household is preliminary to and even commensurate with salvation. He further believed that what applied to the child and the churchgoing family also applied to the nation: "no nation can long thrive by a spirit of conquest; no more can a church" (61). He exhorted his readers to "follow a gentler and more constant method" (62) that would lead child, family, and nation to essential truth and fuse traditional theology and the new sense of freedom in the Jacksonian era.

Bushnell's argument rests on three propositions: infant baptism, the family as an avenue of God's grace, and the importance of nurture in shaping individual thought and behavior.[11] All three tenets have a bearing on literary adoption. Bushnell maintains the importance of infant baptism as the event that signals the inclusion of the child in God's family and initiates the process by which, through "righteousness and love" rather than "brute force," peaceful conversion may be effected (56). Both Ellen Montgomery and Gerty Flint, born to Christian families, can be assumed to have been baptized. Bushnell also emphasizes the importance of early nurture, whereby "more is done to affect, or fix the moral and religious character of children, before the age of language than after" (236). His theory explains why Ellen, who is eight years old at the outset of the novel and lovingly tended by her mother, is initially more receptive to Christian teachings than the recalcitrant Gerty, who is with her mother only a short time before falling into the hands of the abusive Nan Grant. Bushnell argues that because a child is more ready "to be taken by good" than an adult (21), properly nurtured children come to faith gradually from birth onward, rather than abruptly at some appointed time in adulthood. They receive religious sensibility "through their impressions, before they were able to receive it from choice. . . . The spirit of the house is in the members by nurture, not by teaching . . . because it is the air the children breathe" (101). The air Ellen breathes is more spiritually pure than that Gerty breathes, and Ellen is accordingly less angry and more manageable than her counterpart. Ellen benefits more from "full-born intensity of the maternal affection," which Bushnell deems vital in the process of Christian indoctrination. Motherhood as practiced by Mrs. Montgomery rather than by Nan Grant is the "highest and most sacred office" (236).

With its emphasis on nurture, Bushnell's theory aligns with adoption, a recuperative act that demonstrates "the philosophy of religion as a renovated experience." The notion that children raised with gentleness, patience, and love will acquire those same characteristics works with rather than against the concept of original sin. "Assuming the corruption of human nature, when should we think it wisest to undertake or expect a remedy?" Bushnell asks. "When evil is young and pliant to good, or when it is confirmed by years of sinful habit?" (21). The force of heredity loses its grip and the child is not so much "depravated by descent from the parents, who are under the corrupting effects of sin" as it is "within the matrix of the parental life" (27), fully able to benefit from "nurture or cultivation." Then "the Christian life and spirit of the parents . . . shall flow into the mind of the child, to blend with his incipient and half-formed exercises" (30).

Bushnell views adoption, as did Cotton Mather, as an obligation for church members and a saving grace for children: "It is a very great mercy that the children of a bad or irreligious family are sometimes permitted to be inmates elsewhere; to go into virtuous and Christian families, where a better spirit reigns" (120). Bushnell also views the church and the republic in analogous terms, extending the reach of infant baptism from family to nation. In the United States "law makes every infant child a citizen. . . . The baptized child is a believer and a member of the church. . . . [H]e is accepted in God's supernatural economy as a believer; even as the law accepts him, in the economy of society, to be a citizen" (167–68). Home is "the church of childhood" (20), and proper parenting is necessary for sound faith and good citizenship. According to Bushnell, the church is a surrogate, or adoptive, parent: "Whenever there are orphan children, that have been baptized, the church ought to look after them, as being members; see, if possible, that they are not neglected, but trained up in a Christian manner" (193). The purpose of the church is to "take in" members, not exclude them. Believers who are saved "are as fitly to be counted citizens of the kingdom, as they are to be citizens of the state" (175).

INTO THE WORLD

Bushnell's theories of nurture inform Ellen Montgomery's adoption experience in *The Wide, Wide World* (1850). In order to become a godly citizen in the Bushnellian sense, she must separate from her birth parents, who demonstrate outmoded or ineffectual methods of childrearing and nation building. Although critics often focus on the sentimental aspects of *The Wide, Wide World* and laud the loving attachment between Ellen and her mother in contrast to the emotional distance between Ellen and her father, problems inhere in Ellen's relationships with both parents. Her forceful birth father is modeled on a hierarchical Calvinist model that invests men with unquestioned authority. Her retreating birth mother exemplifies a gentler form of Christian faith, but to an extreme: Mrs. Montgomery can do little more than suffer and consign Ellen to the same fate. Warner's portrayals point to the insufficiency of both Calvinist and sentimental approaches to child rearing and clear a path for Ellen to experience a new model of family relations and companionate marriage in keeping with republican ideals.

Mrs. Montgomery is powerless against forces that assail her. Although she resolves never to part from her child, she is persuaded by her doctor of the need for a warm climate and by her husband of the prospect of "a happy home" for Ellen at Fortune Emerson's farm. Ill, meek, and resigned, she knows "that the chance of her ever returning to shield the little creature who was nearest her heart from the future evils and snares of life was very, very small" (12). When Ellen cries at the thought of leaving her mother, Mrs. Montgomery is "too exhausted to either share or soothe Ellen's agitation." The stronger of the two, Ellen effectively becomes the adult. Anguished at the thought of separation, Mrs. Montgomery says, "I cannot bear this any longer" (14), whereupon Ellen spares her mother further distress by calming her own emotions. While her mother sleeps, Ellen assumes the maternal role by laying a kiss on her mother's forehead and stealing "quietly out of the room to her own little bed." The next day, Ellen is "careful" to make no sound that interferes with her mother's sleep; she promises to "grieve her no more with useless expressions of sorrow" (15). She observes from her bedroom window a "poor deformed" orphan on the street; consoles herself that although this child's mother is dead, hers is only going away; and resolves to "work harder" and "mend all my faults" (16) in order "not [to] distress her mother with the sight of her sorrow" (19). Mrs. Montgomery praises Ellen's demonstration of adult responsibility: "It has comforted me greatly . . . that you have shown yourself so submissive and patient under this affliction. I should scarcely have been able to endure it if you had not exerted self-control" (25).

Ellen shows strength in relation to her mother's meekness, but she is powerless in the face of her father's authority. Mr. Montgomery rules with the inscrutable power of a Calvinist deity: "She entertained not the slightest hope of being able by any means to alter her father's will" (20). When he arranges a chaperone to accompany Ellen to her Aunt Fortune's farm with only hours' notice of the departure, Mrs. Montgomery begs to wake Ellen early so that they may spend time together. Mr. Montgomery refuses with a definitive, "I cannot allow it" (59), whereupon Ellen, at the mercy of her father's undisclosed timetable, is jolted from peaceful slumber with only minutes to say goodbye. Abruptly drawn "away from her mother's arms" (64), she is deposited into the Dunscombe carriage and whisked away, comforted only by her mother's naïve understanding that because Fortune's farm is in the country, it "is a very pleasant place," "beautiful and very healthy, and full of charming walks and rides" (22).

Ellen is taught to suffer and relinquish her will to others, a process that trains her, according to Christian doctrine, for ultimate surrender to God. As Ellen's mother tells her, "Perhaps he sees . . . that you never would seek him while you had me to cling to." Ellen's adoptions into a series of homes, none guaranteed or lasting, reinforce the point that "there is a [heavenly] home . . . where changes do not come" (41). Prospective orphancy—and by extension, candidacy for adoption—constitutes Ellen's first important theological lesson. She must not only endure her parents' abandonment but also anticipate and welcome it. Saying goodbye to her father, for whom she feels slight affection, is bearable, but leaving her mother unthinkable: her "love to her mother was the strongest feeling her heart knew" (13). She struggles to acquiesce to her mother's feeling that "if losing your mother might be the means of finding you that better friend [Jesus], I should be quite willing—and glad to go—forever" (23).

Ellen's parents unwittingly foster a dependence that inhibits rather than facilitates her ability to become a spiritually enlightened, self-governing citizen of the republic. Ellen's lack of agency and deference to others is evident when she visits a bookstore and, advised by her mother to "judge for yourself" (31), is gripped by indecision over which Bible to choose. Later, unable to complete their shopping, Ellen and her mother feel "grateful" for the "kind interference" of an old gentleman who helps with the selection of merino wool (51). Ellen's sense of dependency is reinforced when she recites an Old Testament catechism of submission in the form of a hymn about "trials" that "Lay me low, and keep me there" in an abject state:

God in Israel sows the seeds
Of affliction, pain, and toil;

These spring up and choke the weeds
Which would else o'erspread the soil.
Trials make the promise sweet,—
Trials give new life to prayer,—
Trials bring me to his feet,
Lay me low, and keep me there. (56)

Aboard a steamboat, where "she felt very well that nobody there cared in the least for her sorrow" (65), Ellen is reminded by a friendly gentleman that "you can do nothing well without help" (74). She then sings another hymn of submission: "Here now to thee I all resign,—/My body, soul, and all are thine" (75).

Cotton Mather's "Orphanotrophium" represents orphancy as a fortunate fall that allows the child to submit to the power of God. Likewise, in *The Wide, Wide World*, orphancy has disciplinary power not only to curb Ellen's will but also to set the terms for a new model of family and social relations. These ideals are realized through the adoptive parenting by Alice and John Humphreys. However, before Ellen can develop companionate relations with the Humphreys, she must undergo trials devised by her father and his Calvinist proxy, Fortune Emerson. Loaded like "some great bale of goods" (93) onto Mr. Van Brunt's cart, she arrives at Fortune's "neat," "clean," but "comfortless" farm, her dignity reduced (102). Her body and spirit are debased as she endures Fortune's harshness and neglect.

EXTREMES OF NURTURE

Bushnell's theory of Christian nurture resists two extreme tendencies in American society, both of which Fortune Emerson exhibits: Calvinist austerity and Yankee individualism. Like Ellen's father, Fortune is an authoritarian parent figure. Her masculine, rigid management of Ellen is the antithesis of her birth mother's nurturing acceptance. Even though maternal love was popularized as a key ingredient of Christian nurture, Warner shows that masculine force was still prevalent and potent in nineteenth-century culture. As Bernard Wishy confirms, "the supremacy of the father in giving the child clear laws and strong ideals was a fact of momentous importance in the lives of nineteenth-century children."[12] At Fortune's farm, Ellen becomes the fallen child described by Jonathan Edwards, not the divine child of nature.[13] She does not know whether she is good or bad and must suffer what Erica Bauermeister calls "continual mortification" in order to learn what is right.[14] Bushnell also reacted to the extreme individualism, arbitrary supernaturalism, and reliance on emotional revivals that characterized thought and practice in many American churches from the mid-eighteenth century onward. Although liberal, he objected to unchecked liberty and still held to the concept of original sin.[15]

Fortune Emerson takes the ideals of Transcendentalism, promoted by her namesake, Ralph Waldo Emerson, to an extreme. She imposes a too-strict ethos of self-sufficiency on Ellen. When Ellen, accustomed to being pampered, notices her unmade bed, she learns that "the making of it in the future must depend entirely upon herself" (113). When Mr. Van Brunt kisses her, Aunt Fortune does nothing to ward off his inappropriate attentions, nor does she warn Ellen about Nancy Vawse's mischievous pranks. Deprived of schooling, Ellen must "study by myself" (141). Fortune either disciplines Ellen according to outmoded patriarchal Calvinist principles—telling her, "There's nothing in this house but goes through my hand" (113)—or she leaves Ellen completely to her own devices. Both approaches fail because they lack nurture, communal sympathy, and belief in something larger than herself. Too dogmatically Emersonian, Fortune enjoys no uplift from self-reliance. As she bitterly says, "toil, toil, and drive, drive . . . what's the end of it all? . . . One may slave one's life out for other people, and what thanks do you get?" (217).

Fortune's pseudo-adoption of Ellen is the first stop on Ellen's route to higher moral and domestic ground. She first experiences love and gains confidence not at Fortune's farm but in Mrs. Van Brunt's cozy kitchen. Having felt Mrs. Van Brunt's "spirit of kindness" (129), she perceives "a breach" between herself and her aunt "that neither could make any effort to mend" (133). A conversion occurs when, on a mission of charity during a snowstorm, Ellen experiences a debilitating illness. This spiritual as well as physical test of strength transforms Ellen's relationship to herself and her faith. After grudgingly nursing Ellen through a fever and hearing her call for her birth mother, Fortune denigrates her role as adoptive mother with a sarcastic comment that "nobody knows the blessing of taking care of other people's children that ha'n't tried it" (206). Alice Humphreys, on the other hand, understands the blessing of taking in an orphan, and under her tutelage Ellen becomes living proof of the axiom that drives American adoption fiction: saving a child also saves others. Loved by Alice, Ellen learns to love and give to others. While she recovers from her illness, she shares a hymn with Mr. Van Brunt and brings him closer to God. Once well, she reads to Mrs. Vawse; invites her granddaughter, Nancy, to a sewing bee; and treats Aunt Fortune with calm equanimity. These godly gestures put her on a path toward spiritual, social, and economic standing on par with Alice's.

More romantic than fundamentalist, Warner dramatizes the tensions between the old and new theologies to show the shortsightedness of Calvinist methods of child rearing. With Fortune Emerson, Ellen undergoes a series of afflictions and tests that underline her powerlessness and worthlessness; she experiences the severity of Calvinism with its strict demarcation of the saved and damned child. With Alice Humphreys, however, she experiences a gradual process whereby with maternal and sororal affection, guidance, and piety, she can work towards "adoption 'into the family of Christ.'"[16] The misery and abuse she endures with her mean-spirited aunt paves the way for a more loving and nurturing home with Alice and John Humphreys, who together offer her the combination of masculine and feminine qualities needed for a developing republic.

MIDDLE-CLASS AFFECTION

Alice Humphreys relies on feminine benevolence and gentle persuasion rather than masculine control to aid Ellen in "feeling right" (151). Her Bushnellian approach not only corrects Ellen's faults but also strengthens their bond. Alice claims Ellen as her "adopted sister" (225), and the two exchanges tears and kisses at times of parting and reunion in a manner that Carroll Smith-Rosenberg finds characteristic of close female relationships of the period.[17] Their intimacy reaches a new height when Ellen effectively assigns Alice the role of mother as well as sister, allowing Alice to read her mother's letter in order "to feel as if you knew mamma a little" (227).

Alice's model of adoptive care is rooted in a white, middle-class culture of domesticity. She aids Ellen in such a way that supports her own class position while also grooming Ellen for a similar rank. Alice enjoys favored status in her family and society, and she expresses bourgeois, American confidence that others will respond to and meet her needs. At one point she tells Ellen that "nobody ever refuses me any thing" (175) and explains that her English servant Margery, who came to the United States "for love" of her, "looks upon John and me as her own children" (173). She extends class privilege to Ellen, who becomes known as "'an uncommon, well-behaved child'" within the Humphreys' household (266). One outcome of Ellen's new role as Alice's "adopted sister" is her growing awareness that she will never suffer like other orphans, including Nancy Vawse or the poor Irish boy whom she saw on in the street outside her parents' home. Alice's greatest service is to introduce Ellen to John Humphreys, who secures her place in Christian faith, the middle class, and the republic.

Alice offers an appealing alternative to Fortune Emerson's austerity: a fresh start possible through non-kinship adoption. With Ellen's mother dead and her father presumed drowned at sea, Fortune becomes "her sole guardian and owner." Yet Ellen feels little connection to her paternal aunt. An essential ingredient—loving tenderness—is missing, and Ellen "felt sometimes, soberly and sadly, that she was thrown upon the wide world" (381). Fortune teaches only work, duty, and responsibility, but Alice offers the reassuring knowledge that "whenever you can run away from your aunt's this is your home" (163). The Humphreys help Ellen develop a "sweetness of temper" born of "religion and discipline" (418), with the result that Ellen is "happy" for the first time (405). Her father's absence makes her feel only "that she was an orphan," not "that she had lost her father." But Ellen values her new adoptive bond: "Life had nothing now worse for her than a separation from Alice and John Humphreys" (381).

Ellen reaches a milestone when she nurses Aunt Fortune through an illness. She now "felt with great satisfaction that she was trusted and believed. She was no longer an interloper, in every body's way; she was not watched and suspected; her aunt treated her as one of the family and a person to be depended on" (383). Another crisis looms with Alice's impending death, but Ellen is more prepared for this calamity than she was for her mother's death and faces the occasion with true Christian faith. Secure in the Humphreys' home, she follows Alice's advice "to think of it rightly" (431) as going home to God "a little before you" (429). She establishes residence in the Humphreys' parsonage, takes up Alice's "household duties," and prepares to "become the adopted child of the house" (458). Aunt Fortune's illness imposes an obligation on Ellen because the two are blood kin, but Ellen rejects this tie, preferring the bonds of affection and Christian faith constructed with the Humphreys. Foreshadowing the love that will blossom between them, she relaxes in John's presence: "it was pleasure enough to feel that he was there" (468).

Ellen finds love and support with Alice and John Humphreys, demonstrating that although the legal status of adoptees was unclear in 1851, many adoptions were predicated upon strong bonds.[18] Ellen forms multiple relationships—including that of brother and sister as well as daughter and wife—modeling the sense of "spiritual kinship" that Marc Shell finds common in Western literary topography. According to Shell, the idea of "Universal Siblinghood" aligns with Christian believers' sense of themselves as adopted children of God and affirms that "all human beings are siblings, or at least that everyone human is essentially convertible to the same siblinghood."[19] This concept favors adoption over genealogy by questioning the importance of blood as the primary determiner of kinship and by blurring the distinction between incest and chastity, on which kinship structures rely. Shell focuses on the incest taboo and the ways that various works of literature incorporate or challenge it, a theme Warner echoes with her version of the female *Bildungsroman*, in which Ellen passes from being John's daughter or sister to being his wife. Marriage to an adoptive father acknowledges limited options for females at the time, but it also takes Ellen a step further in the direction of democratic individualism, a quality for which the United States became known among Western nations. John takes a developmental approach to faith and balances evangelical authoritarianism with religious liberalism in a manner Bushnell would approve and that was consistent with American ideals. Shaped by multiple relationships—sibling, filial, and spousal—Ellen becomes an exemplary U.S. citizen, her identity shaped not by birthright, which is fixed, but by adoption, which is flexible. She becomes not the person she was born to be but the person she chooses to be. This distinctive American identity takes shape when the Old World meets the New World in the form of Ellen's newly discovered relatives, the Lindsays, who claim her for their own.

FOREIGN RELATIONS

Ellen's adoptive ties to the Humphreys are challenged when she discovers that Aunt Fortune has withheld a letter from her mother instructing Ellen to join her blood relatives in Scotland. She wonders, is her rightful place with her adoptive family, the Humphreys, or with her blood kin, the Lindsays? The push and pull of genealogy is further thematized when Ellen hears the story of the Humphreys and Marshman families' migration from England to America. A European emphasis on primogeniture precipitated their move to the New World. Miss Sophia explains that the elder Mr. Humphreys suffered a disadvantage as "the younger brother," who "in England generally [has] little or nothing" (473). In contrast, in America he found "an excellent situation . . . at one of the best institutions" and prospered (473).

America offers opportunities unavailable in a genealogically bound European culture, although ties between England and the United States endure, especially for the older generation. For example, Mr. Humphreys insists that his son John visit England and Scotland "to see his family and to know his native land" despite John's belief that "he had more important duties at home" (476). Miss Sophia praises Ellen's politeness, declares it "natural to her" (475), and attributes her best qualities—grace, good will, ease, and selflessness—to Ellen's innate, that is, inherited, spirit. Warner focuses on hereditary traits at the very moment Ellen begins to demonstrate what she can accomplish on her own, underlining the tension between inherited and constructed identities in Ellen's life and U.S. society. The novel positions Ellen between biological and adoptive identities, setting the stage for a climactic scene in which she establishes her American identity.

When Ellen discovers the existence of the letter that directs her to Scotland, it creates questions about dual allegiance, framed in the discourse of adoption. Hearing Mr. Humphreys' order to join the Lindsays, she muses, "Must she obey them? . . . I can't be adopted twice." She prefers to stay with the elder Mr. Humphreys, who bestows the prized title of "daughter" on her, but she feels bound to obey her birth parents' wishes, even though they could not have known that would find shelter and happiness under the Humphreys' roof. "May I not judge for myself?" she asks in a typically American fashion (490). This question, like so many others, is settled for her, this time in terms of Old Testament theology rather than romantic individualism: she must obey the Fifth Commandment to honor her mother and father and do her "parents' will" rather than her own (494). Her impulse toward self-reliance checked, she answers the call of Old World obligation rather than New World opportunity.

On the transatlantic voyage that will unite her with her birth grandmother and uncle, Ellen again "wonder[s] how many times one may be adopted" (504). Significantly, she views the reunion with the Lindsays as another adoption rather than a return to family of origin, an interpretation that already marks her as an American with an adoptive rather than strictly genealogical identity. The Lindsays, however, see matters differently. They embrace Ellen as their "own child." An emotional Mrs. Lindsay draws her close, reliving the trauma of losing her daughter to the United States years ago and proclaiming, "I will never let you go!" (502). Ellen is called upon to recite her accomplishments in the New World. On cue, she demonstrates acquisition of an excellent education and upbringing in what her relatives call "the backwoods of America" (505). She impresses her uncle and grandmother with her mastery of horseback riding, French, history, and music. She even takes up her mother's—and her nation's—cause, accepting the label "rebel" and defending her achievements despite the Lindsays' scorn for their "American" provenance. When Mr. Lindsay insists she call him "father" and urges her to "forget you are American . . . you belong to me" (510), Ellen dutifully complies, having "schooled herself" to acquiesce (525, 526). She wisely prevents a "breech [sic] between them that would not readily have been healed" (527).

Inwardly, however, Ellen follows her American training and keeps loyalty to faith, friends, and nation. In the end, she finds that she "can't be adopted twice" (490). She cannot serve both the God of her conscience and the secular sociality of the Lindsays. No matter how appealing the Lindsays' material offerings, she cannot divest herself of American qualities or "forget" the people (534) who make up the nation where she truly feels "*at home*" (513, original emphasis). Ellen rejects an Old World identity. However "excellent people" who "entertain most handsomely and agreeably," the Lindsays exhibit "some peculiarity" (499) and objectify their newly found daughter. She becomes their "pride" (528) and "dear plaything" to be "petted and fondled as a darling possession" (538). Exercising proprietary rights, they say that Ellen belongs to them only, and they insist she renounce her relationship to her "sister" Alice and "brother" John because the Lindsays "do not wish to claim kindred with all the world" (529). They also interfere with Ellen's religious practice. Believing that she is "spoiling herself for life and the world by a set of dull religious notions" (542–43), Ellen's grandmother objects to the one hour that Ellen devotes to morning prayer, requiring her to sleep late and move her bed into Mrs. Lindsay's room. The Lindsays direct Ellen's energies toward a material home, not a heavenly one, but Ellen persists in her faith. She responds to Mr. Lindsay's request that she love them with a hymn that leaves no doubt that her first priority is God and a nonearthly dwelling place: "O Canaan! It is my happy, happy home—/I am bound for the land of Canaan" (546). Ellen keeps two "safeguards" against their materialism: the Bible and thoughts of John.

Ellen also struggles with the Lindsays' hierarchical rather than collaborative model of relationship. For example, deprived of thoughtful, inquiring conversation, she finds herself "talked *to*, but not *with*." She longs for John's "higher style of kindness" (538, original emphasis) and the sense of mutuality it engenders. "At war with herself" over obeying the Lindsays (553), she wonders whether to rebel in order to follow her religious conscience or to resign herself to what amounts to colonization. Although overtly acquiescent, she inwardly resists the Lindsays' influence. In a display of force, Mr. Lindsay frequently lays his fingers on Ellen's lips to enforce compliance. "Cheerful" but not "merry" (548), Ellen tolerates this alien authority, but she refuses to surrender that which she holds most dear: her right to practice her faith in the way that the Humphreys have taught her. She wages a personal revolution in support of an American cause. When John arrives in Scotland, he tells her, "I have no power now to remove you from your legal guardians and you have no right to choose for yourself" (561), but Ellen affirms her bond to him and to her adopted country. She says, "I had given myself to you a great while ago; long before I was his daughter, you called me your little sister" (563). She embraces the United States, not Scotland, and returns from her time abroad in a newly configured role of American daughter and wife.

ADOPTING AMERICA

Ellen joins John as his companion and complement in the New World, where "they try to do the work of life together and help each other be faithful" (576). As critics have noted, Warner's description of John Humphreys establishes a regime of surveillance and control. Ellen observes "two very keen eyes"; "she was quite sure from that one look . . . that he was a person to be feared" (275). John's influence over Ellen is palpable during her stay at the Marshmans', which marks both Ellen's entrance into society and her resolve to reject fashion for piety. Under John's direction, the "breach" she feels between herself and everyone but Ellen Chauncy is, like the "breach" between her and Aunt Fortune, "destined to grow wider" (306). Overcome with remorse for being fashion-conscious and selecting the best swatch of fabric for herself, Ellen admits her fault and surrenders to John's tutelage, heeding the familiar reminder that she must subject her will to masculine power. "You are no worse than before; . . . very, very weak,—quite unable to keep yourself right without constant help," John tells her (296). Combining evangelical piety with sentimental assurance, John paints a picture of divine wrath followed by heavenly bliss. The works of the earth "shall be burned up" (312), but even though man fills the earth "with sin," a world "far more lovely" is available to those with love and faith (313).

Whereas Alice gently instills Christian virtues, John—described as "the Grand Turk" and "the biggest gobbler in the yard" (316)—strips Ellen of autonomy in order to guide her to faith. He addresses her "obstinacy" with methods likened to "chastising" a fine black horse (376–77) in what Jane Tompkins calls a sexualized "dramatization of domination and power."[20] Rather than feel constraint at the prospect of marrying an adoptive father figure, Ellen is satisfied with her circumscribed role: "What [Alice] asked of her Ellen indeed *tried* to do; what John told her *was done*" (351, original emphasis). John's victory in the battle of wills is not only certain but also reassuring. Ellen submits to Bushnell's doctrine that a woman should first and foremost be a Christian. As she accepts John's goals as her own, her "faithfulness began to bring its reward" (335), and she progresses in her drawing, studies, and exercise, all according to John's outline.

The final pages of the novel reinforce Warner's point that Ellen's proper place is not only with John but also with the United States. "When I think of it all at home, how I want to be there," she says about the United States (565). Although "three or four more years of Scottish discipline wrought her no ill," Ellen's proper place is in the New World. With "unspeakable joy," she plans "to spend her life with the friends and guardians she best loved, and to be to them, still more than she had been to her Scottish relations" (569). In the unpublished final chapter that Jane Tompkins includes with the novel, Warner describes the companionate relationship that develops not only between Ellen and John but also between the Old and New Worlds.[21] John readies the house for Ellen, giving her a study with a door that connects to his study. He balances privacy and communion, individualism and family life. The links between the Old World and the New are ensured by the agreed upon plan that Mr. Lindsay "will spend half of his time" (581) near Ellen. They are also represented by the room's cherished furnishings—a combination of family heirlooms and pieces John "picked up . . . in France, Switzerland and Italy" (582) but arranges in a wholly American setting. Thus the room—and the novel—reconciles birth and adoptive identities by demonstrating that true freedom of religion and Christian nurture are possible only in the New World.

Ellen's declaration of allegiance to the United States upholds the myth of national cohesion in vogue at mid century. Popular culture and literature endorsed the idea that Americans joined together to form a union. Bushnell promotes this sense of unity in his conceptualization of family members who form a single national identity: "If we are units, so also are we a race, and the race is one—one family, one organic whole. . . . [I]n all organic bodies known to us—states, churches, sects, armies—there is a common spirit. . . . And we use this word *spirit*, in such cases, to denote a power interfused, a comprehensive will actuating the members." Bushnell also argues for American uniqueness: "How different, for example, is the spirit of France from the spirit of England? The spirit of both from that of the United States?" (102–04, original emphasis).

Paradoxically, however, Bushnell's portrayal of mythic American unity excludes, on the basis of nature, those his argument seeks to include. His emphasis on organicism works against adoption even as it lauds the power of nurture. When he writes that "children fall into their places naturally, as it were, and unconsciously, to do and to suffer exactly what the general scheme of the house requires" (110), he ignores the fact that orphancy and adoption result from specific social, economic, and political circumstances, whether they be parental abandonment or neglect, or death from poverty, addiction, overwork, or some twist of fate. Expressions of middle-class optimism such as Bushnell's barely concealed wide disparities in society at the time he wrote. As Joyce Appleby writes, "a virtual nation materialized out of the repeated messages about effort and accomplishment, virtue and autonomy, national prosperity and universal progress." However, "this imaginative construction of what it meant to be an American" obscured the heterogeneous nature of American life. . . . Ironically the self-conscious pursuit of national unity exacerbated the tensions created by its absence."[22]

The importance of circumstance in shaping adoption narrative is apparent in Susanna Maria Cummins's bestseller, *The Lamplighter*. Like Warner, Cummins popularizes the notion of adoption as a means of saving the child and unifying the nation. Ellen Montgomery and Gerty Flint both undergo a series of adoptions before finding permanent homes. Both negotiate tensions between inherited and acquired identities. However, *The*

Lamplighter complements *The Wide, Wide World* by making Gerty more disadvantaged at the beginning of her journey and more genealogically positioned at the end of it. Both novels promote a Bushnellian theory of nurture, but *The Lamplighter* demonstrates Bushnell's implicit, biological understanding of kinship. His frequent references to the organic nature of family reveal the continuing importance accorded blood kinship in American culture and literature, reinforcing the point that, with regard to adoptive kinship, the overall "American response to change was ambivalent."[23]

IMPOVERISHED

When *The Lamplighter* (1854) opens, eight-year-old Gerty is suffering at the hands of Nan Grant, who has kept and "tolerated"—but not adopted—her since Gerty's mother's death five years previous. Grant's self-serving reasons for taking Gerty into her home become clear at the conclusion of the plot, but the effects of her abuse, which includes "blows, threats, and profane and brutal language," are immediately apparent in Gerty's ragged appearance and violent temper (3). The setting also contributes to Gerty's hardship. She languishes in a filthy section of Boston, an environment antithetical to the child's healthy development. By the end of the day, the city streets are "growing dark," whereas "in the open country it would be light for half an hour or more." Dirt and poverty keep company, with the narrator noting that the snow, "mixed with the mud and filth which abound in those neighborhoods where the poor are crowded together . . . had lost all its purity" (1). Cummins's graphic opening demonstrates what readers of popular fiction well knew: in the Jacksonian era, unprecedented demographic and geographic expansion caused by immigration, urbanization, slavery, and the growing divide between classes threatened the social order. Americans were all too familiar with these conditions and understood, as Emily Graham states later in the novel, "how many children were born into the world amid poverty and privation; how many were abused, neglected and forsaken" (57).

Nominally in Nan Grant's care, Gerty is becoming a street child, a juvenile category found in the discourse of educators, ministers, and doctors, who maintained the importance of the family in preventing crime. Anxious over social upheavals and their effect on domestic life, experts set out to investigate the early years of delinquents and dependents in hope of identifying the root cause of social problems, as historian David Rothman explains.[24] A disproportionate number of people in the cases Rothman cites suffered parental neglect or family disruption when they were children. Separated from birth parents and afforded no opportunity for adoption, these waifs become society's burden. Gerty is such a child: "no one noticed the little girl, for there was no one in the world who cared for her. . . . She was but eight years old and alone in the world" (1–2). Her birth parents missing and unknown, she is one of many orphans on urban streets evoking middle-class compassion and fear. Gerty's need for adoption reflects not only her personal plight but also middle-class anxieties about economic and social change, and the concern that, as Miss Patty Pace says about the socially disenfranchised, "nine-tenths of them will *always* be poor" (210, original emphasis).

Gerty's appearance and demeanor distance her from middle-class standards of cleanliness and decorum. She is shoeless and "scantily clad, in garments of the poorest description." Her hair is "long and very thick; uncombed and unbecoming," and she displays "features which, to a casual observer, had not a single attraction" (1). Amy Schrager Lang notes the novel's "uneven displacement of class across discourses of race and gender."[25] As Gerty's situation improves, she becomes more physically attractive and ladylike. After she recovers from a fever with the benefit of Mrs. Sullivan's "care and kindness," Gerty is "neatly and comfortably dressed, her hair smooth, her face and hands clean" (22). For now, however, she is both "the worst-looking child in the world" and "the worst-behaved" (2).

Gerty's deplorable condition results from poor mothering, a point figuratively represented when Nan Grant beats her for spilling milk, symbol of maternal nurture. Gerty confirms this lack of nurture when she tells a stranger who turns out to be her birth father, "'I *never* was a child'" (276, original emphasis). However, Gerty is not entirely deficient in the qualities that society values in children. By nature kind-hearted and resourceful, she attempts to reverse the narrative of abuse by rescuing a homeless kitten. As Lang writes, "[t]he kitten elicits a maternal and self-sacrificing tenderness . . . from the otherwise belligerent Gerty"; its rescue signals her "specifically feminine fitness to move out of her deprived and depraved surroundings" (19). When Gerty provides the kitten with a makeshift home, she affirms the notion of adoption as an act of salvation that redeems not only the adoptee but also the adopter. She steps boldly away from Nan Grant's control and relies on her own loving authority. However, when Nan discovers the kitten and hurls it into a pot of boiling water, Gerty reverts to typical behavior when "angry or grieved" over injustice (11). Her violent display of aggression—she hits Nan in the head—is at odds with middle-class values of restraint. Two reprehensible acts—Nan's and Gerty's—open the way for a more gentle form of nurture provided by the kindly lamplighter, Trueblood Flint.

NURTURING INDIVIDUALISM

Trueblood Flint makes a dramatic rescue of Gerty—he "picked up and brought home a little ragged child, whom a cruel woman had just thrust into the street to perish with cold, or die a more lingering death in the alms-house" (349)—and becomes "a father to that child" (21). He knows the significance of such a rescue because he once also experienced homelessness. Orphaned at the age of fifteen, he was displaced from his native New Hampshire to Boston. Eventually, he received help from a "wealthy and generous merchant" and found work as a porter in a large store (14). True's story aligns with that of orphaned male protagonists in literature of the period who, rather than be adopted, remain independent and make their way in the world with the aid of a teacher, benefactor, or mentor. Good-natured, productive, and self-supporting, Flint is nonetheless emotionally damaged by the experience of abandonment: he is "naturally silent and reserved, lived much by himself, was known to but few people in the city, and had only one crony, the sexton of a neighboring church" who is known to be "cross-grained and uncompanionable" (15). Nonetheless, True commits himself to caring for Gerty. As he tells his friend Paul Cooper, the Lord raised him up and provided him with friends when he was "lonesome," "fatherless and motherless." Gerty seems "partikerlerly the Lord's, and I could not sarve him more, and ought not to sarve him less, than to share with her the blessins he has bestowed on me" (21).

With Flint's adoption of Gerty, the novel follows a usual pattern of redemption and reform found in American adoption narratives. Flint's partner in "faithful practice of Christian charity" (41) is Mrs. Sullivan, who exemplifies the feminine qualities of Christian nurture espoused by Bushnell: "She was a gentle, subdued sort of woman, with a placid face, that was very refreshing to a child that had long lived in fear" (18). Sewing in tow, she clothes Gerty, nurses her to health, and embodies the notion that a mother's love "is the highest, the holiest, the purest type of God on earth" (108). Flint, Mrs. Sullivan, and her son Willie form an adoptive family that sets a firm foundation for another adoption by Emily Graham. A cultivated, pious, and wealthy young woman, Emily picks up where Flint leaves off, telling him that they "adopted her jointly" (58). Like Alice Humphreys in *The Wide, Wide World*, Emily offers Gerty the opportunity to become a respectable, middle-class woman.

Gerty's potential for change is signaled by her attraction to light—the glow of the street lamp, the natural luminosity of the moon, and the light "within . . . that shall shine through eternity." Innately curious, she gazes out a window and contemplates metaphysical questions, such as "who lit the star." Her adoptive family helps her to believe that because she is "God's child," Christ will "send man or angel to light up the darkness within, to kindle a light that shall never go out" (4). However, in order to embrace faith fully, Gerty must conquer her major flaw: a "violent temper, which, when roused, knew no restraint" (43). Emily helps her rely on a power greater than herself. Tragically blinded, she teaches Gerty to make virtue of misfortune and to see the world positively as a reflection of God's outlook: "she could not see the world without, but there was a world of love and sympathy within her, which manifested itself in abundant benevolence and charity, both of heart and deed. She lived a life of love. She loved God with her whole heart, and her neighbor as herself" (57). Gerty gains the control that leads to inner peace and calm behavior. When girls at school provoke her to another display of violence, Gerty and Emily revisit the incident involving the drowned kitten. Gerty angrily says, "'Did anybody ever drown your kitten? . . . If they had, I know you'd hate 'em, just as I do,'" but Emily advocates restraint: "'If you wish to become good and be forgiven, you must forgive others'" (62). The scene ends with Gerty taking Emily's words to heart, accepting her prayers, and expressing desire to change.

Gerty's greatest challenge is a tendency toward excessive individualism, of which anger is an extreme expression. Throughout his writings, Bushnell is more critical than approving of the increasingly popular "bent toward individualism" (91), writing, "[h]ow trivial, unnatural, weak, and at the same time, violent, in comparison, is that overdone scheme of individualism, which knows the race only as mere units of will and personal action" (216). Instead, he advocates collaboration and a collective consciousness to rekindle a sense of a "national life, a church life, a family life" (91). After six months with Emily, Gerty exhibits the salutary effects of Christian nurture: she "knew what it was to be thought of, provided for, and caressed" (66). Light imagery is associated with her transformation. Whereas earlier, Gerty playfully tells Willie that if she were rich she would have "great big lamps . . . to make the room as *light*—as *light* as it could be!" (47, original emphasis), she now sits at Emily's knee and "received into her heart the first beams of that immortal light that could never be quenched" (67). Internalizing Christian teachings, she begins to "walk patiently in that path which is lit by a holy light" (72). By the end of the novel, Gerty leads others—in particular, her father—to know that "the [spiritual] light is ever burning on high" (277), and when she receives a compliment from Madam Gryseworth "her whole soul shines" (290).

A Bushnellian notion of community develops from Gerty's and Emily's mutual affection. Benefactor and adoptive parent, Emily is also Gerty's kindred spirit and companion. When the two meet at church, they are immediately drawn to each other. Emily's "sweet voice and sympathetic tones went straight to [Gerty's] heart" (55). Emily is moved by the "tone of Gerty's voice" and is compelled to know her better: "something in the child herself . . . excited and interested Emily in an unwonted degree. . . . The impulse to see and know more of her was irresistible" (57). When Gerty prays for help to overcome her anger, Emily recognizes in Gerty's "struggle" her own battle with blindness, recalling how an unchecked temper "might, in one moment of its fearful reign, cast a blight upon a life-time, and write in fearful lines the mournful requiem of earthly joy" (63). Years later, Gerty remains not only Emily's "sort of adopted daughter" (198) but also her "particular friend" (290).

Gerty learns to repay the act of charity that led to her adoption by helping others. Emily teaches her "the power of Christian humility" (73) and provides an opportunity to put faith into practice. In contrast, Nan Grant fails Gerty because she deprives her of meaningful work. Whereas it is not uncommon to see children no older than Gerty "bending under the weight of a large bundle of sticks, a basket of shavings, or, more frequently yet, a stout baby, nearly all the care of which devolves upon them. . . . They were far better off than Gerty, who had nothing to do at all, and had never know [sic] the satisfaction of *helping* anybody" (8, original emphasis). Gerty tidies True's apartment, follows Mrs. Sullivan's example, and learns that to exert oneself "in the cause of cleanliness and order" is also to participate "in the cause of virtue and happiness" (25). Willie gives Gerty a statue of Samuel, based on the biblical child who is dedicated by his mother to faithful service to God (30). Gerty becomes a "faithful little nurse and housekeeper." She "labors untiringly in the service of her first, best friend," inured to others' criticisms and unconcerned with "the outward world," which now "was nothing at all to her" (87–88).

Gerty shows gratitude typically expected of adopted children in nineteenth-century literature and reaps its rewards. Such expressions of appreciation will become problematic for Edith Wharton's heroine in her 1917 novel, *Summer*. Gerty copes with Willie's departure for India, following Emily's injunction that only those who "have learned submission . . . in the severest afflictions, see the hand of a loving Father" (105). She earns a place in the Graham household when True dies, but she is again tested when an embittered servant, Mrs. Ellis, destroys her property. Although only fourteen, she demonstrates forbearance over this injustice and "the first instance of complete self-control" (118). At age eighteen, she helps Mrs. Sullivan and her father, Mr. Cooper, by accepting a teaching position and nursing the ailing family rather than accompany the Grahams on a trip south. This selfless act draws her closer to Willie, who, before he goes abroad, entrusts his family to her care: "'take good care of *our* mother and grandfather—they are *yours* almost as much as mine'" (107, original emphasis). Gerty continues to walk "in the path of duty," earning praise from Emily for her determination "to repay your old obligations" (135). The wealthy but vain Ben Bruce cannot imagine why "an orphan girl, without a cent in the world, would forego such an opportunity" to marry him (206), but Gerty remains committed to service, saying "if there is a person in the world who owes a debt to society, it is myself" (185).

Gerty's adoption succeeds with a combination of nurture and appropriate measures of individualism. She feels "cherished and protected" in Mr. Graham's home and "enjoyed a degree of parental tenderness which rarely falls to the lot of an orphan." The power of nurture is affirmed when she sees "additional proof of the fact that the tie of kindred blood is not always needed to bind heart to heart in the closest bonds of sympathy and affection" (141). The once angry and resentful Gerty can now say that "the world" "has been a good foster mother to its orphan child, and now I love it dearly" (278).

Proper Christian nurture also prepares her for adult responsibility. She acts independently when she resists Mr. Graham's invitation to travel. He "can't see how [the Sullivans'] claim compares with mine" (140), posing the choice as a simple one: to "take care of yourself, or trust to strangers" (146); but Gerty refuses blind loyalty for personal comfort. She intuitively grasps Graham's limitation as a demanding patriarch "not capable of understanding that kind of regard which causes one to find gratification in whatever tends to the present or future welfare of another, without reference to himself or his own interests" (142). She also rejects Dr. Jeremy's pragmatic advice to develop her "independence" so that she might avoid "anybody's hospitality for more than a week or two" (184). Gerty conducts herself in an exemplary way and feels "none of the evils that spring from dependence upon the bounty of strangers" (141). When she chooses Mrs. Sullivan's household over Mr. Graham's, she offers faithful service and acquires quiet strength. She develops "a grace, an ease, [and] a self-possession" (129). As head of the Sullivan household, she finds a doctor, hires a servant, and nurses the dying Nan Grant "with no bitterness or a spirit of revenge" (165). Despite Mr. Graham's displeasure, she remains Emily's "adopted darling" (147) and is referred to as "the life and soul of the place" by the servant Mrs. Prime (148). By the end of the novel, she is "a model to her sex" (358).

ORGANIC FAMILY

Bushnell's progressive views both anticipate modern understandings of child development and make a case for adoption. However, his writings also assert the power of nature over nurture. Like the Puritan model he purports to challenge, Bushnell's theory is rooted in the values of a white, middle class suspicious of anything unlike itself. Adoption provides for basic needs such as food, shelter, and clothing, and emulates God's work by caring for others; but adoptive kinship never fully substitutes for blood ties. Following this direction of thought, *The Lamplighter* reveals its reliance on genealogy and inheritance. This predisposition is evident in a seemingly insignificant remark Nan Grant makes about Gerty: "'I believe she's got an ill-spirit in her'" (12). It also appears in claims that "good taste is inborn, and Gerty had it in her" (47); that Willie and Gerty display a love which is "natural" (48), and that Flint "could not have loved the little adopted one better had she been his own child" (66). More crucially, it is evident in Cummins's resolution of the plot in favor of blood kinship. Gerty benefits from a series of adoptive placements, but in the end, as in European fairy tales, she rejoins her biological father, who has silently watched over her for years. When Gerty's true origins are revealed, her adoptions are undone and her rightful place in the genealogical order is affirmed.

The dual embrace of nature and nurture demonstrates how the novel, as Cindy Weinstein writes, "simultaneously advances an argument in favor of blood not contract even as it seems to give contract not blood the last word."[26] Bushnell promotes a sense of family as a source of God's grace, but he also envisions this family in alignment with nature. The family's "organic unity" derives in part from the fact "that one generation is the natural offspring of another." This fact is undeniable and powerful: "children almost always betray their origin in their looks and features. The stamp of a common nature is on them, revealed in the stature, complexion, gait, form, and dispositions" (97). Bushnell uses the term "organic" to describe not only bloodline but also "a power [that] is exerted by parents over children, not only when they teach, encourage, persuade, and govern, but without any purposed control whatever. . . . Their character, feelings, spirit, and principles, must propagate themselves, whether they will or not" (93).

Because Christian nurture is to begin in infancy and progress toward maturity, children will suffer if nurturing is interrupted. They will not, if left to their own devices, correct themselves. As Bushnell writes, "it is the misery of human children that, as free beings . . . they require some training, over and above the mere indulgence of their natural instincts" (67–68). Bushnell even doubts the power of nurture to counter nature. "How is it possible," he asks, "that the children who are sprung of this distempered heritage, should be as pure in their affinities, as close to the order of truth, as ready for the occupany [sic] of good thoughts, as well governed before all government, as ductile in a word to God, as they that are born of a glorious lineage in faith and prayer and God's indwelling peace." "It is a most dismal and hard lot," he continues, "to be in the succession of a bad, or vicious parentage" (231). Such children stand outside not only the family but also the nation, which is the Christian family "writ in larger and larger letters."[27] In contrast, children of sound stock have an inherent advantage: "it is impossible . . . that the children of a truly sanctified parentage should not be advantaged by the grace out of which they are born. And, if the godly character has been kept up in a long line of ancestry, corrupted by no vicious or untoward intermarriages, the advantage must be still greater and more positive." Children with intact genealogy benefit most from Christian nurture: "how much more such a keeping of inbred grace and faith, in a long line of godly ancestors" (230).

Gerty succeeds through Christian faith and a measure of pluck and self-sufficiency. The novel also advances an argument in favor of faith mixed with materiality. The narrator praises Willie Sullivan, who reads his Bible and is inspired by "a high, a noble, and unselfish motive!" commenting that "those born in honor, wealth, and luxury, seldom achieve greatness" (39). However, even the pious Willie is lured by the possessions of the wealthy and fashionable. He shows Gerty the splendors of affluent urban life along True's lamp lighting route. Whereas conversation "about the church, the minister, the people and the music . . . greatly excited her wonder and astonishment" (43), when Gerty sees the apothecary shop where Willie is apprenticed, her "delight knew no bounds" (44). Even more alluring is the mansion whose fairy-tale opulence Willie and Gerty glimpse through a window: "Rich carpets, deeply-tinted curtains, pictures in gilded frames, and huge mirrors, reflecting the whole on every side, gave Gerty her first impressions of luxurious life" associated with genteel domesticity:

A table was bountifully spread for tea; the cloth of snow-white damask, the shining plate, above all, the home-like hissing tea kettle, had a most inviting look. A gentleman in gay slippers was in an easy-chair by the fire; a lady in a gay cap was superintending a servant-girl's arrangements at the tea-table, and the children of the household, smiling and happy, were crowded together on a window-seat, looking out. (45)

With characteristically American ambition and generosity, Willie and Gerty fantasize about what they will purchase and for whom when they "work and grow rich" (46).

Willie and Gerty attain their dreams by subscribing to a combination of Old and New World values. Willie owes his success not only to the fact that he is enterprising but also to his superior bloodline as the son of an "intelligent country clergyman" (36). Once her birthright is restored, Gerty also enjoys wealth and comfort. Willie staunchly affirms love for Gerty despite her unknown origins, telling Philip Amory that

> You have indeed failed to convince me that Gertrude can in any way be a drawback or disadvantage to the man who shall be so fortunate as to call her his. . . . She has no family, and her birth is shrouded in mystery; but the blood that courses in her veins would never disgrace the race from which she sprung. (358)

However, in the final section of *The Lamplighter*—more like a novel of manners than a romance—European-based, aristocratic manners and fashions compete with democratic, American ones. Gerty has "vivacious originality" and a "vast superiority to most girls of her age" (202), especially the vain Graham cousins, Kitty and Belle. Drawing on European fairy-tale motifs, Cummins depicts her as a Cinderella mistreated by her foster-relatives who emerges victorious when a small-sized India rubber fits her foot perfectly. As an adoptee whose origins are as yet unknown, Gerty patiently bears the insults of the "thoughtless party of fashionables" at the Graham country residence, who call her an "unwarrantable intruder" (247). She comforts Kitty Ray when Ben Bruce rejects her, affirming that "one orphan girl's warm defence of another is but natural" (235), and she refutes Ben's callous view that independence is the most important quality in "a world where people must look out for themselves" (236). Instead of protecting only her own interests, she wins the "cooperation and sympathy" of those who might wish her harm (238).

The novel concludes by affirming blood ties. The reader is prepared for the revelation that Philip Amory is Gerty's father by noting traits the two share: "dark eyes," "a penetrating look," lips that suggest "resolution and strength of will," and a love of walking (258). Cummins also refers to emotional blood ties. Not suspecting that they are related, Gerty is yet conscious of "the strange interest with which this singular man inspired her" (267). From the beginning, their conversation assumes "much ease and freedom from restraint." Gerty "feel[s] confidence in her fellow-traveler" and when he looks at her in "such a benignant, fatherly way . . . she hesitated not to take his offered hand" (268) and "longed to know more of him" (271). Amory acts in a fatherly way, securing rooms for her party in Saratoga (272), quizzing Willie about his intentions for the "unportioned orphan" (353), and rescuing her from a burning boat, with the words, "'My child! My own darling!'" ringing in her ears (336).

Adoptive placements ultimately cannot compare with biological ties. After growing accustomed to being an orphan, "unrecognized, unsought" by her birth family (337), Gerty is elated to discover her roots: "every fibre of her being had thrilled at the thought" that Mr. Amory might be her father (336). Amory underscores the importance of biological kinship and the naming rights it confers when he declares Gerty's adoptive name "a very ugly name, by the way" (352). A hallmark of the romance is the protagonist's ability to rise above circumstances and distinguish herself through her own efforts. Cummins lauds Gerty's resourcefulness and initiative, but the gains facilitated by her adoption lose significance when inherited identity trumps acquired identity. As Lang writes, "the narratives of Willie and Gerty alike turn out to be narratives not of advancement but of recovery, not of mobility but of inheritance: both claim their future by birthright."[28]

In both Warner's *The Wide, Wide World* and *The Lamplighter*, home and marriage are the heroine's destiny and reward. But the novels treat adoption and their heroines' growth differently. The protected and acquiescent Ellen experiences adoption as a means of broadening her horizons. After she experiences cold indifference at Fortune's farm and cloying possessiveness at the Lindsays', she rejects the extremes of both independence and genealogy. Instead she affirms an adoptive identity with the Humphreys that is grounded in tradition. In contrast, the neglected, needy, and angry Gerty stands at first outside the borders of socially accepted childhood. Her adoptive experiences calm her temper, build her faith, and establish an ethos of selfless service. Her excessive independence is finally curbed, however, by inscription in biological kinship. As Lang writes about this ending, "nothing actually changes. No loss is permanent, everything [i.e., parents, children, brothers, sisters] can be recuperated."[29] In both novels adoption is employed to mediate opposing English and American forces. However, Warner's heroine, ostensibly less adventuresome, breaks new ground in defining an American future that is grounded in the past, open to the future, and shaped by adoption.

6

Servitude and Homelessness: Harriet Wilson's *Our Nig*

IN HARRIET WILSON'S autobiographical novel, *Our Nig* (1859), a mixed race girl is abandoned by her mother and taken in by a white family who abuse and exploit her. There is no happy ending for Frado Smith, either through adoption or reunification with her birth family, as there is for countless white children in the fiction of domestic novelists. *Our Nig* demonstrates the limits of adoption for a poor, racially marked Northern child deemed unfit for the middle class. In this, the first African American novel by a woman, child placement is not redeeming but tortuous, offering neither a connection to roots nor a future opportunity.

To narrate Frado's ordeal, Wilson relies on literary conventions of the seduction tale, the slave narrative, and the conversion narrative.[1] She also evokes the tale of indentured service to portray antebellum racism, sexual double standards, and class bias. Indentured service is not the same as adoption, but it was a traditional solution to the problem of orphaned, abandoned, or destitute children in New England.[2] In decline by 1830,[3] indenturing was still practiced in some states well into the twentieth century[4] and remained in legal use until 1917.[5] It resonated with Wilson's own experiences as a domestic servant, which formed the basis for her tale of Frado's trials with the Bellmonts. Wilson would have begun working for the Hayward family around 1830, when the practice still had currency.[6]

By drawing on a literary genre associated with indenturing, Wilson underlines the deep roots of the sort of charity the Bellmonts extend to Frado. Indentured service was a market driven system that usually involved a contract or other mutually understood arrangement that delineated the responsibilities and rights of both parties and that ended after a specific period of time, at which point the indentured individual would be free to earn her or his own living.[7] Frado joins the Bellmont household with no such arrangement and for an indefinite period of time, which Mrs. Bellmont hopes to extend when she warns Frado, upon gaining her freedom, that she will soon wish to be back again. Frado's dependence on the Bellmonts as well as the implied permanence of her situation resembles adoption; however, the fact that Frado labors without renumeration under cruel supervision and neither becomes self-sufficient nor develops a loving attachment to the Bellmonts makes her service closer to slavery. Indeed, blurring the lines between putative freedom in the North and institutionalized slavery in the South, Wilson shows that domestic service can be worse than slavery.

MODELS

Harriet Beecher Stowe's *Uncle Tom's Cabin* (1852) and Wilson's *Our Nig* focus on the same pernicious effects of slavery—the breakup of families—but their geographic focus differs. Stowe's novel demonstrates Southern historical realities: as the expansion of the cotton industry absorbed the investment capital of Southerners, wealth was increasingly situated and realized through the labor and reproductive value of the slaves themselves. Once the profits from cotton rose, the slave's chances of manumission decreased and the chances of families being broken up increased. Hundreds of thousands of African Americans, like the fictionalized Tom, were sold and separated from family members. By 1820, over 1 million Africans had been traded beyond the boundaries of original slave states to Alabama, Mississippi, and Louisiana.[8]

In contrast, Wilson focuses on racism in the free North. State legislators usually granted freedom to African Americans who had served in the Revolution; many freed blacks were able to save enough money to purchase the freedom of others. A gradual abolition process in the North allowed others to gain their freedom. However, blacks took their place behind whites economically and socially. Although Northerners upheld a theory of natural rights that powered abolitionist rhetoric, their call to end racial hostility fell far short of egalitarianism. Inheriting an English concept of race, language, and tradition, they maintained a racialized view of society, fearing both the blurred racial lines suggested by miscegenation and competition in the labor market.[9] Deemed unfit for skilled and professional occupations, free blacks were thought to be naturally "lazy, child-like and immature." A New York merchant even insisted that these laborers be treated as children, under the supervision of adult white guardianship.[10]

Wilson documents the opposition that free blacks faced within a purportedly accepting—but actually hostile—environment. Her depiction of a laboring child who is anything but lazy and yet is unable to exert control over her employment or wages once she reaches adulthood provides a satiric commentary on the treatment of free blacks in North.[11] Wilson asserts in her preface that Frado's "mistress was wholly imbued with *southern* principles" (original emphasis) and suggests her abusiveness in the subtitle: "In A Two-Story White House, North Showing that Slavery's Shadows Fall Even There."[12] Frado is technically free but virtually enslaved by cruel and hypocritical abolitionists. Although she is in need of a home, adoption is never an option, a fact both true of Wilson's time and reflective of adoption practices in the century to follow. Indeed, Wilson anticipates the undesirability of African American "special needs children" in the twentieth-century public welfare system. Such children, Patricia J. Williams writes, are unwanted and disposable.[13]

Wilson's claims were bold for their time and required a new literary form for their expression. In novels such as Susan Warner's *The Wide, Wide World* and Susanna Maria

Cummins's *The Lamplighter*, white middle-class authors use the adoption plot to advance a domestic version of the nineteenth-century American dream. Adoption into a loving family, or its alternative, reunion with the family of origin, affirms familial and social cohesion at a time when society was confronting the unsettling effects of immigration, urbanization, and capitalism. Domestic novels extend the notion of the bourgeois family outward to mutually reinforcing notions of an expanding family and nation. Although these novels acknowledge the difference of class, they seldom take race into account. Stowe, a notable exception, demonstrates, with her depiction of Topsy in *Uncle Tom's Cabin*, that to be adopted and black is to be doubly marginalized in a society that privileges white lineage. Ophelia rescues Topsy from slavery and provides housing and education, but she cannot bring herself to love Topsy or adopt her. Stowe is relatively uncritical of Ophelia's failings. Wilson, in contrast, explores the workings of kinship, class, *and* race to document the failure of the white abolitionist agenda to serve children most in need. As Amy Schrager Lang writes about "the use of race to manage an economic relationship. . . . [T]he orphaned Frado suffers from a homelessness that nothing, it seems, can assuage."[14]

Nor does *Our Nig* describe the escape from servitude found in the slave narrative tradition. Unlike Frederick Douglass or Harriet Jacobs, Frado cannot act independently or benefit from a network of friends or family. African Americans have a tradition of informal methods of kinship adoption that helped to preserve family cohesion in the face of slavery and its disrupting societal challenges;[15] however, Frado has no such support. Unlike post-Civil War novels (e.g., Frances Harper's *Iola Leroy* [1892]) and other narratives of recovery (culminating in Alex Haley's twentieth-century *Roots* [1976]), *Our Nig* describes no "search for roots" or mythic quest. Frado is never more to her adoptive family than a household "nig." Stigmatized by her mother's miscegenation, social isolation, and poverty, she can only bequeath the same legacy to her child. Class and gender play roles in her misfortune, but race trumps both categories. As Frado laments, "I ha' nt got no mother, no home. I wish I was dead" (46); "No mother, father, brother, or sister to care for me . . .— all because I am black!" (75).

Conventions in the slave narrative, orphan's tale, and tale of seduction help to tell Frado's story: both she and her mother are exploited and abandoned as children and seduced as young women. But the tale of indentured service, in which orphans also play a prominent role, is the touchstone for the novel. As Elizabeth Breau notes, the fact that Frado "is not even legally indentured; she is bound by default," allows Wilson to voice outrage "that slavery, or its partner, indentured servitude, can exist among those who congratulate themselves on their moral superiority to Southern slaveholders."[16] When Frado's mother fails to return after leaving Frado at the Bellmonts, ostensibly for the day, the family must decide what to do with their new charge. Mrs. Bellmont declares, "If I could make her do my work in a few years, I would keep her" (26), and Frado is promptly put into service. She is not adopted, nor is her labor legally contracted. Instead, she toils for twelve years without protection or benefit.

The discrepancy between Frado's experience and that of orphaned white children in tales of domestic service is striking. In *Bound Out; or, Abby at the Farm* by Sarah S. Baker [Sarah Schoonmaker] (1824–1926), servitude leads to salvation, both religious and adoptive, when the protagonist is embraced by a family who initially value only her labor. Abby's steadfast service and Christian faith guide her through adversity and bring about the religious conversion of her family. The opposite is true in *Our Nig*. Frustrated in her efforts to find family and faith, Frado remains literally and spiritually orphaned. Unable to overcome the stigma of her roots or race, she leaves the Bellmonts less empowered than when she came and unable to support herself or her son, who is also a victim of racism and social injustice.

MAG'S STORY

Wilson describes the crippling effects of a culture of slavery on three generations: Frado's mother, Frado, and Frado's child. *Our Nig* opens with a story of broken genealogy, as do many domestic novels of the 1850s, including Warner's paradigmatic *The Wide, Wide World*, in which Ellen Montgomery agonizes over leaving her mother. In the first paragraph, the reader meets the "lonely Mag Smith," a white woman defeated sexually, racially, and economically (5). Mag, who is ostracized for bearing an illegitimate child and marrying a black man who has since died, accedes to her common-law husband's suggestion that she abandon Frado in order to ease the couple's financial burden. Before describing Frado's ensuing ordeal, however, Wilson recounts events in Mag's traumatic childhood that led to her abject condition. She draws on the seduction narrative, in which a young woman's loss of virtue is represented as a Christian fall from grace that ends in redemption or in death. However, she also departs from these conventions by emphasizing the role that circumstance rather than character plays in Mag's decision to abandon her daughter.

Mag's fall actually begins in childhood. She is "early deprived of parental guardianship, far removed from relatives." Orphaned and neglected, "she was left to guide her tiny boat over life's surges alone and inexperienced." Early abandonment scars her. Mag "*had* a loving, trusting heart," but without guidance and left "unprotected, uncherished, uncared for," she falls prey to an unnamed "charmer" and false promises of a life "of ease and plenty" (5–6, original emphasis). Pregnant and deserted, Mag is scorned by her community, flees the town, and gives premature birth "among strangers" to a baby girl. When the infant dies, Mag responds with grim practicality rather than faith: she thanks God that "no one can taunt *her* with my ruin" (6, original emphasis). Her reference to the deity is more oath than prayer and one of the first of many expressions of religious doubt in the novel. Equally ambivalent about faith, the narrator at first calls the infant's death fortuitous because the child is illegitimate: "Blessed release! may we all respond.... How many pure, innocent children . . . are heirs . . . of parental disgrace and calumny, from which only long years of patient endurance in paths of rectitude can disencumber them" (6–7). However, the narrator then takes Christians to task for condemning Mag: "How fearful we are to be first in extending a helping hand to those who stagger in the mires of infamy." Self-righteous believers only increase Mag's misery. The narrator asks how many cast off souls "have chosen to dwell in unclean places, rather than encounter these 'holier-than-thou' of the great brotherhood of man!" (7).

The narrator mentions that sins of the fathers are visited upon the children, but it is clear that Mag's problems are rooted in society, not genealogy. Wilson refuses to sentimentalize the infant's death, as do many narratives of the period. She shows that Mag cannot overcome society's negative judgments, even after her child dies and she is free to go on with her life. Although she "resolved to be circumspect, and try to regain in a measure what she had lost," word of her unmarried pregnancy gets out and her "new home was soon contaminated by the publicity of her fall." Disheartened by "some foul tongue [that] would jest of her shame" or by "averted looks and cold greetings," Mag moves again (7). Her dwelling, an ugly "hovel," reflects her self-loathing. Embittered and desperate to preserve her dignity, Mag cuts herself off from humanity. She vows "to ask no favors of familiar faces; to die neglected and forgotten before she would be dependent on any." She ekes out a living, but circumstance again intervenes. Newly arrived immigrants—"foreigners who cheapened toil and clamored for a livelihood"— successfully compete for her job. Consigned to the drudgery of laundry work, she receives occasional offers of better employment from someone in her old life, but the "painful reminder" of former associations only brings more misery (8).

Wilson describes a downward spiral of despair, rage, and alienation. Mag returns from work each day "to her hut morose and revengeful, refusing all offers of a better home than she possessed." Years pass with her "hugging her wrongs, but making no effort to escape" (8). Wilson writes that "[e]very year her melancholy increased, her means diminished." Tackling the subject of miscegenation, Wilson also delivers a critique of race as a socially constructed category. She links two groups in low social positions: sexually disgraced white women and African American men. Mag sinks so low that "at last no one seemed to notice her, save a kind-hearted African." The fact that "no one" except an "African" takes notice signifies that Mag is a nonentity in white society. When Mag and Jim become a couple, her position further deteriorates. This slide into "blackness," or nothingness, begins with sexual transgression, continues with economic failure, and ends in near death. As Mag describes white bigotry: "Folks seem as afraid to come here as if they expected to get some awful disease. I do n't believe there is a person in the world but would be glad to have me dead and out of the way" (9).

Although Mag and Jim love one another, the couple enjoys no happy ending such as found in sentimental romances of the day. Jim wishes to rescue Mag from poverty, but he also knows that marriage to a white woman, even a disgraced one, enhances his value in a racialized economy. He calculates that Mag is "good enough for me" and astutely observes, "She'd be as much of a prize to me as she'd fall short of coming up to the mark with white folks" (11). Complicit in a social order based on skin color, Jim internalizes society's racism and denigrates himself as he attempts to reassure Mag, telling her, "I's black outside, I know, but I's got a white heart inside" (12). Mag likewise understands that marriage to Jim means further degradation. The narrator laments, "Poor Mag. She has sundered another bond which held her to her fellows. She has descended another step down the ladder of infamy." Despite Jim's affection, Mag believes that "nobody on earth cares for *me*" (13, original emphasis).

Werner Sollors notes the mythic significance that nineteenth-century readers attached to black-white intermarriage. White audiences often read representations of interracial couples and their descendants as myths of origins, as "*foundational* stories rather than stories about just *any* couple."[17] Such "primal pairs" appear in Lydia Maria Child's *The Romance of the Republic* (1867), Frank Webb's *The Garies and Their Friends* (1857), and C. W. Mary (Andrews) Denison's *Old Hepsy* (1858). *Our Nig* rejects romantic interpretations of black-white bonds and offers instead an unsentimental, realistic portrait of the marriage. Jim is "truly faithful" (15) to Mag, "proud of his treasure,—a white wife," and "determined she should not regret her union to him" (14). However, poverty strains their love. When Jim falls ill, Mag seems only marginally affected. She "cared for him only as a means to subserve her own comfort." After he dies, Mag continues to suffer. Traditionally, widowhood solidifies a woman's place in society, but Mag feels more, not less, isolated. "A feeling of cold desolation came over her, as she turned from the grave" to face intractable social prejudice against interracial marriage. "She was now expelled from companionship with white people; this last step—her union with a black—was the climax of repulsion." Unnamed sympathizers offer condolences, including "[a] few expressive wishes for her welfare; a hope of better days for her," but these platitudes "were *all* the legacy of miserable Mag" (15, original emphasis). Mag's despair deepens with common-law marriage to Jim's partner, Seth Shipley, who lacks his predecessor's kindness and resourcefulness. Wilson focuses not on the couple's romance but on its economic fragility. Once more "work failed" and means are reduced. "When both were supplied with work, they prospered; if idle, they were hungry together." Wilson unsentimentally shows that poverty is embittering rather than ennobling: "How Mag toiled and suffered, yielding to fits of desperation, bursts of anger, and uttering curses too fearful to repeat" (16). Their bleak union is marked by Mag's decision to move back to her old hovel and, when money is scarce, to abandon her daughter in direct opposition of domestic maternal ideals.

ABANDONMENT

Mag's abandonment of Frado, problematic on many grounds, evokes Hawthorne's depiction of Hester Prynne in *The Scarlet Letter*, published nine years earlier. Both women face disgrace because of sexual transgression and suffer its consequences without fully accepting moral blame. Fiercely independent, Mag "had ceased to feel the gushings of penitence" (16). The scarlet letter, Hawthorne writes, "had not done its office."[18] Both women live on the margins of society, aware of the bigotry that surrounds them. Hester, long after she was obligated to wear the scarlet letter, continues to live in isolation in her small cottage. Likewise, Mag "had no longings" (16), and "[t]hus she lived for years . . . making no effort to escape" (8). However, whereas Hester is a model of motherly devotion and forbearance, compared at one point with the Madonna, Mag relinquishes Frado seemingly without a second thought.

Mag's apparent indifference makes the scene of Frado's abandonment one of the most compelling and chilling in American literature. Such a dereliction of maternal responsibility was inconceivable to white, middle-class audiences that worshiped motherhood on the altar of self-sacrifice. As late as 1899, with Kate Chopin's publication of *The Awakening*, about an affluent white woman who abandons the role of "mother-woman,"[19] demonstrations of maladaptive motherhood could outrage the public. Chopin's novel was censored and her literary career virtually ended. Nineteenth-century adoption stories reserve sympathy for white mothers who are meek, pious victims of poverty, illness, or other misfortunes. Racially or ethnically marked mothers are likely to be depicted as irresponsible, drunken, or immoral. The opposite of the revered mother, Mag is a negative, dark double that makes the positive, angelic aspects of white motherhood possible. By portraying her as enigmatic and monstrous, Wilson acknowledges the underbelly of maternal devotion. "Lurking behind the maternal, Christian ideology of resigned, dogged docility," Stephanie Smith writes about the iconography of nineteenth-century motherhood, "are fires of passionate rage."[20] Wilson's representation of Mag constitutes a critique of constructions of white femininity, which divided women into whores and madonnas and required virtuous women to deny their sexuality and devote body and spirit to indefinite procreation for the good of the nation. As Smith explains, this expectation is "a killing combination, particularly for any woman trapped by slavery, poverty, or an abusive husband."[21] Wilson resists standards of white motherhood that ask women to produce and protect children at all costs.

Mag also stands in juxtaposition to nineteenth-century depictions of African American mothering. Fictional black mothers may abandon their children, or even kill them, as Cassy does in *Uncle Tom's Cabin*, but only under the exigencies of chattel slavery, not in the abolitionist climate of the free North. Mag's relinquishment of Frado runs counter to the behavior of slave mothers, who bore a disproportionately large responsibility to socialize children properly. Although Harriet Jacobs and Sojourner Truth struggle with maternal ties to children who were born of rape, sold away, or termed "bastards" by a Christian slave culture, they endeavor to keep their children close. Rather than escape northward into freedom, Jacobs lives for years in a small attic so that she can see her children, if only through a peephole. Truth uses New York emancipation laws to gain her freedom and appeals to the courts for the return of her five-year-old son. Both rely on community to safeguard their children.[22] In Toni Morrison's *Beloved*, slavery's assault on the family is like a gothic haunting, but kinship is vital, tenacious, and ultimately victorious over circumstance. In contrast, Wilson portrays Frado as "deserted by kindred" (3). When Mag acquiesces to Seth's demand to relinquish Frado, she exhibits no "pluck" or "intrepid resourcefulness" of the kind that David Leverenz finds in Stowe's characterization of Eliza or Cassy.[23]

Mag's passivity also challenges the concepts of nineteenth-century self-reliance. Jean Fagan Yellin and Beth Maclay Doriani note the double bind that African American women such as Jacobs and Wilson faced. They could neither adopt the "conventions of personhood as expressed . . . in the male slave narrative" nor "wholeheartedly embrace the definitions of womanhood that the popular genres of women carried to the American reading public in the 1830s, 1840s, and 1850s."[24] Their projects required narrative strategies of adaptation. Doriani equates the actions of antebellum slave women who display resourcefulness and "take responsibility for the welfare of the children" with those of white males in romantic paradigms. These women are like "the white, male Emersonian hero . . . shapers of their own destinies and responsible for their own survival."[25] Eric Sundquist writes that in a typically American gesture, Frederick Douglass portrays himself as "the self-made man."[26] However, Russell Reising questions this model and points to the limits of Douglass's romanticism in *The Autobiography*. Despite organic metaphors and the embrace of Emersonian transcendence in the notable stand-off with Covey, "nature provides no ultimate foundation for Douglass, no *point d'appui* upon which he can build either a sense of self or his narrative."[27] Ultimately, it is the bonds not of family but of community with other slaves that enable Douglass to imagine and achieve freedom. Mag has no such social framework. Her abandonment of Frado represents both an assault on nature, as understood through Emerson's Transcendentalism, and a failure of community.

Wilson's racialized portrayal of Mag functions, as Smith argues that Stowe's depictions of slave mothers do, to "illustrate the schizophrenia inherent—and still endemic—to that state named 'maternity.'"[28] Racial biases found in nineteenth-century conceptions of motherhood continued through the twentieth century. White mothers, as Melissa Ludtke explains, are traditionally shamed for their motherhood, but black mothers are blamed.[29]

Rickie Solinger notes that through the 1970s white women with illegitimate children were regarded as having made mistakes for which they could redeem themselves by placing their child for adoption.[30] Black women, in contrast, no matter whether they raised their child or placed it for adoption, bore "the unerasable stigma of immorality" that no amount of rehabilitation or redemption could remove.[31]

Mag divests herself of Frado in a brief narrative space, in contrast to pages of tearful mother-child partings in popular sentimental fiction such as Warner's *The Wide, Wide World*. Her abrupt departure mocks the conventions of the nineteenth-century adoption plot, in which white mothers place children with families presumably better able to provide for their children. Throughout *Our Nig*, Wilson rejects a romantic sensibility that elevates suffering associated with family disruption. In *Uncle Tom's Cabin*, Stowe responds to the ravaged genealogies caused by slavery by sanctifying the biological mother-child bond and advocating benevolent foster-parenting of blacks by whites, for example, of Topsy by Ophelia. Stowe holds Cassy accountable for infanticide—chiefly in the form of her confessional narration—and at the end of the novel rewards her with reunification with her children.[32] Wilson offers Mag no such grace. By making Mag more like Stowe's loathed Eva St. Clare than the sympathetic Eliza or Cassy—a woman like Melville's "Bartleby the Scrivener," who would "prefer not to" parent—Wilson rejects sentimental conventions. She does claim for Mag one unspoken privilege of affluent white motherhood: the option to shift the burden of child care onto others.

Mag's abrupt disappearance makes it impossible for the reader to mourn or honor her. It also forestalls any chance of genealogical reconnection. Her name, Mag, evokes another nineteenth-century literary figure likewise named and doomed: Magawisca, the American Indian in Catharine Maria Sedgwick's historical romance, *Hope Leslie* (1824). Caught between the warring Pequods and Puritans, Magawisca defies her father and loses her right arm in an effort to save the life of a Puritan, Everell Fletcher, whom she loves. Her sacrifice produces no personal gain, however. At the end of the novel Magawisca retreats to the wilderness, unable to live either with Indians or whites. Wilson's portrayal of a white mother with a mixed race child viewed only as "our nig" reinforces the bondage of black motherhood enforced legally through slavery, in which the child's condition follows that of its mother. It also presages the essentialist thinking of the century to come. As Sollors points out, under slavery the closest of blood relations could be undermined. Some relatives counted more than others, and "kin relations could be obscured in the name of race, a category that ironically tended to usurp the terms of blood and kinship."[33] This dissonance of race and family appears in a semantic confusion that results when mixed race children are classified as belonging to the purportedly inferior race. Such marking of children continues today. As F. James Davis writes about race trumping parentage in interracial families: "it is as if the child has only African ancestors, as if the white parent's family and white ancestry do not exist."[34] Although she is white, Mag cannot control how society defines or treats her daughter.

SERVICE

Indenturing has a long history in the United States, beginning in colonial times. As a general practice, it dates far earlier. John Boswell claims that in ancient and medieval Europe, most abandoned children were taken in by adults for the purposes of extracting work from them.[35] The American system of indentured service, most representative in the Chesapeake colonies, served a variety of needs. It offered shelter, food, and clothing to poor, illegitimate, and orphaned children who might otherwise become burdens on the community. It also provided labor while giving the indentured individual purposeful work, skills, and improved religious and moral character. New England practices were similar to those in other regions except that New England colonists took care to prevent burdensome individuals from entering their ranks or weeded them out in an attempt to reduce the number of people requiring town assistance.[36] Indentured children did not assume the name of their master, nor were they given inheritance rights. The responsibility of the master ended when the child reached adulthood and received the proverbial $50, a Bible, and two suits of clothing.[37]

Although indenturing was on the decline by the mid-nineteenth century, the practice of "putting out" orphaned or poor children with childless couples or families needing labor appeared on a large scale in the United States with orphan trains, organized by Charles Loring Brace. Trains transported indigent and orphaned children without indenture contracts from New York City to Midwestern and Western farm families from the 1860s to the early 1900s.[38] Some of these children were legally adopted by families and lovingly cared for, but others labored in exchange for food and shelter and experienced varying degrees of abuse or neglect.

Frado's "unofficial indenture," as Gretchen Short writes, is "informed by a long tradition going back to the colonial New England of the seventeenth century which practiced a kind of militantly exclusionary domesticity."[39] It is also consistent with nineteenth-century attitudes toward child placement and labor. Until the beginning of the twentieth century, when the concept of childhood gradually changed from "productive" to "priceless," it was expected that children taken in by families would contribute to the household.[40] These arrangements also represented opportunities for exploitation. Progressive-era reformers disparagingly referred to indentured servitude as "binding-out," connecting it to "the days when slavery and serfdom were tolerated."[41] The practice left many children vulnerable and put female children especially at risk of sexual abuse. Barbara White writes that Wilson was likely abused by the family for whom she worked.[42] Frado is confined and severely beaten, possibly raped,[43] and her skin darkened to accentuate her blackness. Her experiences reflect the abhorrent rather than salutary aspects of contemporary placing-out practices and their historical underpinnings.

American literature provides accounts of indentured service and offers insight into the role of race in setting its terms. For example, Cotton Mather owned slaves and housed a Spanish-Indian girl servant. He was by no means an abolitionist, yet he denounced the brutal aspects of the colonial slave trade and asked Boston residents to examine their consciences and consider whether slaves are "always treated according to the Rules of Humanity? . . . Are they treated as those, that are of one Blood with us?"[44] In *The Negro Christianized* (1706), he reminded slaveowners that "'They are *Men*, and not *Beasts* that you bought.'"[45]

Emphatic on the issue of religion, Mather worked in England and America to promote the Christianizing of black slaves and took specific interest in the spiritual well-being of those dependent upon him. In 1706 parishioners purchased for him a young black man, whom he named Onesimus, after the runaway slave in the New Testament who was converted and became a virtual son to Paul. Mather adhered to clearly delineated expectations and responsibilities for taking in servants and slaves. Kenneth Silverman notes about him and other Puritans, "servants were to be treated as family members—as persons, that is, for whose salvation the householder was obliged to be deeply concerned."[46] In colonial America, denying subordinates access to religion was unheard of. Even the most self-serving Northerners believed that Christianizing slaves would allow them to serve their white masters more dutifully. In contrast to the Bellmonts' treatment of Frado, Mather permitted Onesimus to work outside the house and earn an independent income. Respect for slaves and indentured servants fell short of unconditional trust, however, and Puritans found honorable ways of disencumbering themselves of troublesome charges. Around 1716, annoyed that Onesimus was proving difficult, unreliable, and rebellious, Mather allowed him to purchase his freedom by putting up money for his replacement, a young boy whom Mather named Obadiah.[47]

American literature also provides accounts of indentured service from the servant's perspective. Elizabeth Sampson Sullivan Ashbridge (1713–55), was born in England, married at age fourteen, widowed a few months later, and spent time in Dublin with relatives. Shortly after, she embarked alone for Pennsylvania, intending to locate her mother's brother, but instead she found herself bound as an indentured servant without fully knowing what her contract entailed. She describes the coercive circumstances under which she was forced to pay for the transatlantic crossing:

> The captain got an indenture and demanded of me to sign it, at the same time threatening me if I refused it. I told him I could find means to satisfy him for my passage without being bound, but he told me I might take my choice: either to sign that or have the other in force which I signed in Ireland. I therefore in a fright signed the latter, and though there was no magistrate present it proved sufficient to make me a servant for four years. In two weeks time I was sold, and were it possible to convey in characters a scene of the sufferings of my servitude, it would affect the most stony heart with pity for a young creature who had been so tenderly brought up.[48]

Although Ashbridge and Frado begin their service at different ages, their experiences are similar: both are unwillingly indentured, endure physical abuse, and struggle to keep religious faith.

The damaging effects of cruelty on Ashbridge's body and spirit resonate with Frado's sufferings. Ashbridge writes that her master "was so inhuman that he would not suffer me to have clothes to be decent in, making me to go barefoot in the snowy weather, and to be employed in the meanest drudgery, wherein I suffered the utmost hardships that my body was able to bear."[49] Frado suffers not cold but heat when Mrs. Bellmont orders her hatless so that the sun will darken her skin and exaggerate her difference from the Bellmont family: "no matter how powerful the heat when sent to rake hay or guard the grazing herd, she was never permitted to shield her skin from the sun. . . . Mrs. Bellmont was determined the sun should have full power to darken the shade which nature had first bestowed upon her as best befitting" (39). Ashbridge is disgusted by the hypocrisy of a master who denigrates her while praying and taking the sacrament. Our Nig likewise exposes Mrs. Bellmont's hypocrisy. Twice referred to as a "professor of religion," she nevertheless forbids Frado to attend church, claiming that "religion was not meant for niggers" (68), and seeks to benefit from Frado's Sunday labor (89). Both Ashbridge and Frado struggle with their faith. Ashbridge begins to "believe there was no such a thing as religion, and that the convictions I had felt in my youth were nothing more than the prejudice of education. . . . [N]ow I began to be hardened and for some months don't remember I felt any such thing, so that I was ready to conclude there was no God."[50] Frado likewise believes that "she was unfit for any heaven, made for whites or blacks" (85) and rejects a God who made the Bellmont women white and her black (51). Despite abuse, Ashbridge concludes her narrative by affirming Christian faith. Frado likewise ends by "reposing on God [with whom] she has thus far journeyed securely" (130) although she enjoys few comforts associated with piety or church membership.

Nineteenth-century debate over the servant's place in U.S. society revealed a conflict between democratic ideals and an entrenched perception of deserved Anglo-European hegemony. "A servant," Harriet Beecher Stowe wrote, "can never in our country be the mere appendage to another man; . . . he must be a fellow-citizen, with an established position of his own, free to make contracts, free to come and go, and having in his sphere titles to consideration and respect just as definite as those of any trade or profession whatever."[51] At the time, Stowe's subject was fair treatment of the Irish servant class, which she deemed essential not only for domestic harmony but also for American republican ideals of equality and democracy. However, her egalitarianism had distinct limits. Her "projected assimilation of Irish servants into American domestic economy . . . is not an option for emancipated slaves," as Gillian Brown notes, citing the history of Topsy as an illustration of a black child who remains outside the orbit of "sentimental possession."[52] Brown emphasizes the segregationist aspects of Stowe's reform agenda. In *Uncle Tom's Cabin*, an orphaned black child can become, under the auspices of a well-positioned Northern foster mother, an educated and respectable member of society. But rather than integrate the mature Topsy into white society, Stowe sends her to Africa to live. Stowe's domestic program is decidedly different for whites and blacks, a point Rafia Zafar makes, citing Chloe and Tom's inability to live as free citizens in their home.[53] Confined to an attic or closet, Frado is likewise imprisoned.

By the mid-nineteenth century, religious sentiments congealed around national pride built on a sense of the republic's past as well as its future. However, Americans paid tribute to a collective cultural genealogy that worked against the welfare of black and mulatto children such as Frado, who were of uncertain or scorned lineage. Even Horace Bushnell, noted proponent of childhood nurture, makes heritage a condition of godliness. In *Christian Nurture* he affirms that some races are disadvantaged because they do not have the "long continuance" of the "qualities of education, habit, feeling, and character" that over time "become thoroughly inbred in the [Anglo] stock."[54] Lacking this continuity, Frado can only depend on the Bellmonts' sense of fairness, which is deficient.

Wilson suggests a close connection between the indentured service of African Americans and slavery. Indeed, indenturing of *all* people was decried by many as a form of slavery, although the practice continued for some years after slavery's abolition.[55] African American children were especially affected during the antebellum period, when few options existed for those who needed homes. The Colonial Orphan Asylum, founded in 1836, was the first orphanage for African American children, but asylums were not readily available for African American orphans and orphans of other racial and ethnic minorities until the late nineteenth century.[56] African American children were often considered ineligible for adoption; it was not until well into the twentieth century, with the 1948

Child Welfare League of America Conference on Adoption, that any significant headway was made in expanding the definition of adoptable child to include African Americans or other minorities, or disabled, older, or foreign-born children.[57] Since the colonial days, in lieu of institutional support, African American children were raised in their own communities in extended families, where children born out of wedlock were less stigmatized than white children were in their social groups.[58] Frado, alienated from both the white and African American communities, benefits from none of these supports.

BOUND OUT AND ADOPTED

Sarah S. Baker's *Bound Out; or, Abby at the Farm* (1859) follows a pattern typical of white, middle-class adoption fiction of the period: a child is separated from her home, endures trials in one or more placements, and eventually joins a loving adoptive family, often through religious conversion. In contrast, *Our Nig* describes Frado's abuse in the Bellmont home, her lack of access to Christianity, and her failure to achieve either love or independence. Whereas Abby proves her worth through self-effacement, Frado, in the eyes of white society, has no worth to prove.

Bound Out opens with Abby Blake having spent six of her ten years in an orphan asylum before she is bound out to a farm family for a term of at least eight years. Although she is sad to leave the kind asylum matron and friends "among whom she was a great favorite,"[59] Abby looks forward to her new home and resolves to be a model daughter. Her expectations prove to be too high. Mr. Potter's forbiddingly broad back as he sits in the carriage bodes ill for Abby's new life. "What an important character he was to be to her for some years to come!" the narrator muses, underlining Abby's powerlessness. Despite his indifference to her needs, Abby resolves "to like Mr. Potter; even more, she thought she should love him." She even convinces herself that "he must have taken a fancy to her, or he never would have chosen her out of all the twenty children at the Asylum." The farmer notices only Abby's qualities that will profit him: "her square, well knit little figure, and her broad, strong hands . . . she was a healthy child, and likely to be a good worker—and with this he was satisfied. . . . The fact was, the farmer had not once thought of Abby," so preoccupied was he with "his purchases and his crops, the work he had finished yesterday, and the work he should begin to-morrow" (4–5). The Potters provide food, clothing, shelter, and church attendance in exchange for labor but make no emotional investment in their new ward.

Like Abby, Frado has high hopes for her stay with her new family. She dreams of being adopted and fantasizes that "she should, by remaining, be in some relation to white people she was never favored with before" (28). She marvels at a home more luxuriously furnished than any she has ever seen; passes through "nicely furnished rooms" that are "a source of great amazement"; and contemplates living in such splendor. However, the wished-for "relation" never comes about. Instead of having a room in the main section of the house, Frado is relegated to the attic, a cramped "L chamber" that Mrs. Bellmont deems "good enough for a nigger" (26). This "unfinished" space, with its "roof slanting" and a "small half window" (27) accessible through a dark passage and by a ladder, recalls the dark attic in which Nan Grant locks her ward, Gerty Flint, in Cummins's *The Lamplighter*. Before her rescue by Flint, Gerty is "scolded, beaten, deprived of the crust which she usually got for her supper, and shut up in her dark attic for the night."[60] More prison than refuge, the room evokes spaces associated with slavery, namely, the ship that transported Africans to America and the attic where Harriet Jacobs spends seven years before escaping to freedom.

Both Abby Blake and Frado Smith suffer from their mistress's abuse. Unchecked by intimidated or distracted husbands, Mrs. Bellmont and Mrs. Potter torture their wards under the guise of administering discipline. Abby must answer to the demanding, "shrill" voice of Mrs. Potter (9), who on one occasion confines Abby to the pantry and spies to ensure that she has not stolen food and on another occasion, in a fit of jealousy, cuts off her beautiful long braids. Without her hair, Mrs. Potter tells Abby, "you can comb your hair in less than no time in the morning," and start work earlier (24). Likewise, Frado endures Mrs. Bellmont's verbal and physical cruelty, is denied every pleasure of childhood, and is overworked to the point of ill health. Fearful that Frado's good looks outshine those of her biological daughter, Mrs. Bellmont avoids "the calamity" of a comparison between the two girls by exposing Frado to sunlight to "darken the shade which nature had first bestowed" (39).[61] Both Mrs. Potter and Mrs. Bellmont favor their biological children, whom they allow to bully their charges. Abby is tormented by four-year-old Rehoboam, and Frado by teenaged Mary. Consistent with Zafar's observation that countless slaves "saw wild areas as free zones,"[62] both girls seek refuge out of dors. Abby loves the farm animals (43); Frado finds sanctuary in the woods and spends the night in "a thick cluster of shrubbery" (20).

Despite similarities, there are essential differences in the girls' experiences. Abby suffers from the Potters' ignorance and material ambition rather than from their deliberate cruelty, and her situation improves once her caretakers awaken to their Christian responsibilities. The narrator of *Bound Out* states that hearts are closed to Abby because they are as yet unenlightened by the Bible. In contrast, no amount of time or religion ameliorates Mrs. Bellmont's racist sensibility. Her brutality is as egregious as any found in the slaveholding South.

The heroines also respond differently to adversity. Abby braves her trials with the humility of a true Christian believer. She comes to the Potter farm armed with knowledge of the Bible and unwavering faith: she "had not presumed to think herself better than others: she had given no advice,—she had but loved and lived as Christian" (89). Lacking earthly parents, she turns to a heavenly one. She looks "to the 'God of the fatherless' as her Guide and her Comforter," thinks of herself as God's child, and even finds it possible to thank him for placing her on the farm. In keeping with sentimental conventions, Christian acceptance has the power to conquer social injustice. Abby's active faith eventually halts the march of self-centered materialism bred by capitalism on the farm and begins to right its wrongs. The narrator says that Mr. Potter, intent on business and profits, "would have been . . . astonished to know that some one had been praying in his great covered wagon, where many bargains had been made, and an oath been heard now and then" (6–7). Abby's prayers effect the spiritual conversion of Mr. Potter as well as that of his family and hands.

Abby's capacity for redemptive suffering is clear when her finger becomes infected from a needle prick. She bears the pain silently and faints rather than complain. Mr. Potter responds to this medical emergency and witnesses a prostate Abby. At first relieved that the problem is with Abby and not with his biological son, he then gazes at Abby "lying pale and helpless on the floor" and begins to realize his fondness for her (49–50). Abby's tale of being "bound out" is transformed into a story of being spiritually "bound up" as Mr. Potter dresses Abby's wound:

> [He] had cared for the wounds of many a dumb animal, and his heart had been touched by their sufferings; but when he had bound up Abby's finger, and laid it gently on her lap, he felt tenderly, more tenderly than he could ever have believed possible, towards the little girl whom he had brought home to work for him, much as he would have led a new ox to the stall. (51–52)

The guiding rule in Baker's novel is Christian and democratic: "the first step towards ruling others wisely, is to be able to rule one's own self" (61). No one is more culpable or deserving than another, and all can be saved. When Mr. Potter reads the Bible to his son, "truth came into his own soul" (65) and he embraces Abby as his daughter. As a result, Abby becomes a female version of the American ideal—self-reliant, pious, optimistic, and anchored in domesticity.

In contrast, Frado is frustrated in her quest for family and faith. Whereas Abby surrenders to the will of others and follows the Christian mandate to turn the other cheek, Frado's spunky, "mirthful" (53) personality is temperamentally at odds with the servile role she is forced to play. When reciting her catechism, she challenges James about God, asking, "Who made me so?" "Why didn't he make us *both* white?" (51, original emphasis). When she is permitted to attend services, she does so as "a pleasant release from labor" rather than with a sense of reverence (69). Having internalized Mrs. Bellmont's racism, she "hardly believed she had a soul" (86). She inquires, "*is* there a heaven for the black?" (84, original emphasis). Rather than undergo a spiritual conversion or lead others to faith, Frado persists in believing her "unfitness for heaven" (99). She equates hell with blackness and views death not as a pathway to salvation but as an escape or punishment. She entertains impious death wishes when Mrs. Bellmont beats her, when James dies, and when she falls ill. After Mary dies, Frado feels only a sense of "thanksgiving." She imagines Mary in a hell "as black as I am!" and relishes the surprised look on Mrs. Bellmont's face at such a prospect (107).

Both Abby and Frado receive sympathy from Christian relatives and friends, but Frado benefits little from it in the long run. A farmhand named Bill comes to Abby's aid in *Bound Out*; James and Aunt Abby encourage Frado in *Our Nig*. James believes that Frado's native traits, "if restrained properly, might become useful in originating a self-reliance which would be of service to her in after years" (69). However, like other white characters in the novel, he fails to act on Frado's behalf, denying her fervent prayer for "release" into his custody. The likewise ineffectual Aunt Abby sees "a soul to save, an immortality of happiness to secure" (69) and reminds Frado about "doing good to those who hate us" (80), but she does not work to ameliorate Frado's situation. The climax of Christian tales of indentured service occurs when the protagonist affirms faith and leads others to convert. Frado, unlike Abby, cannot improve herself or others. She becomes resentful and "reckless of her faith and hopes and person" (119) when, after achieving long-awaited freedom, poverty and illness force her return to the Bellmonts.

Unsentimental in her treatment of the Bellmonts' failings, Wilson shows that Christian salvation cannot work alone. It must be accompanied by social justice and self-sufficiency.

Frado progresses only after she leaves the Bellmont home and learns how to make a living by sewing straw bonnets. Then her "devout and Christian exterior invited confidence from the villagers" and she "grows in the confidence of her neighbors and new found friends" (125). When Wilson writes that "[n]othing turns her from her steadfast purpose of elevating herself" (130), she means self-improvement in an economic as well as a spiritual sense. Faith alone cannot set Frado free.

HOMELESS

Even if indentured service is not contractual, it involves mutual obligation. At the end of their terms, indentured servants are prepared to earn their own living. Instead, the Bellmonts make a mockery of the custom of giving two suits of clothing, a Bible, and $50 by giving Frado one suit of clothing, a Bible, and 50 cents. As Frado says about the Bellmonts, "they owe me something," but she cannot make them pay. She leaves their home debilitated, dependent, and unable to support herself.

Frado's story continues in three appended letters. Like prefaces to slave narratives, these documents authenticate the author's claims, generate reader sympathy, and mobilize abolitionist support, but their appearance at the end rather than at the beginning of the text is a "parodic inversion" that suggests Wilson's skill as creative storyteller, not simply autobiographer.[63] The appendices also demonstrate that even though she has reached adulthood, Frado is like a child in need of a home. In the first appendix, a writer identified as "Allida" writes that "truth is stranger than fiction," alerting the reader that Frado's tale is a story in search of a form. Allida settles on the sentimental orphan tale and its happy ending, adoption, but the fit is forced. A grown woman, Frado is finally "adopted" by a kindly woman, Mrs. Walker, who takes her in, nurses her through illness, and helps her obtain work as a hat maker. With Mrs. Walker, Frado enjoys the comfort and security of adoption for the first time. She writes to aunt J—, "I have at last found a *home*,—and not only a home, but a *mother*." As is typical in nineteenth-century adoption fictions, this home is described as a gift of God's mercy that warrants thanks, with Frado marveling, "What shall I render to the Lord for all his benefits?" (133, original emphasis).

Allida writes that Frado is "truly happy" (133), but the plot veers in the direction of the seduction tale when Frado falls in love, marries, and is deserted. Homeless again, Frado moves to the inauspicious County House, not a proper home but an institution, where her son is born in surroundings no better than the attic space to which Frado was consigned with the Bellmonts. The text flirts with the possibility of marital harmony when Frado's husband returns, but after he abandons her without providing for their son, Allida reverts a final time to the sentimental tradition of the orphan's tale. An infantilized Frado is taken in by "a kind gentleman and lady" who help her earn a living by giving her a formula for dying hair (136). Again the formulaic narrative of salvation through adoption fails to reach its proper conclusion when poor health renders Frado unable to work.

Although Allida proclaims the healing powers of home and models Frado's story on the sentimental tale of the white orphan, such as *The Wide, Wide World* or *The Lamplighter*, the novel itself describes disenfranchisement common to African American experience in the context of slavery. The traditional orphan's tale insufficiently describes Frado's experience. A free but abandoned mulatto child living in the North, she is destined not for adoption but for poverty and isolation. The adoption plot, Wilson demonstrates, is of little use to children of color.

At the end of the novel, Frado assumes another role: that of an author seeking a home for her story as well as for herself. This quest is described in the second appendix, by Margaretta Thorn. Like Allida, Thorn emphasizes Frado's juvenile qualities: "The writer of this book has seemed to be a child of misfortune" (138). However, cognizant of racism in a way that Allida is not, Thorn urges readers "not to look at the color of the hair, the eyes, or the skin," and to acknowledge that Frado "was indeed a slave, in every sense of the word" (138–39). Finding readers for Frado's narrative will be difficult, for those who buy her book must also buy her story. That is, they must admit that cruelties such as those committed by the Bellmonts exist in the abolitionist North. They must acknowledge that whereas adoption normally provides a foundation for unbroken lineage of future genera-tions, for Frado or other children living under "slavery's shadows," there is no such gene-alogical cohesion. Frado keeps her child and hopes to raise him, unlike Mag, who abandons her daughter. However, a little more than five months after *Our Nig* is published, the child dies. He is nearly eight, just a little older than Frado was when she arrived at the Bellmonts. With this death, Wilson calls for a different kind of adoption. She asks not white but "colored brethren" to "rally around me a faithful band of supporters and defenders" (3) who will adopt her book and give it a home.

The author of the third appendix, known only by initials, likewise endorses Frado's book, "hoping that its circulation will be extensive." The writer adds, "I hope no one will refuse to aid her in her work, as she is worthy the sympathy of all Christians, and those who have a spark of humanity in their breasts" (140). Because the writer says that Frado's "complexion is a little darker than mine" and "esteem[s] it a privilege to . . . assist her whenever an opportunity presents itself," Henry Louis Gates deduces that the writer's race is white. However, Gates notes that "'C. D. S.' was also a *legal* abbreviation for 'Col-ored Indentured Servant.'"[64] If Wilson intended the latter meaning, she literally uses a mark of indentured service to end her tale.

Wilson draws on conventions associated with white middle-class adoption narratives and tales of indentured service, but she undermines the sentimental aspects of both genres, just as she rejects the emancipatory strategies of the slave narrative and the cau-tionary lessons of the seduction story. Frado's failed adoptions chronicle a reality for antebellum black and mulatto children: their undesirability in a white society. By docu-menting the cruelty of domestic service for African American children and exposing the abuse disguised as discipline that these children face, Wilson, like Stowe, portrays African American children in circumstances that warrant and allow legal adoption. But unlike Stowe, she demonstrates the shallowness of abolitionist rhetoric, for despite putative freedom, Frado is spurned by the white family that can help her and is treated worse than a slave. The felicitous endings found in bourgeois narratives about domestic service and adoption are unavailable to African American children living in the context of slavery.

7

The Limits of Nurture: Louisa May Alcott's Adoption Fiction

LITTLE WOMEN (1868–69) and its sequels established Louisa May Alcott as a leading author of fiction about white, middle-class childhood in the tradition of nineteenth-century domestic novelists such as Susan Warner and Susanna Maria Cummins. Orphans, adoptees, and adoptive parents figure prominently in her work. Although critics debate whether Alcott's plots support or subvert prevailing codes of femininity,[1] few have noticed how her fictional representations of children and naturalized or denaturalized families reveal ongoing tensions in her writing between acceptance and rejection of mainstream social values. The sheer number and range of nonbiological kinship structures in Alcott's fiction point to her awareness of the family as socially as well as biologically constructed and to her enthusiasm for alternatives to the traditionally structured family. Alcott's adoption plots promote an ethos of care consistent with nineteenth-century sentimental reform ideologies and offer a platform from which to deliver a feminist critique of patriarchal family structures. These reconstructed families, however, also express concern that the powers of nurture are insufficient to overcome those of nature.

Alcott commonly presents a view of family as crucial to the formation and maintenance of genteel American society, but she also describes an intimate family unit threatened by corrosive forces from both within and without. Her focus on adoption, a process by which original birth ties are sundered and reconstituted, reveals the extent to which she perceives the naturalized family—even one so idealized as in Little Women—as vulnerable at every point to dispossession and disconnection. Such threats to family safety could be externally motivated: witness the March family on the brink of dissolution without adequate funds or the means to raise them in the context of the Civil War and a materialistic, increasingly aggressive economy from which the key family player, Father March, is absent. Witness also the fragility of patriarchal ties, demonstrated by the fact that the deaths of soldiers in the Civil War left thousands of children technically orphaned, forcing the realignment of biological family structures.[2] Or consider the threat to family integrity generated internally, for example, as emotional attachments become unleashed when the taboos associated with blood kinship are suspended. Such themes of risk and danger run rampant in Alcott's sensational fiction, in which mentors or guardians exploit their power over their usually female, juvenile wards. They also appear in Alcott's domestic narratives: note Jo March's pathological investment in Laurie and its strain on the acceptable limits of brother and sister relations, or motherly Mrs. Jo's projection of erotic desire onto her wayward adoptive son, Dan Kean, in *Jo's Boys* (1886). Applauding family life, Alcott also registers alarm over its vulnerabilities.

Adoptive families in Alcott's fiction perform the same cultural work as most nineteenth-century adoption fiction: they show how the expanded nuclear family serves affective purposes by providing a model of reassurance to a nation uneasy about unprecedented economic growth and demographic change. Her portrayals of adoption also reflect a white, middle-class bias toward biological kinship. Alcott views children as capable of improvement with nurture and education designed to inculcate personal habits such as cleanliness, courtesy, and self-restraint as well as public virtues such as hard work and responsibility. But she is ambivalent about the reaches of reform and, responding to the scientific discoveries of Darwin regarding inherited characteristics, she shows the failures as well as successes of families reconfigured through adoption. Despite adoptive parents' best efforts, she demonstrates, especially in *Jo's Boys*, that some children are critically limited by their biology. Caught between sentimentality and science, adoption benefits adults and children, but the law of nature dictates that some adoptions must fail. The children in these adoptions are as vulnerable and damaged as the most beleaguered victims in Alcott's sensational fiction.

REFORM

Alcott felt great sympathy for the plight of orphans. Her compassion for homeless children developed in part from her experience of being chronically misunderstood and unappreciated in her own family. Although she was not adopted, she was repeatedly encouraged by strong-willed, idealistic parents—a genteel, philanthropic mother and a reform-minded Transcendentalist father—to put her own needs last.[3] Sensitive to the predicaments of those who differ from parents or siblings and feel trapped in environments they cannot change or control, she became active in the support of children, especially orphans. Just as the March sisters are persuaded by Marmee in *Little Women* to practice Christian charity by giving their Christmas breakfast to a poor immigrant family, Alcott absorbed her parents' habit of taking in "lost girls, abused wives, [and] friendless children."[4] As an adult, she visited New York City institutions that helped orphaned and abandoned children, making particular mention of a tour of the Newsboys' Lodging House in an 1875 letter to her nephews.[5] She endorsed the efforts of the Children's Aid Society, which not only sheltered orphans but also sent them to live with rural families in the West. Throughout adulthood, Alcott cultivated an interest in philanthropy and reform informed by feminism. She also experienced adoption firsthand when she adopted her niece, Louisa May (Lulu), after her sister, May Alcott Nieriker, died in 1879. She bestowed all possible maternal affection upon Lulu, writing to Mary Mapes Dodge in May, 1880, that "I fancy I shall feel as full of responsibility as a hen with one chick, & cluck & scratch industriously for the sole benefit of my daughter."[6] In a letter to editor and publisher Horace Chandler, she wrote, "I am more anxious to do my duty by her than if she were my own."[7] Alcott also legally adopted her nephew, John Pratt, so that he could receive royalties from her writing after her death.[8] Adoption routinely appears in her personal, literary, and social agenda.

Alcott's advocacy of adoption as a private as well as public means of doing good aligned with the middle-class values with which she was raised. Adoption integrated an ethos of service instilled by her parents with a commitment to philanthropy mobilized by the perceived threat of juvenile homelessness and waywardness created by immigration and urbanization. Social contexts for adoption could be found in various reform movements as well as in more extreme social experiments in which communities of people aimed to bridge the widening gap between private and public spheres through utopian societies. The preamble to the Articles of Agreement and Association at the experimental community, Brook Farm, with which the Alcotts were involved, announced the intention "to substitute a system of brotherly cooperation for one of selfish competition."[9] John Humphrey Noyes, founder of the Oneida Community, declared his hope of extending the sincerity of the "family union beyond the little man-and-wife circle to large corporations."[10] The idea of adoption as reform also appeared in mainstream discourse. Theologians and educators such as Horace Bushnell outlined a theory of white, middle-class childhood that emphasized adoption-as-salvation and promoted nurture as a means of achieving domestic, religious, and social harmony.[11]

This emphasis on adoption as a means of saving children, although optimistic, reflected social anxiety. Most middle-class writers held to a romantic view of children as inherently good and capable of infinite improvement. However, collective social qualms were evident in the work of reformers such as Charles Loring Brace, founder of the Children's Aid Society. His work, from the late 1850s until the end of the century, documented in his book, *The Dangerous Classes of New York*, generated a complementary portrait of American childhood among the urban underclass. Brace saw his fears for the nation embodied in the bands of street children driven from dirty, overcrowded tenements onto New York streets, where they begged, stole, fought, drank, gambled, prostituted themselves, and spread depravity and disease. He founded the Children's Aid Society and a multitiered system of assistance that included the organization of orphan trains to escort children out of the slums and westward, where they were taken in by waiting families. Brace's primary purpose was to move at-risk children away from their Catholic, neglectful parents and into Protestant farm homes, where their labor would benefit both the children and their families. His plan, although philanthropic, amounted to removal, a term applied to the dislocation of American Indians. Just as whites justified the relocation of the Indian population by branding them savage and civilized, so Brace cited the "wild natures" of poor and homeless children sent westward.[12]

Brace's rhetoric reveals a sense of urgent threat: he envisioned growing bands of roaming boys, "an unconscious society" that endangered the real society.[13] What will happen, Brace worried, when this unregulated horde of boys, already well versed in combative arts, grows up? He feared for New York City's very survival, writing: "if the opportunity offered, we should see an explosion from this class which might leave this city in ashes and blood."[14] His contradictory assessment of poor or orphaned children as both needy and threatening reveals an overall ambivalence toward adoption in American public discourse. On the one hand, Brace describes animals with "wolfish habits"[15] and violent revolutionaries capable of apocalyptic destruction and the overthrow of an American way of life:

> It has been common, since the recent terrible Communistic outbreak in Paris, to assume that France alone is exposed to such horrors; but, in the judgment of one who has been familiar with our "dangerous classes" for twenty years, there are just the same explosive social elements beneath the surface of New York.[16]

On the other hand, he sees children so neglected and destitute that they require immediate, drastic assistance. As Amy Lang notes, Brace rails against the national threat posed by poor, immigrant, and orphaned children at the same time that he hails the children's American character.[17]

Ultimately, Brace sides with optimism. Unlike their European counterparts, whose identity is "fixed and inherited," American street children are malleable. Their criminal tendencies are "not so deeply stamped in the blood," and they have resourcefulness— what he refers to as the "intensity of the American temperament"—to "overcome all obstacles."[18] As Lang observes, "Brace uses nationality to bring class orthodoxy and class heresy into an altogether new relationship: the promise of mobility, widely touted as the foundation of class harmony."[19] "Passionately committed" to education, he believed "the destitute and/or immigrant child was a source of contamination . . . that might be neutralized by retraining," as Claudia Nelson notes.[20] Relocation, which might lead to adoption, was one mechanism by which this social reform could take place.[21]

Brace's adoptive project was rooted in issues of class; his concern for child welfare hinged as much on socioeconomic status as on actual orphancy. In fact, fewer than half the children Brace helped were true orphans.[22] Most had parents who were ill, unemployed, addicted to alcohol, or too disabled by poverty to care for their children. For Brace, the family's economic situation—and middle-class values associated with it—was the deciding factor in assessing the children's emotional and social health. As Lang argues, Brace's insistence on defining poor or neglected children as orphans reflected "a particular understanding of what constitutes a home, an understanding framed by the rapidly consolidating culture of domesticity."[23] A home with an attentive mother and employed father was thought to be the best measure of a healthy family and nation, and the best solution for the containment of class antagonism.[24] Louisa May Alcott shared Brace's outlook about the importance of family and championed, as did he, middle-class domesticity. Unlike Brace, Alcott favored a form of adoption that kept the child close to home and intimate with the mother. When Alcott examined conditions in the asylums established by the Children's Aid Society, she looked for evidence of feminine domesticity and order such as the kind that Mrs. Jo establishes with the Plumfield orphans in *Jo's Boys*. When she writes about successful adoptions, she emphasizes the connections between the child and feminine care.

Alcott's embrace of adoption, a form of activism that demonstrated the triumph of nurture over nature, was but one manifestation of her larger efforts toward revisionist domestic politics. Raised with liberal values, she worked for social reform and challenged the status quo on a number of fronts, including evolution, abolition, Transcendentalism, and, most importantly, women's rights. She was, as Madeleine Stern writes, "a writer sensitive to the cultural and social currents of her time. . . . Always present . . . are examples of the struggle between the sexes, reflecting the rise of feminism."[25] Elizabeth Keyser notes that "the case for Alcott's programmatic feminism can readily be supported by biographical fact and fictional expression."[26] Some of her fictional adoptions are accomplished by traditionally structured families, but in many narratives Alcott portrays successful adoptions by single women or sibling groups. In these stories, adoption grants women autonomy: they choose when and how to parent without the requirement of marriage.[27] As progressive as Alcott's feminist reform agenda is, however, it is deeply embedded in mainstream culture and genteel values. Her vision of reform falls short of radical reconfigurations of family or society.

FEMINIST ADOPTION

Alcott's feminist portrayals of adoption include advocacy for birth mothers, support of female children, and alternatives to traditionally structured families. As Nina Auerbach notes, Alcott's fictional kinship structures are often matriarchal and self-sustaining.[28] Her figurations of family align with the breakdown of patriarchal ideals that Mintz and Kellogg note were well underway by mid-nineteenth century.[29] Relatively few of her adopted children join traditional, nuclear families; a good number find homes with unmarried women or siblings. For example, in the sketch, "My Girls," in the collection *Aunt Jo's Scrap-Bag*, Alcott traces the development of seven young women, one of whom becomes a doctor and, unmarried, adopts a daughter, whom she likewise educates to pursue a vocation. Alcott publicly advocated for unmarried women, whom she describes as "busy, useful, independent spinsters" who chose to be single, "for liberty is a better husband than love to many of us."[30] She often rewards such fictional women by giving them children through adoption and by making their primary adult relationships sororal and fraternal rather than marital.

Even adoption stories that take place within the context of marriage—such as those of Jo and Professor Bhaer in *Little Men* and *Jo's Boys*—depict family structures that are large and communal rather than strictly nuclear. In *Little Women*, Laurie is adopted by his grandfather but becomes a favorite of the entire March family. Later he and Amy provide funding for Jo's Plumfield School, an ambitious enterprise that opens its doors to a wide range of orphaned and needy boys. The self-replicating aspect of Alcott's adoption fiction—many of her adopted children grow up to adopt others—points to her skill as inventor, through literature, of a form of reproduction without men. In the story, "Fancy's Friend," published in *Morning-Glories, and Other Stories*, an orphaned girl who is cared for by Aunt Fiction and Uncle Fact conjures up a mermaid whom she wishes to adopt. In the novel, *Eight Cousins*, Rose, who is raised by six aunts and an uncle, takes an untutored servant under her wing. And in the sequel, *Rose in Bloom*, Rose continues the pattern of adoption by visiting orphan asylums and adopting a baby whose father is in prison and whose mother has died. Alcott often suggests the superiority of maternal adoptive bonds over paternal ones, a belief she herself put into practice: When her sister May died, Alcott's niece Lulu was sent from her father and placed with the Alcott family. "May left me her little daughter for my own," Alcott wrote to her editor and friend, Mary Mapes Dodge, about her adoption of Lulu.[31]

Alcott's feminism also appears in her depiction of female characters struggling with society's sexual double standards. She shows sympathy for scorned or fallen women with sensitive portrayals of birth mothers and with plots that reverse adoption by reuniting the child with this mother. Alcott is especially understanding of mothers who, in a story such as "Ruth's Secret" (1856), are ill and poor and have no choice but to place their child with others. She also responds warmly toward women who innocently follow their hearts and become victims of male deceit. "A New Year's Blessing" (1856), for example, opens with a disheartened, ill, and disgraced mother pleading with her father to safeguard her daughter. Drawing on a sentimental tradition in which a mother's love is measured by the pain she feels upon separating from her child, Alcott emphasizes the heroism of women willing to relinquish their children to ensure their survival. She likewise describes the child's attachment to this mother, underscoring the strength of mother-child ties.

Many of Alcott's stories show her versatility: she depicts adoption as a permanent placement that heralds fresh starts—a typically American ending—and she depicts adoption as a temporary placement that leads to discovery of lineage—a typically European ending. Some of her narrative solutions favor genealogy and include happy endings such as those found in fairy tales and Shakespearean plays such as *Pericles, The Winter's Tale*, and *Cymbeline*, romances with which Alcott was familiar and that influenced nineteenth-century writers on both sides of the Atlantic.[32] For example, in "A New Year's Blessing," the need for origins is validated when a mother, disinherited for making a forbidden marriage, is forgiven and welcomed back into the family home. The story affirms blood-line, with both the mother and child returning to the father's house and recovering fortune and status.

Alcott also advocates for wronged women in "Little Genevieve" (1856), a lurid tale res-onant with her anonymously published thrillers. In this story, a man seduces a woman and absconds with their child, whom he places in the custody of a stranger. Eventually, the child comes to live with her birth mother, Natalie, a well-known actress who mourns the daughter she believes she has lost forever. Natalie showers Genevieve with love and affection, unaware that she is her biological daughter. Although the duplicitous lover tries to keep Genevieve's identity secret, Natalie learns the truth and permanently reunites with her child. Alcott cleverly writes the plot as both an adoption story *and* a tale about recovery of origins. She shows that a mother's love can be the same for a biological child or an adopted child, but she concludes the story by affirming the primacy of genea-logical connection.

Of Alcott's early stories, none displays the elements of popular nineteenth-century adoption fiction more prominently than "Marion Earle; or, Only an Actress!" (1858). She takes up the cause of two groups of maligned women, orphans and actresses, demonstrates the power of feminine sacrifice, and reaffirms traditional family bonds. When the story opens, Marion Earle, a "friendless and poor" orphan who is *"but an actress,"*[33] is supporting herself and her sister through an acclaimed acting career. When her sister dies, Marion takes in a stranger named Agnes, who is pregnant and has been abandoned by her lover. A conversation over whether acting is a suitable profession for women occurs between a sympathetic male character, Mr. Lennox, and a haughty and wealthy woman, Mrs. Leicester, who callously comments about Marion's grief over her sister's death: "such people [actresses] never feel these things very deeply."[34] Mrs. Leicester turns out to be the mother of Agnes's lover. Her son, Robert Leicester, becomes engaged to Marion, but when Marion discovers that he is the father of Agnes's child, she breaks her engagement and insists that Robert marry Agnes. Robert contracts a contagious fever and is nursed by Marion, as well as by Mrs. Leicester, who undergoes a change of heart toward Marion and Agnes. When Robert recovers from his illness, he likewise experiences an emotional conversion and proclaims his love for Agnes and his child. Marion, however, becomes fatally infected with the contagious disease. The tale demonstrates the transformative power of motherly love, as do many domestic fictions of the period. Alcott praises Marion, who is self-sacrificing, in contrast to Mrs. Leicester, who is demanding and self-serving. However, Alcott withholds true happiness from her heroine. Although Marion's adoptive care of Agnes is superior to Mrs. Leicester's indulgence of her biological son, Alcott favors genealogy in the end. Marion dies, and birth parents Agnes and Robert reunite, supported by the birth grandparent, Mrs. Leicester.

Rivalry between birth and adoptive mother figures is also the subject of "Ruth's Secret" (1856). In this tale, an imperious woman named Barbara, who lives with her brother, Robert, hires a young girl, Ruth, as a servant. Although Ruth performs her duties conscientiously and cheerfully, Barbara is annoyed that Ruth refuses to explain why she stays up working late or whom she visits in her free hours. Obsessed with knowing Ruth's secret, Barbara enlists Robert's help. Robert learns that Ruth secretly cares for her dissipated mother, who is coincidentally the friend Barbara wronged years ago when the two women loved the same man. When the suitor chose Ruth's mother, Barbara sought revenge and fabricated lies that led to her rival's disinheritance and poverty. After the wronged woman's husband and all of her children except for Ruth died, the distraught widow turned to alcohol and ruined her health. She dies shortly after Robert visits her. When Barbara hears this story from Robert, who is in love with Ruth, she feels remorse. Barbara conquers her ancient jealousy and blesses Robert and Ruth's marriage, thus correcting the wrong she committed against Ruth's mother. Alcott portrays Ruth, orphaned for a brief time, as the redemptive force that heals Barbara's jealousy. She portrays Robert, an adoptive father who becomes Ruth's husband, as saving Ruth twice, once through adoption and once through marriage.

"Ruth's Secret" explores a vexed issue in nineteenth-century adoption literature: the fact that some female adoptees marry their adoptive fathers. In this and other early stories, Alcott portrays the guardian-turned-husband plot as beneficial for all concerned. However, by the end of the century, in particular in Edith Wharton's novel *Summer* (1917), this plot is presented more realistically, as incest. In Alcott's "Bertha" (1856), an orphaned child is taken in by two brothers, who both love her. When one is killed in a duel, the other one courts Bertha; the surviving brother and Bertha happily marry at the end of the story. The lines between father and husband are also happily erased in "Love and Self-Love" (1860). In this tale, a woman who cares for a sixteen-year-old girl named Effie is dying. She asks the narrator, Basil Ventnor, to help by either adopting the girl or marrying her. The elderly narrator decides to marry Effie, even though he loves another woman, with whom he begins an affair after the marriage. The emotionally wounded Effie remains steadfast in her love and eventually wins her husband back. In both "Bertha" and "Love and Self-Love," the roles of father and suitor conflate in sentimental, unproblematic portrayals of adoption and marriage. These plots raise questions about the extent of Alcott's feminism. On the one hand, she defends female adoptees by revealing their limited choices: they must make the transition from father to husband without ever leaving home. On the other hand, she portrays marriage to an adoptive father as the best possible outcome for her characters.

The adoption-to-marriage theme acquires sinister overtones in thrillers published during the 1860s, in which male guardianship is akin to abduction. For example, in *Moods*, a guardian holds his niece, a presumed orphan, captive in his home. The heroine hears warnings from her mother, who is also imprisoned, and by heeding them manages to escape. *Moods* contrasts the abusive power of the adoptive uncle with the innocent vulnerability of the adoptee, dramatizing the perils for girls inherent in patriarchal family structures. In *Moods*, both adoption and marriage are forms of Gothic imprisonment. Alcott's portrayals of the master-slave dynamic met a popular demand for the lurid, but they also reflect a personal melodrama: the battle of wills between father and daughter that developed when Alcott herself rebelled against the tyranny of her father's utopian ideals. Her sensational stories affirm the kind of life of which father would certainly disapprove,[35] but these narratives also open a space for what Elizabeth Keyser calls an erotics of family relations in Alcott's fiction, in which romantic interests extend to mothers and sons and as well as to fathers and daughters. As Alcott herself said, "I'm fond of boys, as you may have discovered, & always want one some where handy."[36] Focusing not on the thrillers but on the *Little Women* books, Keyser notes numerous ways in which Alcott safely inscribes the erotic in her domestic fiction.[37] In *Little Women*, for example, Laurie must become an honorary fifth March sister and follow its ways before he can also be a love object for Amy. His pseudo-adoption allows Alcott to reinforce a bourgeois family system and eroticize family ties without the outright risk of incest.

"PRACTICAL CHRISTIANITY"

A cultural ethos of family as key to social reform developed among upper- and middle-class Americans in the mid-nineteenth century, as historians Charles Strickland and Kathryn Sklar note.[38] Reform was present in the visionary philosophies young Alcott daily absorbed from her Transcendentalist father. Her ideas about adoption may have had their source in Bronson Alcott's Fruitlands experiment, which was based on the belief that by making proper families into cultural asylums, the next generation might be saved from poverty and ignorance.[39] However, Alcott had mixed feelings about her father's plan, having suffered extreme poverty as a result of his failure to realize his utopian ideals; she later savagely satirized his efforts in her book, *Transcendental Wild Oats*. It is more likely that Alcott's attitudes toward social reform were based on what she called "a practical Christianity" and the concomitant gifts of "time, sympathy, help."[40] The idea that proper families might open their homes to children of the poor, especially orphans, was also practiced in the Alcott home and witnessed in her reform-minded mother's work at a Boston social service agency from 1848 to 1852. Like Abba, Alcott took a concrete, somewhat conservative rather than ideological approach to reform. She expressed little interest, as did her father, in socialist alternatives to capitalism. She believed in promoting social purity and eradicating polluting vices such as dime novels, sexual promiscuity, alcohol, and excessive greed through the influence of the moral and social elite. And she believed that cultivated women, in particular, had an obligation to regenerate society through the family.[41]

A transformation of faith in the nineteenth century affected attitudes toward adoption and reform. Domestic writers of Alcott's generation turned the theology inherited from seventeenth-century Calvinism into sentimental forms of love and charity, as Ann Douglas has noted.[42] They adapted and secularized the notion of God's salvation by portraying adoptive families as saviors of children. Acting in godly ways, women, in particular, transform their homes into sanctified spaces in which adopted children become objects of salvation and living proof of God's grace. Those who care for these needy or homeless children also reap benefits, as Alcott demonstrates in "The Sisters' Trial" (1856), in which a woman labors faithfully as the governess of a wealthy man's children and is rewarded when he proposes marriage.

Combining Christian charity and feminine care, Alcott also shows how acts of benevolence that originate in a woman-centered family emanate outward to society as a whole. If an orphan enters a home where he or she is not valued or protected—as a servant, for example—Christian lessons might still be learned from the adoptive placement. The story, "Patty's Place," published in *Aunt Jo's Scrap-Bag* (1872–82), demonstrates this interplay of sacrifice and salvation. Patty, a thirteen-year-old girl, waits futilely in an orphan asylum while younger and more attractive children are adopted. She is repeatedly passed over because of her physical deformity and plain appearance. Alcott describes adoption as a process that treats the child as a commodity rather than a being with inherent value: "people who came for pets chose the pretty little ones; and those who wanted servants took the tall, strong merry-faced girls. . . . Nobody guessed what a hungry, aspiring young soul lived in that crooked little body."[43] Eventually Patty is taken in by a family in need of a servant. Like Abby in Sarah Baker's novel, *Bound Out*, the "industrious, docile, and faithful" Patty slaves for the family but receives no love in return.[44] Eventually a spinster aunt helps her relatives realize Patty's value, and at the end of the story, Patty, like Cinderella with whom she is compared, is adopted and rewarded with a loving "place" with her adoptive family. Alcott shows that kindness, honesty, and hard work—qualities romantically associated not only with faithful service but also with childhood itself—win the hearts of indifferent adults. Through adoption, adults come to know God and experience an expansive love that allows them to embrace the adoptee as their own. Alcott's romantic belief in childhood's purifying power appears in her journal: when asked by her father what was God's "noblest work," Alcott's sister responded, "*men*," but Alcott answered, "*babies*. Men are often bad; babies never are."[45]

THE LIMITS OF NURTURE

Alcott's philanthropy revolved around the difference that reconstructed families could make in society, but her magnanimity had limits. If necessary, she knew how to say no. For example, when she was asked to take in one of four children whose mother had died and whose father was a drunkard, Alcott refused, saying, "Lu is all we can manage now."[46] She fictionalizes this episode in *Jo's Boys*, in which Jo sets aside fan mail from "a lady who wants you to adopt her child and lend her money to study art abroad for a few years."[47] Alcott believed that a family should be supportive of adoption but must protect itself from potentially harmful or intrusive influences. She also made distinctions between the worthy and unworthy poor that bordered, in Strickland's view, on the "smug."[48] She held prejudices against certain ethnic groups, such as the Irish, and she preferred lending aid to the temporarily rather than the chronically destitute. She approved of helping those who were most like herself: "needy, but respectable."[49] Her sentiments, like Ralph Waldo Emerson's doctrine of "self-reliance," reflect philanthropic skepticism and received endorsement from popularizations of Darwinism and rising class consciousness.

Alcott's class consciousness affected her attitudes toward adoption. Her fiction reveals faith not only in sentimental self-sacrifice, but also in an increasingly market-driven economy and bourgeois materialism.[50] Even narratives ostensibly emphasizing the spiritual dimensions of adoption have material components. For example, when adopted children join a household, they help middle-class adults take stock of their good fortune—in the form of comfortable furnishings, adequate food, or clothing—and thereby reinforce the status quo. In "The Cross on the Church Tower" (1857), a sickly, bedridden orphan finds comfort from looking out at a cross on a church tower and inspires a struggling, discouraged writer. The narrator begins with a spiritually uplifting message about the boy: "poverty and pain seemed to have no power to darken his bright spirit, for God's blessed charity had gifted him with that inward strength and peace" (214). However, when the writer develops his career by publishing his work and joining the ranks of middle class, the orphan has fulfilled his mission. Likewise, in Alcott's vignette, "Our Little Newsboy," helping a poor but enterprising boy both saves the child and fuels the economy. When a child named Freddy hears about a poor newsboy selling papers, he sympathetically declares, "'If I saw that poor little boy, Aunt Jo, I'd love him lots!'" The narrator responds, not by encouraging the family's adoption of the boy but by asking "busy fathers" hurrying home from work at night to "buy their papers of the small boys. . . . For love of the little sons and daughters safe at home, say a kind word, buy a paper, even if you don't want it." By bringing home the paper rather than the boy, middle-class philanthropists extend charity but also set its limits. The newsboy is left "to sleep forgotten in the streets at midnight, with no pillow but a stone" whereas the middle-class boy rests comfortably at home, satisfied with his family's expression of compassion.[51]

The limits of nurture are also apparent in Alcott's novel, *Under the Lilacs* (1878). A part of the *Little Women* series, it was written during a time of great productivity and in response to readers' demands for more uplifting family stories like those about the Marches. At the time, Alcott was also anonymously writing fiction for adults. For example, she revised and published the sensation thriller, *A Modern Mephistopheles*, in 1877, just months before beginning *Under the Lilacs*. Both tales have ominous overtones.[52] The protagonist, a twelve-year-old boy named Ben Brown, performs with his father in a circus until his father goes West to purchase horses and is reported missing. Mistreated by the circus entertainers, Ben runs away and is informally adopted by the kindly Miss Celia. Celia's Christian influence is so positive that by the end of the novel, Ben prefers his newly found family over life in the circus.

Under the Lilacs extols the virtues of domesticity and features a young protagonist compliant with its requirements. Having known only an itinerant life, Ben feels an occasional urge to wander, but he "is well pleased by all he saw" of Celia's home.[53] His "thirst for information" is satisfied by the education Celia provides (48); he finds solace in church; and he quickly makes friends with other children. Ben's conversion to "respectable" family life is accomplished easily under Celia's tutelage (97, 218), with Ben's rough edges—and his distinctiveness—smoothed out as he learns to be a conventionally pious, well-mannered bourgeois boy. Celia instructs Ben to "forget the harmful part" of his past "while learning to be more like our boys, who go to school and church, and fit themselves to become industrious, honest men" (97). Ben, in turn, determines to "start afresh" (228). Celia, like Jo in *Jo's Boys*, shares qualities with Alcott. For example, she is credited with writing "My Kingdom," a poem that Alcott wrote when she was fourteen, and she owns a house like the one that Alcott purchased for her sister Anna. Ben's broken genealogy and adoption provide the occasion for his moral and social makeover. Ben even comes to view his presumed orphancy as a blessing: "his longing for the father whom he had seen made it seem sweet and natural now to love and lean, without fear, upon the Father whom he had not seen" (115).

Under the Lilacs is a faux adoption story because Ben's father, presumed dead, returns at the end of the narrative to claim his son. In a further emphasis on the value of home, Alcott portrays the father establishing domestic roots. He finds work in a livery stable and eventually marries the widowed woman whose two daughters have become Ben's friends. Alcott makes home so attractive in this novel that even the most inveterate wanderers are drawn toward it. She also glorifies the hearth by repeatedly demonstrating dangers outside its protective circle. The most obvious threat to family structure is the circus, which beckons seductively not only to Ben but also to other children who sneak away without permission to see an afternoon performance. As is typical in didactic juvenile fiction, the children soon regret their disobedience and impulsivity: a rainstorm drenches them; two of them must walk home tired and footsore; and Ben's valued pet, a dog named Sancho, is abducted by a circus performer who dyes the dog's beautiful white coat black and cuts off its tail. Sancho eventually finds his way home to Ben, but his mutilated body and distrust of humans serve as a warning to those who would venture too far from the family circle.

On the one hand, Alcott affirms the sanctity of family in *Under the Lilacs;* on the other, she portrays its fragility. Accidents, or simple forces of nature extracted from a popular understanding of Darwinian notions of competition for survival, threaten to undermine even the strongest bonds: those between parent and child. In the main plot, Ben's adoption occurs as a result of his father's accident, which prevents the father from contacting his son. In a subplot, Celia finds money missing and unjustly accuses Ben before discovering that a mouse is the culprit. A mother mouse has stolen and chewed the bills to make a nest for her babies. She perishes when she is caught in a trap, and her orphaned babies are devoured by a cat. Survival, even when parental bonds are strong, is by no means guaranteed. Celia also tells the children a harrowing historical tale about an Indian attack in which a father who is about to be captured tries to safeguard his daughter by hiding her inside a hollowed tree. Years later, when he is released and returns home to reunite with his family, he locates the tree and discovers the girl's shoe buckles and an arrow, evidence of her death. In this novel, myriad forces and circumstances disrupt birth families and leave children vulnerable.

JO'S BOY

In her early fiction, Alcott validates adoption as a beneficial way to structure a family, even a nontraditional one. In *Under the Lilacs*, for example, none of the family groups is organized with mother, father, and children under one roof, although at the end of novel

Ben is reunited with his birth father. Celia raises her younger brother and Ben alone. Ben's father and Mrs. Moss are single parents, and their marriage produces a blended family of stepparents and stepchildren. Alcott continues to advocate the expansion of families through adoption in her last two novels about the March family, *Little Men* (1871) and *Jo's Boys* (1886). She introduces Plumfield School in *Little Women* when Jo and Professor Bhaer open a school for boys on the estate that Jo inherits from her aunt March. The spirit of the school is philanthropic, idealistic, and American. Jo looks upon her "family as a small world,"[54] a possible allusion to John Winthrop's notion of a family as a little commonwealth. Plumfield School is welcoming enough to include orphaned, poor boys as well as wealthy, fashionable ones. Both adoptive and biological kinship is the norm. Nevertheless, even a school as magnanimous as Plumfield displays a preference for genealogy.

A year after Jo announces her long-held vision for the enterprise, the school is up and running. Five years later it is flourishing, with Jo's own boys, Rob and Teddy, added to the mix of students. Jo has postponed her writing career—which in comparison seems "selfish, lonely, and cold"—for the tumble of large-scale family life.[55] For all of its altruism, however, Plumfield relies on tangible resources. Wealth has built the school and keeps it running. As an experiment loosely akin to Bronson Alcott's Fruitlands venture, Plumfield is described in the romantic language of nature, but Alcott's description links organic growth to a market economy: the school will be "profitable" by producing a "crop," not in grain, but in boys.[56] Poverty may be the starting point for learning life's lessons, but it is never the goal. In Alcott's later fiction, money—and the comfort it provides—becomes essential to acts of selfless service. As Meg comments in *Jo's Boys* about the bright futures of boys who have graduated from Plumfield: "this is the sort of magic that money and kind hearts can work" (1). Plumfield students enjoy "all the advantages that *wealth*, wisdom, and benevolence could give them" (2, emphasis added).

Although the Plumfield curriculum is academic, Jo teaches an elusive quality specific to good breeding, what Alcott refers to as "that better wisdom which makes good men."[57] The school accepts a range of boys, both rich and poor, both orphaned and with living parents. Jo assumes the roles of mother, instructor, comforter, and confidante to all of them. A secularized minister, she has "faith in the good spot which exists in the heart of the naughtiest . . . ragamuffin"; endless capacity for "forgiving"; and an ear open to the boys' "confidences" and "penitent sniffs and whispers after wrong-doing." However, she has her favorites. The poor boy rather than the orphan "is the style of boy in which she most delighted,"[58] not because he is the most needy, but because, coming from good, known stock, he has the greatest potential to improve. Jo notes the credentials that have led to Laurie becoming a pride and honor to his family. She points to his worldly success, polite manners, and refined taste as models for her boys: "here you are, a steady, sensible businessman, doing heaps of good with your money. . . . But you aren't merely a businessman,—you love good and beautiful things, enjoy them yourself, and let others go halves."[59] Laurie, in turn, views Plumfield in terms of philanthropic entrepreneurship. As he affirms in *Little Women*: "It's not half so sensible to leave a lot of legacies when one dies, as it is to use the money wisely while alive, and enjoy making one's fellow-creatures happy with it. We'll have a good time ourselves, and add an extra relish to our own pleasure by giving other people a generous taste."[60] The school brings joy to the March family members in large part because it replicates comfortable middle-class values.

When *Jo's Boys* opens, the first crop of boys has graduated, and Amy and Laurie have realized their philanthropic goal: their lives are "earnest, useful, and rich in the beautiful benevolence which can do so much when wealth and wisdom go hand in hand with charity" (19). Plumfield opens its doors at a time of growing class consciousness in the United States, created in part by increases in post–Civil War immigration and urbanization. The nation was in transition from the belief that class is determined by genealogy or roots to a notion of class as a function of achievement. This tension was enacted in Alcott's own family. Her mother was of genteel background, and even in the worst of times, Louisa was reminded never to forget where she came from; her interest in reform and philanthropy developed from a position of entitlement.

A particular experience Alcott recorded in her journal sensitized her to the needs of those less fortunate than herself. When ten years old, she was read a story called "The Judicious Father," about an experiment in inherited and constructed identities such as Mark Twain would explore in *Pudd'nhead Wilson*, in which a slave's child and a master's child are switched at birth. In Alcott's story, an affluent gentleman observes his daughter warning a poor girl not to look over their fence at their beautiful garden. Chagrined at her lack of charity, he makes his daughter exchange clothes with the poor girl. Alcott summarizes the two girls' reactions as well as her own: "The poor one was glad to do it, and he told her to keep them. But the rich one was very sad; for she had to wear the old ones a week, and after that she was good to shabby girls. I liked it very much, and I shall be kind to poor people."[61] Focusing on the lesson that the rich girl learns, Alcott suggests that philanthropy benefits the giver as much as the receiver. By the same token, she suggests that not all poor people are capable of a transformation simply because charity is extended to them. Self-improvement cannot be "put on" like a new set of clothes.

In *Jo's Boys*, the boys at Plumfield who lack inherited status must earn it, but even the most determined boys might not succeed because "people cannot be moulded like clay" according to plan (66). The limited success of characters in humble circumstances demonstrates Alcott's class bias, born of the deep conviction that nurture cannot completely conquer nature. This belief is succinctly stated by Jo's sister Amy, who is sure that Nat, an orphan at Plumfield, is not good enough to marry her biological daughter, Daisy: "Nat was not man enough, never would be, no one knew his family, a musician's life was a hard one" (29). Jo attempts to ease Nat's disappointment by describing a family as a clan. She is oblivious to the wound her words inflict on an orphan with no hope of finding biological kin: "we Marches, though we have been poor, *are*, I confess, a little proud of our good family. We don't care for money; but a long line of virtuous ancestors *is* something to desire and to be proud of" (100, original emphasis). Even though Jo admits that "some of our boys are failures" (321), Nat's story ends happily—as do other narratives of boys who receive adequate family support. Displaying musical talent—a "natural" gift that suggests superior biology after all—Nat is sent by Professor Bhaer to Germany to study with a tutor. After a lengthy "probation" (277), he returns to Plumfield, "surprising the most critical by his progress in music even more than by the energy and self-possession which made a new man of [him]" (321). Having proven himself, he earns the right to marry Daisy; his and "all the [Plumfield] marriages turned out well" (322).

The narrator, promising that "a few words will tell the history of each," explains how the twelve original Plumfield boys has fared (3). The outcomes are mixed, suggesting that neither biology nor adoption alone is sufficient to ensure success. The boys with sponsors, teachers, or relatives do considerably better than the boys without them. Nat flourishes under the Fritz's tutelage. Other boys have blood relations to help them. For example, Franz, with a merchant kinsman, is succeeding in Hamburg at age twenty-six. Emil is sent to sea by his uncle and given a good opportunity by a German relative. Jack is attempting to make a fortune in business with his father. Others, like Dolly, George, and Ned, who are in college and reading law, manage by relying on one another. Some, however, fare poorly. Tom struggles to make a career in medicine although his heart is not in it. Dick and Billy have died, but the narrator forestalls reader sympathy with the fatalistic pronouncement, "no one could mourn for them, since life would never be happy, afflicted as they were in mind and body" (3).

The boy most resistant to Jo's reformist agenda is Dan Kean, a street orphan who first appears in *Little Men* when he is taken in on a trial basis and who is later expelled for organizing a party with cards, beer, and cigars. "A wanderer still" at the beginning of *Jo's Boys* (3), Dan has pursued geological research in South America, sheep farming in Australia, and mining in California. He returns to Plumfield having made a small fortune in mining and ponders his next step. Dan is the most troubled and most romantic of Jo's boys. Although he has the benefit of a Plumfield education, his sense of adventure and wanderlust make it difficult for him to settle on a career path like the other boys do. Dan is fundamentally different, that is, different by nature, and no amount of adoptive care can bridge the gap between his original, wild state and the evolved, cultivated young man that Mrs. Jo and Professor Bhaer wish him to become. In short, Dan is too independent, too severed from genealogical supports, to benefit from adoption.

Of all Alcott's orphans in the *Little Women* series, Dan is conspicuously bereft of kin to help him discover and develop his talent. He has no legacy to draw upon and must invent himself, in a broad American sense. His independent spirit and taste for unsettled lands align him with nineteenth-century heroes such as Cooper's Leatherstocking, but Alcott associates this robust form of masculinity with failure, not success. Her portrait of Dan reflects a growing tension in American literature between glorification of the gentle, compliant, self-sacrificing child and celebration of the adventurer and risk taker. As Alice Fahs points out, at a time when the Civil War played an increasingly large role in the production of children's literature, authors began to change from depicting children in supportive roles such as drummer boys to actually imagining male children as war heroes, capable of major activity outside the family circle.[62]

At the same time, a culture of domesticity in place since the 1830s drew the knot tight between parent and child and warned of the dangers inherent in a child's transition from youth to adulthood. As Mary Ryan explains, writers "construed youth in largely negative, defensive, and moral terms, fearing their sons and daughters would not withstand the shock of entrance into the difficult and corrupting world outside the home."[63] Catherine Beecher's young brother, Henry Ward, spoke of the menaces associated with growing up male in the nineteenth-century United States. Unsuspecting young men were embarking on a world of "snares and temptations"—many located in the cities—populated by "spiders" and "monsters" ready to lure them into saloons, gambling halls, brothels, and dens of iniquity.[64] Beecher implored young men to protect themselves from such temptation by seeking the safety of home. Studies show that the campaign worked. In Hamilton, Ontario, and in Utica, New York, a higher percentage of young people stayed in their parents' homes at mid-century than in the past, the longer period of time under their parents' roof allowing for more moral influence.[65] Alcott joins this group of worriers in *Jo's Boys* with her portrayal of an adoptive mother who insists on her boys' attachment to home.

All the Plumfield boys are depicted as uncivilized beings who must be tamed, but the school works its magic, as Caroline Levander notes about *Little Men*, by having the boys first acknowledge their animalistic nature, a notion derived from Darwin, and then work to remediate it: "By tracking the way the bourgeois family wields sentiment to ensure that even the most 'savage' boys successfully develop into upstanding middle-class citizens, *Little Men* illustrates how bourgeois culture in turn uses the scientific models that depend upon sentiment to construct its values as 'natural.'"[66] Acknowledging their savageness allows the boys sympathetic identification with one another, which is important because they learn "to treat other people as they like to be treated themselves."[67] Reflecting the latest theories, Jo practices the "science of teaching" by knowing which children "to mix" with whom (111). However, her experiment fails with Dan, who, even after a Plumfield education, is "in the rough as yet, and always will be" (84). Dan's unruly nature is at odds with Jo's vision of domesticity. She prefers orphans with kinship or other close ties that maximize the boy's potential for assimilation into the American mainstream. Dan is subjected to the rigors of Jo's domesticating agenda and model of adoption, which derive from theories of science as well from sentimental religion and social reform, but he fails to profit from them.

Dan grows more animal-like, not less. A self-described "wild buffalo," he has a "shaggy black head" and beard (54). He is also a "colt [that] was not thoroughly broken yet" (66) and a cat with "nine lives" (290). His animal nature suggests a discomfiting sexuality at odds with Jo's genteel standards. "I'm glad he's going away," she says about his rugged good looks, "He's too picturesque to have here among so many romantic girls" (84). When Dan's charm begins to affect Plumfield girls, such as Nan and Bess, Jo hastens to forestall any romantic encounters. Dan, like Nat, is deemed unworthy of joining Jo's family. Stressing lineage, Jo fears Dan will become what "she suspected his father had been—a handsome, unprincipled, and dangerous man" (310).

Dan's nonconforming ways are racially as well as behaviorally marked. Although his origins are unknown, Jo "often thought that Dan had Indian blood in him, not only because of his love of a wild, wandering life, but because of his appearance; for as he grew up, this became more striking" (54). Dan challenges Jo when he asks, "What should you say if I brought you an Indian squaw some day?" and seems satisfied with her promise to "welcome her heartily, if she was a good one" (56). But he also understands that Jo believes that Indians are wild, and biology is destiny. She hopes to reform him, but she "feared while she hoped, knowing that life would always be hard for one *like him*" (66, emphasis added).

Dan's values are at odds with the Plumfield's bourgeois ideals. He cares nothing for the money that his small investments in California have made. He contemplates farming and the stabilizing effect that will follow from a prudent investment of his newly won fortune and admits that "a little money sort of ballasts a fellow and investing it in land anchors him" (59–60). However, he has "doubts about it suiting" him for very long (60). The antithesis of a bourgeois materialist, Dan lives in the moment, with a fatalistic sense of the future: "No use to lay up; I shan't live to be old and need it—my sort never do" (55). Money, instead of freeing him, "rather oppressed him" (55). As the "black sheep" of the Plumfield family (322), Dan identifies with outsiders, both the peaceful Montana Indians who are quietly starving because they "don't get their share," and the proud Sioux Indians who are still "fighters" even though the government has cheated them out of their land. His concern for the needy strikes a sympathetic cord in Jo, "for misfortune was much more interesting to her than good luck" (62–63), but there is a difference in their outlooks. Jo's compassion comes from a position of security obtained by birthright whereas Dan experiences life as an outsider. Sadly, he proves to be more like the martial Sioux than the complacent Montana. As he tells Jo, foretelling the crime that will land him in jail: "I get excited, and then this devilish temper of mine is more than I can manage. . . . I shall kill someone some day" (108).

Many nineteenth-century juvenile fictions about the adoption of boys follow a plot line similar to that of *Jo's Boys*: with the help of mentors, teachers, or adoptive parents— and sometimes without these supports—boys set off independently to make their fortunes, their futures hopeful even if unknown.[68] The West, in particular, beckoned: a vast geographic and imaginative space and the source of the United States's bright future. Its meaning for Alcott as a qualified site of riches, opportunity, and independence is evident in a description in an 1875 letter she composed after visiting the Newsboys' Lodging House in New York City. She viewed migration westward positively, but only as one step in a socializing process that also involved hard work, economic fitness, hygiene, and domestic order. These are qualities aligned not with adventure but with feminized bourgeois life. In *Jo's Boys*, Alcott insists that Dan return home again, enveloping him in what Mary Ryan has termed "the empire of the mother."[69]

Alcott's fantasy—of the frontier as finishing school—appears in her description of the daily protocol in the New York shelter for homeless boys. When she visited this facility, she was impressed by the orderly efficiency and upright appearance of the boys:

> Each boy on coming in gives his name, pays six cents, gets a key, and puts away his hat, books, and jacket (if he has 'em) in his own cubby for the night. They pay five cents for supper, and schooling, baths, etc. are free. They were a smart-looking set, larking round in shirts and trousers, barefooted, but the faces were clean, and the heads smooth, and clothes pretty decent, yet they support themselves, for not one of them has any parents or home but this.[70]

One of the boys at the lodge sets an example for others when he goes westward, flourishes, and returns to invite his sister to join him on the frontier. In Alcott's view, the West was not only an antidote for the perils of city life but also a training ground for the acquisition of genteel, bourgeois ideals:

> [A] neat, smart young man came in, and said he was one of their boys who went West with a farmer only a little while ago; and now he owned eighty acres of land, had a good house, and was doing well, and had come to New York to find his sister, and to take her away to live with him. Was n't that nice? Lots of boys do as well. Instead of loafing round the streets and getting into mischief, they are taught to be tidy, industrious, and honest, and then sent away into the wholesome country to support themselves.[71]

Dan's experience is the opposite of this fantasy. During his jaunt in the Wild West, he makes and loses a fortune, kills a man, and aligns himself with Indians. In 1860, in a letter to Alfred Whitman, Alcott describes a quality of boyhood she perceived in herself and sets forth a model for boys in general: "There was always something very brave & beautiful to me in the sight of a boy when he first 'wakes up' & seeing the worth of life takes it up with a stout heart & resolves to carry it nobly to the end through all disappointments & seeming defeats."[72] Dan never manages this integration. His adoption is problematic, and his imaginative return to roots anything but palliative. He is a child who fits nowhere.

Jo presses Dan to join her domestic program. She adjures him to read the Bible not only for his own sake but also "for love of mother Bhaer, who always loved her 'fire-brand' and hoped to save him" (111). She attempts to draw him out with a more romantic narrative. Knowing that it "was always hard for him to show his inner self" because Dan conceals his feelings "as an Indian does," she reads him the story about a volatile character named Sintram who climbs a hill accompanied by Death and the Devil. Jo asks Dan to identify his condition with that of the "danger and sin" surrounding the driven Sintram. She also encourages him to revisit a primal scene of loss involving his father's abandonment and his mother's death. Jo painfully awakens the past by urging Dan to remember "the bad father [who] left you to fight alone" (111).

Little is gained by this guided genealogical journey; Dan only feels more alone. Neither does he derive comfort from Jo's advice to "recollect *your* mother," from whom Jo feels sure "all the good qualities you possess come from." She tells Dan that maternal benevolence is so powerful and encompassing that it extends from beyond the grave, but Dan is skeptical. He tells her, "I don't take much stock in the idea of meeting folks in heaven. Guess mother won't remember the poor little brat she left so long ago; why should she?" (112, original emphasis). At the tale's conclusion, "where Sintram kneels at his mother's feet, wounded but victorious over sin and death," Dan compliantly produces the desired "great tear"; and Jo is "well pleased" to have "touched Dan to the heart's core" (112–13). Just as quickly, however, with a "sweep of the arm," Dan brushes away the tear and Jo's sentimental project, rebuffing her domesticating overtures (113). He remains unreformed, his adoption incomplete. Jo, her heart's desire unfulfilled, is left "clinging fast to her black sheep although a whole flock of white ones trotted happily before her" (322).

Alcott's fiction exhibits an extraordinary commitment to nonhierarchical, charitable, and mutually empowering family relations. Her adoptive families are among the happiest and most satisfying in American fiction in part because they strike a balance lacking in much popular fiction. She reinterprets Calvinism for a romantic age, replacing its patriarchal precepts with sentimental creeds of female-centered sympathy but retaining the importance of effort and duty. She also portrays myriad circumstances under which adoption is undertaken, and she sensitively portrays all three members of the adoption triangle: birth parents, adoptees, and adoptive parents. Adoption has salutary effects for the child, who improves with proper nurturing and education, and for the adoptive parents, who grow spiritually as they help others. At the same time, however, Alcott's representations of adoption reflect a deeply rooted, white, middle-class anxiety about unknown origins. Even the most loving adoptive influences are no match for the forces of nature, which appear with Darwinian intensity in her late fiction. Her philanthropy is based on sympathetic identification and belief in reform; but throughout her fiction, the power of biology, filtered through the lens of race and class, counter adoption's beneficial effects.

8

Charity Begins and Ends at Home: Edith Wharton's *Summer*

THE PLOT OF Edith Wharton's adoption novel, *Summer* (1917), would seem to qualify it for a place in the tradition of nineteenth-century domestic adoption fiction. A five-year-old girl is rescued from a sordid Mountain community and given a home with a childless lawyer and his wife in the New England town of North Dormer. However, Wharton eschews sentimentality by denying her heroine, Charity Royall, the happy ending common to nineteenth-century adoption fiction and the female *Bildungsroman*.[1] Charity enjoys little solace or opportunity as lawyer Royall's ward, and her adolescent hopes for love are dashed when she begins an affair with a young visitor, becomes pregnant, and ends her misadventures with a quasi-incestuous marriage to her adoptive father. Unlike heroines in popular nineteenth-century fiction, whose adoptions illustrate the resourcefulness of the heroine and the flexibility of the family in the context of national expansion, Charity remains uneducated and entrapped in a small, isolated world.

Wharton writes a realistic rather than romantic account of adoption and in so doing sounds the death knell for sentimental portraits of juvenile homelessness. Refusing to idealize adoption or offer her heroine its emotional consolations, she questions a literary tradition that assumes the beneficence of adopters, the gratitude of adoptees, and the equation of adoption and nurture. Wharton's adoptee is alienated and inarticulate, reflecting shifts in literary history toward modernism and corresponding changes in cultural perceptions of childhood.

Sentimentality, a mainstay of mid-nineteenth–century fiction, played a role in "creating full human reality for children" and others who were historically subject to cruelty and neglect, as Philip Fisher argues.[2] However, Viviana Zelizer notes that, beginning in the 1870s, there was a change from the literary figure of the dying child to actual figures of children hurt or dying in accidents. Such a shift was concurrent with literary realism and was "part of a cultural process of 'sacralization' of children's lives" to levels of public policy.[3] Jane Thrailkill likewise observes that the brutalized child is a common image in media today, concluding that the "sentimental has . . . given way to the traumatic."[4] And in a related study, the United Nations High Commissioner for Refugees refers to the twentieth century as a period of crisis for the refugee. Wars and revolutions, decolonization, and economic globalization uprooted and displaced millions of people worldwide, including children, contributing to migrations of unprecedented size.[5] Such displacements, a tragic and traumatic phenomenon of the past 100 years, are interpreted by some scholars as important, constitutory elements of modernity. A child who is sheltered but not legally adopted, Charity is more a modern refugee and trauma victim described by Zelizer, Thrailkill, and the United Nations than an idealized child found in the domestic tradition of fiction Wharton inherited.

Wharton's intention to write a novel different from those of her predecessors, who depict felicitous adoptions or uplifting returns to origins, is well known. She was determined, she writes in her autobiography, to "draw life as it really was" rather than present it through "rose-coloured spectacles" as Sarah Orne Jewett and Mary Wilkins Freeman did.[6] The result is an adoption narrative with neither the healing quality of nurture nor the recuperative power of roots found in novels such as Susan Warner's *The Wide, Wide World* and Susanna Maria Cummins's *The Lamplighter*. Harsh birth circumstances as well as adult self-interest limit Charity's opportunity for fresh starts, leaving her displaced, damaged, and defeated. The struggle to reconcile personal and social identities is a common theme in Wharton's fiction. Many of her most memorable characters—Lily Bart in *The House of Mirth*, Mattie and Ethan in *Ethan Frome*, and Newland Archer in *The Age of Innocence*—fail to balance their own desires with those of conventional family members or peers. *Summer* reflects Wharton's interest not only in environment and the "ethnography of manners" but also in the forces of biology.[7] Battling genetic as well as social aspects of identity, Charity survives her adoptive experience enervated and battle scarred.

Wharton's martial imagery is not accidental. *Summer* bears the imprint of its time period: World War I and the massive relief efforts that Wharton organized on behalf of French and Belgian citizens who lost homes and family during the German offensive.[8] She composed the novel "at a high pitch of creative joy, but amid a thousand interruptions, and while the rest of my being was steeped in the tragic realties of the war."[9] Witnessing suffering and destruction as Germany violated national borders, she reimagined the plight of ravaged European countries through the construction of a young girl's quest for safety, identity, and independence. From the vantage point of war-torn France, in moments stolen from "charities," she crafted "Charity's" story. Charity never fully controls her life and often is at the mercy of others. Reflecting wartime aggression and dislocation, Wharton portrays her adoption as a war zone, with Charity first in the role of a refugee seeking shelter, then in the role of a rebel seeking autonomy.

The war was horrifying for its physical violence and its threat to civilization. To Wharton as well as her compatriots, the unprecedented brutality put an end to the notion of social progress that Victorians had hitherto taken for granted. Charity's drama registers this shift from a mid-nineteenth-century belief in the salutary powers of nurture and reform to an early twentieth-century preoccupation with the hostile forces of nature and science. On the question of whether civilized society could be perfected through social refinement and the control of erotic impulses, *Summer* upholds the rules of biology. From her blossoming sexuality to her pregnancy and instinctive resolve to carry her child to term, Charity acts in accordance with dictates of the body. Adoption, which is predicated on the power of culture and choice, proves to be no match for these biological imperatives.

NEED

Edith Wharton's twenty-eight-year marriage produced no children. However, Wharton expressed a life-long interest in the welfare of the young through her creation of characters adversely affected by poor parenting. *Summer* is Wharton's most fully developed fiction about adoption, but Charity is but one of many vulnerable figures who suffer from unmet emotional and physical needs. Other notably neglected females include the homeless socialite Lily Bart in Wharton's first bestseller, *The House of Mirth* (1905), the naïve Mattie Silver in *Ethan Frome* (1911), the itinerant governess Sophy Viner in *The Reef* (1912), and the displaced Ellen Olenska in *The Age of Innocence* (1920). Homelessness and suspicions of illegitimacy appear in Wharton's biography as well. The last and presumably unexpected child born with two nearly grown brothers, the artistically gifted and intellectually curious Wharton was an anomaly in her society-minded New York family. She was so unlike family members and peers that rumors circulated that she was the illegitimate child of her brothers' tutor.[10] Wharton eventually became estranged from her socialite mother, Lucretia Jones, who demanded conformity to New York conventions and offered scant encouragement for her daughter to pursue her literary ambitions. Wharton alludes to the difficulties of being different from her family in an early short story about adoption.

In "The Mission of Jane" (1902),[11] a prominent New York couple not unlike Wharton's parents adopt a baby girl and become alarmed when the precocious child shows signs, as Wharton did, of being intellectual and independent. Jane attempts to please her parents although she instinctively knows their interests are not her own; her parents struggle in turn to fit her into their mold. The ongoing battle of wills is finally settled when Jane's parents succeed in marrying her off. The fictional marriage has unmistakable parallels to Wharton's life: both courtships are arranged by parents who put their needs ahead of their child's, and both unions trap the bride with an incompatible mate.[12] In Wharton's story, Jane successfully fulfills her "mission," not when she finds her own happiness, but when she facilitates the happiness of her parents. With her marriage, "she had drawn them together at last."[13] Wharton repeats this motif in *Summer*, in which Charity's adoption and then her marriage ostensibly serve her needs but also have the effect of alleviating lawyer Royall's loneliness and bolstering his stature in the town. North Dormer is socially and geographically far removed from elite, "Old New York" society, but in "The Mission of Jane" as well as in *Summer*, adoptive parenting is aligned with self-interest that inhibits rather than supports a young girl's development.

Wharton also explores illegitimacy and adoption in her novella, *The Old Maid* (1924), part of the quartet, *Old New York*. This tale describes a situation Charity might have faced had she refused to marry Royall. Charlotte Ralston is an unwed mother with no resources to raise her child. She secretly agrees to switch roles with her affluent and socially prominent, married cousin, becoming aunt rather than mother to her illegitimate daughter. Unlike Charity Royall, Tina never learns the truth about her origins and is spared the shame that plagues Charity Royall. Instead, Wharton focuses on the embittering effect that relinquishing a child has on Charlotte.

Wharton also explores adoptive kinship in *The Children* (1928), a novel about a cohort of undisciplined waifs abandoned by narcissistic parents, foster parents, and stepparents who are too busy marrying, divorcing, and gallivanting across Europe to attend to their children. Reminiscent of Henry James's *What Maisie Knew*, about a child shuttled between her parents and stepparents, *The Children* focuses on the teenaged Judith Wheater, who, because she is older than the others, is sensitive to the effects of parental neglect. Despite this awareness, however, Judith is naïve about the intentions of Martin Boyne, a man several years her senior who befriends the children and becomes their champion. In a scene reminiscent of the one in *Summer* in which Royall proposes marriage to Charity, Boyne declares his intention to take care of Judith, with whom he becomes infatuated. Judith thinks he is offering to adopt, not marry, her. In the awkward confusion that ensues, a chagrined Boyne departs for South America, setting the Wheater brood adrift again. In this novel, unlike in *Summer*, Wharton draws firm boundaries between adoption and marriage, saving Judith from premature marriage to a father figure. With Boyne gone, she allows for the possibility that Judith will eventually marry a man her own age. In contrast, she limits Charity's options, giving her only a brief chance at romance with Lucius Harney before permanently consigning her to Royall and the stifling town of North Dormer.

Wharton became personally familiar with adoption when she helped orphaned and needy children during World War I. Among her diverse charities were hostels and workrooms for displaced Belgian refugee women and children. Her work was expansive, ably administered, and matched by ceaseless fundraising efforts aimed at an American population still wary of U.S. military engagement. When the war ended and the Belgian government resumed responsibility for the children, Wharton personally supervised the care and education of four boys who had been abandoned by their mother and placed in charitable care by their father, who had been "severely gassed during the war" and could not care for them. Wharton's extensive involvement included signing a formal agreement with the father that made her responsible for the boys' education.[14] Wharton's charities—ambitious and effective—earned such great admiration from the French people that the government recognized her work by awarding her the Legion of Honor. She was the first American ever so honored.[15]

Summer, written during periods of respite from relief work, is a striking example of what critics call the circuitous route by which women document an experience that affected them deeply but from which they were largely excluded. Barred from combat, women faced unique interpretive challenges that often resulted in their choosing to represent violence and aggression obliquely.[16] Wharton wrote that the actuality of war eluded the female observer, who is "a bewildered looker-on" whether she is at home or, in Wharton's case, near the front. The magnitude and devastation of the fighting fueled the literary imagination, its horror "a spectacle" at once abhorrent and stimulating to the artist's eye. Wharton wrote about the "unfolding frieze" of a marching army or a French countryside ravaged by battle while struck by the "utter impossibility of picturing how the thing *really happens*."[17] She was especially distressed by the plight of the large number of displaced and traumatized Belgian and French children. She began composing *Summer* in 1916 as an escape from these horrors in "fits and starts because of the refugees."[18] A sexual coming-of-age story, *Summer* is often viewed in feminist terms.[19] However, Charity's compelling struggle with emergent womanhood originates in juvenile rather specifically feminine vulnerability. Wharton's critical vision of childhood, which developed throughout her career, crystallized at the moment she wrote *Summer*. Her firsthand knowledge of the traumas children face when they are separated from home and family is portrayed in Charity's efforts to reconcile biological and adoptive aspects of her identity.

A prototype for Charity appears in Wharton's *The Book of the Homeless* (1915), a compilation of writings and artwork that she requisitioned to raise funds for her charities. In the preface to the volume, Wharton details the fate of a refugee child who was uprooted from his home and deposited in a new and strange environment in Paris. The boy had been trained as an acrobat in a circus. Separated from his family for the first time, he knew life "only in terms of the tent and the platform, the big drum, the dancing dogs, the tight-rope and the spangles." After being rescued, he was put to work as a page in a large [Paris] hotel. Although he was "given good pay, and put into a good livery, and told to be a good boy," he found it impossible to adjust to his new surroundings. The difficulties of relocation were too great. As Wharton explains, he "tried . . . he really tried . . . but the life was too lonely." The boy's outcome was predictable and regrettable: one night, he stole into the hotel attic, broke into trunks stored by wealthy guests, "and made off with some of the contents. He was caught, of course, and the things he had stolen were produced in court," where he was tried for theft.[20] Wharton ends the vignette with a telling detail: the pilfered items were spangled dresses and embroidered coats, the same kind of clothing found in the circus that he missed so much. These garments represented his only connection to the home he had lost.

The story of the circus boy is a testament to the importance of home and roots. Wharton writes that her vignette is meant to remind readers that those working on behalf of refugees "are trying, first and foremost, to *help a homesick people*." Sensitive to the effects of dislocation, she writes that aid is needed not only "to feed and clothe and keep alive" a displaced population but also "to console for the ruin of their old life a throng of bewildered fugitives."[21] The refugees are stranded individuals longing for their homeland. Wharton's purpose in producing *The Book of the Homeless* was political as well as humanitarian: she was arguing for the need for the United States to end its policy of isolationism and enter the war against German aggression. In so doing, she also documents the psychological stress precipitated by displacement of large numbers of adults and children and the pull of roots that follows these dislocations. These same tensions appear in *Summer*. Just as the circus boy gravitates toward a wardrobe that reminds him of home, so, too, Charity feels drawn to her roots in the Mountain community, despite relative security in North Dormer.

Charity seesaws dangerously, like the disrupted nations Wharton worked to defend, between basic survival and higher states of autonomy. War marked a dividing point in Wharton's consciousness, leading her to question the progress of Western civilization. "Hasn't it shaken all the foundations of reality for you?" she wrote to her friend Bernard Berenson in August, 1914.[22] Likewise, Charity's world divides at the point of her affair with Lucius Harney and out-of-wedlock pregnancy, which causes her to reassess her relationship to herself and others. She is both rescued by lawyer Royall and in a precarious struggle for power with him. Echoed in their troubled relationship is the mixture of gratitude and resentment that characterizes the efforts of weaker nations to preserve their political and cultural integrity in the face of larger, more dominant forces.

Wharton's novel explores two experiences of war: that of the refugee and that of the rebel. Like a refugee, Charity is delivered from dire straits on the Mountain to relative safety in North Dormer. As a rebellious adolescent, she resists the colonizing effects of her adoption and seeks to establish her identity by returning to her roots. This desire for return is consistent with Wharton's understanding of the refugee's experience. Contrary to the assumptions of receiving nations who accept displaced populations, the refugees, Wharton writes in *The Book of the Homeless*, are no "army of volunteer colonists."[23] They are individuals driven from their homeland and seeking to rejoin it. Wharton adds texture to Charity's situation in her depiction of the Mountain people as a group of colonists who voluntarily withdrew from New England society to form their own outlaw community. Moreover, she sets her tale in Massachusetts, the birthplace of a republic that broke away from its birth country and the site of the first battle in the War of Independence. The Mountain people, a subset of the original English colonists at first grateful to the crown and then rebellious against it, continue to wage war for independence. Their history forms the backdrop for Charity's simultaneous quest for origins and freedom.

Charity lives in two worlds. Adoption inscribes her in the small, conventional community in North Dormer, but genealogy connects her to the Mountain folk who form "a queer colony . . . a little independent kingdom" that has "nothing to do with the people in the valleys" and remains "outside [their] jurisdiction." The Mountain people are an enclave of holdouts dating from the railway-building days, conspicuously different from the town residents: "No school, no church—and no sheriff ever goes up to see what they're about."[24] Charity has been raised to scorn her roots, but because she comes from this outlaw nation, she is, as Rhonda Skillern writes, "literally born into rebellion."[25] She is in conflict with both the place of her birth and the place of her adoption, and her difficulties only intensify as she moves from childhood to womanhood. The child Charity carries within her is the fruit of her rebellion, but marriage to Royall legitimizes her pregnancy and inscribes her in conventional patriarchy. Her narrative ends as it begins: in Royall's home and under his domain. Charity has yet to reconcile the biological and adoptive aspects of her identity.

Charity's less-than-optimal domestic arrangements also reflect Wharton's ambivalence about her native American culture and that of her adopted nation, France. The years spent in war relief efforts were but one phase of a life devoted to Europe. In the 1890s, Wharton began making regular trips abroad, immersing herself in European art, history, and culture. Soon she was living permanently in France, enjoying literary and personal freedoms impossible in conventional New York society. When World War I broke out, she committed her energies to the Allied cause, convinced that German aggression not only jeopardized the political autonomy of France and Belgium but also threatened the future of Western civilization. She viewed France as a place of opportunity, "a landscape across which the imagination might follow its own lead, its psychic space free of predetermined expectations."[26] But she also felt the pangs of dislocation, referring to herself as one of the "wretched exotics"[27] who suffer alienation as a result of being culturally transplanted. The novel's troubled ending expresses not Wharton's expansive optimism but her anxiety about this personal and national border crossing. Embedded in Charity's cultural and personal homelessness is the larger question of whether identity is a function of blood or experience. Citizenship, Wharton concludes, is predicated not only on shared commitments but also on genealogical continuity. Just as German aggression during World War

I placed questions of nationalism on the world stage, Wharton's fictional exploration of loyalty as a function of blood or culture situates her novel at the forefront of questions about race and nationhood of her day.

REFUGE

Charity's discontent is signaled in her first, repeated utterance, "How I hate everything!" (159, 162). Having been "ill of a fever," she cannot remember the event that brought her from the Mountain to lawyer Royall's home when she was five years old; she only remembers "waking one day in a cot at the foot of Mrs. Royall's bed" (168). However, she understands that crime and shame play a role in becoming Royall's ward. The child of a convicted criminal and a derelict mother, she was "given" to Royall by her birth father before he began a jail sentence for a violent crime. Taken by Royall as a favor to her father rather than chosen for her own sake, she is a token of exchange between two men in a transaction Gayle Rubin calls "traffic in women." Drawing on Freud and Lévi-Strauss, Rubin writes that such exchanges are essential to kinship systems in capitalist and noncapitalist societies and occur in order to create more male alliances, which in turn limit women's abilities to form their own connections with themselves or one another.[28]

In nineteenth-century fiction, adopted children are expected to appreciate their new families, but Charity has difficulty feeling thankful for the refuge extended to her. The Royalls advertise their benevolence by christening her "Charity," a name intended "to commemorate Mr. Royall's disinterestedness in 'bringing her down.'" The name also serves a disciplinary function: "to keep alive in her a becoming sense of her dependence" (168). As Barbara Katz Rothman notes, the myth of the adopted child as a "chosen" child circulates around adoption and makes an appealing bedtime story, but it accentuates the adopted child's difference from biological children. The fact that the child has been selected among others is intended to make up for the inescapable fact that it was once abandoned. However, the child might ask what it was chosen for and "suddenly parenthood becomes contingent. Chosen for being pretty, sweet, cute, for any given characteristic, means if you lose that characteristic, your chosen status is at risk."[29] Charity feels neither chosen nor cherished despite the fact she "had always been told that she ought to consider it a privilege that her lot had been cast in North Dormer" (161). She is especially ambivalent about acknowledging Royall as the source of her privilege. The neighbor, Miss Hatchard, drills her: "you must never cease to remember that it was Mr. Royall who brought you down from the Mountain" (161). However much Charity would like to comply, doing so means internalizing Royall's negative judgments about her birthplace and herself. The Mountain, outside the jurisdiction of the tiny republic of North Dormer, is a place about which she is "not very clear" except to know "that it was a bad place, and a shame to have come from, and that, whatever befell her in North Dormer, she ought . . . to remember that she had been brought down from there, and hold her tongue and be thankful. She looked up at the Mountain, thinking of these things, and tried as usual to be thankful" (161), but she cannot.

Charity's refugee status is signaled by the first line of the novel: "A girl came out of lawyer Royall's house" (159). Charily lives not in her own home, but in Royall's. This liminal status is underscored by the fact that she was not legally adopted. As an attorney,

Royall can easily file the paper work necessary to adopt Charity. Wharton offers no reason for his failure to do so, but she allows for the possibility that Royall wishes to weaken the normal parent-child bond in order to accomplish the incestuous marriage that occurs at the end of the novel. This being the case, Royall's actions run counter to prevailing thinking about kinship at the turn of the twentieth century. Western nations were tightening controls against incest by end of the nineteenth century. Michel Foucault observes a new politics of procreativity and family governance, noting that "there was a systematic campaign being organized against the kinds of incestuous practices that existed in rural areas or in certain urban quarters inaccessible to psychiatry."[30] Michael Grossberg likewise writes that in the United States an earlier nineteenth-century commitment to individual choice and environment as key aspects in child rearing gave way to a more biologically based reductionism and an emphasis on authoritarian solutions to regulating family life. By the end of the century, medical and scientific arguments motivated passage of new prohibitions banning unions that threatened hereditary lines. Grossberg notes two developments: the number of states banning first-cousin marriages increased, and some states expanded nuptial codes to bring all possible family members, including adopted ones, under the incest ban. As he explains, "Respect for the sanctity of the family grew so intense that even adopted children found themselves under statutory supervision: the new laws prohibited marriages between adopted children and their new parents or siblings."[31] Despite these laws and Royall's power to implement them, Charity enjoys no protection against incest.

North Dormer, with spruces, a white church, and houses arranged in a common, suggests a sense of local community and continuity that Thomas Bender finds typical of New England towns with Calvinist histories.[32] As an adoptee, Charity lacks connection to the town or its history. For her, it is an "empty," exposed place that "lies high and in the open" (160, 159). Known for its annual celebrations of "Old Home Week," North Dormer evokes "Old New York," the society Edith Wharton found likewise stifling as a child. Wharton, unlike her heroine, could appreciate her community's longevity. In *A Backward Glance*, she proudly notes that she descends from venerable Americans who arrived early in the nation's history and established the stock from which her elite society emerged: "on both sides our colonial ancestry goes back for nearly three hundred years." This mercantile society was so settled and secure, Wharton adds, that the American Revolution did "little" to "revolutionize" it.[33] Charity, in contrast, remains alienated. Twice a week she works at Hatchard Memorial Library, named for the town's illustrious author, where she is reminded of a past in which she played no part. She sits under an engraving of the deceased author for whom the building is named and "wonder[s] if he felt any deader in his grave than she did in his library" (162).

Charity is a child of nature, not culture; her quest for knowledge cannot be sated by books. A year earlier, a trip to the town of Nettleton "developed in her a thirst for information that the position as custodian of the village library had previously failed to excite" (160) and for a brief period afterward, she read avidly among the "dusty volumes" in the library in order to improve herself. But once the impression of Nettleton fades, inertia sets in and, with it, timidity. When Charity sees Lucius Harney for the first time, she instinctively retreats into Royall's house with a "shrinking that sometimes came over her when she saw people with holiday faces." She then shyly regards herself in a mirror, over which hangs "a gilt eagle" (159), a symbol of Eagle County and the republic into which she has been adopted. But this watchful bird, reminiscent of the eagle in Hawthorne's "The Custom House," offers no protection. At the library, Harney requests information about "Eagle County," but Charity cannot locate the volume in question, about which she admits to holding a "grudge" (165). Ever the outsider, she is "ashamed of her old sun-hat," "sick of North Dormer, and jealously aware" that her rival Annabel Balch, of Springfield, has a genealogical and geographical advantage over her (161).

The library, rather than serving as a source of nourishment, is for Charity a "prison-house" (162). She flings her hat over a plaster bust of Minerva, ancient goddess of wisdom, and opens the shutters to check for signs of life in a swallow's nest outside the window. She has been monitoring the nest for eggs, more interested in the teachings of nature than of books. Finding nothing, she resigns herself to crocheting lace, the same task performed by Belgian women refugees in the workrooms that Wharton organized during World War I. Like another orphaned laborer, Lily Bart in *The House of Mirth*, Charity is ill suited for her task. "Not an expert workwoman," she crochets "with furrowed brow," chagrined that "it had taken her many weeks to make the half-yard of narrow lace" (162). Ironically, she wraps her handiwork around the buckram back of Cummins's novel, *The Lamplighter*. In contrast to the resourceful Gerty Flint, Charity ends her adventures neither with loving reunion with her birth father nor with marriage to a suitable young man.

Charity's refugee status is complicated by her gender. Wharton knew well the difficult choices women face in a society with double sexual standards and masterfully documents the debilitation that occurs when women must barter their charms and bodies to secure their social position. Such is the premise of *The House of Mirth*, in which Lily, besieged by self-serving materialists, makes a moral choice but fails to save her reputation or herself. It is also the theme of a short story Wharton wrote about World War I, "Coming Home." In this tale, a French woman in a German occupied zone prostitutes herself with a German officer so that she can ensure the safety of her family; it is she rather than her fiancé who fights "at the front" and executes a heroic mission. Wharton describes a similar case of prostitution in her novella, *New Year's Day*, in which Lizzie Hazeldean scandalizes New York, ostensibly for the sake of the husband she loves. In *Summer*, the specter of prostitution looms in the form of Julia Hawes, the disgraced sister of Charity's friend, whose place Charity unthinkingly offers to fill when she encounters the drunken Royall in Nettleton and says to him, "come home with me" (235). Although reciprocity is implied in the statement that "lawyer Royall ruled in North Dormer; and Charity ruled in lawyer Royall's house," the balance of power is not equal. Charity's lack of agency is foreshadowed when, after Mrs. Royall dies, lawyer Royall gives Charity her bedroom, grooming her as a substitute wife. Charity's power is limited: "she knew what it was made of, and hated it" (167).

Royall places Charity in the position of surrogate wife in a form of child sexual abuse prevalent in nineteenth-century fiction. Linda Gordon calls the practice "domestic incest," in which "girls became virtual housewives, taking over not only wifely sexual obligations but also housework, child care, and general family maintenance."[34] The role is aligned with another plot convention outlined by Karen Sánchez-Eppler, in which the child saves the alcoholic adult from ruin. Authors of temperance literature frequently employ the child as a symbol of purity and vehicle of reform that effects spiritual conversion and, in turn, promotes abstinence. However, Sánchez-Eppler notes that the female child performs this function at a cost. In fiction after fiction, the girl is positioned in the bed of the drunken father, showering him with kisses and embraces aimed to calm a potential and often explicit scene of domestic violence. Such portraits of domestic intimacy produce an artificially inflated concept of the child but also render it susceptible to adult abuse, especially sexual abuse of the daughter by the father. Sánchez-Eppler writes, "structured by their own logic of conversion," these temperance stories "make drunks temperate by transforming . . . scenes of pederasty and incest into loving mechanisms of redemption." Although moving, these rescues do "not fundamentally alter the structures of power. . . . [T]he child's love works to enforce a bourgeois patriarchal order that leaves the child as vulnerable as ever."[35] The position of the adopted child is especially precarious. She not only can save the father from loneliness, dissolution, and rage, but she also can legally shift roles from daughter and object of erotic desire to wife.

Charity has long understood her place in her alcohol-ridden family and resigns herself to a sacrifice on Royall's behalf. By the time she is twelve or thirteen, she "had taken the measure of most things about her. She knew that Mrs. Royall was sad and timid and weak; she knew that lawyer Royall was harsh and violent, and still weaker" (168). She anticipates Royall's moods and learns to meet his needs.[36] When Miss Hatchard recommends boarding school for "other" unmentionable reasons that Charity "is too young to understand" (169), Charity complies with Royall's wish that she stay home. When he returns from a school interview with "a black face; worse . . . than she had ever seen him" and angrily asserts, "you ain't going," Charity is "disappointed" (168) but acknowledges her "dependence" (167) on his will. The headmistress's ambivalently worded rejection letter, "under the circumstances," suggests that Royall has sabotaged Charity's candidacy for admission—perhaps by divulging sordid details about her Mountain origins. Charity sacrifices her future again when Miss Hatchard offers to find an appropriate school for her. Charity "cut[s] her short with the announcement that she had decided not to leave North Dormer." She makes this decision for Royall's sake: "she was conscious that he was superior to the people about him, and that she was the only being between him and solitude." Charity "pitie[s] him" and explains, "I guess Mr. Royall's too lonesome" (168-69), whereupon Royall rewards her as a lover might, with the gift of a Crimson Rambler.

Royall's alcoholic indiscretions culminate when Charity is seventeen. The evening begins benignly enough with Royall arriving home from Nettleton elated by a rare success with a case. "In high-good humour" he talks "impressively at the supper-table of the 'rousing welcome' his old friends had given him" (170). However, a stray thought deflates his mood, and he begins to rant against his late wife, blaming her for his lackluster career. An astute Charity "immediately perceived that something bitter had happened to him" and attempts to ward off the inevitable alcoholic binge by hiding the liquor cabinet key. "Experience" tells her (168) to expect drunkenness; it does not, however, prepare her for a knock at her bedroom door. Charity's response is swift and sure. She halts Royall with a restraining arm, saying, "This ain't your wife's room any longer." As he turns away, Charity feels "deep disgust," then "fear," then "consciousness of victory" (170–71).

Charity wins the battle against Royall's advance and is in the position to demand concessions. She bargains events of "that hateful night" to obtain a housekeeper, even though her request "was far less for her own defense than for his humiliation" (176). Her victory is short lived, however. A few days later, Royall counters with a proposal of marriage. She contemptuously refuses his offer, which is proffered more as a command than a question—"I want you to marry me"—and sees him "as a hideous parody of the fatherly old man she has always known" (173). Nonetheless, by the novel's end she will become his wife. Her fate is foreshadowed when Charity seeks a library position in order that she might "earn money enough to get away" (171). "'To get away?'" Miss Hatchard puzzles. "'You want to leave Mr. Royall? . . . I know [he] is trying at times; but his wife bore with him; and you must always remember, Charity, that it was Mr. Royall who brought you down from the Mountain'" (167).

REBELLION

Summer is a coming-of-age narrative with a double quest plot. As a female, Charity seeks romance that leads to marriage and motherhood. As an adoptee, she seeks integration of her dual identities as the adopted daughter of lawyer Royall and the child of derelict birth parents. Lucius Harney is the catalyst for both processes of development: he represents a vibrant, appropriate sexual alternative to Royall, and he offers Charity the opportunity to explore her Mountain culture. Until Harney appears, Charity has vague, negative feelings about her birthplace. The Mountain looms, a "scarred cliff that lifted its sullen wall above the lesser slopes of Eagle Range, making a perpetual background of gloom." "Like a great magnet drawing the clouds," it "cast[s] its shadow over North Dormer" and Charity's troubled aspirations (161). She has a grand but undefined plan to escape and frequently speculates about her relatives on the Mountain. Like the circus boy in Wharton's *The Book of the Homeless* who longs for home, she feels "something in her blood that made the Mountain the only answer to her questioning" (282). Her rebellion against her adoption begins when Harney awakens this native interest.

On the day Harney arrives in North Dormer, Charity is musing about her origins (161). She has tenuous connections to the Mountain through Liff Hyatt, to whom she might be related (186), and through Royall, who assures her that because of his importance, the Mountain people would never harm her (185), but she feels only shame when she thinks of her birthplace. Wharton writes that she "knew nothing of her early life, and had never felt any curiosity about it: only a sullen reluctance to explore the corner of her memory where certain blurred images lingered," but meeting Harney "had stirred her to the sleeping depths. She had become absorbingly interesting to herself, and everything that had to do with her past was illuminated by this sudden curiosity" (187). Harney's enthusiasm for Mountain architecture sparks a sense of pride and prompts her to think of her roots in a new way. When she hears his admiring opinion that the ramshackle houses "must have a good deal of character," she feels a "deepened" and "dawning curiosity" about herself (190). She still "hated more than ever the fact of coming from the Mountain; but it was no longer indifferent to her. Everything that affected her was alive and vivid: even the hateful things had grown interesting because they were a part of herself" (187).

Charity enters a stage of self-absorption that is common to adolescents and especially to adopted adolescents, who, because they are estranged from their biological parents, struggle without clear genetic answers to the question, "Who am I?" The adoptee's bond to the same-sex birth parent is especially complex. Once Harney awakens Charity's curiosity about her roots, her birth mother surfaces in her consciousness as never before: "She had always thought of her mother as so long dead as to be no more than a nameless pinch of earth; but now it occurred to her that the once-young woman might be alive." In closed adoptions, in which children have no knowledge or memory of the birthparents, it is not uncommon for the adoptee to fantasize about the unknown parent. Charity contemplates this mystery mother, imagining her "once young and slight," "wrinkled and elf-locked," like the woman she and Harney meet when they visit the brown house (187). She reaches for details that will connect her, even in a token way, with the mother she never knew. She later acts on one of the few facts she knows about this mother by replicating her out-of-wedlock pregnancy.

Charity's self-exploration is derailed, however, when lawyer Royall violates her privacy by telling Harney her birth story. The story of Charity's adoption is hers alone to tell, but Royall divulges personal details without her consent. Humiliated, Charity hides in silence while the two men engage in after-dinner conversation. "Why the Mountain's a blot," Royall declares, and the people who inhabit it "scum [who] ought to have been run in long ago." He rages "against a gang of thieves and outlaws living over there, in sight of us, defying the laws of their country" and excoriates the authorities for lacking courage to bring the renegade community under local control. In "somewhat technical language" he explains how the "little colony of squatters had contrived to keep the law at bay" and live according to its own rules. As Royall appropriates Charity's story, he inflates his own importance so that he rather than she emerges as the hero of the tale. When Harney asks whether Royall has ever ventured up the Mountain, he answers with bravado, "Yes, I have. . . . The wiseacres down here told me I'd be done for before I got back; but nobody lifted a finger to hurt me" (193–94).

Royall further aggrandizes himself when he describes Charity's birth father as an impulsive, violent man who worked as a logger, squandered his earnings, and fought in a row that caused another man's death. Royall boasts about his successful prosecution of the case. The convicted father judged his defense attorney to be a "'chicken-livered son of a—'" and turned instead to the prosecution for help. Royall quotes the father as saying that Royall was "'the only man I seen in court that looks as if he'd do it.'" As Royall tells it, Charity's birth father was so impressed with Royall that he asked him, the prosecuting attorney, to adopt his child. Royall magnanimously tells Harney that he felt "sorry for the fellow," "went up and got the child," and "reared her like a Christian" according to the father's wishes. Royall then callously dismisses Charity's mother: "Oh, yes: there was a mother. But she was glad enough to have her go. She'd have given her to anybody. They ain't half human up there" (194). Royall places himself at the center of Charity's adoption narrative in order to impress Harney.

Royall's retelling of Charity's birth story reveals an obsession to control renegade behavior. Charity, the child of an outlaw colony, is likewise subject to "Royall" will. As Sandra Gilbert writes, she is "a living manifestation of the father's wealth, the charity to which he is culturally entitled."[37] A child with a "swarthy" complexion (159), she is also the dark other, associated, as Homi Bhabha and Edward Said note in studies of colonialism, with sexual license and made the object of desire in an effort by the colonizer to exhibit and maintain conquest.[38] To assert her independence, she must rebel, as did the American colonies when they formed the republic from which the Mountain people have since seceded. Her bid for independence begins with her attraction to Harney. When they spend a day visiting the Mountain people who live in the brown house, Charity gains access to her birth culture and a lost part of herself. She realizes that the independent spirit of the

Mountain is a resource from which she can draw. She also aligns with nature in defiance of the culturally constructed relationships with Royall in North Dormer. The day of the visit begins "without a cloud" (196). Charity, in harmony with natural elements throughout the novel, feels a "triumphant sense of being a part of the sunlight and the morning" (197). She thinks of Harney in natural terms: as "an undercurrent as mysterious and potent as the influence that makes the forest break into leaf before the ice is off the pools" (195).

Charity's growing self-acceptance goes hand in hand with her increasing trust in Harney. Although this confidence proves misplaced, it helps her temporarily overcome her sense of inferiority. "What did it matter where she came from or whose child she was, when love was dancing in her veins, and down the road she saw young Harney coming toward her?" (197). She continues to wrestle with "shame," wishing Harney not "to see the people she came from while the story of her birth was fresh in his mind." Still, Charity realizes that her Mountain roots have positive value: they grant Harney access to the architectural specimens he wants to see. With "forced defiance" Charity assets that "[h]e'd better know what kind of folks I belong to" (198) and even finds the courage to declare, "[t]hose people back there are the kind of folks I come from. They may be my relations, for all I know." She delivers this comment as a challenge so that Harney will not "think that she regretted having told him her story" (202). He assures her that he does not believe half the things people say about the Mountain, and for a moment Charity views the dilapidated brown house as Harney does, without embarrassment, as a structure more or less "typical" of those in the region (186).

The visit to the brown house foreshadows Charity's return to the Mountain at the end of novel, when she searches for her birth mother. A rainstorm forces the couple to take refuge inside the house, giving Charity opportunity to compare the Mountain home with the one in North Dormer. A woman crudely welcomes her, asking, "You're the girl from Royall's, ain't you?" An unconscious play on words suggests biological connection as she tells Charity, "You kin stay." The jolt of confronting her troubled past produces mind-numbing confusion. Charity feels "oppressed" by the "bare and miserable" furnishings and the ragged inhabitants of the house. She instinctively recoils from the squalid room and feels a "loathing of the place and the people" (200). Their poverty contrasts with the "vision of peace and plenty" of her adoptive home, leaving her unable to imagine life among these people. The bourgeois décor of lawyer Royall and Miss Hatchard, once seemingly "so poor and plain," seems opulent in contrast to these miserable surroundings. She struggles to affirm her birth identity: "This is where I belong—this is where I belong," she silently chants, but the words "had no meaning." She cannot reconcile the person she has become with the place she has come from. "Every instinct and habit made her a stranger among these poor swamp-people living like vermin in their lair" (201). Desperate to preserve her dignity, she tells Harney with choking sobs, "I ain't—I ain't ashamed. They're my people." His embrace and ambiguous "My dear . . ." (202) comfort her, but seeing a look of "constraint" in his eyes, Charity questions his "reason for holding her close" (206).

As Charity's relationship with Harney deepens, so do her conflicts over her identity. Her importance to him depends on her Mountain origins, but her alignment with the Mountain affirms her low status in the town. Unable to reconcile the Mountain and North Dormer parts of herself, she and Harney forge a bond in private, outside the boundaries of North Dormer. When they meet in public in the town, conversation is strained, with Charity at a clear disadvantage. At the library, she senses Harney's alarm when the minister mentions Annabel Balch's name. Excluded from the social maneuvering that results in the couple's engagement, she is left to her own "restless imagination" to answer the question, "why did he leave the library with Mr. Miles?" She feels "the uselessness of struggling against unseen influences in Harney's life." When Harney is invited but fails to arrive for dinner at Royall's house, she suspects Royall's interference, but again she is powerless: "she had no means of finding out whether some act of hostility on his part had made the young man stay away, or whether he simply wished to avoid seeing her again after their drive back from the brown house" (207–208).

Charity takes matters into her own hands by keeping a silent vigil outside Harney's window, but her plan backfires. The scene is important because for the first time Charity grasps the meaning of the sexual journey before her. Seeing Harney stretched out on his bed, she "suddenly understood what would happen if she went in. . . . It was what had happened to Ally Hawes's sister Julia" (211). She fears pregnancy, abortion, and "people never mentioning her name." Her fate is foreshadowed when she thinks with dread of other "worse endings": marriages made for the sake of convention and the "mean, miserable, unconfessed fates" of those whose "lives . . . went on drearily, without visible change, in the same cramped setting of hypocrisy" (211). Charity holds fast to her virginal ideals, doing nothing "to deface the image of her that he [Harney] carried" (212). However, the next morning Royall accuses her of spending the night with Harney and claims witnesses saw her enter his house. Charity retorts that it "was you that put the lie in their mouths" (215), but Royall counters with a proposal of marriage and a threat to force Harney's hand. Humiliated, she feels the deep sense of "shame" and "lassitude" that she will also experience at the end of the novel. As she contemplates her defeat, "there flitted through her mind the vision of Liff Hyatt's muddy boot coming down on the white bramble-flowers" (218).

Charity's most valiant act of rebellion occurs when she accompanies Harney to Nettleton on the Fourth of July. Their kiss at the fireworks celebration follows a fortnight of "simple friendship" (223) and awakens Charity's passion. The kiss leads not to historic freedom, however, but to further restriction.[39] Wharton composes the scene carefully, with Charity "determined to assert her independence" (222) and preparing as a bride would for a wedding. She wears a hat "of white straw" with a "cherry-coloured lining that made her face glow" (221). Ally Hawes serves as attendant, but when she helps Charity dress and remembers her sister's near death from an abortion in Nettleton, a shadow falls over Charity's enthusiasm. Charity shrugs off the resemblance, saying "Poor Julia! . . . The pity of it was that girls like Julia did not know how to choose, and to keep bad fellows at a distance," but the aura of prostitution lingers over her day with Harney. Intent on evading Royall's surveillance, Charity slips "unnoticed" out of the house to enjoy sightseeing pleasures with Harney (222), but she does not escape Royall's notice for long. Inebriated, with Julia Hawes on his arm, he publicly condemns her: "you damn—bareheaded whore, you!" (235). The hypocritical attack—Royall is with a prostitute while accusing Charity of prostitution—brings Charity, as Lev Raphael notes, from the heights of ecstasy "into the depths of shame."[40] "Her mind" "still in a fog of misery," she returns home with the "secretive instinct of the animal in pain" (237). The next day, like the wounded retreating from battle, she thinks only of escape. She tosses clothing and Harney's letters into a bag, resolving, as she "always" does in "moments of revolt," to retrace her past: "I'll go to the Mountain—I'll go back to my own folks." Leaving North Dormer for a more promising destination is impossible because "[s]he had never learned any trade that would have given her independence in a strange place" (239).

Charity never reaches the Mountain because Harney intervenes and takes her to the "abandoned house" that becomes their love nest (243). Their trysts, like the Nettleton Independence Day celebration, offer only momentary freedom. Intimacy with Harney also means "fatalistic acceptance of his will" that they meet secretly (248). Pregnant with his child and aware of his engagement to Annabel, she refuses to encumber him, with the result that she again becomes subject to Royall's dominion, this time not as daughter but as wife. The outcome is foreshadowed in the Old Home Week celebration, in which Charity glimpses Annabel and Harney sitting together and hears Royall's speech about returning to North Dormer "for good" (257–59). The ambiguous "good," with its sense of finality as well as virtue, signals her defeat.

SURRENDER

Charity journeys to the Mountain in a final effort to evade Royall's grasp. This return to roots and search for the mother figure is a familiar plot device, with analogues in sentimental and Gothic fiction. In these stories, the quest for the lost maternal is an inner search, with the pursued heroine finding in the image of the mother both a version of herself and the other.[41] The motif appears in Alcott's thriller, in "A Whisper in the Dark," in which the heroine hears her imprisoned mother's cries and escapes by heeding her warnings. Wharton rejects positive connotations of maternal connection, however, creating instead what Monika Elbert calls a "matriphobic atmosphere."[42] Citing Henry Adams's observation that "an American virgin would never dare command; an American venus would never dare exist," Stephanie Smith notes the general failure of feminine ideals by the turn of twentieth century.[43] The image of the maternal was purged of sentimentality, and associations with either the devil or the angel of the house gave way to more unstable, modernist representations. Smith describes this symbol's new, multivalent qualities: "the mother can still be mobilized in contemporary narrative both as a symbol of the shared, liberal democratic bond of natural and genetic or hereditary affections and also as a sign of rankling violence, a historical sign of horrific dependencies or the bondage of the flesh."[44] Wharton participates in this modernist trend, which introduced a new dynamism in human relations and with it an instability that brought both rupture and potentially freeing innovations.[45] She does so, as Nancy Bentley writes, "by severing the conventional marriage plot from local place and supplanting it with stories of divorces, remarriage, abandonment, and adoptions that transpire across time and place."[46] Charity's encounter with the mother reenacts the scene of maternal desertion. Seeking solace, Charity finds not a welcoming mother but a dead carcass, an unrecognizable mass of flesh with "no sign in it of anything human" (290).

In the brutal moment that she confronts her mother's dead body, as Rhonda Skillern writes, "[w]hatever answer, comfort, or community Charity hoped to find is denied."[47] The story she has been told about her mother seems confirmed. The words Royall used with Harney to debase her mother and imply Charity's promiscuity come to her with sterling clarity: "They all know what she is, and what she came from. They all know her mother was a woman of the town from Nettleton, that followed one of those Mountain fellows up to his place and lived there with him like a heathen. . . . I went to save her from the kind of life her mother was leading" (266). In shock, Charity perfunctorily follows the minister's cues, disconnected from the funeral service and her feelings.

However, out of the scene's trauma comes an epiphany about the significance of the maternal. For the first time, the refrain, "This is where I was born . . . this is where I belong," which previously meant nothing, "now had become a reality" (288). Despite the minister's protests, Charity resolves to stay on the Mountain. She goes home with Liff Hyatt and his mother, briefly joining the Mountain community in a pseudo-replication of her mother's experience: she "lay on the floor on a mattress, as her dead mother's body had lain" (294). Vicarious contact with the mother's body creates a new understanding of maternal love and fresh insight about her adoptive situation. She recalls Royall's statement, "Yes, there was a mother; but she was glad to have the child go. She'd have given her to anybody," but the words now take on positive meaning. For the first time, Charity understands the difficult decision that led to her relinquishment. She realizes that her mother must have loved her enough to consign her to a better home, and she forgives her for abandoning her. As she does so, her sense of shame subsides. "Well! after all, was her mother so much to blame? . . . What mother would not want to save her child from such a life?" (295).

What mother indeed. For the first time, Charity views her mother's abandonment of her as an act of love, not callous indifference, and she uses that realization to develop a loving attitude toward her unborn child. With the mystery of roots solved, Charity is free to move forward. She contemplates her next step. "Charity thought of the future of her own child, and tears welled into her aching eyes. . . . If she had been less exhausted . . . she would have sprung up there and then." When she awakens in the Hyatt home, it is with fresh awareness of possibilities: "A new day to live, to choose" (295–96). Although her choices are complicated and far from ideal, rebellion is no longer an option. "In her fagged and floating mind only one sensation had the weight of reality; it was the bodily burden of her child" (297).

Charity puts her child first, as does her literary counterpart, Charlotte Lovell, in Wharton's *The Old Maid*. She also resembles Isabel Archer in James's *The Portrait of a Lady*—Isabel returns to a controlling husband out of concern for Osmond's child, Pansy. Like James, Wharton solidifies this mother-child bond in a realistic rather than sentimental way. Initially, Charity is guided by fantasy. She rejects abortion as an option, paying Dr. Merkle $20 to redeem the brooch that serves as down payment for services, and now feels "as though, to save her child from such a fate, she would find strength to travel any distance, and bear any burden life might put on her." She also sentimentally considers adoption: she "would find some quiet place where she could bear her child, and give it to decent people to keep." Like Charlotte Lovell in *The Old Maid*, she envisions herself as an ennobled, fallen birth mother. She becomes an impossible version of Julia Hawes, who earns her living and supports her child: "every other consideration disappeared in the vision of her baby, cleaned and combed and rosy, and hidden away somewhere where she could run and kiss it" (295). She also fantasizes about escape from North Dormer: "on one point she was still decided: she could not remain at North Dormer, and the sooner she got away from it the better." However, "everything beyond was darkness" (297).

In fact, Charity has few viable options. Like the rootless Lily Bart in *The House of Mirth*, Charity is "a mere speck in the lonely circle of the sky" (297). But unlike Lily, who embraces an imaginary child as she drifts into drugged-induced sleep and death, Charity carries a living child. Whereas Lily is "mere spin-drift of the whirling surface of existence,"[48] Charity has real connection to life. With an animal-like instinct for survival, she grabs a piece of bread intended for the Hyatt children. She "did not care" that she was depriving others as needy as herself: "She had her own baby to think of" (296). Without it, she "would have felt as rootless as the whiffs of thistledown the wind blew past her. Her child was like a load that held her down, and yet like a hand that pulled her to her feet" (297). One vexing problem remains: how to reconcile these competing forces of drag and lift.

The solution presents itself with Royall's carriage outlined against the morning sky. Charity's first impulse is to hide, but the refugee's need for rescue overwhelms all others: "the instinct of concealment was overruled by the relief of feeling that someone was near her in the awful emptiness." Charity and Royall negotiate the same arrangement as years ago when Charity relinquished an education in return for Royall's companionship and protection. Now Charity sacrifices independence for dependence. She feels "softness" and gratitude for Royall, "which no act of his had ever produced since he had brought her the Crimson Rambler because she had given up boarding-school to stay with him" (298). The rescue also recalls the day that Royall first brought Charity down from the Mountain. Then, as now, her physical safety is assured, but her emotional well-being is at risk.

Images of passivity convey Charity's powerlessness. Throughout the novel she is inarticulate, for example, when Royall accuses her of spending the night with Harney, when Harney embraces her at the Fourth of July celebration, and when she struggles to compose a brief postcard to him. She is quiet again when Royall sets the carriage in the direction of Hamblin, her muteness a recognized strategy that women adopt to cope with the incommunicability of war. She falls into an "apathetic musing" and "half unconsciously" gets out of the buggy at Mrs. Hobart's house, where she accepts her hospitality with a "feeling of complete passiveness." Wharton emphasizes the demands of the body; all thought of escape vanishes. "A feeling of complete passiveness had once more come over her, and she was conscious only of the pleasant animal sensations of warmth and rest." When the effects of the meal take hold, "her thoughts cleared and she began to feel like a living being again; but the return to life was so painful that the food choked in her throat and she sat staring down at the table in silent anguish" (299). Charity faintly protests when Royall proposes marriage but acquiesces to the train trip to Nettleton, defeated: "his voice had the grave persuasive accent that had moved his hearers at the Home Week festival" (300).

Wharton is ambiguous about whether Royall represents a benevolent rescue or further colonization, with his tone of "mournful tolerance" and "composed and kindly" face as well as Charity's "dread of her own weakness" and dismay. "Bewildered," Charity struggles to speak, but Royall completes her sentences, subordinating her will to his. "What's all this about wanting? . . . You want to be took home and took care of. And I guess that's all there is to say" (300). He simultaneously commands and reassures. "His tone was so strong and resolute that it was like a supporting arm about her. She felt her resistance melting, her strength slipping away from her as he spoke" (301) and she allows herself to sink into a sensation of being swept along a current "as a refuge from the torment of thought." "A tired child" (302), more refugee than bride, she is filled with disgrace and is "ashamed to look at herself" in the mirror at the clergyman's house (304).

Charity's choice to marry is not surprising given the stigma attached to unwed motherhood at the turn of the century. Regina Kunzel writes that social workers attached new importance to the problem, viewing it "against a background of widespread concern over the state of moral life in an urban industrial society, a concern that coalesced around the future of the family." Few issues, she argues, were as charged for Progressive reformers and social critics as that of illegitimate births.[49] Although Charity's pregnancy prompts Cynthia Griffin Wolff to celebrate the novel's "generativity,"[50] Wharton depicts her wedding as more funereal than life-affirming. The image of Royall turning the horses' heads toward Hamblin recalls the line in Emily Dickinson's poem, "Because I could not stop for Death—," in which "the Horses' Heads/Were toward Eternity—." In the poem, death calls in a carriage in the persona of a seductive and cordial yet uncompromising gentleman. Like the speaker in the poem, who relinquishes earthly ambitions as she passes familiar scenes, Charity is an inert passenger who "felt herself sinking into deeper depths of weariness." Just as "Fields of Gazing Grain" give way to starkness in Dickinson's poem, Charity "seemed to be sitting beside her lover with the leafy arch of summer bending over them. But this illusion was faint and transitory." In reality, she stares through the train window "at the denuded country." Summer is over; her hopes dashed. Only two days ago, "the trees still held their leaves; but . . . the lines of the landscape were as finely penciled as in December. A few days of autumn had wiped out all trace of the rich fields and languid groves through which she had passed on the Fourth of July." Like Dickinson, who writes of consciousness beyond the grave, Charity has a postdeath experience and with it, a feeling of bodily alienation: "She could no longer believe that she was the being who had lived [the fervid hours of before]." She reviews events as Dickinson's speaker does, as both immediate and having happened long ago. "She was someone to whom something irreparable and overwhelming had happened, but the traces of the steps leading up to it had almost vanished" (302).

Charity's marriage to Royall occurs, as it were, from beyond the grave. The witness to the ceremony is "raking dead leaves on the lawn" and the clergyman's reading "had the same dread sound of finality" as Mr. Miles's words at her mother's funeral (304). The description of the wedding night is equally somber. In the hotel room, Charity is finally free of "the long turmoil of the night and day" and sits with closed eyes, "surrendering herself to the spell of warmth and silence." She opens her eyes to a picture over the bed that shows "a young man in a boat on a lake overhung with trees. He was leaning over to gather water-lilies for the girl in a light dress. . . . The scene was full of a drowsy midsummer radiance." This romantic scene, a reminder of her summer love affair, drives home her painful reality, and she "avert[s] her eyes." She paces the room, only to realize that the window overlooks Nettleton Lake, where she and Harney celebrated Independence Day. Stricken "for the first time [by] a realization of what she had done," Charity feels "the old impulse of flight," but now "it was only the lift of a broken wing" (305–306).

Charity's sense of defeat contrasts sharply with Royall's certain victory. Freshly coifed, his "shaggy grey hair . . . trimmed," he enters the room "strongly and quickly, squaring his shoulders and carrying his head high, as if he did not want to pass unnoticed." He authoritatively suggests dinner, and Charity, not daring to "confess" that the "thought of food filled her with repugnance," meekly "followed him" to the lift (306). That night Royall sleeps in an armchair, delaying consummation of the marriage and granting Charity a measure of autonomy. However, as wife, Charity is as dependent upon him as she was as daughter. The battle of wills—marked by offensives, counterattacks, truces, and stalemates—ends in a negotiated peace in which Charity surrenders her freedom in return for her child's legitimacy and security.

Summer's portrayal of an adoption-turned-marriage is troubling for many reasons, not least of which is an ending that infantilizes the main character. Adoption provides a homeless child with a window of opportunity for growth, but adoption followed by marriage closes the door on that opportunity. At the moment that she is about to assume the most important role of adulthood—that of parent—Charity is treated as a child. Her subordinate status is marked by Royall's paternalistic approval, "You're a good girl, Charity" and her acquiescent, "I guess you're good, too" (311).

The novel's conclusion reflects not only Charity's conflicted adoption but also the strife Wharton faced when she worked to retain control of her charities in the wake of the United States's engagement in World War I. In particular, she battled the bureaucratic machinery of the American Red Cross and felt vulnerable to its size and power when the United States entered the war, similar to the way that Charity feels vulnerable to Royall. Wharton had urged the United States to enter the war, writing articles, raising funds, and lobbying friends to advocate intervention and support her relief work, but mobilization required, as in any corporate takeover, that Wharton's charities fall under the domain of the American Red Cross. In exchange for governmental help, Wharton was forced to relinquish control of hostels, hospitals, and workrooms. The transition from a female- to male-dominated government institution, as Alan Price writes, meant that the charities lost their independence and separate identities.[51] Wharton grew especially skeptical of the American Red Cross in the summer of 1917, the year she published *Summer*. Her concerns over the appropriation of feminine autonomy by masculine authority appear in her portrayal of Royall. His marriage to Charity, equivalent to a government agency's takeover, is expedient and irrefutable. Wharton described the American Red Cross takeover as a kind of death over which she had no choice, saying that she "was somewhat in the position of the man of whom his wife was asked by the clergyman if he was 'resigned' when he died, and who said: 'I guess he had to be.'"[52]

Although she lamented a loss of autonomy, Wharton was also sensitive to the need for stability in a time of crisis. She understood that capitulation has its benefits. Her regard for Royall appears in a comment made to her friend, Bernard Berenson, "Of course *he's* the book!"[53] His declaration that Charity is "a good girl," followed by Charity's weak reply that he is "good, too" suggests guarded optimism about the new alliance (311). Charity is exhausted by the time Royall reaches her. Wharton likewise felt so fatigued just before the government-sponsored relief agency arrived that she said she was willing "to give our whole planet" to the American Red Cross.[54] Moreover, surrender was not without erotic appeal. Wharton worried that increasing donations to large, governmental or corporate agencies meant fewer resources for private war charities such as hers, yet she could not help but find the director of the Rockefeller Foundation's tuberculosis effort, Dr. Livingston Farrand, "perfectly charming."[55] In accepting the Red Cross's intervention, Wharton embraced the inevitable. She hoped that something "good" would come of the takeover. However, she also acted defensively and kept some charities under her control. She signed an agreement that turned the American Hostels over to the Red Cross, but she retained the Children of Flanders and American Convalescent Homes for women and children. Charity does the same when she safeguards her unborn child.

SCIENCE

Charity's impending motherhood represents another battle, which was raging in the fields of evolutionary science and eugenics. Wharton would have been aware of the Victorian belief, which Marianne Novy notes dates to the Renaissance, about the impact of circumstances on conception. Popular science held that the state of mind of the parents and the degree of their affection for one another at the time of conception affected the personality of the engendered child.[56] Charity's sordid beginnings among the Mountain outlaws constitute, for North Dormer residents, a fixed and negative feature of her identity. Wharton was well aware of the eugenics movement, which was influenced by Darwinian science. Supporters of eugenics maintained that the best stock should reproduce itself and thus perfect the race. In contrast, they argued that inferior human beings should be discouraged or prevented from reproducing. By the turn of the twentieth century, some writers fretted over the possibility of "race suicide" as the birth rate of immigrants and other less favored types surpassed that of those presumed to be more fit—namely, educated, middle-and upper-class Anglo Protestants. At its height, the eugenics movement attracted notable Americans, including Wharton's friend, Theodore Roosevelt, whose political rhetoric included descriptions of superior and inferior races. By 1910 there was a privately run Eugenics Record Office at Cold Spring Harbor, Long Island, backed by Mrs. E. H. Harriman's considerable wealth. By 1917, sixteen states had laws permitting the sterilization of certain kinds of unfortunates presumed capable of passing on hereditary defects.

North Dormer's bias against Charity's sordid origins reflects thinking of self-proclaimed experts such as John H. Kellogg, a promoter of eugenics whose lack of scientific data in no way deterred him from drawing definitive conclusions about the negative effect of environment on sexual reproduction. In the following passage, he hypothesizes about a man who might well be Charity's birth father:

> Who can tell how many of the liars, thieves, drunkards, murderers, and prostitutes of our day are less responsible for their crimes against themselves, against society, and against Heaven, than those who were instrumental in bringing them into the world? Almost every village has its boy "who was born drunk," a staggering, simpering idiotic representative of a drunken father, beastly intoxicated at the very moment when he should have been most sober.
>
> It is an established physiological fact that the character of the offspring is influenced by the mental as well as the physical conditions of the parents at the moment of the performance of the generative act.[57]

Theories such as these, Ronald Walters writes, "flourished in something of a free enterprise atmosphere . . . with little systematically gathered evidence to hinder them."[58] Eugenics shaped the course of twentieth-century literature about adoption, with experts free to apply lists of inheritable diseases, defects, and moral failings to children of unknown, criminal, or impoverished parents. By the time Wharton published *Summer*, readers were likely to judge Charity by her bloodline rather than to accept the sentimental fictional conventions of childhood innocence and healing qualities of nurture.

Science also explains Charity's choice to bear and raise her child. Although her pregnancy is socially transgressive, it secures motherhood for the continuation of the race.

Kate Chopin makes a similar point in *The Awakening*, about a woman trapped by marriage and maternity. However, whereas Edna Pontellier eludes her children through suicide, Charity becomes fiercely attached to her unborn child and determined to protect it. Moreover, from a Darwinian perspective she improves her lineage. Whereas eugenicists would classify her as unfit for procreation on the grounds that *"like tends to beget like . . .* and we desire to make parenthood the privilege of those whom we regard as *inherently* the best,"[59] Charity invigorates her bloodline by choosing to mate with Harney, who bests Royall in age, energy, and ambition.

Nature and culture combine to direct Charity's course. Charity and Harney's sexual attraction is an undeniable force, and as Charity remembers each stage of "her poor romance," the distinctions among passion, body, and nature begin to blur:

> All these memories, and a thousand others, hummed through her brain till his nearness grew so vivid that she felt his fingers in her hair, and his warm breath on her cheek as he bent her head back like a flower. These things were hers; they had passed into her blood, and become a part of her, they were building the child in her womb; it was impossible to tear asunder strands of life so interwoven. (279)

Charity likewise feels the immutable power of social forces when she realizes that Harney will marry Annabel Balch, and "the more she thought of these things the more the sense of fatality weighed on her: she felt the uselessness of struggling against circumstances. She had never known how to adapt herself" (273).

The plot of *Summer* is cyclical—and conservative. Charity's unborn child is at the end of the novel in the same position that Charity was. Conceived out of wedlock, both depend on Royall for shelter and security, a situation that validates the primacy of patriarchy and regulates the moral purity of women. Experts at the time Wharton wrote the novel debated the best methods by which society would advance—through individual efforts or government interventions. Quietly enacted social conformity was tacitly preferred. Noted physician and adoptive mother Elizabeth Blackwell added her voice in preference of private supervision. The job of perfecting humankind, she argued, resides in the regulation of sex in the home, not in challenging the social order.

> The value of a nation . . . must always be judged by the condition of its masses; and the test of that condition is the strength and purity of home virtues—the character of the women of the nation. . . . [M]oral development must keep pace with the intellectual, or the race degenerates. . . . We learn that the early and faithful union of one man with one woman is the true ideal of society.[60]

Charity's marriage to Royall ensures compliance with this national agenda.

Summer ushers in a new age of adoption literature. Unlike nineteenth-century novelists who herald the transformative powers of nurture and hail fresh starts, *Summer* aligns adoption neither with doctrines of salvation nor with national expansiveness. Charity has a vexed relationship with her roots, and the stigma of broken genealogies persists even as she continues the race. Like countless American writers before her, Wharton portrays an orphan leaving an impoverished situation for a more promising one, but Wharton is realistic about the losses as well as the gains associated with family displacement.

Charity remains, like Wharton in her adoptive nation of France, "a wretched exotic." Whereas for domestic writers, the benefits of adoption outweigh the trials of orphancy, Wharton is unflinching about the pain of separation from the birth family and the risk of new kinship attachments. The power of the wounded child is great, as Jane Thrailkill notes, because it refutes the ideal, and in juxtaposition to that ideal, points to its precariousness.[61]

Nonetheless, if Charity begins and ends at home, it is significant that home is an adoptive one. Twentieth-century writers after Wharton would continue to probe the complex demands of blood and bonds. In 1932, fifteen years after the publication of *Summer*, William Faulkner sets another illegitimate pregnancy against the fullness of the summer season in his novel, *Light in August*, with Lena on a slow, steady search for the father of her child. Like Wharton, Faulkner explores the confounding pulls of blood and environment. He also explores the stigma of illegitimacy and racialized difference with his portrayal of an orphan, Joe Christmas, who is abandoned, adopted, and alienated from his society. Other twentieth-century writers followed Wharton's lead in exploring the implications of the growing commodification of childhood, vividly illustrated in a 1924 sales campaign of an Oklahoma department store, which displayed bassinettes with babies borrowed from a local adoption placement agency. A 1930 article in the *Saturday Evening Post* likewise referred to adoption as a "big bull market" with "baby securities" promising "investors" ample "dividends" paid out in smiles and giggles.[62] Playwright Edward Albee dramatizes the psychological damage of commodification in his autobiographical play, *The American Dream* (1961). Wharton's realism exposes the tensions between inherited and constructed identity that earlier American literatures, with their rhetoric of salvation, minimize. Her work anticipates a twentieth-century body of fiction in which adoption is treated skeptically, as a genetically inflected, psychologically complex negotiation of the bonds of care and blood.

NOTES

INTRODUCTION

1. Herman Melville, *Moby-Dick, or The Whale* (1851; repr., New York: Penguin, 1992), 525, 535, 625.

2. Mark Twain, *Adventures of Huckleberry Finn* (1884; repr., New York: Norton, 1977), 7.

3. Ellen Herman, *Kinship by Design: A Modern History of Adoption in the United States* (Chicago: University of Chicago Press, 2008), 6.

4. Barbara Melosh, *Strangers and Kin: The American Way of Adoption* (Cambridge, Mass.: Harvard University Press, 2002), 2.

5. Adam Pertman, *Adoption Nation: How the Adoption Revolution is Transforming America* (New York: Basic Books, 2000).

6. Caroline Field Levander and Carol J. Singley, eds., *The American Child: A Cultural Studies Reader* (New Brunswick, N.J.: Rutgers University Press, 2003), 4.

7. Caroline Field Levander, *Cradle of Liberty: Race, the Child, and National Belonging from Thomas Jefferson to W. E. B. Du Bois* (Durham, N.C.: Duke University Press, 2006); Karen Sánchez-Eppler, *Dependent States: The Child's Part in Nineteenth-Century American Culture* (Chicago: University of Chicago Press, 2005).

8. John Winthrop, "A Defense of an Order of Court." In Alan Heimert and Andrew Delbanco, eds., *The Puritans in America: A Narrative Anthology* (Cambridge, Mass.: Harvard University Press, 1985), 166.

9. Claudia Nelson, *Little Strangers: Portrayals of Adoption and Foster Care in America, 1850–1929* (Bloomington: Indiana University Press, 2003); Diana Loercher Pazicky, *Cultural Orphans in America* (Jackson: University Press of Mississippi, 1998); Cindy Weinstein, *Family, Kinship, and Sympathy in Nineteenth-Century American Literature* (New York: Cambridge University Press, 2004).

10. Lawrence Stone, *The Family, Sex and Marriage in England, 1500–1800* (London: Weidenfield & Nicolson, 1977); Philippe Ariès, *Centuries of Childhood: A Social History of Family Life*, trans. Robert Baldick (New York: Vintage, 1962); Edmund Sears Morgan, *The Puritan Family: Religion and Domestic Relations in Seventeenth-Century New England* (Boston: Trustees of the Public Library, 1944); John Demos, *A Little Commonwealth: Family Life in Plymouth Colony* (New York: Oxford University Press, 1970); Bernard W. Wishy, *The Child and the Republic: The Dawn of Modern American Child Nurture* (Philadelphia: University of Pennsylvania Press, 1967).

11. Viviana A. Rotman, *Pricing the Priceless Child: The Changing Social Value of Children* (New York: Basic Books, 1985); Stephanie Coontz, *The Way We Never Were: American Families and the Nostalgia Trap* (New York: Basic Books, 2000); James R. Kincaid, *Child-Loving: The Erotic Child and Victorian Culture* (New York: Routledge, 1992); and Lauren Gail Berlant, *The Queen of America Goes to Washington City: Essays on Sex and Citizenship* (Durham, N.C.: Duke University Press, 1997).

12. Marianne Novy, *Reading Adoption: Family and Difference in Fiction and Drama* (Ann Arbor: University of Michigan Press, 2005); Marianne Novy, ed., *Imagining Adoption: Essays on Literature and Culture* (Ann Arbor: University of Michigan Press, 2001); Judith S. Modell, *Kinship with Strangers: Adoption and Interpretations of Kinship in American Culture* (Berkeley and Los Angeles: University of California Press, 1994); Herman, *Kinship by Design*; Melosh, *Strangers and Kin*; Julie Berebitsky, *Like Our Very Own: Adoption and the Changing Culture of Motherhood, 1851–1950* (Lawrence: University Press of Kansas, 2000); E. Wayne Carp, *Family Matters: Secrecy and Disclosure in the History of Adoption* (Cambridge, Mass.: Harvard University Press, 1998); E. Wayne Carp, ed., *Adoption in America: Historical Perspectives* (Ann Arbor: University of Michigan Press, 2002).

13. Jay Fliegelman, *Prodigals and Pilgrims: The American Revolution Against Patriarchal Authority, 1750–1800* (New York: Cambridge University Press, 1982); Jerome Griswold, *Audacious Kids: Coming of Age in America's Classic Children's Books* (New York: Oxford University Press, 1992).

14. Alexis de Tocqueville, *Democracy in America*, ed. Arthur Goldhammer, vol. 2 (1835; repr., New York: Library of America, 2004).

15. Herman, *Kinship by Design*, 8.

16. Anne Scott MacLeod, *A Moral Tale: Children's Fiction and American Culture, 1820–1860* (Hamden, Conn.: Archon, 1975), 9.

17. Harris Interactive for the Adoption Institute and Dave Thomas Foundation for Adoption, *National Adoption Attitudes Survey Research Report, Executive Summary* (New York: Evan B. Donaldson Institute, 2002), 1, http://www.adoptioninstitute.org/publications/index.php#adoptionattitude (accessed June 10, 2010).

18. David M. Schneider, *A Critique of the Study of Kinship* (Ann Arbor: University of Michigan Press, 1984) writes that two prominent assumptions of kinship theory are that "genealogical relations are the same in every culture," and "Blood Is Thicker Than Water," making "genealogical relations unlike any other social bonds" (174). Kinship, he argues, is therefore seen as an aftereffect of sexual reproduction, when in fact "the notion of a pure, pristine state of biological relationships 'out there in reality' which is the same for all mankind is sheer nonsense" ("Kinship and Biology," in *Aspects of the Analysis of Family Structure*, ed. Ansley J. Coale et al. [Princeton: Princeton University Press, 1965], 97).

19. Modell, *Kinship with Strangers*, 21; original emphasis. Modell expands on the work by Canadian sociologist David H. Kirk, *Adoptive Kinship: A Modern Institution in Need of Reform* (Toronto: Butterworths, 1981).

20. Benedict R. Anderson, *Imagined Communities: Reflections on the Origin and Spread of Nationalism*, rev. and extended ed. (New York: Verso, 1991), 6–7.

21. Gayle Rubin, "The Traffic in Women: Notes on the 'Political Economy' of Sex." In *Toward an Anthropology of Women*, ed. Rayna R. Reiter (New York: Monthly Review Press, 1975), 157–210.

22. Marilyn Strathern, *After Nature: English Kinship in the Late Twentieth Century* (Cambridge: Cambridge University Press, 1992), 17, 82–83; *Reproducing the Future: Essays on Anthropology, Kinship and the New Reproductive Technologies* (New York: Routledge, 1992), 16–17.

23. Stefan Helmreich, "Kinship in Hypertext: Transubstantiating Fatherhood and Information Flow in Artificial Life." In *Relative Values: Reconfiguring Kinship Studies*, ed. Sarah Franklin and Susan McKinnon (Durham, N.C.: Duke University Press, 2001), 135.

24. Sylvia Yanagisako and Carol Delaney, "Naturalizing Power." In *Naturalizing Power: Essays in Feminist Cultural Analysis*, ed. Sylvia J. Yanagisako and Carol Delaney (New York: Routledge, 1995), ix–x.

25. Marianne Novy, *Reading Adoption: Family and Difference in Fiction and Drama* (Ann Arbor: University of Michigan Press, 2005), 47.

26. For information on the history of U.S. adoption law, see Stephen B. Presser, "The Historical Background of the American Law of Adoption," *Journal of Family Law* 11 (1971–72): 443–516; reprinted in *Law, Society and Domestic Relations: Major Historical Interpretations*, ed. Kermit L. Hall (New York: Garland, 1987), 455–558. See also Carp, *Family Matters*, 11–12.

27. See Samuel G. Goodrich, *Peter Parley's Short Stories for Long Nights* (Boston: Allen & Ticknor, 1834), 11, 14, quoted in MacLeod, *Moral Tale*, 58–59. The Irish were a staple of Jacksonian-era fiction, their dire poverty eliciting both prejudice and charity. As MacLeod notes, anti-Catholic, anti-Irish sentiment ran high against these "unlettered, unskilled, and often unruly" immigrants, who represented an entirely new and disturbing urban underclass (103).

28. Amy Schrager Lang, *The Syntax of Class: Writing Inequality in Nineteenth-Century America* (Princeton, N.J.: Princeton University Press, 2003), 5.

29. Susanna Cummins, *The Lamplighter*, ed. Nina Baym (1854; repr., New Brunswick, N.J.: Rutgers University Press, 1988), 57.

30. Wishy, *Child and the Republic*, 32–33.

31. James Marten, *The Children's Civil War* (Chapel Hill: University of North Carolina, 1998), 14.

32. Fliegelman, *Pilgrims*, 182.

33. Ibid., 235.

34. Michael Grossberg, *Governing the Hearth: Law and the Family in Nineteenth-Century America* (Chapel Hill: University of North Carolina Press, 1985), 234–35.

35. Ibid., 218.

36. Philip Greven, *The Protestant Temperament: Patterns of Child-Rearing, Religious Experience, and the Self in Early America* (New York: Knopf, 1977), 6, 22–24.

37. Mary P. Ryan, *The Empire of the Mother: American Writing about Domesticity, 1830 to 1860*, Women and History 2/3 (New York: Institute for Research in History and Haworth Press, 1982), 47–49.

38. Daniel Walker Howe, *Making the American Self: Jonathan Edwards to Abraham Lincoln* (Cambridge, Mass.: Harvard University Press, 1997), 125.

39. Appleby, *Inheriting the Revolution*, 170–73. See also Steven Mintz and Susan Kellogg, *Domestic Revolutions: A Social History of American Family Life* (New York: Macmillan, 1988), 17.

40. Wishy, *Child and the Republic*, 26, 28.

41. Mary P. Ryan charts the rise of domesticity among the middle class in *Cradle of the Middle Class: The Family in Oneida County, N.Y., 1790–1865* (New York: Cambridge University Press, 1981). As she observes in *Empire of the Mother*, "the feminization of child-rearing, in literature and in practice, dovetailed neatly with the gender system enshrined in the cult of domesticity. The true woman was the perfect candidate for the role of child nurturer. She was loving, giving, moral, pure, and consigned to the hearth" (56). On the character of the emerging middle class, see Stuart M. Blumin, *The Emergence of the Middle Class: Social Experience in the American City, 1760–1900* (New York: Cambridge University Press, 1989). On middle-class gentility and domesticity, see Richard L. Bushman, *The Refinement of America: Persons, Houses, Cities* (New York: Vintage, 1992).

42. Gail Parker, ed., *The Oven Birds: American Women on Womanhood, 1820–1920* (Garden City, N.Y.: Anchor, 1972), 149.

43. Ann Douglas, *The Feminization of American Culture* (New York: Knopf, 1977). On the cult of domesticity and attendant views toward children, see, in addition to Wishy, *Child and the Republic*: Nancy Cott, *The Bonds of Womanhood: "Woman's Sphere" in New England, 1780–1835* (New Haven, Conn.: Yale University Press, 1977), 41–48; Barbara Welter, "The Cult of True Womanhood: 1800–1860," *American Quarterly* 18 (1966): 151–74; Barbara Welter, *Dimity Convictions: The American Woman in the Nineteenth Century* (Athens: Ohio University Press, 1976); and Ryan, *Cradle of the Middle Class*.

44. "A family is a little commonwealth, and a commonwealth is a great family," in John Winthrop, "A Defense of an Order of Court," in Alan Heimert and Andrew Delbanco, eds., *The Puritans in America: A Narrative Anthology* (Cambridge, Mass.: Harvard University Press, 1985), 164–68.

45. MacLeod, *Moral Tale*, 9.

46. Jacob Abbott, *Rollo on the Atlantic* (Boston: W. J. Reynolds, 1853), quoted in Wishy, *Child and the Republic*, 58–59. See also publications of the Sunday School Union. Founded in 1824 as part of the Protestant evangelical movement, the Union quickly established branches in many states and became a formidable publisher of literature for children of all ages, including adoption literature. The books it published were not narrowly religious but broadly moral and didactic, dealing with realistic rather than fantastical subjects, and devoted to developing moral character.

47. Franklin and McKinnon, introduction, *Relative Values*, 6.

48. Priscilla Wald, *Constituting Americans: Cultural Anxiety and Narrative Form* (Durham, N.C.: Duke University Press, 1995), 2.

49. Nathaniel Hawthorne to William Ticknor, January 19, 1855, *The Centenary Edition of the Works of Nathaniel Hawthorne*, vol. 17, *The Letters: 1855–1856*, ed. Thomas Woodson, James A. Rubino, L. Neal Smith, and Norman Holmes Pearson (Columbus: Ohio State University Press, 1984), 304.

50. Jane P. Tompkins, *Sensational Designs: The Cultural Work of American Fiction, 1790–1860* (New York: Oxford University Press, 1985).

51. Horace Bushnell, *Christian Nurture* (1847; repr., Grand Rapids, Mich.: Baker Book House, 1979).

52. For a detailed legal history of sealed records, see Elizabeth J. Samuels, "The Idea of Adoption: An Inquiry into the History of Adult Adoptee Access to Birth Records," *Rutgers Law Review* 53 (2001): 367–436.

CHAPTER 1

1. John Winthrop, "A Defense of an Order of Court," in Alan Heimert and Andrew Delbanco, eds., *The Puritans in America: A Narrative Anthology* (Cambridge, Mass.: Harvard University Press, 1985), 166.

2. E. Wayne Carp writes that "colonial Americans showed little preference for the primacy of biological kinship, practiced adoption on a limited scale, and frequently placed children in what we would call foster care" (*Family Matters: Secrecy and Disclosure in the History of Adoption* [Cambridge, Mass.: Harvard University Press, 1998], 5).

3. Linda Ann Babb, *Ethics in American Adoption* (Westport, Conn.: Greenwood, 1999), 36.

4. Cotton Mather, *Magnalia Christi Americana*, quoted in Sacvan Bercovitch, *The Puritan Origins of the American Self* (New Haven, Conn.: Yale University Press, 1975), 113.

5. Thomas Shepard, *Autobiography*, in *God's Plot: The Paradoxes of Puritan Piety; Being the Autobiography and Journal of Thomas Shepard*, ed. Michael McGiffert (Amherst: University of Massachusetts Press, 1972), 56–60, quoted in Bercovitch, *Puritan Origins*, 118.

6. Diana Loercher Pazicky, *Cultural Orphans in America* (Jackson: University Press of Mississippi, 1998), 8.

7. Patricia Caldwell, *The Puritan Conversion Narrative: The Beginnings of American Expression* (Cambridge: Cambridge University Press, 1985), 133–34.

8. Donald Wharton, *In the Trough of the Sea: Selected American Sea-Deliverance Narratives, 1610–1766* (Westport, Conn.: Greenwood, 1979), 4.

9. Eileen Simpson, *Orphans: Real and Imaginary* (New York: Weidenfeld & Nicolson, 1987), 221.

10. Edward Johnson, "Wonder-Working Providence of Sion's Savior in New England," quoted in David Cressy, *Coming Over: Migration and Communication between England and New England in the Seventeenth Century* (Cambridge: Cambridge University Press, 1987), 194–95.

11. Thomas Shepard, *Thomas Shepard's Confessions, Collections*, ed. George Selement and Bruce C. Woolley, vol. 58 (Boston: Colonial Society of Massachusetts, 1981), 66 vols., 1895–1993, 179, quoted in Pazicky, *Cultural Orphans*, 16.

12. John Winthrop et al., "The Company's Humble Request," in *Chronicles of the First Planters of the Colony of Massachusetts Bay, 1623–1636*, ed. Alexander Young (Boston: Little, Brown, 1846), 296.

13. John Cotton, "God's Promise to His Plantations" (1630; Boston: Samuel Green, 1686), 18, *Early American Imprints, 1639–1800*, first series, no. 402, http://docs.newsbank.com/s/Evans/eaidoc/EAIX/0F3015709CDF3C40/0DC2EA1C6DFCA835 (accessed October 7, 2010).

14. Pazicky, *Cultural Orphans*, 5.

15. Robert Filmer, *Patriarcha and Other Writings*, ed. Johann P. Sommerville (Cambridge: Cambridge University Press, 1991), 2, 7, 4.

16. On conflicts between the merchant class and the Puritan establishment, see Bernard Bailyn, *The New England Merchants in the Seventeenth Century* (New York: Harper & Row, 1955), 16–44. On transatlantic politics, see Richard A. Johnson, *Adjustment to Empire: The New England Colonies, 1675–1715* (New Brunswick, N.J.: Rutgers University Press, 1981) and Michael Garibaldi Hall, *Edward Randolph and the American Colonies, 1676–1703* (Chapel Hill: University of North Carolina Press, 1960).

17. Edwin G. Burrows and Michael Wallace, "The American Revolution: The Ideology and Psychology of National Liberation," *Perspectives in American History* 6 (1972): 168.

18. Kai Erikson, *Wayward Puritans: A Study in the Sociology of Deviance* (New York: Wiley, 1966), v–vi.

19. Heimert and Delbanco, *Puritans in America*, 108.

20. John Cotton, "The Way of Congregational Churches Cleared" (London: Matthew Simmons, 1648), 22, quoted in Pazicky, *Cultural Orphans*, 8.

21. See Elizabeth Wade White, *Anne Bradstreet: The Tenth Muse* (New York: Oxford University Press, 1971), 116 ff.

22. Anne Bradstreet, "To My Dear Children," *The Works of Anne Bradstreet*, ed. Jeannine Hensley (Cambridge, Mass.: Belknap Press of Harvard University Press, 1967), 241.

23. Adrienne Rich, foreword, *Works of Anne Bradstreet*, xiv.

24. Bradstreet, *Works of Anne Bradstreet*, 180–81.

25. William Bradford, *Of Plymouth Plantation*, in Heimert and Delbanco, *Puritans in America*, 56–57.

26. Ursula Brumm, "Transfer and Arrival in the Narratives of the First Immigrants to New England," *The Transit of Civilization from Europe to America*, ed. Winifred Herget and Karl Ortsifen (Tübingen, Germany: Gunter Narr, 1986), 32, quoted in Pazicky, *Cultural Orphans*, 7.

27. Bradford, *Of Plymouth Plantation*, in Heimert and Delbanco, *Puritans in America*, 58.

28. Heimert and Delbanco, *Puritans in America*, 102.

29. Thomas Morton, *New English Canaan or New Canaan*, in Heimert and Delbanco, *Puritans in America*, 50.

30. Robert Douglas Mead, *New Promised Land: The Story of American Civilization* (New York: New American Library, 1974), 2.

31. Pazicky, *Cultural Orphans*, 10.

32. Thomas Hooker, "The Danger of Desertion," *Writings in England and Holland, 1626–1633*, ed. George H. Williams, Norman Pettit, Winfried Herget, and Sargent Bush, Jr. (Cambridge, Mass.: Harvard University Press, 1975), 244.

33. John Winthrop, "Reasons to be Considered for Justifying the Undertakers of the Intended Plantation," quoted in Heimert and Delbanco, *Puritans in America*, 71.

34. Caldwell, 26.

35. Heimert and Delbanco, introduction, *Puritans in America*, 15; original emphasis.

36. Thomas Hooker, *The Christians Two Chiefe Lessons, viz. Self-Denial, and Selfe-Tryall* (London: 1640), quoted in David Leverenz, *The Language of Puritan Feeling: An Exploration in Literature, Psychology, and Social History* (New Brunswick, N.J.: Rutgers University Press, 1980), 119; original emphasis.

37. Jay Fliegelman, *Prodigals and Pilgrims: The American Revolution against Patriarchal Authority, 1750–1800* (New York: Cambridge University Press, 1982), 173.

38. John Winthrop, "A Model of Christian Charity," in Heimert and Delbanco, *Puritans in America*, 92.

39. Markus Barth, introduction, trans. and commentary, *The Anchor Bible: Ephesians 1–3* (Garden City, N.Y.: Doubleday, 1982), 80–81.

40. Pazicky, *Cultural Orphans*, 10.

41. Kenneth Silverman, *The Life and Times of Cotton Mather* (New York: Harper & Row, 1984), 426.

42. Christopher D. Felker, *Reinventing Cotton Mather in the American Renaissance:* Magnalia Christi Americana *in Hawthorne, Stowe, and Stoddard* (Boston: Northeastern University Press, 1993), 12–13.

43. See, for example, Perry Miller, *The New England Mind: From Colony to Province* (Cambridge, Mass.: Harvard University Press, 1953), 402; Vernon Louis Parrington, *Main Currents in American Thought: An Interpretation of American Literature from the Beginnings to 1920*, 3

vols. (1927; New York: Harcourt, 1930), 1:106–17; and Peter Gay, *A Loss of Mastery: Puritan Historians in Colonial America* (Berkeley and Los Angeles: University of California Press, 1966), 53–87. Recent revisionary accounts such as Richard Lovelace's *The American Pietism of Cotton Mather: Origins of American Evangelicalism* (Grand Rapids, Mich.: Christian University Press, 1979), chaps. 4–7, identify him as a forerunner of the religious revival known as the Great Awakening. Robert Middlekauff's *The Mathers: Three Generations of Puritan Intellectuals, 1596–1728* (New York: Oxford University Press, 1971), 306–19, likewise places Mather's religious enthusiasm in the context of American Puritanism. More balanced portraits that emphasize his personal, theological and literary complexity include those by Mitchell Robert Breitwieser, *Cotton Mather and Benjamin Franklin: The Price of Representative Personality* (Cambridge: Cambridge University Press, 1984), chap. 1; Kenneth Silverman, *Life and Times of Cotton Mather*, 424–26; and Sacvan Bercovitch, "Cotton Mather and the Vision of America," in *The Rites of Assent: Transformations in the Symbolic Construction of America* (New York: Routledge, 1993), 90–167. Constance J. Post reviews the critical reception of Mather's work in *Signs of the Times in Cotton Mather's* Paterna: *A Study of Puritan Autobiography*, AMS Studies in Religious Tradition, no. 2 (New York: AMS Press, 2000), xviii–xxiv. On Mather's *Paterna*, see also Sacvan Bercovitch, "Cotton Mather," in *Major Writers of Early American Literature*, ed. Everett Emerson (Madison: University of Wisconsin Press, 1972), 90–146.

44. Adam Pertman, *Adoption Nation: How the Adoption Revolution is Transforming America* (New York: Basic Books, 2000).

45. The distinction made today between foster care and adoption did not hold in Puritan times. Today, foster parenting is understood as temporary whereas adoptive parenting is permanent. Foster parents have limited rights and must defer many decisions about a child's welfare to a state or county social worker, whereas adoptive parents have the same parental rights and obligations as birth parents do when the child is born to them. In Puritan society the terms might interchangeable (Christine Adamec and William Pierce, "Foster Care," in *The Encyclopedia of Adoption*, 2nd ed. [New York: Facts On File, 2000], 112), http://encyclopedia. adoption.com/entry/foster-care/144/1.html (accessed March 10, 2010).

46. Silverman, *Life and Times of Cotton Mather*, 76.

47. Ibid., 290.

48. Ibid., 94.

49. Post, *Signs of the Times*, 80.

50. Cotton Mather, "Orphanotrophium. Or, Orphans well-provided for.: An essay, on the care taken in the divine Providence for children when their parents forsake them.: With proper advice to both parents and children, that the care of heaven may be the more conspicuously & comfortably obtained for them.: Offered in a sermon, on a day of prayer, kept with a religious family, (28.d. 1.m. 1711) whose honourable parents were lately by mortality taken from them" (Boston: B. Greene, 1711), 67. Subsequent page citations appear parenthetically in the text. Original emphasis throughout.

51 . Mather, Cotton. [*Bonifacius*] *Essays To Do Good: Addressed to all Christians, Whether in Public or Private Capacities* (1711; repr., New York: American Tract Society, 1820).

52. Cotton Mather, undated MS sermon on Col. IV.5., ca. 1685, Brown University Library, quoted in Silverman, *Life and Times of Cotton Mather*, 228; original emphasis.

53. Cotton Mather, *Diary of Cotton Mather*, ed. Worthington Chauncey Ford, *Collections of the Massachusetts Historical Society*, 7th ser., vols. 7–8 (Boston: 1912), 263, 41–42, quoted in Silverman, *Life and Times of Cotton Mather*, 230.

54. Silverman, *Life and Times of Cotton Mather*, 232.

55. Cotton Mather, *Ornaments for the Daughters of Zion*, ed. and introd. Pattie Cowell (Delmar, N.Y.: Scholars' Facsimiles & Reprints, 1978), vii–viii.

56. Bradstreet, "Before the Birth of One of her Children," *Works of Anne Bradstreet*, 224.

57. David E. Stannard writes that the fear of separation from parents because of death must have been devastating for children (*The Puritan Way of Death: A Study in Religion, Culture, and Social Change* [New York: Oxford University Press, 1977], 61–71). Increase Mather, in contrast to his son Cotton, used death as a powerful instructional theme in *An Earnest Exhortation to the Children of New England to Exalt the God of their Fathers*. In this sermon, death poses a greater horror of separation of parent and child than that created by mere loss of worldly comfort and sustenance because a discriminating God does not hesitate to break apart families and send one to Heaven and one to Hell. Increase Mather explores the possibility that, having lost parents, one will not be adopted by God: "what a dismal thing it will be when a Child shall see his Father at the right Hand of Christ in the day of Judgment, but himself at His left Hand: . . . And when after the Judgment, children shall see their Father going with Christ to Heaven, but themselves going away into Everlasting Punishment!" ([Boston, 1711], 35, quoted in Stannard, *Puritan Way of Death*, 63–64).

58. Edmund S. Morgan, *The Puritan Family*, rev. ed. (1944; New York: Harper & Row, 1966), 65.

59. Cotton Mather, *Paterna*, ed. Ronald A. Bosco (Delmar, N.Y.: Scholars' Facsimiles & Reprints, 1976), 232.

60. Cotton Mather, "What the Pious Parent Wishes," in *A Course of Sermons on Early Piety* (Boston: S. Kneeland, 1721), 9, quoted in Morgan, *Puritan Family*, 87. Ironically, Mather died intestate, and the task of the administration of his estate fell to probate judge Samuel Sewall. Mather's failure to perform for his own family that which he mandated in "Orphanotrophium" may follow from the meager earthly possessions he had to distribute at his death, but it also suggests that taking proper steps to provide for the eventual adoption of one's child was in fact difficult to accomplish. Despite a theology that directed attention heavenward, most parents could not easily envision themselves dying and abandoning their children.

61. Mather writes in *Paterna* that the "*First Chastisement*" for misbehavior is "*To Lett ye Child See and hear me in an Astonishment*, and hardly able to Beleeve, that the Child could Do so *Base a Thing; but Beleeving, that they will never do it again*" (194).

62. Ibid., 195. Mather also emphasizes acquainting children with the goodness of God and his angels and minimizing evil angels, writing, "The *Slavish* way of *Education*, carried on, with Raving, and Kicking, and Scourging, (in *Schools* as well as *Families;*) Tis Abominable, and a dreadful Judgment of God upon ye world."

63. Ibid., 194.

64. Carp, *Family Matters*, 3; Ellen Herman, *Kinship by Design: A History of Adoption in the Modern United States* (Chicago: University of Chicago Press, 2008), 4.

65. See Ps. 127:3: "Children are an heritage of the Lord: and the fruit of the womb is his reward."

66. Elaine Tyler May, *Barren in the Promised Land: Childless Americans and the Pursuit of Happiness* (New York: Basic Books, 1995), 23.

67. Laurel Thatcher Ulrich, *Goodwives: Image and Reality in the Lives of Women in Northern New England, 1650–1750* (New York: Knopf, 1982), 146–47.

68. Margaret Marsh and Wanda Ronner, *The Empty Cradle: Infertility in America from Colonial Times to the Present* (Baltimore: Johns Hopkins University Press, 1996), 11. The average white woman bore seven living children as late as 1800.

69. May, *Barren in the Promised Land*, 32.

70. Ibid., 30.

71. Ibid. Marsh and Ronner note that in one Chesapeake county, almost 20 percent of the children were orphaned before the age of thirteen, and more than 30 percent by the age of eighteen (*Empty Cradle*, 18).

72. Benjamin Coleman, *The Duty and Honour of Aged Women* (Boston: B. Green, 1711), quoted in May, *Barren in the Promised Land*, 26.

73. Marsh and Ronner, *Empty Cradle*, 17–18. The rate of infertility is unclear. Marsh and Ronner question the 2 percent rate arrived at by the genealogical studies performed by Frederick S. Crum, "The Decadence of the Native American Stock," *American Statistical Association Journal* 14 (1916–17): 215–22. They follow the 8 percent figures suggested by Steven Mintz and Susan Kellogg, *Domestic Revolutions: A Social History of American Family Life* (New York: Free Press, 1988), 12.

74. On legal changes in adoption from the colonial period through the mid-twentieth century, see Helen L. Witmer, Elizabeth Herzog, Eugene A. Weinstein, and Mary E. Sullivan, *Independent Adoptions* (New York: Russell Sage Foundation, 1963), 19–54.

75. May, *Barren in the Promised Land*, 31.

76. See Philippe Ariès, "The Family and the City in the Old World and the New," and John Demos, "Images of the American Family Then and Now," both in Virginia Tufte and Barbara Myerhoff, ed., *Changing Images of the Family* (New Haven, Conn: Yale University Press, 1979), 29–41, 43–60. On guardianship and American inheritances practices, see Toby L. Ditz, *Property and Kinship: Inheritance in Early Connecticut, 1750–1820* (Princeton, N.J.: Princeton University Press, 1986). On placing out, see "Bonds of Apprenticeship, 1655–1705, Kent County, Maryland, 1655," in Donald M. Scott and Bernard Wishy, eds., *America's Families: A Documentary History* (New York: Harper & Row, 1982), 160.

77. May, *Barren in the Promised Land*, 30–31.

78. Ditz, *Property and Kinship*, 148.

79. Judith S. Graham, *Puritan Family Life: The Diary of Samuel Sewall* (Boston: Northeastern University Press, 2000), 48.

80. Ibid., 15.

81. Ibid., 3, 50, 252n1.

82. Harriet Wilson, *Our Nig; or, Sketches from the Life of a Free Black, in a Two-Story White House, North* (1859), ed. Henry Louis Gates (New York: Vintage, 1983), 43–44.

83. Graham, *Puritan Family Life*, 135–37; original emphasis.

84. Ibid., 136.

85. Ibid., 139.

86. Ibid., 141–42.

87. Ibid., 137–38.

88. Ibid., 15–16.

89. Ibid., 140.

90. Ibid., 137.

91. Ibid., 141, 166.

92. In the late nineteenth century, a Baltimore orphanage referred to contracts for indentured service as adoptions (Nurith Zmora, *Orphanages Reconsidered: Child Care Institutions in Progressive Era Baltimore* [Philadelphia: Temple University Press, 1994], 111).

93. Alan Macfarlane, *The Family Life of Ralph Josselin, a Seventeenth-Century Clergyman: An Essay in Historical Anthropology* (New York: Norton, 1970), 112–25; Morgan, *Puritan Family*, 75.

94. Cotton Mather, *Selected Letters of Cotton Mather*, ed. Kenneth Silverman (Baton Rouge: Louisiana State University Press, 1971), 294.

95. Beatrice Gottlieb, *The Family in the Western World from the Black Death to the Industrial Age* (New York: Oxford University Press, 1993), 160. Ilana Krausman Ben-Amos argues that apprenticeship began at ages ten or twelve, although younger children might be boarded out for reasons that included schooling, outbreaks of disease, poverty, or parental death (*Adolescence and Youth in Early Modern England* [New Haven, Conn.: Yale University Press, 1994], 54–64). For a confirming view see Paul Griffiths, *Youth and Authority: Formative Experiences in England, 1560–1640* (Oxford: Clarendon Press, 1996), 33.

96. Lawrence Stone, *The Family, Sex and Marriage in England, 1500–1800* (New York: Harper & Row, 1977), 107.

97. John Demos, *A Little Commonwealth: Family Life in Plymouth Colony* (New York: Oxford University Press, 1970), 120.

98. Graham, *Puritan Family Life*, 165; David Hackett Fischer, *Albion's Seed: Four British Folkways in America* (New York: Oxford University Press, 1989), 101–102.

99. Graham, *Puritan Family Life*, 4.

100. Helena M. Wall, *Fierce Communion: Family and Community in Early America* (Cambridge, Mass.: Harvard University Press, 1990), 97–125.

101. Roger Thompson, "Adolescent Culture in Colonial America," *Journal of Family History* 9 (Summer) (1984): 140.

102. Stone, *Family, Sex and Marriage*, 108; Macfarlane, *Family Life of Ralph Josselin*, 92–93, 112–25; Joseph E. Illick, "Child-Rearing in Seventeenth-Century England and America," in *The History of Childhood*, ed. Lloyd deMause (New York: Psychohistory Press, 1974; repr., New York: Peter Bedrick Books, 1988), 321–23.

103. Graham, *Puritan Family Life*, 149.

104. Major studies of childhood that touch in this issue include Philippe Ariès, *Centuries of Childhood: A Social History of Family Life*, trans. Robert Baldick (New York: Vintage, 1962); Stone, *Family, Sex and Marriage*; David Hunt, *Parents and Children in History: The Psychology of Family Life in Early Modern France* (New York: Basic Books, 1970); and Edward Shorter, *The Making of the Modern Family* (New York: Basic Books, 1975). Ariès, Stone, and Shorter take an evolutionary approach to the family and find little emotional involvement between parents and child until the mid-seventeenth century. Analyzing the journal of the physician and mentor to Louis XIII, Hunt likewise concludes that parents treated children with indifference or aversion. These authors primarily address French and English families, but their findings are relevant in as much as American families bear the imprint of their European predecessors. For example, see Fischer, who argues for the persistence of English folkways in colonial America. Alan Macfarlane, examining the diary and papers of the English Puritan Ralph Josselin, refutes Stone's and others' thesis that the parents in early families lacked emotional feeling for their children (*The Family Life of Ralph Josselin: A Seventeenth-Century Clergyman: An Essay in Historical Anthropology* [New York: Norton, 1970], 112–25). Linda A. Pollock, in *Forgotten Children: Parent-Child Relations from 1500 to 1900* (Cambridge: Cambridge University Press, 1983), analyzes English and American diaries and autobiographies from the sixteenth through nineteenth centuries and finds little change over time in the intensity of interest parents took in their children.

105. This theory originates with Morgan, *Puritan Family*, 75–78. It is endorsed by John Demos, *Little Commonwealth*, 71–75; by Michael Zuckerman, *Peaceable Kingdoms: New England Towns in the Eighteenth Century* (New York: Knopf, 1970), 81–83, who adds that placing out

contributed to Puritan social cohesiveness; and by Stannard, who notes the Puritan parent's need for emotional distance because of the high incidence of child death and the Puritan conviction that every human being, including children, was "polluted with sin and natural depravity" (Stannard, *Puritan Way of Death*, 59).

106. John Wall, "Animals and Innocents: Theological Reflections on the Meaning and Purpose of Child-Rearing," *Theology Today* 59(4) (2003): 566.

107. Winthrop, "A Model of Christian Charity," in Heimert and Delbanco, *Puritans in America*, 91.

108. Cotton Mather, *A Family Well-Ordered* (Boston: B. Green & J. Allen, 1699), 3–4, quoted in Graham, *Puritan Family Life*, 5; original emphasis. In foundational work, historians Edmund Morgan, John Demos, Michael Zuckerman, and Philip Greven also view colonial society from the perspective of the family. Demos finds in the Puritan household a microcosm of the commonwealth, a place where children learned the values, skills, and behaviors they would need in the larger community. Zuckerman interprets the attitudes toward children and family as efforts to promote harmony, order, and unity. Greven distinguishes three methods of child rearing—evangelical, moderate, and genteel—each of which corresponded to a family's socioeconomic status and religious outlook and resulted in attitudes of discipline that ranged from authoritarian to indulgent. David Hackett Fischer notes the persistence of family-oriented English folkways in colonial America.

109. Morgan, *Puritan Family*, 168.

110. Post, *Signs of the Times*, 17.

111. Wall, *Fierce Communion*, 86.

112. Thomas Bender, *Community and Social Change in America* (New Brunswick, N.J.: Rutgers University Press, 1978), 64.

113. Ibid., 67–68.

114. Graham, *Puritan Family Life*, 50–51.

115. Alice Morse Earle, *Home Life in Colonial Days, 1898* (New York: Macmillan, 1900), 391–92.

116. David J. Rothman, *The Discovery of the Asylum: Social Order and Disorder in the New Republic*, rev. ed. (Boston: Little, Brown, 1990), 22, 19.

117. Pazicky, *Cultural Orphans*, 27. See also Larzer Ziff, *Puritanism in America: New Culture in a New World* (New York: Viking, 1973), 81.

118. Rothman, *Discovery of the Asylum*, 20.

119. Robert H. Bremner, ed., *Children and Youth in America: A Documentary History*, 3 vols. (Cambridge, Mass.: Harvard University Press, 1970), 2:64.

120. Pollock, *Forgotten Children*, 204–11. Other historians affirming parents' positive attitude toward children include Demos, *A Little Commonwealth*, who argues that children were greatly indulged until the age of about one year, at which point they began to experience their parents' efforts to curb their wills (131–38) and Graham, *Puritan Family Life*, whose examination of Samuel Sewall's diary reveals a parent-child relationship "marked by warmth, sympathy, and love" (4).

121. Graham, *Puritan Family Life*, 61.

122. Winthrop, "Defense of an Order," in Heimert and Delbanco, *Puritans in America*, 166.

123. Herman, *Kinship by Design*, writes that a "national reporting system existed only between 1945 and 1975, when the U.S. Children's Bureau and the National Center for Social Statistics collected data supplied voluntarily by states and territories," 303 n.5.

124. Babb, *Ethics in American Adoption*, 36.

125. Massachusetts Laws of 1672, 55, quoted in Morgan, *Puritan Family*, 130. Morgan quotes from the case of Elizabeth Wells, whose child was reportedly fathered by a servant, Andrew

Robinson, but who named the father as James Tufts, her master's son. Goodman Tufts, defending his son, testified, "Elizabeth Wells hearing of the sayd law she sayed unto us that If shee should bee with child shee would bee sure to lay it un to won who was rich enough abell to maytayne it wheather it wear his or no" (Middlesex Files, folder 52, group 2).

126. See Rickie Solinger, *Wake Up Little Susie: Single Pregnancy and Race before* Roe v. Wade (New York: Routledge, 1992).

127. Morgan, *Puritan Family*, 130.

128. Richard Godbeer, *Sexual Revolution in Early America* (Baltimore, Md.: Johns Hopkins University Press, 2002), 256.

129. May, *Barren in the Promised Land*, 32.

130. Lyle Koehler, *A Search for Power: The "Weaker Sex" in Seventeenth-Century New England* (Urbana: University of Illinois Press, 1980), 203.

131. Ibid., 204.

132. Ibid., 201.

133. Graham, *Puritan Family Life*, 55–56.

134. Roger Thompson, *Sex in Middlesex: Popular Mores in a Massachusetts County, 1649–1699* (Amherst: University of Massachusetts Press, 1986), 22–31, quoted in Graham, *Puritan Family Life*, 56.

135. Edmund S. Morgan, "The Puritans and Sex," *New England Quarterly* 15(4) (1942): 602–603.

136. Graham, *Puritan Family Life*, 61.

137. Post, *Signs of the Times*, 16.

138. Thomas Shepard, "The Church-Membership of Children, and their Right to Baptisme" (Cambridge: Samuel Green, 1663), 1, *Early American Imprints, 1639–1800*, first series, no. 82, http://docs.newsbank.com/s/Evans/eaidoc/EAIX/0F3015710870EF38/0DC2EA1C6DFCA835 (accessed October 15, 2010).

139. Winthrop, "A Defense of an Order of Court," in Heimart and Delbanco, *Puritans in America*, 166.

140. Thomas Cobbett, *Fruitfull and Usefull Discourse*, 59, quoted in Morgan, *Puritan Family*, 177.

141. Ibid., 197.

142. William Stoughton, *New Englands True Interest, Not to Lie* (Cambridge, Mass., 1670), 33; original emphasis, quoted in Morgan, *Puritan Family*, 178.

143. Increase Mather, *An Earnest Exhortation*, 35, quoted in Morgan, *Puritan Family*, 179.

144. Morgan, *Puritan Family*, 178.

145. Ibid., 182.

146. John Cotton, *Covenant of Gods Free Grace*, 19–20, quoted in Morgan, *Puritan Family*, 180; original emphasis.

147. Morgan, *Puritan Family*, 182.

148. Ibid., 174.

149. Ibid., 168.

150. Ibid., 186. Philip Greven also notes the extraordinary emphasis Puritans placed on obedience to parents and finds this tendency particularly among evangelicals, who emphasized the nuclear family, in contrast to moderates, who favored extended families (*The Protestant Temperament: Patterns of Child-Rearing, Religious Experience, and the Self in Early America* [New York: New American Library, 1977], 32–43).

151. Thomas, *Summa Theologica*, III, Q.68, a.9, quoted in Wall, "Animals and Innocents," 563.

152. Increase Mather, *Pray for the Rising Generation* (Cambridge, Mass.: Samuel Green, 1678), 12, *Early American Imprints, 1639–1800*, first series, no. 255, http://docs.newsbank.com/s/Evans/eaidoc/EAIX/0F3014515321C808/0DC2EA1C6DFCA835 (accessed October 1, 2010).

CHAPTER 2

1. Benjamin Franklin, *The Autobiography of Benjamin Franklin*, ed. Leonard Labaree, Ralph L. Ketcham, Helen C. Boatfield, and Helene H. Fineman (New Haven, Conn.: Yale University Press, 1964), 46. Subsequent page citations appear parenthetically in the text.

2. Willard Sterne Randall, *A Little Revenge: Benjamin Franklin and his Son* (Boston: Little Brown, 1984), 35.

3. Ibid.

4. Constance J. Post (*Signs of the Times in Cotton Mather's* Paterna: *A Study of Puritan Autobiography*, AMS Studies in Religious Tradition No. 2 [New York: AMS Press, 2000]), notes similarities in theme, structure, and composition between Franklin's *Autobiography* and Mather's spiritual autobiography, *Paterna*. Both exhibit the Puritan value of constant improvement; both are "pattern books," intended to model behavior on that of Christ and set an example for future generations. Both are directed to sons who disappointed them. Franklin began *The Autobiography* in 1771, before the Revolutionary War caused father and son to part ways. Mather began *Paterna* shortly after the birth of his son Increase in 1699, labored on it for three years, and set it aside until 1717, when he felt he had already lost influence on "Creasy," who eventually died at sea in 1724. Mather then redirected his discourse to his other son, Samuel, who was born in 1706 (35, 169–70).

5. Silence Dogood [Benjamin Franklin], "Silence Dogood," No. 4 in *The Papers of Benjamin Franklin*, ed. Leonard W. Labaree, Whitfield J. Bell, Jr., Helen C. Boatfield, and Helene H. Fineman, 37 vols. (New Haven, Conn.: Yale University Press, 1959), 1:15.

6. Franklin continues this theme in a 1784 pamphlet, "Information to Those Who Would Remove to America": "Much less is it advisable for a person to go thither who has no other quality to recommend him but his birth. In Europe it has indeed its value; but it is a commodity that cannot be carried to a worse market than to that of America, where people do not inquire concerning a stranger, 'What is he?' but 'What can he do?'" (*Benjamin Franklin:* The Autobiography *and Other Writings*, ed. Herbert W. Schneider [Indianapolis, Ind.: Bobbs-Merrill, 1952], 195).

7. Benjamin Franklin, "Last Will and Testament, Codicil" [1789] in *The Writings of Benjamin Franklin*, ed. Albert Henry Smyth, 10 vols. (New York, 1905–07), 10:502.

8. Esmond Wright, ed., *Benjamin Franklin: His Life as He Wrote It* (Cambridge, Mass.: Harvard University Press, 1989), 1.

9. Carl Van Doren, *Benjamin Franklin* (New York: Viking, 1938), 91.

10. J. A. Leo Lemay, *The Life of Benjamin Franklin*, vol. 2, *Printer and Publisher, 1730–1747* (Philadelphia: University of Pennsylvania Press, 2006), 4.

11. James Parton, *Life and Times of Benjamin Franklin*, 2 vols. (Boston: Osgood, 1864), 1:177.

12. Lemay, *Life of Benjamin Franklin*, 4.

13. Ibid., 4–5.

14. Sheila L. Skemp, *William Franklin: Son of a Patriot, Servant of a King* (New York: Oxford University Press, 1990), 4.

15. Lemay, *Life of Benjamin Franklin*, 4–5.

16. Gordon S. Wood, *The Americanization of Benjamin Franklin* (New York: Penguin, 2004), 101.

17. Francis Folger Franklin was born on October 20, 1732, and died of smallpox on November 21, 1736. He was greatly mourned. Sarah ("Sally") was born September 11, 1743. Franklin's family was small for the times.

18. Lemay, *Life of Benjamin Franklin*, 7.

19. Daniel Walker Howe, *Making the American Self: Jonathan Edwards to Abraham Lincoln* (Cambridge: Cambridge University Press, 1997), 114.

20. Larry E. Tise, ed., *Benjamin Franklin and Women* (University Park: Pennsylvania State University, 2000), xx. Tise writes that with the help of his landlady, Margaret Stevenson, Franklin took in the ailing Sarah Franklin (ca. 1753–81), provided her with schooling, and "treated her . . . as his own daughter." He also describes the myriad "young women [Franklin] loved to guide through life" and calls him "without question one of the world's first and best mentors" (2).

21. Jan Lewis, "Sex and the Married Man: Benjamin Franklin's Families," in Tise, *Benjamin Franklin and Women*, 81.

22. Lemay, *Life of Benjamin Franklin*, 22.

23. Howe, *Making the American Self*, 112.

24. Lemay, *Life of Benjamin Franklin*, 5.

25. Ibid., 23.

26. Ibid., 7.

27. Lewis, "Sex and the Married Man, 79. He imagined William marrying the English Polly Stevenson; his grandson William Temple betrothed to the French Cunégonde Brillon; and Sally wed to William Strahan, Jr., the son of a London friend and business associate.

28. Esmond Wright, ed., *Benjamin Franklin: His Life as He Wrote It* (Cambridge, Mass.: Harvard University Press, 1989), 4.

29. J. A. Leo Lemay, ed., *Benjamin Franklin's Autobiography* (New York: Norton: 1986), xiii–xiv.

30. Wright, *Benjamin Franklin*, 9.

31. Abigail Adams to Isaac Smith, Jr., April 20, 1771, in *The Meridian Anthology of Early American Women Writers: From Anne Bradstreet to Louisa May Alcott, 1650–1865*, ed. Katharine M. Rogers (New York: Penguin, 1991), 153.

32. Marianne Novy, *Reading Adoption: Family and Difference in Fiction and Drama* (Ann Arbor: University of Michigan, 2005), 48.

33. Wood, *Americanization of Benjamin Franklin*, 9–10.

34. Ibid.

35. Philip Dray, *Stealing God's Thunder: Benjamin Franklin's Lightning Rod and the Invention of America* (New York: Random House, 2005), 219.

36. Robert Middlekauff, *Benjamin Franklin and His Enemies* (Berkeley and Los Angeles: University of California Press, 1996), 208.

37. Lord Howe's Conference with the Committee of Congress, September 11, 1776, in Labaree, *Papers of Franklin*, 22:601–605.

38. Sheila L. Skemp, *Benjamin and William Franklin: Father and Son, Patriot and Loyalist* (Boston: Bedford, St. Martin's, 1994), 31.

39. Ibid., 90, 85.

40. Benjamin Franklin, *London Chronicle*, May 9, 1759, in Labaree, *Papers of Benjamin Franklin*, 8:342.

41. Wood, *Americanization of Benjamin Franklin*, 71, 57.

42. Ibid., 68.

43. Franklin, "Observations Concerning the Increase of Mankind," 1751, in *Benjamin Franklin: Writings*, ed. J. A. Leo Lemay (New York: Library of America, 1987), 374; original emphasis.

44. Benjamin Franklin to William Franklin, August 16, 1784, in *Benjamin Franklin: Writings*, 1097; original emphasis.

45. Franklin, "Last Will," *Writings of Benjamin Franklin*, 10:494.

46. Randall, *Little Revenge*, 494.

47. Thomas Bender, *Community and Social Change in America* (New Brunswick, N.J.: Rutgers University Press, 1878), 79–80.

48. Jay Fliegelman, *Prodigals and Pilgrims: The American Revolution against Patriarchal Authority* (New York: Cambridge University Press, 1982), 3.

49. Joyce Appleby, *Inheriting the Revolution: The First Generation of Americans* (Cambridge, Mass.: Harvard University Press, 2000), 21.

50. J. M. Opal, *Beyond the Farm: National Ambitions in Rural New England* (Philadelphia: University of Pennsylvania Press, 2008).

51. W. A. Wheeler, III, "Ann Sargent Gage," paper presented to the Waterford, Historical Society in Waterford, Maine, August 8, 1996, 2. The paper is on file at the American Antiquarian Society, Worcester, Mass.

52. Ibid., 3. Ann recounts this experience in a letter to Lucius Manlius Sargent, January 8, 1852, box 1, folder 15, Ann Sargent Gage Papers, American Antiquarian Society, Worcester, Massachusetts.

53. Ann Sargent Gage to Lucius Manlius Sargent, January 8, 1852, box 1, folder 15. Gage Papers.

54. Wheeler, "Gage," 3–4.

55. Ibid., 3.

56. Lucius Manlius Sargent to Ann Sargent Gage, January 18, 1852, box 2, folder 13, Gage Papers.

57. Wheeler, "Gage," 4.

58. Ibid., 4–5.

59. Ibid., 5.

60. Ann Sargent Gage to Lucius Manlius Sargent, January 15, 1852, box 1, folder 15, Gage Papers.

61. Wheeler, 5.

62. Michael Grossberg, *Governing the Hearth: Law and the Family in Nineteenth-Century America* (Chapel Hill: University of North Carolina Press, 1985), 197.

63. *Juvenile Miscellany*, n.s. 4 (1830): 236, quoted in Anne Scott MacLeod, *A Moral Tale: Children's Fiction and American Culture, 1820–1860* (Hamden, Conn.: Archon Books, 1975), 94.

64. Catharine Maria Sedgwick, *Boy of Mt. Rhingi* (1848), 181, quoted in MacLeod, *Children's Fiction*, 94.

65. Richard L. Bushman, *The Refinement of America: Persons, Houses, Cities* (New York: Knopf, 1992), 276.

66. Appleby, *Inheriting the Revolution*, 4.

67. Bushman, *Refinement of America*, xiii.

68. Appleby, *Inheriting the Revolution*, 148.

69. Phyllis Cole, *Mary Moody Emerson and the Origins of Transcendentalism: A Family History* (New York: Oxford University Press, 1998), 163–64.

70. Ann Sargent Gage to Phebe Ripley, n.d., box 1, folder 1, Gage Family Papers.

71. Cole, *Mary Mood Emerson*, 131.

72. Wheeler, "Gage," 6.

73. Cole, *Mary Moody Emerson*, 254.

74. Phebe Ripley to Ann Sargent Gage, n.d., box 1, folder 3, Gage Papers.

75. Wheeler, "Gage," 6.

76. Cole, *Mary Moody Emerson*, 290.

77. Quoted in Wheeler, "Gage," 6.

78. Ann Sargent Gage to Phebe Ripley, n.d., box 1, folder 3, Gage Papers; original emphasis.

79. Cole, *Mary Moody Emerson*, 13, 144.

80. Wheeler, "Gage," 9.

81. Ibid., 10.

82. Howe, *Making the American Self*, 73, 113. See also Linda Kerber, *Women of the Republic* (Chapel Hill: University of North Carolina Press, 1980), 199–200; Kathryn Kish Sklar, "The Founding of Mount Holyoke College," in *Women of America: A History*, ed. Carol Berkin and Mary Beth Norton (Boston: Houghton Mifflin, 1979), 177–201.

83. Harriet Beecher Stowe, "How Shall I Learn to Write?" *Hearth and Home*, January 16, 1869, 56, quoted in Richard H. Brodhead, *Cultures of Letters: Scenes of Reading and Writing in Nineteenth-Century America* (Chicago: University of Chicago Press, 1993), 114.

84. Benjamin Rush, "Thoughts upon Female Education," (1787), repr., Frederick Rudolph, ed., *Essays in Education in the Early Republic* (Cambridge, Mass.: Belknap Press of Harvard University Press, 1965), 28, quoted in Cathy N. Davidson, *Revolution and the Word: The Rise of the Novel in America* (New York: Oxford University Press, 1986), 62.

85. Jane Greer, ed., *Girls and Literacy in America: Historical Perspectives to the Present* (Santa Barbara, Calif.: ABC-CLIO, 2003), xviii.

86. *New England Primmer Improved, for the More Easy Attaining the True Reading of English* (New York: Naphtali Judah, 1799), 13, *Early American Imprints, 1639–1800*, first series, no. 35872; *The Child's First Primer; or, A New and Easy Guide to the Invaluable Science of A, B, C* (Philadelphia: W. Jones, 1800), n.p. *Early American Imprints, 1639–1800*, first series, no.37176.

87. Ann Sargent Gage to Lucius Manlius Sargent, January 15, 1852, box 1, folder 15, Gage Family Papers.

88. Cole, *Mary Moody Emerson*, 152.

89. Ibid., 153.

90. Wheeler, "Gage," 8.

91. Ann Sargent Gage to Daniel Sargent Curtis, 1854, box 1, folder 17, Gage Family Papers.

92. Ann Sargent Gage to Mary Walker, November 28, 1834, box 1, folder 9, Gage Family Papers. Mary responded in a detailed letter that she had no memory of Hepzibah, as her mother had died when she "was only two or three years old," but she confirmed "that D. Sargent of this city [Boston] was your Father" (Mary Walker to Ann Gage, August 11, 1834, box 1, folder 10, Gage Family Papers).

93. Ann Sargent Gage to Mary Walker, Thomas Oliver Walker, July 3, 1834, box 1, folder 10, Gage Family Papers.

94. Ann Sargent Gage to Lucius Manlius Sargent, September 13, 1854, box 1, folder 17, Gage Family Papers.

95. Ann Sargent Gage to Lucius Manlius Sargent, January 15, 1852, box 1, folder 15, Gage Family Papers.

96. Cole, *Mary Moody Emerson*, 251. Leander Gage (1792–1842) was the son of Amos (1758–1833) and Lois Hovey Gage (1759–1842) of Bethel, Maine. One of Leander and Ann's children,

Thomas Hovey Gage (1826–1909), became a notable physician, surgeon, and community leader in Worcester, Massachusetts.

97. Barbara Welter, "The Cult of True Womanhood: 1820–1860," *American Quarterly* 18 2(1) (1966): 151–74.

98. Wheeler, "Gage," 11, 15.

99. Cole, *Mary Moody Emerson*, 271.

100. Bruce A. Rhonda, *Elizabeth Palmer Peabody: A Reformer on Her Own Terms* (Cambridge, Mass.: Harvard University Press), 164, 252.

101. Wheeler, "Gage," 19.

102. Cole, *Mary Moody Emerson*, 252.

103. Ann Sargent Gage, untitled ms. "The contest between the soul," n.d., box 7, folder 2, Gage Family Papers, quoted in Cole, *Mary Moody Emerson*, 252–53.

104. Ann Sargent Gage to Samuel Ripley, June 5, 1838, box 1, folder 11, Gage Family Papers.

105. Cole, *Mary Moody Emerson*, 251.

106. Mary Moody Emerson to Phebe Gage, March 2, [1840], in *The Selected Letters of Mary Moody Emerson*, ed. Nancy Craig Simmons (Athens: University of Georgia Press), 416.

107. Wheeler, "Gage," 23.

108. Lucius Manlius Sargent to Ann Sargent Gage, July 20, 1852, box 2, folder 13, Gage Family Papers.

109. Ann Sargent Gage to "My dear son," Februrary 17, 1852, box 1, folder 2, Gage Family Papers.

110. Wheeler, "Gage," 24–26.

111. Quoted in Wheeler, "Gage," 24.

112. Wheeler, "Gage," 22.

113. Betty Jean Lifton, *Twice Born: Memoirs of an Adopted Daughter* (New York: McGraw-Hill, 1975).

114. Wheeler, "Gage," 9.

115. David M. Brodzinsky, Marshall D. Schechter, and Robin Marantz Henig, *Being Adopted: The Lifelong Search for Self* (New York: Doubleday, 1992).

116. Cole, *Mary Moody Emerson*, 271.

117. Gouverneur Morris to John Jay, January 10, 1784, in *The Correspondence and Public Papers of John Jay*, ed. Henry P. Johnston (New York: Putnam, 1891), vol. 3, 104–105, quoted in Appleby, *Inheriting the Revolution*, 3.

118. Nancy F. Cott, *The Bonds of Womanhood: "Woman's Sphere" in New England, 1780–1835* (New Haven, Conn.: Yale University Press, 1977), 5–9.

119. Ann Sargent Gage to Phebe Ripley, n.d. box 1, folder 2, Gage Family Papers; original emphasis.

120. Michael Ragussis, *Acts of Naming: The Family Plot in Fiction* (New York: Oxford University Press, 1986), 231, 233.

121. Claudia Nelson, *Little Strangers: Portrayals of Adoption and Foster Care in America, 1850–1929* (Bloomington: Indiana University Press, 2003).

122. Grossberg, *Governing the Hearth*, 205, 207.

123. Ibid., 218.

CHAPTER 3

1. Nathaniel Hawthorne, *The Scarlet Letter*, ed. Seymour Gross, Sculley Bradley, Richmond Croom Beatty, and E. Hudson Long., 3rd critical ed. (New York: Norton, 1988), 69. Subsequent page citations appear parenthetically in the text.

2. Bernard Wishy, *The Child and the Republic: The Dawn of Modern American Child Nurture* (Philadelphia: University of Pennsylvania Press, 1968), 1–10.

3. See T. Walter Herbert, Jr., "Nathaniel Hawthorne, Una Hawthorne, and *The Scarlet Letter*: Interactive Selfhoods and the Cultural Construction of Gender," *PMLA* 103(3) (1988): 285–97.

4. "America is now wholly given over to a d—d mob of scribbling women, and I should have no chance of success while the public taste is occupied with their trash." Hawthorne mentions Susanna Maria Cummins's *The Lamplighter*, which sold 40,000 copies in two months, and 70,000 the first year (Nathaniel Hawthorne to William Ticknor, January 19, 1855, *The Centenary Edition of the Works of Nathaniel Hawthorne*, ed. William Charvat, Roy Harvey Pearce, and Claude M. Simpson, vol. 15, *The Letters: 1813–1843*, ed. Thomas Woodson, L. Neal Smith, and Norman Holmes Pearson [Columbus: Ohio State University Press, 1984], 304).

5. Henry Nash Smith, "The Scribbling Women and the Cosmic Success Story," *Critical Inquiry* 1(1) (1974): 51.

6. Hawthorne addresses what adoption expert Katarina Wegar calls "the most tragic of injustices—the predicament of mothers compelled to give up their children for reasons beyond their choosing" (Katarina Wegar, *Adoption, Identity, and Kinship: The Debate over Sealed Birth Records* [New Haven, Conn.: Yale University Press, 1997], x). See also historian Rickie Solinger, *Wake Up Little Susie: Single Pregnancy Before* Roe v. Wade, 2nd ed. (New York: Routledge, 2000), and Laura R. Woliver, *The Political Geographies of Pregnancy* (Urbana: University of Illinois, 2002), 5, 14, 115–35.

7. Emily Miller Budick, "Hester's Skepticism, Hawthorne's Faith; Or, What Does a Woman Doubt? Instituting the American Romance Tradition," *New Literary History* 22(1) (1991): 201.

8. Michael Davitt Bell, *Hawthorne and the Historical Romance: The Sacrifice of Relation* (Princeton, N.J.: Princeton University Press, 1971).

9. Gloria C. Erlich, *Family Themes and Hawthorne's Fiction: The Tenacious Web* (New Brunswick, N.J.: Rutgers University Press, 1984), 76. Also see Edgar A. Dryden, *Nathaniel Hawthorne: The Poetics of Enchantment* (Ithaca, N.Y.: Cornell University Press, 1977), 145–72.

10. Nathaniel Hawthorne, "Etherege," *Centenary Edition of the Works of Nathaniel Hawthorne*, vol. 12, *The American Claimant Manuscripts*, ed. Edward H. Davidson, Claude M. Simpson, and L. Neal Smith (Columbus: Ohio State University Press, 1997), 257–58.

11. T. Walker Herbert, *Dearest Beloved: The Hawthornes and the Making of the Middle-Class Family* (Berkeley and Los Angeles: University of California Press, 1993), 64.

12. Hawthorne to Elizabeth C. Hawthorne, June 18, 1821, *Letters: 1813–1843*, 151.

13. Elizabeth N. Goodenough, "'Demons of Wickedness, Angels of Delight': Hawthorne, Woolf, and the Child," in *Hawthorne and Women: Engendering and Expanding the Hawthorne Tradition*, ed. John L. Idol, Jr., and Melinda M. Ponder (Amherst: University of Massachusetts Press, 1999), 229.

14. Julian Hawthorne, *Nathaniel Hawthorne and his Wife: A Biography*, 2 vols. (Boston: Houghton Mifflin, 1884), 1:429.

15. Herbert, *Dearest Beloved*, 40.

16. Ibid., xviii.

17. Ibid., 55.

18. Ibid., xvi. On Hawthorne's fiction and the middle-class values of professionalism, property and privacy see Joel Pfister, *The Production of Personal Life: Class, Gender, and the Psychological in Hawthorne's Fiction* (Stanford, Calif.: Stanford University Press, 1991); Michael T. Gilmore, "Hawthorne and the Making of the Middle Class," in *Rethinking Class:*

Literary Studies and Social Formations, ed. Wai Chee Dimock and Michael T. Gilmore (New York: Columbia University Press, 1994), 215–38; Milette Shamir, "Hawthorne's Romance and the Right to Privacy," *American Quarterly* 49(4) (1997): 746–79.

19. Herbert, *Dearest Beloved*, xvi.

20. Karen Sánchez-Eppler, "Hawthorne and the Writing of Childhood," *The Cambridge Companion to Nathaniel Hawthorne*, ed. Richard H. Millington (New York: Cambridge University Press, 2004), 143.

21. Nathaniel Hawthorne to Samuel Longfellow, March 21, 1838, in Samuel Longfellow, *The Life of Henry Wadsworth Longfellow*, vol. 1 (Boston: Ticknor, 1886), 280, 298, quoted in Richard A. Hathaway, "Hawthorne and the Paradise of Children," *Western Humanities Review* 59 (1961): 163.

22. On Hawthorne's cultivation of childhood imagination, see Ellen Butler Donovan, "'Very capital reading for children': Reading as Play in Hawthorne's *Wonder Book for Girls and Boys*," *Children's Literature* 30 (2002): 19–41.

23. Nathaniel Hawthorne, "The Wayside," *Centenary Edition of the Works of Nathaniel Hawthorne*, vol. 7, *A Wonder-Book and Tanglewood Tales*, ed. William Charvat, Roy Harvey Pearce, and Claude M. Simpson (Columbus: Ohio State University Press, 1972), 179.

24. Julian Hawthorne, *Nathaniel Hawthorne and His Wife*, 1:462. On *A Wonder-Book* and *Tanglewood Tales* as expression of myths of Eden, see Hathaway, "Hawthorne and the Paradise of Children," 161–72.

25. Sánchez-Eppler, "Hawthorne and the Writing of Childhood," 150, 143.

26. Goodenough, "'Demons of Wickedness,'" 227.

27. Gillian Brown, "Hawthorne and Children in the Nineteenth Century," in *A Historical Guide to Nathaniel Hawthorne*, ed. Larry J. Reynolds (New York: Oxford University Press, 2001), 80; Laura Laffrado, *Hawthorne's Literature for Children* (Athens: University of Georgia Press, 1992), 4.

28. Herbert, *Dearest Beloved*, xix.

29. Brown, "Hawthorne and Children," 89–90.

30. Jamie Barlowe notes that in both cases Hester's power is constrained. Her first outburst is tamed by drugs administered by Chillingworth; her second by lectures about her moral responsibilities to Pearl (*The Scarlet Mob of Scribblers: Rereading Hester Prynne* [Carbondale: Southern Illinois University Press, 2000], 18).

31. See Edmund S. Morgan, *The Puritan Family*, rev. ed. (1944; New York: Harper & Row, 1966), 130; Richard Godbeer, *Sexual Revolution in Early America* (Baltimore, Md.: Johns Hopkins University Press, 2002), 256.

32. Michael Grossberg, *Governing the Hearth: Law and the Family in Nineteenth-Century America* (Chapel Hill: University of North Carolina Press, 1985), 198–99.

33. Benjamin Franklin, *The Speech of Polly Baker* [1747], in *The Papers of Benjamin Franklin*, ed. Leonard W. Labaree, Whitfield J. Bell, Jr., Helen C. Boatfield, and Helene H. Fineman, 37 vols. (New Haven, Conn.: Yale University Press, 1959–), 3: 124–25; original emphasis.

34. Grossberg, *Governing the Hearth*, 207.

35. Eleanor Boatright, "The Political and Civil Status of Women in Georgia, 1783–1860," *Georgia Historical Quarterly* 25 (1941): 317, quoted in Grossberg, *Governing the Hearth*, 207.

36. *People v. Landt*, 2 Johns. 375, 376 (New York: 1807), quoted in Grossberg, *Governing the Hearth*, 209.

37. Grossberg, *Governing the Hearth*, 212.

38. Ibid., 234–35.

39. Ibid., 218.

40. Wishy, *Child and the Republic*, 32–33.

41. Shirley Samuels, *Romances of the Republic: Women, the Family, and Violence in the Literature of the Early American Nation* (New York: Oxford University Press, 1996), 16–17.

42. Stephanie A. Smith, *Conceived by Liberty: Maternal Figures and Nineteenth-Century American Literature* (Ithaca, N.Y.: Cornell University Press, 1994), 11–13. See also Martha Banta, *Imaging American Women: Idea and Ideals in Cultural History* (New York: Columbia University Press, 1987), and Annette Kolodny, *The Lay of the Land: Metaphor as Experience and History in American Life and Letters* (Chapel Hill: University of North Carolina Press, 1975). For analysis of national iconography, see Lauren Berlant, *The Anatomy of National Fantasy: Hawthorne, Utopia, and Everyday Life* (Chicago: University of Chicago Press, 1991). On democratic theory, see Anne Phillips, *Engendering Democracy* (University Park: Pennsylvania State University Press, 1991).

43. Smith, *Conceived by Liberty*, 1.

44. Ibid., 8.

45. Ibid., 13.

46. Berlant, *Anatomy of National Fantasy*, 28.

47. *San Francisco Chronicle*, June 25, 1989, quoted in Smith, *Conceived by Liberty*, 219. The case was decided by a court ruling that denied Whitehead custody but granted her visiting rights and also found in favor of the biological father. The claim to motherhood based on the sacredness of biology does not have as much standing in the United States as the claim of an adoptive mother, or a mother who rears or wants to rear her birth child as opposed to deciding to rear it after entering a contract to bear it for money; surrogate motherhood has a smaller role than adoptive motherhood in this American cultural narrative.

48. Ann Douglas, *The Feminization of American Culture* (New York: Knopf, 1977); Mary P. Ryan, *The Empire of the Mother: American Writing about Domesticity, 1830–1860* (New York: Institute for Research in History and Haworth Press, 1982).

49. Herbert, *Dearest Beloved*, 111.

50. Parallels exist today, as attention to so-called "family values" intensify public vituperation against unmarried women that society dubs "welfare mothers" (Rickie Solinger, *Beggars and Choosers: How the Politics of Choice Shape Adoption, Abortion, and Welfare in the United States* [New York: Hill & Wang, 2001]). The single birth mother has been singled out, Solinger notes, for social humiliation and has often been deprived of the economic means by which she can parent her child. In the late twentieth century the stigma on illegitimacy has lessened and the terms "single mother" and "working mother" have become common usage and are no longer seen as contradictory (94). See also Rayna Rapp, "Toward a Nuclear Freeze? The Gender Politics of Euro-American Kinship Analysis," in *Gender and Kinship: Essays Toward a Unified Analysis*, ed. Jane Fishburne Collier and Sylvia Junko Yanagisako (Stanford, Calif.: Stanford University Press, 1987), 119–31.

51. Gillian Brown, "Hawthorne, Inheritance, and Women's Property," *Studies in the Novel* 23(1) (1991): 113.

52. Horace Bushnell, *Christian Nurture* (1847; repr., Grand Rapids, Mich.: Baker Book House, 1979), 256.

53. Barbara Garlitz, "Pearl: 1850–1955," *PMLA* 72(4) (1957): 689.

54. Reinhard Kuhn, *Corruption in Paradise: The Child in Western Literature* (Hanover, N.H.: University Press of New England, 1982), 41, 60–61.

55. Ibid., 40–41.

56. Goodenough, "'Demons of Wickedness,'" 230–31.

57. Cindy Lou Daniels, "Hawthorne's Pearl: Woman-Child of the Future," *American Transcendental Quarterly* 19(3) (2005): 226.

58. See, for example, Robert Emmet Whelan, Jr., "Hester Prynne's Little Pearl: Sacred and Profane Love." *American Literature* 39(4) (1968): 488–505, and Charles Fiedelson, Jr., *Symbolism and American Literature* (Chicago: University of Chicago Press, 1953).

59. Darrell Abel, "Hawthorne's Pearl: Symbol and Character," *ELH* 18(1) (1951): 50–66.

60. Hawthorne, *Centenary Edition of the Works of Nathaniel Hawthorne*, vol. 8, *The American Notebooks*, ed. Claude M. Simpson (Columbus: Ohio State University Press, 1972), 430–31.

61. Bushnell, *Christian Nurture*, 244; emphasis added.

62. See Richard H. Brodhead, "Sparing the Rod: Discipline and Fiction in Antebellum America," *representations* 21(Winter) (1988): 67–96; reprinted in Brodhead, *Cultures of Letters: Scenes of Reading and Writing in Nineteenth-Century America* (Chicago: University of Chicago Press, 1993), 13–47.

63. Herbert, *Dearest Beloved*, 205.

64. Michael Ragussis, *Acts of Naming: The Family Plot in Fiction* (New York: Oxford University Press, 1986), 12, 72.

65. Ibid., 69–70.

66. Erlich, *Family Themes*, 27.

67. David Leverenz, *Manhood and the American Renaissance* (Ithaca, N.Y.: Cornell University Press, 1989), 274.

68. Steven Mintz and Susan Kellogg write that "latent tensions" arose in the nineteenth-century "democratic family" as a result of constrictions of the father's role (*Domestic Revolutions: A Social History of American Family Life* [New York: Free Press, 1988], 53–55).

69. Carol Delaney, "Cutting the Ties that Bind: The Sacrifice of Abraham and Patriarchal Kinship," in *Relative Values: Reconfiguring Kinship Studies*, ed. Sarah Franklin and Susan McKinnon (Durham, N.C.: Duke University Press), 458–60.

70. Henry James, *The Portrait of a Lady* (1881; New York: Penguin, 1984), 35.

71. Edith Wharton, *Novels: The House of Mirth, The Reef, The Custom of the Country, The Age of Innocence* (New York: Library of America, 1986), 1079.

72. Chillingworth's legacy also evokes a Greek myth about contested child custody that Hawthorne retells in "The Pomegranate Seeds," in his 1853 collection, *Tanglewood Tales*. In Hawthorne's version of the tale, a mother grieves for the daughter abducted by the god of the underworld, a dark force who values power over natural beauty and who manipulates the targets of his affection. Pearl, like Persephone, is claimed by a mother's unconditional love and by a father's wealth. Chillingworth, who resides deep within his own heart, resembles the Greek god Hades. His legacy makes Pearl wealthy but also exiles her to a remote land comparable to the underworld found in the Greek myth.

73. Daniels, "Hawthorne's Pearl," 232.

74. Bushnell, *Christian Nurture*, 243.

75. T. Walter Herbert Jr., cites passages in Hawthorne's notebook to establish his cultural concerns with gender in the period. The name of his daughter, Una, alluding to Spenser's *Faerie Queen*, embodies and helps to maintain one-half of the dichotomous view of womanhood ("Nathaniel Hawthorne, Una Hawthorne," 287).

76. Goodenough, "Demons of Wickedness," 231.

77. Fanny Nudelman, "'Emblem and Product of Sin': The Poisoned Child in *The Scarlet Letter* and Domestic Advice Literature," *Yale Journal of Criticism* 10(1) (1997): 195.

78. Monika Elbert, "Bourgeois Sexuality and the Gothic Plot in Wharton and Hawthorne," in *Hawthorne and Women: Engendering and Expanding the Hawthorne Tradition*, ed. John L. Idol, Jr., and Melinda M. Ponder (Amherst: University of Massachusetts Press, 1999), 259, 265.

79. Erlich, *Family Themes*, 76.

80. Herbert, "Nathaniel Hawthorne, Una Hawthorne," 287.

CHAPTER 4

1. Cindy Weinstein, "'A Sort of Adopted Daughter': Family Relations in *The Lamplighter*," *ELH* 68(4) (2001): 1029. The Massachusetts adoption law defined family in terms of a contract and "reflect[ed] the republican ideal in which each family member possesses individual rights which are guaranteed, not by one's status in the family, but by the contractual obligations family members have toward one another" (1023–24). Ellen Herman notes that "in the early years of the American republic, adoption did not exist as a legal method for forging family ties." Kinship among non-blood kin was defined by wills and indentures, which specified the inheritance of property and parental responsibilities. In Massachusetts, 101 bills changing children's name were passed between 1781 and 1851, and the transaction was explicitly called "adoption" after 1823 (*Kinship by Design: A History of Adoption in the Modern United States* [Chicago: University of Chicago, 2008], 21). See also William Whitmore, *The Law of Adoption in the United States, and Especially in Massachusetts* (Albany, N.Y.: Joel Munsell, 1876).

2. On sentimentality and the death of children, see Karen Sánchez-Eppler, "Then When We Clutch Hardest: On the Death of a Child and the Replication of an Image," in Mary Chapman and Glenn Hendler, eds., *Sentimental Men: Masculinity and the Politics of Affect in American Culture* (Berkeley and Los Angeles: University of California Press, 1999), 64–85.

3. Edward Hicks, *Memoirs* (Philadelphia: Merrihew & Thompson, 1851), 19–21, quoted in Joyce Appleby, *Inheriting the Revolution: The First Generation of Americans* (Cambridge, Mass.: Harvard University Press, 2000), 190.

4. The number of institutions began to rise in the 1830s as a result of social reform. See Timothy A. Hacsi, *Second Home: Orphan Asylums and Poor Families in America* (Cambridge, Mass.: Harvard University Press, 1997) on nineteenth-century welfare; David J. Rothman, *The Discovery of the Asylum: Social Order and Disorder in the New Republic*, rev. ed. (1971; repr., Boston: Little, Brown, 1990) on antebellum reform; James Marten, *The Children's Civil War* (Chapel Hill: University of North Carolina, 1998), 14–15, 211–20, on the rise of post-Civil War institutions to care for the children of soldiers; and Nurith Zmora, *Orphanages Reconsidered: Child Care Institutions in Progressive Era Baltimore* (Philadelphia: Temple University Press, 1994), 8–10, on progressive era reform.

5. Jane Tompkins, *Sensational Designs: The Cultural Work of American Fiction, 1790–1860* (New York: Oxford University Press, 1985).

6. See Laura Peters, *Orphan Texts: Victorian Orphans, Culture and Empire* (Manchester, England: Manchester University Press, 2000), 6–18. See also Carolyn Steedman, *Childhood, Culture and Class in Britain: Margaret McMillan, 1860–1931* (New Brunswick, N.J.: Rutgers University Press, 1990) and Hugh Cunningham, *The Children of the Poor: Representations of Childhood since the Seventeenth Century* (Oxford: Blackwell, 1991).

7. See Karen Sánchez-Eppler, "Playing at Class," *English Literary History* 67 (2000): 819–42; reprinted in *The American Child: A Cultural Studies Reader*, ed. Caroline F. Levander and Carol J. Singley (New Brunswick, N.J.: Rutgers University Press, 2003), 40–62.

8. Rothman, *Discovery of the Asylum*, xxx.

9. Ibid., 76.

10. Ibid., xxxv.

11. Anne Scott MacLeod, *A Moral Tale: Children's Fiction and American Culture, 1820–1860* (Hamden, Conn.: Archon, 1975), 59, 67. For example, in Catharine Maria Sedgwick's *Stories for Young Persons* a woman prefers any alternative to relying on public charity (New York: Harper & Brothers, 1841). For a history of orphanages, see Richard B. McKenzie, ed., *Home Away from Home: The Forgotten History of Orphanages* (New York: Encounter, 2009). On Catholic support of needy families between the Civil War and World War II, see Dorothy M. Brown and Elizabeth McKeown, *The Poor Belong to Us: Catholic Charities and American Welfare* (Cambridge, Mass.: Harvard University Press, 1997).

12. Harriet Beecher Stowe, *Uncle Tom's Cabin* (1852; repr., New York: Penguin, 1981), 624.

13. Daniel Walker Howe, *Making the American Self: Jonathan Edwards to Abraham Lincoln* (Cambridge, Mass.: Harvard University Press, 1997), 4–5.

14. Appleby, *Inheriting the Revolution*, 10.

15. On Protestant bias against Catholic immigrants, see Ray Allen Billington, *The Protestant Crusade, 1800–1860: A Study of the Origins of American Nativism* (New York: Macmillan, 1938).

16. Catharine Maria Sedgwick, *Love Token* (New York: Harper & Brothers, 1838), 53, quoted in MacLeod, *A Moral Tale*, 93.

17. Mary P. Ryan, *The Empire of the Mother: American Writing about Domesticity, 1830–1860*, Women and History 2/3 (N.Y.: Institute for Research in History and Haworth Press, 1982), 49.

18. Edouard de Montulé, *A Voyage to North America, and the West Indies in 1817* (London: Sir R. Phillips, 1821), quoted in Appleby, *Inheriting the Revolution*, 126.

19. Stuart M. Blumin, *The Emergence of the Middle Class: Social Experience in the American City, 1760–1900* (New York: Cambridge University Press, 1989), 240–49.

20. Diana Loercher Pazicky, *Cultural Orphans in America* (Jackson: University Press of Mississippi, 1998), 120.

21. Ibid., 121.

22. Edward Pessen, *Riches, Class, and Power: America before the Civil War* (1973; repr., New Brunswick, N.J.: Transaction Publishers, 2009), 42.

23. Karen Halttunen, *Confidence Men and Painted Women: A Study of Middle-Class Culture in America, 1830–1870* (New Haven, Conn.: Yale University Press, 1982), 29, quoted in Pazicky, *Cultural Orphans*, 122.

24. George Wallingford Noyes, comp., and Lawrence Foster, ed., *Free Love in Utopia: John Humphrey Noyes and the Origin of the Oneida Community* (Urbana: University of Illinois Press, 2001), 147.

25. Martin Swales, *The German Bildungsroman from Wieland to Hesse* (Princeton, N.J.: Princeton University Press, 1978), 14; emphasis added.

26. Gillian Brown, "Child's Play," *differences* 11(3) (2000): 76–106; reprinted in *The American Child: A Cultural Studies Reader*, ed. Caroline F. Levander and Carol J. Singley (New Brunswick, N.J.: Rutgers University Press, 2003), 24. See also Henry A. Giroux, who writes that myths of childhood innocence are "constructed around the notion that both childhood and innocence reflect a natural state, one that is beyond the dictates of history, society, and politics," and are deployed in contemporary culture to relieve adults of responsibility toward children (*Stealing Innocence: Youth, Corporate Power, and the Politics of Culture* [New York: St. Martin's Press, 2000], 2). See also cultural theorist Marina Warner, who defines children as "innocent because they're outside of society, pre-historical, pre-social, instinctual, creatures of unreason, primitive, kin to unspoiled nature" (*Six Myths of Our Time: Little Angels, Little Monsters, Beautiful*

Beasts, and More [New York: Vintage, 1994], 57). On the constructed rather than universalized notion of childhood innocence, see Philippe Ariès, *Centuries of Childhood: A Social History of Family Life*, trans. Robert Baldick (New York: Vintage, 1962).

27. On idealized childhood, see Chris Jenks, *Childhood*, 2nd ed. (New York: Routledge, 2005), 121–31, and Anne Higonnet, *Pictures of Innocence: The History and Crisis of Ideal Childhood* (New York: Thames & Hudson, 1998).

28. Carolyn Steedman, *Strange Dislocations: Childhood and the Idea of Human Interiority, 1780–1930* (Cambridge, Mass.: Harvard University Press, 1995), 42; Franco Moretti, *The Way of the World: The* Bildungsroman *in European Culture* (London: Verso, 1987), 6–8.

29. Franco Moretti, "Kindergarten," in *Signs Taken for Wonders: Essays in the Sociology of Literary Forms*, trans. Susan Fischer, David Forgacs, and David Miller (London: Verso, 1983), 157.

30. Ibid., 162; original emphasis.

31. Ibid., 163.

32. On the use of internally generated constraints to achieve republican ends in the nineteenth century, see G. M. Goshgarian, *To Kiss the Chastening Rod: Domestic Fiction and Sexual Ideology in the American Renaissance* (Ithaca, N.Y.: Cornell University Press, 1992), 39–43. On the use of sentimental nurture for political ends in Revolutionary America, see Jay Fliegelman, *Prodigals and Pilgrims: The American Revolution against Patriarchal Authority, 1750–1800* (Cambridge: Cambridge University Press, 1982), 23–26.

33. Samuel Langhorne Clemens [Mark Twain], *Adventures of Huckleberry Finn*, ed. Sculley Bradley, Richmond Croom Beatty, E. Hudson Long, and Thomas Cooley, 2nd critical ed. (New York: Norton, 1977), 7.

34. Eliza M. French, *The Two Orphans: A Story for Little Children* (New York: Kiggins & Kellogg, 1849–1856?), 46; Julia A. Mathews, *Nettie's Mission: "Our Father in Heaven, Hallowed Be Thy Name"* (1866; repr., New York: Robert Carter & Brothers, 1869), 140.

35. John G. Cawelti, *Adventure, Mystery and Romance: Formula Stories as Art and Popular Culture* (Chicago: University of Chicago Press, 1976), 35–36.

36. Sarah S. Baker [Sarah Schoonmaker], *Coming to the Light; or, The Story of Fidgety Skeert* (New York: Anson D. F. Randolph, 1862); Asa Bullard, comp., *The Lighthouse* (Boston: Lee & Shepard, 1863).

37. Rachel Blau DuPlessis, *Writing Beyond the Ending: Narrative Strategies of Twentieth-Century Women Writers* (Bloomington: Indiana University Press, 1985), 5.

38. Ibid., 9.

39. Gillian Beer, *The Romance* (New York: Methuen, 1970), 78. See also Janice Radway, *Reading the Romance: Women, Patriarchy, and Popular Culture* (Chapel Hill: University of North Carolina Press, 1984).

40. Humphrey Carpenter, *Secret Gardens: A Study of the Golden Age of Children's Literature* (Boston: Houghton Mifflin, 1985), 86.

41. Shirley Samuels, ed. and introd., *The Culture of Sentiment: Race, Gender, and Sentimentality in Nineteenth-Century America* (New York: Oxford University Press, 1992), 4.

42. Glenn Hendler, *Public Sentiments: Structures of Feeling in Nineteenth-Century American Literature* (Chapel Hill: University of North Carolina Press, 2001), 4–5.

43. Tompkins, *Sensational Designs*, 160.

44. For example, in a sampling of twenty-one juvenile fictions catalogued under the subject heading "adoption" in the collection at the American Antiquarian Society, Worcester, Massachusetts, thirteen had female protagonists, only four had male protagonists, and four had both male and female protagonists.

45. MacLeod, *Moral Tale*, 31. Evidence points to the importance of gender throughout literature and history. On the prevalence of girls in adoption, a *Slate* article finds 105 boys for every 100 girls in the general population of biological children but 89 boys for every 100 girls in the adopted population (John Gravois, "Bringing up Baby: Why do Adoptive Parents Prefer Girls?" *Slate* [January 14, 2004], http://www.slate.com/id/2093899/ [accessed October 24, 2008]). Barbara Melosh notes a historical preference for girls in American adoption because they are viewed as more malleable or affectionate. From the 1930s to 1960s, however, some adoptive parents sought boys because they wanted more spirited and athletic children (*Strangers and Kin: The American Way of Adoption* [Cambridge, Mass.: Harvard University Press, 2002], 54–68). Marianne Novy observes a gender difference in Renaissance literature: "the image of the bastard is mostly gendered masculine and the image of the adoptee is more often gendered feminine" (*Reading Adoption: Family and Difference in Fiction and Drama* [Ann Arbor: University of Michigan Press, 2005], 82).

46. Similar divisions occur in children's play. Melanie Dawson notes that boys are more active than girls and are encouraged "to envision themselves as agents in shaping their own destinies," whereas girls are depicted in forms of domestic play or "miniaturized womanhood" that position them for adult responsibility as wives, mothers, and homemakers ("The Miniaturizing of Girlhood: Nineteenth-Century Playtime and Gendered Theories of Development," in *The American Child: A Cultural Studies Reader*, ed. Caroline F. Levander and Carol J. Singley [New Brunswick, N.J.: Rutgers University Press, 2003], 65, 68–69).

47. Lois Keith, *Take Up Thy Bed and Walk: Death, Disability and Cure in Classic Fiction for Girls* (New York: Routledge, 2001), 120–21.

48. Nina Baym, *Woman's Fiction: A Guide to Novels by and About Women in America, 1820–1870* (Ithaca, N.Y.: Cornell University Press, 1978), 11–12.

49. Robert L. Griswold, *Fatherhood in America: A History* (New York: Basic Books, 1993), 13–15.

50. Appleby, *Inheriting the Revolution*, 170–73.

51. Lois Keith, *Take Up Thy Bed*, 120–21.

52. *Little Bob True, the Driver Boy* (Philadelphia: Presbyterian Board of Publication, 1858?).

53. Asa Bullard, comp., *My Teacher's Gem* (Boston: Lee & Shepard, 1863?), 43, 47.

54. *Orphan Willie, and Other Stories* (Fitchburg, Mass.: S. & C. Shepley, 1847), 32–33.

55. Clemens, *Adventures of Huckleberry Finn*, 229.

56. Ann Douglas, *The Feminization of American Culture* (New York: Knopf, 1977), 1–312. On the battle between Calvinism and sentimental Christianity see also Barbara Welter, "The Cult of True Womanhood: 1800–1860," *American Quarterly* 18 (1966): 151–74; Barbara Welter, *Dimity Convictions: The American Woman in the Nineteenth Century* (Athens: Ohio University Press, 1976), 83–102; and James Turner, *Without God, without Creed: The Origins of Unbelief in America* (Baltimore, Md.: Johns Hopkins University Press, 1985), 82–95.

57. Richard H. Brodhead, "Sparing the Rod: Discipline and Fiction in Antebellum America," *representations* 21(Winter) (1988): 67–96; rpt. in Brodhead, *Cultures of Letters: Scenes of Reading and Writing in Nineteenth-Century America* (Chicago: University of Chicago Press, 1993), 13–47; Wishy, *The Child and the Republic*, 94–114.

58. According to Samuel Goodrich, in 1820 30 percent of the books published in the United States were by American authors and 70 percent by British authors. By 1850 this ratio had reversed (Samuel G. Goodrich, *Recollections of a Lifetime* [New York: Miller, Orton, 1856], 2:388–90).

59. Catharine Maria Sedgwick, *Means and Ends; or, Self-Training* (Boston: Marsh, Capen, Lyon, and Webb, 1840), 260, quoted in Mary P. Ryan, *Empire of the Mother*, 49.

60. Heman Humphrey, *Domestic Education* (Amherst, Mass.: J. S. & C. Adams, 1840), 43, 47, and Catherine Beecher, *Suggestions Respecting Improvements in Education* (Hartford, Conn.: Packard and Butler, 1829), 45, both quoted in Ryan, *Empire of the Mother*, 50.

61. The number of infant adoptions was low but was motivated by affection and a sense of responsibility. Julie Miller writes that with no legal provision for adoption in New York until passage of an 1873 adoption law, "families wanting to adopt foundlings as full family members could use the only legal instrument available: the indenture agreement used for apprenticeship." "Even so," she writes, "most infant adoptions in this period . . . were guided more by sentiment than by venal motives, since an infant, unlike an older child, could not work" (*Abandoned: Foundlings in Nineteenth-Century N.Y. City* [New York: New York University Press, 2008], 56).

62. Maria J. B. Browne, *Laura Huntley* (Boston: Massachusetts Sabbath School Society, 1850), 29. Subsequent page citations appear parenthetically in the text.

63. Cotton Mather, "Orphanotrophium. Or, Orphans well-provided for: An essay, on the care taken in the divine Providence for children when their parents forsake them.: With proper advice to both parents and children, that the care of heaven may be the more conspicuously & comfortably obtained for them.: Offered in a sermon, on a day of prayer, kept with a religious family, (28.d. 1.m. 1711) whose honourable parents were lately by mortality taken from them" (Boston: B. Greene, 1711). Mather explains, "In the Oracles of God, the Distressed Christian has that *Motto* provided for him; *not forsaken.* Behold, a Bereaved Orphan challenging that Glorious *Motto; Not Forsaken*" (1). The line also provides the title for adoptee David Klinghoffer's memoir, *The Lord Will Gather Me In*, which discusses his religious conversion (New York: Free Press, 2002).

64. *The Three Darlings: or, The Children of Adoption* (New York: American Female Guardian Society, 1854), 24–25.

65. Pattie Cowell, "Introduction," in *Ornaments for the Daughters of Zion* by Cotton Mather (Delmar, N.Y.: Scholars' Facsimiles & Reprints, 1978), vii–viii.

66. The conservative position on this debate was established by H. Ross Brown, *The Sentimental Novel in America, 1789–1860* (Durham, N.C.: Duke University Press, 1940) and was reinvigorated by Douglas, *Feminization of American Culture.* An early advocate of the subversive aspects of domestic fiction was Helen Waite Papashvily, *All the Happy Endings: A Study of the Domestic Novel in America, the Women Who Wrote It, the Women Who Read It, in the Nineteenth Century* (New York: Harper & Brothers, 1956), who calls the novels "a witches broth, a lethal draught brewed by women and used by women to destroy their common enemy, man" (xvii). Tompkins continues this line of argument, arguing that as spiritual caretakers, women wielded genuine power. She calls Stowe's portrayal of women in *Uncle Tom's Cabin* a "new matriarchy" (*Sensational Designs*, 142). Those believing that domesticity worked to constrain women under a continuing system of patriarchy include Linda Kerber, "Separate Spheres, Female Worlds, Woman's Place: The Rhetoric of Women's History," *Journal of American History* 75 (1988): 9–39, and Carroll Smith-Rosenberg, *Disorderly Conduct: Visions of Gender in Victorian America* (New York: Oxford University Press, 1985). More recently, Lora Romero challenged the dichotomous nature of the critical debate (*Home Fronts: Domesticity and its Critics in the Antebellum United States* [Durham, N.C.: Duke University Press, 1997]).

CHAPTER 5

1. Both novels met with immediate success. *The Wide, Wide World* went into twenty-two editions in only three years; *The Lamplighter* sold 40,000 copies within two months, and was second in popularity only *Uncle Tom's Cabin*.

2. See Elaine Tyler May, *Barren in the Promised Land: Childless Americans and the Pursuit of Happiness* (New York: Basic Books, 1995), 30; Robert Griswold, *Fatherhood in America: A History* (New York: Basic Books, 1993), 10; and Phillip J. Greven, Jr., ed., *Child-Rearing Concepts, 1628–1861: Historical Sources* (Itasca, Ill.: F. E. Peacock, 1973), 4–5.

3. Susan Warner, *The Wide, Wide World*, ed. and afterword Jane Tompkins (1850; New York: Feminist Press, 1987), 12, 41; original emphasis. Subsequent page citations appear parenthetically in the text.

4. Susanna Maria Cummins, *The Lamplighter; or, An Orphan Girl's Struggles and Triumphs*, ed. and introd. Nina Baym (1850; repr., New Brunswick, N.J.: Rutgers University Press, 1988), 322. Subsequent page citations appear parenthetically in the text.

5. Critics note other differences between the novels. Nina Baym notes "Cummins' rewriting of Warner's story in a more benevolent and rationalist mode, a returning to the [Catharine] Sedgwick camp" in her introduction to *The Lamplighter*, xvii. Erica R. Bauermeister, in "*The Lamplighter, The Wide, Wide World*, and *Hope Leslie*: Reconsidering the Recipes for Nineteenth-Century American Women's Novels," *Legacy* 8(1) (1991), seeks to "dispel the image of homogeneity which surrounds American women writing prior to 1860" and likewise argues that the heroines in *Hope Leslie* and *The Lamplighter*, who take counsel from their own hearts, have more in common than the heroines in *The Wide, Wide World* and *The Lamplighter* (18–19).

6. John M. Mulder, ed. and introd., *Christian Nurture* by Horace Bushnell (1847; repr., Grand Rapids, Mich.: Baker Book House, 1979), xv.

7. Ibid., xvii.

8. Jonathan Edwards, "Feast of Tabernacles," *Upon the Types of the Old Testament*, ed. Charles W. Mignon (Lincoln: University of Nebraska Press, 1989), 542.

9. Paul Siogvolk, "The Rights of Children," *Knickerbocker* 39(June) (1852): 489–90, quoted in Bernard Wishy, *The Child and the Republic: The Dawn of Modern American Child Nurture* (Philadelphia: University of Pennsylvania Press, 1868), 23.

10. Horace Bushnell, *Christian Nurture*, ed. and introd. John M. Mulder (1847; Grand Rapids, Mich.: Baker Book House, 1979), 118. Subsequent page citations appear parenthetically in the text.

11. Ibid., xxii–xxiv.

12. Wishy, *Child and the Republic*, 25.

13. Luther A. Weigle distinguishes Edwards's view of children from Bushnell's: they "were held to be lost in sin, depraved by nature, and in need of a wholly new heart. . . . Older folk can do nothing for them, then, save to seek to deepen in them a sense of their need, and to pray on their behalf for the gift of conversion" (Luther A. Weigle, in *Christian Nurture* by Horace Bushnell, ed. and introd. Luther A. Weigle [New Haven, Conn.: Yale University Press, 1967]), xxxiii.

14. Bauermeister, "Lamplighter," 27.

15. Wishy, *Child and the Republic*, 22.

16. "The Conversion of my Little Daughter," *Mother's Assistant* 4(April) (1844): 74–81, quoted in Wishy, *Child and the Republic*, 31.

17. Carroll Smith-Rosenberg, "The Female World of Love and Ritual: Relations between Women in Nineteenth-Century America," *Signs* 1(1) (1975): 1–29.

18. Massachusetts passed the nation's first adoption law safeguarding the interests of the child in 1851, but legal and social policies remained vague until the early twentieth century. See Cindy Weinstein, "'A Sort of Adopted Daughter': Family Relations in *The Lamplighter*," *ELH* 68(4) (2001): 1023–47.

19. Marc Shell, *The End of Kinship: Measure for Measure, Incest, and the Idea of Universal Siblinghood* (Stanford, Calif.: Stanford University Press, 1988), 11.

20. Tompkins, afterword, *Wide, Wide, World*, 599.

21. In her "Note on the Text," Tompkins explains that the publisher advised omitting the last chapter because the book was longer than expected and the chapter "did not contribute substantially to the novel" (8). Susan S. Williams argues that it was omitted because its worldliness conflicted with the novel's moral message ("Widening the World: Susan Warner, Her Readers, and the Assumption of Authorship," *American Quarterly* 42[4] [1990]), 577).

22. Appleby, *Inheriting the Revolution*, 263.

23. Anne Scott MacLeod, *A Moral Tale: Children's Fiction and American Culture* (Hamden, Conn.: Archon, 1975), 9.

24. David J. Rothman, *The Discovery of the Asylum: Social Order and Disorder in the New Republic*, rev. ed. (1971; Boston: Little, Brown: 1990), 71–76.

25. Amy Schrager Lang, *The Syntax of Class: Writing Inequality in Nineteenth-Century America* (Princeton, N.J.: Princeton University Press, 2003), 8.

26. Weinstein, "'A Sort of Adopted Daughter,'" 1026.

27. Mulder, introduction, *Christian Nurture*, xxvi.

28. Lang, *Syntax of Class*, 28.

29. Ibid.

CHAPTER 6

1. R. J. Ellis writes that *Our Nig* "fractures generic boundaries" of the sentimental conversion genre in "Body Politics and the Body Politic in William Wells Brown's *Clotel* and Harriet Wilson's *Our Nig*," in *Soft Canons: American Women Writers and Masculine Tradition*, ed. Karen L. Kilcup (Iowa City: University of Iowa Press, 1999), 100. Rachel Carby analyzes the novel as an allegory of the slave narrative in *Reconstructing Womanhood: The Emergence of the Afro-American Woman Novelist* (New York: Oxford University Press), 43. See also Elizabeth J. West, "Reworking the Conversion Narrative: Race and Christianity in *Our Nig*," *MELUS* 24(2) (1999): 3–27; and Henry Louis Gates, who writes that Wilson "combines the received conventions of the sentimental novel with certain key conventions of the slave narratives, then combines the two into *one new form*" (ed. and introd., *Our Nig* [New York: Random House, 1982], lii; original emphasis).

2. Marcus Wilson Jernegan, *Laboring and Dependent Classes in Colonial America, 1607–1783* (Chicago: University of Illinois Press, 1931), 179; Robert Francis Seybolt, *Apprenticeship and Apprenticeship Education in Colonial New England and New York* (New York: Teachers College, Columbia University, 1917), 36, 49; E. Wayne Carp, *Family Matters: Secrecy and Disclosure in the History of Adoption* (Cambrdge, Mass.: Harvard University Press, 1998), 6.

3. David W. Galenson, *White Servitude in Colonial America: An Economic Analysis* (New York: Cambridge University Press, 1981), cites the following as reasons for the decline: low levels of English migration, slow economic growth, low costs of transatlantic passage followed by large-scale migration of free workers, and the arrival of Asian, indentured migrants (179–81). See also David Northrup, *Indentured Labor in the Age of Imperialism, 1834–1922* (New York:

Cambridge University Press, 1995), 4; and David W. Galenson, "The Rise and Fall of Indentured Servitude in the Americas: An Economic Analysis," *Journal of Economic History* 44(1) (1984): 1–26.

4. Ellen Herman, *Kinship by Design: A History of Adoption in the Modern United States* (Chicago: University of Chicago Press, 2008), 23.

5. Galenson, "Rise and Fall of Indentured Servitude," 1.

6. See Barbara A. White, who asserts that Wilson was born between 1824 and 1828 and most likely appeared as a "free colored person" in the Nehemiah Hayward home in the 1840 census of Milford, when she was between ten and twenty-four years old ("'Our Nig' and the She-Devil: New Information about Harriet Wilson and the 'Bellmont' Family," *American Literature* 65(1) [1993]: 22).

7. Galenson, *White Servitude*, 97.

8. Joyce Appleby, *Inheriting the Revolution: The First Generation of Americans* (Cambridge, Mass.: Harvard University Press, 2000), 70.

9. Ibid., 16, 158–60.

10. Leon F. Litwack, *North of Slavery: The Negro in the Free States, 1790–1860* (Chicago: University of Chicago Press, 1961), 156; A New York Merchant, *The Negro Labor Question* (New York: J. A. Gray, 1858): 5–6, 21–22, quoted in Litwack, 156.

11. See Gabrielle Forman's analysis of labor, class structure, and the autobiographical aspects of the novel in "Recovered Autobiographies and the Marketplace: *Our Nig's* Generic Genealogies and Harriet Wilson's Entrepreneurial Enterprise," in *Harriet Wilson's New England: Race, Writing, and Region*, ed. JerriAnne Boggis, Eve Allegra Raimon, and Barbara A. White (Durham: University of New Hampshire Press, 2007), 123–38.

12. Harriet Wilson, *Our Nig; or, Sketches from the Life of a Free Black, In A Two-Story White House, North*, ed. and introd. Henry Louis Gates (1859; repr., New York: Vintage, 1983), n.p. Subsequent page citations appear parenthetically in the text.

13. Patricia J. Williams, *The Rooster's Egg* (Cambridge, Mass.: Harvard University Press, 1995), 223. The history of transracial adoption in the United States reads like a chronicle of race relations. "Matching" the racial, ethnic, and religious qualities of children and adoptive families was the leading principle behind placements throughout most of the twentieth century, when segregation laws and practices were common. In response to increasing numbers of transracial adoptions and perhaps to the 1965 Moynihan Report, describing the black family as a threatened institution, in 1972 the National Association of Black Social Workers (NABSW) began to defend a policy of placing African American orphans only in African American families. The NABSW defended its policy as protecting the black family and community as a legitimate and viable institution and attacked transracial adoption as a "form of genocide" (Rita James Simon and Howard Altstein, *Transracial Adoption* [New York: Wiley, 1977], 50–52). These essentialist views see race as a fixed category identical to culture. In 1977, the Interracial Family Association issued a statement defending transracial adoption, but, as Margaret Homans points out, supporters of this practice "still see it as second best after inracial adoption" ("Adoption and Essentialism," *Tulsa Studies in Women's Literature* 21[2] [2002], 260). Proponents of transracial adoption include Simon and Altstein, *Transracial Adoption*; Elizabeth Bartholet, *Family Bonds: Adoption and the Politics of Parenting* (Boston: Houghton Mifflin, 1993), 86–117. Opponents include Sandra Patton, *BirthMarks: Transracial Adoption in Contemporary America* (New York: New York University Press, 2000), 154–56.

14. Amy Schrager Lang, *The Syntax of Class: Writing Inequality in Nineteenth-Century America* (Princeton, N.J.: Princeton University Press, 2003), 63–64.

15. Herman, *Kinship by Design*, 231.

16. Elizabeth Breau, "Identifying Satire: *Our Nig*," *Callaloo* 16(2) (1993): 456.

17. Werner Sollors, *Neither Black Nor White Yet Both: Thematic Explorations of Interracial Literature* (New York: Oxford University Press, 1997), 34–35; original emphasis.

18. Nathaniel Hawthorne, *The Scarlet Letter*, ed. Seymour Gross, Sculley Bradley, Richmond Croom Beatty, and E. Hudson Long, 3rd critical ed. (New York: Norton, 1988), 114.

19. Kate Chopin, *The Awakening*, ed. Margot Culley, 2nd critical ed. (New York: Norton, 1994), 9.

20. Stephanie A. Smith, *Conceived by Liberty: Maternal Figures and Nineteenth-Century American Literature* (Ithaca, N.Y.: Cornell University Press, 1994), 97.

21. Ibid., 100.

22. Appleby (*Inheriting the Revolution*, 177–78) writes that legal, physical, and emotional restrictions that enslaved men and women faced

> . . . created strong emotional ties, their shared suffering encouraging a sense of kinship that quickly embraced new members of the community. With slave sales increasingly breaking up married couples and dividing parents from their children, the larger extended families in slave communities came to play a more important role in the intimate lives of black Americans at the same time that their influence was diminishing among white Americans. . . . [T]he slave population on larger plantations became an intricate network of cousins, aunts, and uncles.

23. David Leverenz, *Manhood and the American Renaissance* (Ithaca, N.Y.: Cornell University Press, 1989), 196.

24. Beth Maclay Doriani, "Black Womanhood in Nineteenth-Century America: Subversion and Self-Construction in Two Women's Autobiographies," *American Quarterly* 43(June) (1991): 203.

25. Ibid., 219.

26. Eric J. Sundquist, "Frederick Douglass: Literacy and Paternalism," *Raritan* 6(2) (1986): 109.

27. Russell Reising, *The Unusable Past: Theory and the Study of American Literature* (New York: Methuen, 1986), 270.

28. Smith, *Conceived by Liberty*, 99.

29. Melissa Ludtke, *On Our Own: Unmarried Motherhood in America* (New York: Random House, 1997), 51.

30. Rickie Solinger, *Wake Up Little Susie: Single Pregnancy and Race Before Roe v. Wade* (New York: Routledge, 1992), 3–6, 26.

31. Ludtke, *On Our Own*, 52.

32. On Cassy's possible figuration of subversive female power, see Ann Douglas, *The Feminization of American Culture* (New York: Knopf, 1977), 293–309; Elizabeth Ammons, "Heroines in *Uncle Tom's Cabin*," *American Literature* 49(2)(May) (1977): 166–79, repr., in Ammons, ed., *Critical Essays on Harriet Beecher Stowe* (Boston: G. K. Hall, 1980), 152–65; Gillian Brown, "Getting in the Kitchen with Dinah: Domestic Politics in *Uncle Tom's Cabin*," *American Quarterly* 36(4) (Fall) (1984): 503–23; and Jane Tompkins, *Sensational Designs: The Cultural Work of American Fiction, 1790–1860* (New York: Oxford University Press, 1985), 123–39.

33. Sollors, *Neither Black Nor White*, 43–44.

34. F. James Davis, *Who is Black? One Nation's Definition* (University Park: Pennsylvania State University Press, 1991), 144.

35. John Boswell, *The Kindness of Strangers: The Abandonment of Children in Western Europe from Late Antiquity to the Renaissance* (New York: Pantheon, 1988), 225–27.

36. Jernegan, *Laboring and Dependent Classes*, 179, 191–93.

37. Christine A. Adamec and William L. Pierce, eds., "Introduction," in *The Encyclopedia of Adoption*, 2nd ed. (New York: Facts on File, 2000), xxi.

38. Carp, *Family Matters*, 9–10.

39. Gretchen Short, "Harriet Wilson's *Our Nig* and the Labor of Citizenship," *Arizona Quarterly* 57(3)(Autumn) (2001), relates Frado's failure to achieve self-sufficiency and full citizenship through her labor to "domestic imperialism" (8).

40. Herman, *Kinship by Design*, 26. Viviana A. Zelizer describes the movement from productivity to pricelessness in *Pricing the Priceless Child: The Changing Social Value of Children* (New York: Basic Books, 1985).

41. Herman, *Kinship by Design*, 26.

42. White, "'Our Nig,'" 31–32.

43. Cassandra Jackson, "Beyond the Page: Rape and the Failure of Genre," in *Harriet Wilson's New England*, ed. Boggis, Raimon, and White, 140; Ronna C. Johnson, "Said but Not Spoken: Elision and the Representation of Rape, Race, and Gender in Harriet E. Wilson's *Our Nig*," in *Speaking the Other Self: American Women Writers*, ed. Jeanne Campbell Reesman (Athens: University of Georgia Press, 1997), 96–116.

44. Cotton Mather, *Diary of Cotton Mather*, ed. Worthington Chauncey Ford, *Collections of the Massachusetts Historical Society*, 7th ser., VII–VIII (Boston, 1912), 687, quoted in Kenneth Silverman, *The Life and Times of Cotton Mather* (New York: Harper & Row, 1984), 264.

45. Cotton Mather, *The Negro Christianized; An essay to excite and assist the good work, the instruction of Negro-servants in Christianity* (Boston: B. Green, 1706), 23; original emphasis, *Early American Imprints, 1639–1800*, first series, no. 1262, http://docs.newsbank.com/s/Evans/eaidoc/EAIX/0F2FD4175B2416F0/0DC2EA1C6DFCA835 (accessed July 1, 2010).

46. Silverman, *Life and Times of Cotton Mather*, 264.

47. Ibid., 290.

48. Elizabeth Ashbridge, *Some Account of the Fore Part of the Life of Elizabeth Ashbridge* (Nantwich, England: J. Bromley, 1774), in *The Meridian Anthology of Early American Women Writers: From Anne Bradstreet to Louisa May Alcott, 1650–1865*, ed. Katharine M. Rogers (New York: Penguin, 1991), 113. Although Ashbridge concludes with an affirmation of Christian faith, she chronicles the effect of steady abuse on her spirit.

49. Ibid., 114.

50. Ashbridge, *Some Account*, 114.

51. Harriet Beecher Stowe, "Servants," *House and Home Papers* by Christopher Crowfield [pseud.] (Boston: Ticknor & Fields, 1865), 221, quoted in Gillian Brown, *Domestic Individualism Imagining Self in Nineteenth-Century America* (Berkeley and Los Angeles: University of California Press, 1990), 55.

52. Brown, *Domestic Individualism*, 55.

53. Rafia Zafar, *We Wear the Mask: African Americans Write American Literature, 1760–1870* (New York: Columbia University Press, 1997), 132.

54. Bushnell, *Christian Nurture* (1847; Grand Rapids, Mich.: Baker Book House, 1979), 202.

55. Adamec and Pierce, eds., *Encyclopedia of Adoption*, xxi.

56. Ibid., xxvii–iii. Herman notes in *Kinship by Design* that although the number of asylums proliferated until 1900, children of color needing placement faced exclusion or segregation until the post-1945 era (22).

57. E. Wayne Carp, *Family Matters: Secrecy and Disclosure in the History of Adoption* (Cambridge, Mass.: Harvard University Press, 1998), 32.

58. Jon Butler, *Becoming America: The Revolution before 1776* (Cambridge, Mass.: Harvard University Press, 2000), 45.

59. Sarah S. Baker [Sarah Schoonmaker], *Bound Out; or, Abby at the Farm* (New York: Anson D. F. Randolph, 1859), 3. Subsequent page references are cited parenthetically in the text.

60. Susanna Maria Cummins, *The Lamplighter*, ed. Nina Baym (1854; repr., New Brunswick, N.J.: Rutgers University Press, 1988), 3. Both characters also rage at injustice. Gerty screams, "I hate you, Nan Grant!" (3) and takes refuge in the wood yard. Frado also runs outside to escape Mrs. Bellmont's wrath. Gerty is maligned by other children, who feel "their advantage" and upon seeing her being beaten, tell her she is "ugly, wicked" and "belonged to nobody." Frado likewise is taunted by other children and seldom interacts with them.

61. See Mary Niall Mitchell's "'Rosebloom and Pure White,' Or So It Seemed," on Civil War–era pictorial juxtapositions of black and white children (*American Quarterly* 54(3) [2002]). Such images, enlisted in the abolitionist cause, also shored up "an idealized white childhood" (382) and sounded Northerners' alarm over "the precarious future of their divided nation" (374).

62. Zafar, *We Wear the Mask*, 139.

63. Breau, "Identifying Satire," 458.

64. Gates, introduction, Wilson, *Our Nig*, xix–xx; original emphasis.

CHAPTER 7

1. For example, Elizabeth Lennox Keyser, *Whispers in the Dark: The Fiction of Louisa May Alcott* (Knoxville: University of Tennessee Press, 1993), argues that although Alcott is not overtly subversive, "she does consistently supply the means of dismantling the system of values that her more or less conventional plots, characters, and narrators appear to support" (xv). She cites Ann Douglas, Judith Fetterley, Karen Halttunen, Eugenia Kaledin, and Martha Saxton as critics who think that Alcott's anonymous composition of thrillers opened avenues for artistic expression about the constraints on women. She includes Sarah Elbert, Alfred Habegger, Joy A. Marsella, Ruth MacDonald, and Charles Strickland among those less convinced that the tensions Alcott faced in the two kinds of writing produced positive results (191, n. 4). See also Ann B. Murphy, in "The Borders of Ethical, Erotic, and Artistic Possibilities in *Little Women*" (*Signs* 15[3] [1990], 562–85), for a review of this criticism.

2. Alice Fahs notes in *The Imagined Civil War: Popular Literature of the North and South, 1961–1865* (Chapel Hill: University of North Carolina Press, 2001), 316, that *Little Women* was a notable exception to popular literature of the period in describing the home-front efforts of women and girls. According to James Marten (*The Children's Civil War* [Chapel Hill: University of North Carolina, 1998], 211), there are no statistics on the number of children entering orphanages and asylums due to the deaths of soldier-fathers, but the evidence suggests thousands. The plight of war orphans and half-orphans inspired a patriotic call of responsibility as the country sought to provide for these children as a kind of memorial or debt repaid to their dead fathers.

3. Martha Saxton describes Alcott's troubled childhood: "taught that her own desires should count for nothing," but by nature independent and rebellious, she struggled with anger

and resentment (*Louisa May: A Modern Biography of Louisa May Alcott* [Boston: Houghton Mifflin, 1977], 14–15). See also Madelon Bedell, *The Alcotts: Biography of a Family* (New York: Clarkson Potter, 1980), 243–44.

4. *The Journals of Louisa May Alcott*, introd. Madeleine B. Stern, ed. Joel Myerson and Daniel Shealy (Boston: Little, Brown, 1989), 67.

5. Louisa May Alcott to Frederick and John Pratt, December 4, 1875, *The Selected Letters of Louisa May Alcott*, ed. Joel Myerson and Daniel Shealy, assoc. ed. Madeleine B. Stern (Boston: Little, Brown: 1987), 202–204. Later that month she made a Christmas visit to the orphanage and hospital at Randall's Island, distributing candy and presents to children and seeing "faces and figures that will haunt me a long time" (Louisa May Alcott to the Alcott Family, December 25, 1875), 211. See also Alcott's letter to the Randall's Island director, Mrs. Anna Rice Powell, in Aaron M. Powell, *Personal Reminiscences of the Anti-Slavery and Other Reforms* (New York: Caulon Press, 1899), 240–41, and Madeleine B. Stern, *Louisa May Alcott* (Norman: University of Oklahoma Press, 1950), 254–56.

6. Louisa May Alcott to Mary Mapes Dodge, May 29, [1880], *Selected Letters*, 248.

7. Louisa May Alcott to Horace P. Chandler, November 8, [1881], *Selected Letters*, 256n.

8. Madeleine B. Stern, introduction, *Selected Letters of Louisa May Alcott*, xli.

9. William Alfred Hinds, *American Communities*, rev. ed. (Chicago: Kerr, 1902), 226.

10. John Humphrey Noyes, ed., *The American Socialist* 1(2) (April 6, 1876), 1.

11. Horace Bushnell, *Christian Nurture* (1847; repr., Grand Rapids, Mich.: Baker Book House, 1979), 193.

12. Charles Loring Brace, *The Dangerous Classes of New York, and Twenty Years' Work among Them*, 1872 (New York: Wynkoop & Hallenbeck, 1880; repr., Montclair, N.J.: Patterson Smith, 1967), 23. For assessment of Brace's work as founder of the modern foster system and for testimonies of some of the 250,000 children sent on orphan trains, see Stephen O'Connor, *Orphan Trains: The Story of Charles Loring Brace and the Children He Saved and Failed* (Boston: Houghton Mifflin, 2001).

13. Ibid., 13.

14. Ibid., 29.

15. Charles Loring Brace, "Wolf-Reared Children," *St. Nicholas* 9(May) (1882): 544

16. Brace, *Dangerous Classes*, 29.

17. Amy Schrager Lang, *The Syntax of Class: Writing Inequality in Nineteenth-Century America* (Princeton, N.J.: Princeton University Press, 2003), 100.

18. Ibid., 26–27.

19. Ibid., 100.

20. Claudia Nelson, *Little Strangers: Portrayals of Adoption and Foster Care in America, 1850–1929* (Bloomington: Indiana University Press, 2003), 20.

21. See Marilyn Irvin Holt, *The Orphan Trains: Placing Out in America* (Lincoln: University of Nebraska Press, 1992), who notes that despite an increase in legal adoptions in the late nineteenth century, many children sent on orphan trains were not adopted and "existed in a kind of no man's land of legal status" (141).

22. O'Connor, *Orphan Trains*, xx.

23. Ibid., 15.

24. As Christine Stansell describes it, laboring mothers and children in the streets violated the "moral geography of family life" as it was understood by the middle class: "men at work, women at home, children inside" (*City of Women: Sex and Class in New York, 1789–1860* [Chicago: University of Illinois, 1987], 213).

25. Madeleine B. Stern, introduction, *A Double Life: Newly Discovered Thrillers of Louisa May Alcott*, ed. Madeleine B. Stern, Joel Myerson, and Daniel Shealy (Boston: Little, Brown, 1988), 10.

26. Keyser, *Whispers in the Dark*, xiii.

27. Catherine Beecher and Harriet Beecher Stowe write that a woman who "earns her own livelihood, can institute the family state, [and] adopt orphan children . . . and then to her will appertain the authority and rights that belong to man as the head of a family" (*The American Woman's Home; or, Principles of Domestic Science* [New York: J. B. Ford, 1869]), 204.

28. Nina Auerbach, *Communities of Women: An Idea in Fiction* (Cambridge, Mass.: Harvard University Press, 1978), 36.

29. Steven Mintz and Susan Kellogg, *Domestic Revolutions: A Social History of American Family Life* (New York: Macmillan, 1988), xv.

30. *Journals of Louisa May Alcott*, 165.

31. Katharine Susan Anthony, *Louisa May Alcott* (New York: Knopf, 1938), 279.

32. Madeleine B. Stern notes Alcott's lifelong fascination with theatre, art, and the occult, noting that "the theme of theatricality in general, and of Shakespeare in particular, run markedly through nearly all [her thrillers]" (Stern, *Double* Life, 12). On Shakespeare and the importance of blood ties, see Marianne Novy, *Reading Adoption: Family and Difference in Fiction and Drama* (Ann Arbor: University of Michigan Press, 2005), ch. 3. On Shakespeare's influence on nineteenth-century British writers, especially George Eliot, see chapter 5.

33. Louisa May Alcott, "Marion Earle; or, Only an Actress!," in *The Early Stories of Louisa May Alcott: 1852–1869*, ed. and introd. Monika Elbert (New York: Ironweed, 2000), 255, 274; original emphasis.

34. Alcott, "Marion Earle," *Early Stories*, 257.

35. On Alcott's father-daughter conflict, see Stern, *Double Life*, 24, and Karen Halttunen, "The Domestic Drama of Louisa May Alcott," *Feminist Studies* 102(Summer) (1984): 233.

36. Louisa May Alcott to Alfred Whitman, January 6, 1869, *Selected Letters of Louisa May Alcott*, ed. Joel Myerson and Daniel Shealy, assoc. ed. Madeleine B. Stern (Boston: Little, Brown: 1987), 120.

37. Keyser, *Whispers in the Dark*, 94–99.

38. Charles Strickland, *Victorian Domesticity: Families in the Life and Art of Louisa May Alcott* (Tuscaloosa: University of Alabama Press, 1985), 145, and Sklar, *Catherine Beecher*, 166–67.

39. Strickland, *Victorian Domesticity*, 151.

40. *Journals of Louisa May Alcott*, 67.

41. Strickland, *Victorian Domesticity*, 144–45.

42. Ann Douglas, *The Feminization of American Culture* (New York: Knopf, 1977), 1–9.

43. "Patty's Place," *Aunt Jo's Scrap Bag*, 6 vols. (1871–82), vol. 4, *My Girls and Other Stories* (Boston: Roberts, 1878), 163.

44. Ibid., 169.

45. *Journals of Louisa May Alcott*, 45; original emphasis.

46. Louisa May Alcott to Mrs. Bond, 1886, in Ednah D. Cheney, ed., *Louisa May Alcott: Her Life, Letters, and Journals* (1889; repr., Boston: Little, Brown, 1910), 376.

47. Louisa May Alcott, *Jo's Boys* (1886; repr., New York: Bantam, 1995), 41–42. Subsequent page references appear parenthetically in the text.

48. Strickland, *Victorian Domesticity*, 153.

49. Cheney, *Alcott*, 270.

50. On the emphasis on wealth, material goods, and social status in *Little Women*, see Sarah Way Sherman, "Sacramental Shopping: *Little Women* and the Spirit of Modern Consumerism," *Prospects: An Annual of American Cultural Studies* 26 (2001): 183–237.

51. Louisa May Alcott, "Our Little Newsboy," *Aunt Jo's Scrap Bag*, 6 vols. (1871–82), vol. 2, *My Boys* (Boston: Roberts, 1871), 191–92. Sánchez-Eppler says of this scene, "the emotional traits of interest and concern [are] indistinguishable from the economic processes of purchase and ownership" ("Playing at Class," *English Literary History* 67 [2000]: 823; repr., *The American Child: A Cultural Studies Reader*, ed. Caroline F. Levander and Carol J. Singley [New Brunswick, N.J.: Rutgers University Press, 2003], 44).

52. Encouraged by Mary Mapes Dodge, the editor of *St. Nicholas* magazine, Alcott began *Under the Lilacs* in August 1877 and finished it in September, earning $3,000 for her work. The novel appeared in monthly installments between December 1877 and October 1878 and appeared as a book by published by Roberts Brothers in October 1878, when Alcott was forty-six. The speed at which she wrote the novel was due in part to the "exigency" of her mother's failing health. As she wrote in her journal, "I foresaw a busy or a sick winter, and wanted to finish while I could" (*Journals of Louisa May Alcott*, 205). Abba Alcott became seriously ill in September and died in late November, attended by Louisa, who was herself battling fatigue and poor health.

53. Louisa May Alcott, *Under the Lilacs* (1878; repr., Boston: Little, Brown, 1936), 38. Subsequent page citations appear parenthetically in the text.

54. Louisa May Alcott, *Little Men* (1871; repr., Boston: Little, Brown, 1903), 378.

55. Louisa May Alcott, *Little Women* (1868–69; repr., New York: Penguin, 1989), 489.

56. Ibid., 481.

57. Alcott, *Little Men*, 28.

58. Alcott, *Little Women*, 485.

59. Ibid., 484.

60. Ibid., 460.

61. Alcott, *Journals of Louisa May Alcott*, 45.

62. Fahs, *Imagined Civil War*, 283–85. Alcott's Civil War writings include "Hospital Sketches," "M.L.," "Nelly's Hospital," and peripherally *Little Women*.

63. Mary P. Ryan, *The Empire of the Mother: American Writing about Domesticity, 1830–1860*, Women and History 2/3 (New York: Institute for Research in History and Haworth Press, 1982), 59.

64. Henry Ward Beecher, *Lectures to Young Men: On Various Important Subjects* (Boston: J. P. Jewett, 1867): 242, quoted in Ryan, *Empire of the Mother*, 59.

65. Ryan, *Empire of the Mother*, 60.

66. Caroline F. Levander, "The Science of Sentiment: The Evolution of the Bourgeois Child in Nineteenth-Century American Narrative," *Modern Language Studies* 30(1) (2000): 37.

67. Alcott, *Little Men*, 120.

68. Carol J. Singley, "Building a Nation, Building a Family," in *Adoption in America: Historical Perspectives*, ed. E. Wayne Carp (Ann Arbor: University of Michigan Press, 2002), 67–70.

69. Ryan, *Empire of the Mother*, 18.

70. Louisa May Alcott to Frederick and John Pratt, December 4, 1875, *Selected Letters*, 203.

71. Ibid., 204

72. Louisa May Alcott to Alfred Whitman, March 2, [1860], *Selected Letters*, 51.

CHAPTER 8

1. As outlined by Nina Baym, *Woman's Fiction: A Guide to Novels by and about Women in America, 1820–1870* (Ithaca, N.Y.: Cornell University Press, 1978), 11–12.

2. Philip Fisher, *Hard Facts: Setting and Form in the American Novel* (New York: Oxford University Press, 1985), 99. See also Lawrence Stone, *The Family, Sex and Marriage in England*

1500–1800 (New York: Harper & Row, 1977), 658–66, and Edward Shorter, *The Making of the Modern Family* (New York: Basic Books, 1975).

3. Viviana A. Zelizer, *Pricing the Priceless Child: The Changing Social Value of Children* (New York: Basic Books, 1985), 11.

4. Jane F. Thrailkill, "Traumatic Realism and the Wounded Child," in *The American Child: A Cultural Studies Reader*, ed. Caroline F. Levander and Carol J. Singley (New Brunswick, N.J.: Rutgers University Press, 2003), 133.

5. United Nations High Commissioner for Refugees, *The State of the World's Refugees: A Humanitarian Agenda* (New York: United Nations, 1997), http://www.unhcr.org/3eb7bbd04. html (accessed September 28, 2009).

6. Edith Wharton, *A Backward Glance* (New York: Scribner's, 1934), 293.

7. Nancy Bentley, *The Ethnography of Manners: Hawthorne, James, Wharton* (New York: Cambridge University Press, 1995).

8. For a discussion of Wharton's World War I relief work, see Alan Price, *The End of the Age of Innocence: Edith Wharton and the First World War* (New York: Macmillan, 1996).

9. Wharton, *Backward Glance*, 356.

10. R. W. B. Lewis, *Edith Wharton: A Biography* (New York: Harper & Row, 1975), 254, 535–39.

11. The story appeared in *Harper's Magazine* 106(December) (1902), 63–74, and is reprinted in Wharton's collection, *The Descent of Man and Other Stories* (New York: Scribner's, 1904), 37–68.

12. Lucretia Jones choreographed her daughter's marriage to a prominent Bostonian, Edward (Teddy) Wharton, to whom Wharton remained unhappily wed for twenty-eight years. The tale's subtext—that the child is less important than the parents—was vividly represented in Wharton's case when her wedding invitation was printed and mailed without mention of the bride's name (Hermione Lee, *Edith Wharton* [New York: Knopf, 2007], 74).

13. Edith Wharton, "The Mission of Jane," in *The Collected Short Stories of Edith Wharton*, ed. R. W. B. Lewis. 2 vols. (New York: Scribner's, 1968), 1:379.

14. Price, *End of the Age*, 169–70.

15. For discussions of Wharton's war writings, see Julie Olin Ammentorp, *Edith Wharton's Writings from the Great War* (Gainesville: University of Florida Press, 2004); Mary Carney, "Wharton's Short Fiction of War: The Politics of 'Coming Home,'" in *Postmodern Approaches to the Short Story*, ed. Farhat Iftekharrudin, Joseph Boyden, Joseph Longo, and Mary Rohrberger (Society for the Study of the Short Story, Contributions to the Study of World Literature 118) (Westport, Conn.: Praeger, 2003), 109–20; Deborah Lindsay Williams, *Not in Sisterhood: Edith Wharton, Willa Cather, Zona Gale and the Politics of Female Authorship* (New York: Palgrave, 2001); and Judith Sensibar, "Edith Wharton as Novelist and Propagandist: Competing Visions of 'The Great War'", in *A Forward Glance: New Essays on Edith Wharton*, ed. Clare Colquitt, Susan Goodman, and Candace Waid (Newark: University of Delaware Press, 1999) 141–71. For a discussion of *Summer* as a reflection of Wharton's views of World War I and U.S. isolationism, see Emilie Mindup, "The Mnemonic Impulse: Reading Edith Wharton's *Summer* as Propaganda," *Edith Wharton Review* 18(1) (2002): 14–22.

16. Revisionist scholarship challenging findings that there is an unbridgeable gap between women's experiences and war include Trudi Tate, *Modernism, History and the First World War* (New York: St. Martin's Press, 1998); Suzanne Raitt and Trudi Tate, eds., *Women's Fiction and the Great War* (New York: Oxford University Press, 1997); Miriam Cooke and Angela Wollacott, eds., *Gendering War Talk* (Princeton, N.J.: Princeton University Press, 1993); Lynne Hanley, *Writing War: Fiction, Gender, and Memory* (Amherst: University of Massachusetts Press, 1991);

Claire Tylee, *The Great War and Women's Consciousness: Images of Militarism and Womanhood in Women's Writings, 1914–1964* (Iowa City: University of Iowa Press, 1990); Helen M. Cooper, Adrienne Auslander Munich and Susan Merrill Squire, eds., *Arms and the Woman: War, Gender, and Literary Representation* (Chapel Hill: University of North Carolina Press, 1989); and Margaret Randolph Higonnet, Jane Jenson, Sonya Michel, and Margaret Collins Weitz, eds., *Behind the Lines: Gender and the Two World Wars* (New Haven, Conn.: Yale University Press, 1987). These studies complement and in some cases challenge findings in the classic androcentric accounts of war: Malcolm Cowley, *Exile's Return: A Narrative of Ideas* (New York: Norton, 1934); Stanley Cooperman, *World War I and the American Novel* (Baltimore, Md.: Johns Hopkins University Press, 1967); and Paul Fussell, *The Great War and Modern Memory* (New York: Oxford University Press, 1975).

17. Edith Wharton, *Fighting France, from Dunkerque to Belfort* (New York: Scribner's, 1915), 209, 82, 89; original emphasis.

18. Edith Wharton to André Gide, August 10, [1917], *The Letters of Edith Wharton*, ed. R. W. B. Lewis and Nancy Lewis (New York: Scribner's, 1988), 397.

19. For a discussion of the novel as female romance, see Barbara A. White, "Edith Wharton's *Summer* and 'Women's Fiction,'" in *Essays in Literature* 11(2) (1984): 223–35. Critics also have analyzed the novel in the context of Progressive Era politics and women's rights, including suffrage. The ending, with Charity's marriage to her guardian, has engendered intense controversy. Cynthia Griffin Wolff calls it "a hymn to generativity" (*A Feast of Words: The Triumph of Edith Wharton* [New York: Oxford University Press, 1977; repr., New York: Addison Wesley, 1995], 285); Candace Waid writes that it affirms "the benevolence of paternal authority" (*Edith Wharton's Letters from the Underground: Fictions of Women and Writing* [Chapel Hill: University of North Carolina Press, 1991], 115). Elizabeth Ammons declares the marriage "not merely depressing" but also "sick" and calls the novel "Wharton's bluntest criticism of the patriarchal sexual economy" (*Edith Wharton's Argument with America* [Athens: University of Georgia Press, 1980], 133). Shari Benstock calls the union "psychologically, if not in fact, incestuous" (*No Gifts from Chance: A Biography of Edith Wharton* [New York: Scribner's, 1994], 328). Jennie A. Kassanoff, reading the novel through the lens of Wharton's conservative politics of race and gender, notes that the incest achieves social cohesion (*Edith Wharton and the Politics of Race* [New York: Cambridge University Press, 2004], 113, 138). Wendy Gimbel writes that "forbidden [incestuous] energy provides the central dynamic" of the novel and adds that Royall "is quite possibly [Charity's] biological parent as well" (*Edith Wharton: Orphancy and Survival* [New York: Praeger, 1984], 104, 96). Taking an anthropological approach, Nancy Bentley argues that the transformation of incest into marriage is Wharton's attempt "to uncover and master . . . the 'deep structure' of culture" ("'Hunting for the Real': Wharton and the Science of Manners" in *The Cambridge Companion to Edith Wharton*, ed. Millicent Bell [New York: Cambridge University Press, 1995], 61).

20. Edith Wharton, ed., *The Book of the Homeless* (New York: Scribner's, 1916), xix.

21. Ibid., xx; original emphasis.

22. Wharton to Bernard Berenson, August 11, 1914, *Letters of Edith Wharton*, 333.

23. Wharton, *Book of the Homeless*, xx.

24. Edith Wharton, *Summer*, in *Novellas and Other Writings*, ed. Cynthia Griffin Wolff (New York: Library of America, 1990), 190–91. Subsequent references appear parenthetically in the text.

25. Rhonda Skillern, "Becoming a 'Good Girl': Law, Language, and Ritual in Edith Wharton's *Summer*," in *The Cambridge Companion to Edith Wharton*, ed. Millicent Bell (New York: Cambridge University Press, 1995), 120.

26. Shari Benstock, "Expatriate Modernism: Writing on the Cultural Rim," in *Women's Writing in Exile*, ed. Mary Lynn Broe and Angela Ingram (Chapel Hill: University of North Carolina Press, 1989), 28.

27. Wharton to Sara Norton, June 5, [1903], *Letters of Edith Wharton*, 84.

28. Gayle Rubin, "The Traffic in Women: Notes on the 'Political Economy' of Sex," in *Toward an Anthropology of Women*, ed. Rayna R. Reiter (New York: New Monthly Review Press, 1975), 157–210.

29. Barbara Katz Rothman, *Genetic Maps and Human Imaginations: The Limits of Science in Understanding Who We Are* (New York: Norton: 1998), 204.

30. Michel Foucault, *The History of Sexuality: An Introduction*, trans. Robert Hurley, vol. 1 (1978; repr., New York: Vintage, 1990), 129.

31. Michael Grossberg, *Governing the Hearth: Law and the Family in Nineteenth-Century America* (Chapel Hill: University of North Carolina Press, 1985), 145.

32. Thomas Bender, *Community and Social Change in America* (New Brunswick, N.J.: Rutgers University Press, 1978), 63–68.

33. Wharton, *Backward Glance*, 11.

34. Linda Gordon, *Heroes of Their Own Lives: The Politics and History of Family Violence, Boston 1880–1960* (New York: Viking, 1988), 227.

35. Karen Sánchez-Eppler, "Temperance in the Bed of a Child: Incest and Social Order in Nineteenth-Century America," *American Quarterly* 47(1) (March 1995): 2–3. For discussions of sexual attraction to children, see James Kincaid, *Child-Loving: The Erotic Child and Victorian Culture* (New York: Routledge, 1992); and G. M. Goshgarian, *To Kiss the Chastening Rod: Domestic Fiction and Sexual Ideology in the American Renaissance* (Ithaca, N.Y.: Cornell University Press, 1992).

36. Emphasizing the sacrifice of self, Monika Elbert writes that Charity "sells her body as surely as does her friend Julia, another fallen woman, in order to ensure the welfare of her child" ("Bourgeois Sexuality and the Gothic Plot in Wharton and Hawthorne," in *Hawthorne and Women: Engendering and Expanding the Hawthorne Tradition*, ed. John L. Idol, Jr., and Melinda M. Ponder [Amherst: University of Massachusetts Press, 1999], 262). Charity's sacrifice for Royall's sake is suggested by "Roman Charity," in which a daughter keeps her incarcerated father alive by breastfeeding him. With her extensive knowledge of Renaissance and seventeenth-century painting, Wharton would surely have known Rubens's versions of the scene and Caravaggio's inclusion of it in *The Seven Acts of Mercy*.

37. Sandra Gilbert, "Life's Empty Pack: Notes Toward a Literary Daughteronomy," *Critical Inquiry* 11(3) (1985): 371.

38. See Homi K. Bhabha, *The Location of Culture* (1994; repr., London: Routledge, 2004), 96, and Edward Said, *Orientalism* (New York: Pantheon, 1978), 188.

39. Charity and Harney's transgressive romance alludes to Wharton's extramarital affair with London *Times* correspondent Morton Fullerton Fullerton. Wharton's "brief summer" with Fullerton took place in 1907 and 1908 and included a night spent in a dilapidated hotel, which may have inspired the fictional account of the summer house. Although Wharton's affair did not end in pregnancy, as Charity's does, it brought disillusionment and betrayal. Fullerton, like Harney, was an inconstant lover involved in relationships with both men and women; he was engaged to his cousin when he began seeing Wharton. When the romance ended, Wharton refused to blame Fullerton, instead extending the hand of friendship, as does Charity when she fails to hold Harney accountable as the father of her child and releases him to marry the more cosmopolitan Annabel Balch.

40. Lev Raphael, *Edith Wharton's Prisoners of Shame* (New York: St. Martin's Press, 1991), 296.

41. See Claire Kahane, "The Gothic Mirror," in *The (M)Other Tongue: Essays in Feminist Psychoanalytic Criticism*, ed. Shirley Nelson Garner, Claire Kahane, and Madelon Sprengnether (Ithaca, N.Y.: Cornell University Press, 1985), 337.

42. Monika Elbert, "The Politics of Maternality in *Summer*," *Edith Wharton Review* 7(2) (1990): 4–9, 24.

43. Henry Adams, *The Education of Henry Adams*, ed. Ernest Samuels (1918; repr., Boston: Houghton Mifflin, 1973), 385, quoted in Stephanie Smith, *Conceived by Liberty: Maternal Figures and Nineteenth-Century American Literature* (Ithaca, N.Y.: Cornell University Press, 1994), 215.

44. Stephanie Smith, *Conceived by Liberty: Maternal Figures and Nineteenth-Century American Literature* (Ithaca, N.Y.: Cornell University Press, 1994), 216.

45. Anthony Giddens, *Modernity and Self-Identity: Self and Society in the Late Modern Age* (Stanford, Calif.: Stanford University Press, 1991), 16–20.

46. Nancy Bentley, "Wharton, Travel, and Modernity" in *The Historical Guide to Edith Wharton*, ed. Carol J. Singley (New York: Oxford University Press, 2003), 1.

47. Skillern, "Becoming a 'Good Girl,'" 120.

48. Edith Wharton, *The House of Mirth* (1905; repr., New York: Penguin, 1985), 319.

49. Regina G. Kunzel, *Fallen Women, Problem Girls: Unmarried Mothers and the Professionalization of Social Work, 1890–1945* (New Haven, Conn.: Yale University Press, 1993), 51.

50. Wolff, *Feast of Words*, 285.

51. Price, *End of the Age*, 124–25.

52. Wharton to Elisina Tyler, July 27, 1917, quoted in Price, *End of the Age*, 126.

53. Wharton to Bernard Berenson, September 4, 1917, *Letters of Edith Wharton*, 398; original emphasis.

54. Wharton to Elisina Tyler, July 27, 1917, quoted in Price, *End of the Age*, 126.

55. Wharton to Mary Cadwalader Jones, August 8, 1917, quoted in Price, *End of the Age*, 126. See also William M. Morgan, who writes that Royall is a complex character whom Wharton never reduces "to either his vulgar or redeeming qualities alone," in *Questionable Charity: Gender, Humanitarianism, and Complicity in U.S. Literary Realism* (Lebanon, N.H.: University Press of New England, 2004), 149; and Carol J. Singley, who argues that Royall embodies Whitman-like respect for imperfection, a belief "that what *is* is ultimately good" (*Edith Wharton: Matters of Mind and Spirit* [New York: Cambridge University Press, 1995], 156; original emphasis).

56. Marianne Novy, *Reading Adoption: Family and Difference in Fiction and Drama* (Ann Arbor: University of Michigan, 2005), 96.

57. John Harvey Kellogg, *Plain Facts about Sexual Life* (Battle Creek, Mich.: Office of the Health Reformer, 1877), 64–69, quoted in Ronald G. Walters, ed., *Primers for Prudery: Sexual Advice to Victorian America*, rev. ed. (Baltimore, Md.: Johns Hopkins University Press, 2000), 152.

58. Walters, *Primers for Prudery*, 151.

59. Caleb Williams Saleeby, *Parenthood and Race Culture: An Outline of Eugenics* (New York: Moffat, Yard, 1911), 113; original emphasis.

60. Dr. Elizabeth Blackwell, *Counsel to Parents on the Moral Education of Their Children* (New York: Brentano's Literary Emporium, 1879), 76–77, 79, 81–82, quoted in Walters, *Primers*, 156.

61. Thrailkill, "Traumatic Realism," 142.

62. Julie Berebitsky, *Like Our Very Own: Adoption and the Changing Culture of Motherhood, 1851–1950* (Lawrence: University Press of Kansas, 2000), 4.

INDEX